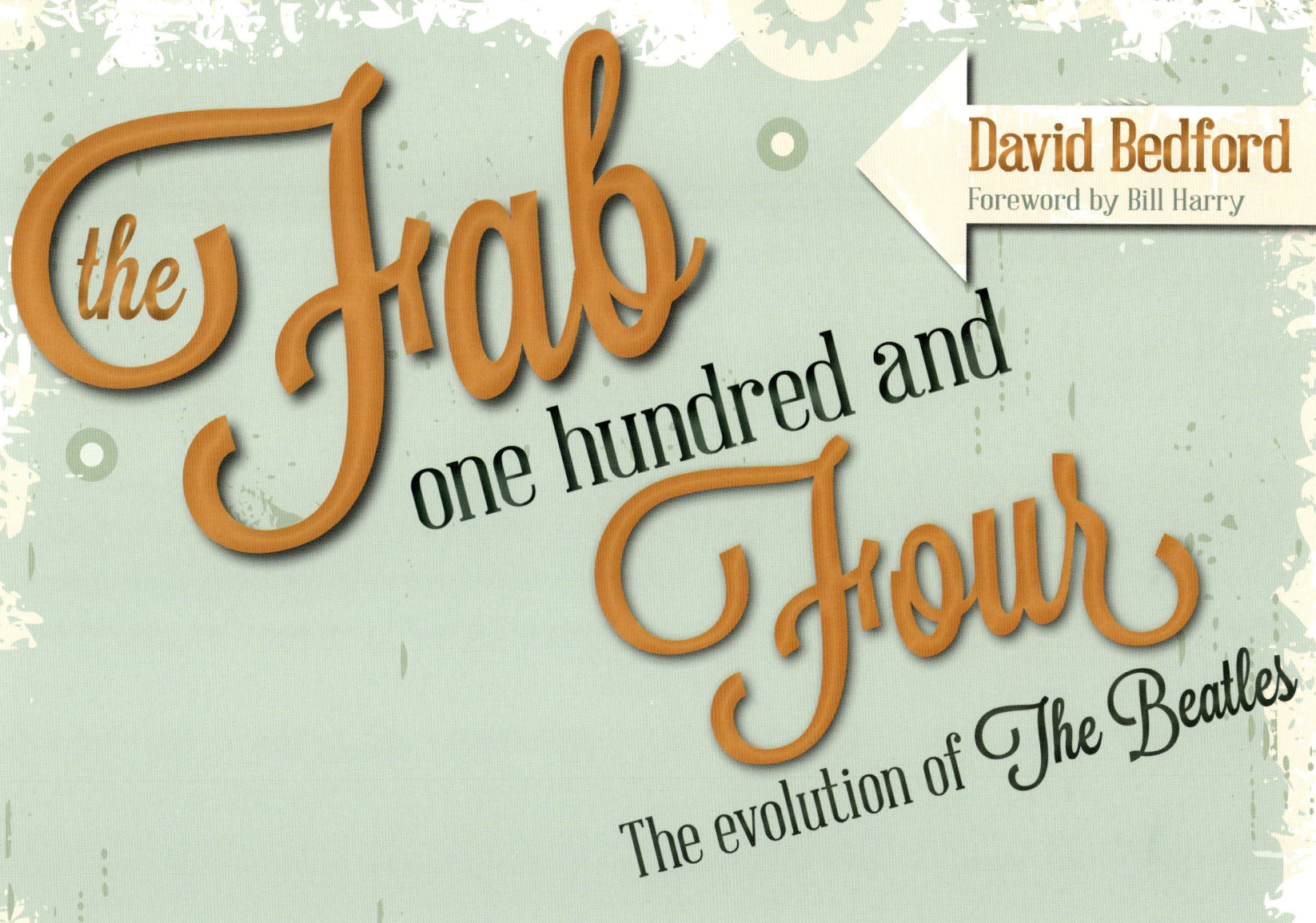

This book is dedicated to my wife, Alix
and daughters, Philippa, Lauren and Ashleigh
and to the memory of my sister, Judy [1967-2007],
my father, Colin Bedford [1935-2009] and
my friend, Jim Atkisson [1951-2012].

The *Fab* one hundred and *Four*
David Bedford

Published 2013

© Dalton Watson Fine Books Limited
ISBN 978-1-85443-264-3

All rights reserved. Apart from any fair dealing for the purpose of private study, research, criticism or review, as permitted under the terms of the Copyright, Design & Patents Act of 1988, no part of this book may be reproduced or transmitted in any form or by any means, electronic, electrical, chemical, mechanical, optical including photocopying, recording or by any other means placed in any information storage or retrieval system, without prior permission of the publisher.

Printed in Hungary
Interpress Co. Ltd. for the Publisher

Dalton Watson Fine Books
Deerfield, IL 60015 USA
info@daltonwatson.com

www.daltonwatson.com

John Lennon once stated,
"I met Paul, and said,
'Do you wanna join me band',
and then George joined,
and then Ringo joined.
We were just a band that made it
very, very big, that's all.
We were four guys."

...or were there only four?

Contents

	Introduction	10
	Foreword	13
	From The Quarrymen to The Fab Four – The Musicians & Performers: 1956-1962	14
	The Fab one hundred and Four The evolution of The Beatles from The Quarrymen to The Fab Four: 1956-1962.	16
	The Story of the Cunard Yanks: how Liverpool groups discovered American records	24
	Quarry Bank High School	34
	Liverpool Institute High School for Boys and Liverpool Art College	40
July 1956 – October 1959	The Quarrymen	48
	Geoff "George Henry" Lee	50
July 1956	John Lennon, Julia Lennon, Uncle George Smith and Arthur Pendleton	53
	Pete Shotton	64
	Bill Smith	67
	Eric Griffiths	72
	Rod Davis	74
	Colin Hanton	78
	Ivan Vaughan	83
	Nigel Walley	89
	Michael Hill	94
	Len Garry	97
Spring 1957	The Blackjacks	100
22 June 1957	Charlie Roberts photographs The Quarrymen	102
6 July 1957	John Lennon meets Paul McCartney	107
	Paul McCartney and Jim McCartney	120
	Paul McCartney and Ian James	127
August 1957	The McCartney Brothers – Paul and Mike	139
	Paul McCartney and Jim Gretty	142
7 December 1957	George Harrison, Harold Harrison and Len Houghton	146
	George Harrison and Geoff Nugent	151
	The Rebels – George and Peter Harrison, Arthur Kelly and Alan Williams	154
	George Harrison, Colin Manley and Don Jefferson	158
7 December 1957	George Harrison joins The Quarrymen	161
8 March 1958	John Lennon, Paul McCartney, George Harrison and Dennis Littler	164
Spring 1958	John Duff Lowe joins The Quarrymen	167
12 July 1958	Percy Phillips records The Quarrymen	170
July 1958	Paul McCartney, George Harrison, John Brierley and Aneurin Thomas	174
February 1959	The Les Stewart Quartet – Les Stewart, Ray Skinner, George Harrison and Ken Brown	175
29 August 1959	The Quarrymen – George Harrison, Ken Brown, John Lennon and Paul McCartney	177
26 October 1959	Johnny and the Moondogs to The Silver Beatles	179
December 1959	Stuart Sutcliffe and Rod Murray are invited to join John Lennon, Paul McCartney and George Harrison	181
January 1960	The Beatals	203
23 April 1960	The Nerk Twins – John Lennon and Paul McCartney	206
May 1960	From Trinidad to Toxteth – The Black roots of The Beatles: Lord Woodbine, Everett Estridge, Jimmy James, Vinnie Ismael, Odie Taylor, and Zancs Logie	208
10 May 1960	Cheniston K. Roland photographs The Silver Beetles	228
10 May 1960	John Lennon, Paul McCartney, George Harrison, Stuart Sutcliffe and Tommy Moore	233
10 May 1960	John Lennon, Paul McCartney, George Harrison, Stuart Sutcliffe and Johnny Hutchinson	240
14 May 1960	The Silver Beats – John Lennon, Paul McCartney, George Harrison, Stuart Sutcliffe and Cliff Roberts	244
20 May 1960	John Lennon, Paul McCartney, George Harrison, Stuart Sutcliffe and Johnny Gentle	246
June 1960	John Lennon, Paul McCartney, George Harrison, Stuart Sutcliffe and Janice the Stripper	254

14 June 1960	John Lennon, Paul McCartney, George Harrison, Stuart Sutcliffe and Ronnie 'The Ted'	256
18 June 1960	John Lennon, Paul McCartney, George Harrison, Stuart Sutcliffe and Norman Chapman	258
24 June 1960	Royston Ellis and The Beetles	265
August 1960 – August 1962	The Beatles to The Fab Four	273
12 August 1960	The unknown drummer nearly joins The Beatles	275
12 August 1960	John Lennon, Paul McCartney, George Harrison, Stuart Sutcliffe and Pete Best	276
4 October 1960	Derry and the Seniors – Howie Casey, Derry Wilkie, Stan Foster, Brian Griffiths, Billy Hughes, Paul Whitehead, Jeff Wallington and The Beatles	282
15 October 1960	Lu Walters, John Lennon, Paul McCartney, George Harrison and Ringo Starr	287
November 1960	Howie Casey, Derry Wilkie, Stan Foster, Stuart Sutcliffe plus a German drummer	289
November 1960	John Lennon, Paul McCartney, Stuart Sutcliffe and Pete Best	290
17 December 1960	Mona Best becomes The Beatles' Manager	292
17 December 1960	John Lennon, Paul McCartney, George Harrison, Pete Best and Chas Newby	296
Spring 1961	John Lennon, Paul McCartney, George Harrison, Stuart Sutcliffe, Pete Best and Steve Calrow	299
15 March 1961	Rory Storm and The Wild Ones: Rory Storm, Lu Walters, Johnny Guitar, Ty Brian, Ringo Starr, John Lennon, Paul McCartney and George Harrison	300
April 1961	Klaus Voormann – almost The Beatles' bass player	302
Spring 1961	The Beatles back Tanya Day and Buddy Britten in Hamburg	304
24 June 1961	John Lennon, Paul McCartney, George Harrison, Pete Best and Tony Sheridan	306
27 July 1961	The Beatles and Cilla Black	312
17 August 1961	The Beatles and Johnny Gustafson	315
17 October 1961	Paul McCartney and Pete Best	316
19 October 1961	The Beatmakers – John Lennon, Paul McCartney, George Harrison, Pete Best, Gerry Marsden, Freddie Marsden, Les Chadwick, Les Maguire and Karl Terry	318
24 November 1961	The Beatles and Davy Jones	322
1 February 1962	Paul McCartney, George Harrison, Pete Best and Rory Storm	324
5 April 1962	John Lennon, Paul McCartney, George Harrison, Pete Best, Ringo Starr, Ray McFall, Billy Hatton, Dave Lovelady and Brian O'Hara	326
April 1962	The Beatles and Gene Vincent	329
April 1962	John Lennon, Paul McCartney, George Harrison, Pete Best and Roy Young	332
20 June 1962	Paul McCartney and The Strangers – Joe Fagin, Harry Hutchings and George Harper	336
16 August 1962	Pete Best is dismissed from The Beatles	338
	Ringo Starr, Harry Graves, Marie Maguire, a "Teacher" and Red Carter	345
	The Eddie Clayton Skiffle Group – Eddie Myles, Roy Trafford, Peter Healey, John Dougherty and Micky McGrellis and Richy Starkey	350
	The Cadillacs with Richy Starkey	353
	The Darktown Skiffle Group with Richy Starkey	355
	Rory Storm and the Hurricanes and Richy Starkey	356
18 August 1962	The Fab Four – John Lennon, Paul McCartney, George Harrison and Ringo Starr	364
11 September 1962	John Lennon, Paul McCartney, George Harrison, Ringo Starr and Andy White	370
12 September 1962	The Beatles and Simone Jackson	373
21 October 1962	The Beatles and The Chants – Joe Ankrah, Eddie Ankrah, Edmund Amoo, Nat Smeda and Alan Harding	374
28 October 1962	The Beatles and Craig Douglas	386
November 1962	John Lennon plays solo in Hamburg	388
31 December 1962	The Beatles with Horst and Freddie Fascher	390
	And in the end...	393
	The Fab one hundred and Four (in order of appearance)	394
	Index of The Fab one hundred and Four	396
	Image Credits	398
	Bibliography	399

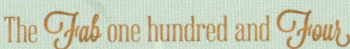

Introduction

It all started with a simple question: "How did they go from The Quarrymen to The Beatles?" An easy one to answer, or so I thought.

David's first book, *Liddypool: Birthplace of The Beatles*.

When my first book, *Liddypool: Birthplace of The Beatles* was published in 2009, it was a dream come true. Just to see it on a bookstore shelf was enough for me. If it did not sell, I would still have been happy, even if my publisher was not! However, when it went into a second print run within two years, it was clear that I had written a book that Beatles fans wanted to read. I can look back at seven amazing trips to America to speak at Beatles conventions, plus guest appearances in the UK and Europe. I've also met so many nice Beatles fans who I can now call friends, proving that when you have a common interest, there are no international borders.

Since *Liddypool* was published, I have appeared on several radio shows, been filmed for TV and involved in several Beatles projects, including writing the foreword to a Beatles book and editing *John Lennon: The Boy Who Became a Legend* by John's school friend, Michael Hill. I have also helped establish the Beatles Social Network (www.beatlessocialnetwork.com) and Beatles information site, The Beatles Website (www.thebeatleswebsite.com), as well as continuing to write for the British Beatles Fan Club magazine.

Friends and fans had a genuine fascination with the early history of The Beatles. Encouraged by their enthusiasm, and with the writing bug coursing through my veins, it did not take long to start writing again. This time, I promised, it wouldn't take nine years as it did with *Liddypool*.

One of the chapters in *Liddypool* that most interested me – as well as many of those with whom I'd spoken – was the evolution of the group from John's first lineup to Ringo's arrival as the final member in 1962. The chapter, called "The Story of the Fab 27", showed how the personnel of the group changed. It brought home the realization that at the heart of The Beatles' story is the tale of a long line of musicians who came and went through the band until it became The Fab Four we all know and love by the end of 1962.

A friend of mine, Mark Naboshek, who has done an incredible job editing this book, told me how he came to know and write about Ian James. Ian was Paul McCartney's school friend who had taught the future Beatle to play guitar. I became fascinated with the story

Ian James, who taught Paul McCartney to play guitar.

The Chants performing at The Cavern in 1963.

of how The Beatles were inspired and encouraged to begin their musical journey. I can still remember my first piano lessons when I was eight and how much I hated them! I also remember how my parents supported my musical ambitions by buying several guitars and other musical equipment for me over the years. I have fond memories of friends like Gary and Derek, who encouraged me and helped me to learn and improve my guitar playing. I still have recordings we made of our band, which I keep for purely sentimental reasons, as opposed to their technical merit. They remind me of a fun time when I was young.

I therefore decided to find every musician who had played with The Beatles in their formative years, plus those who influenced them, like Paul McCartney's dad Jim and John Lennon's mum Julia. There are the school friends like Ian James, plus the founding members of The Quarrymen and the other musicians who were part of the group. Then there were the musicians like Tony Sheridan (who The Beatles referred to as the "Teacher") from whom they learned many of their performing skills. Finally, there were the various acts like Davy Jones, The Shades – who achieved fame as The Chants – and even an unknown exotic dancer named Janice the Stripper, whom they once backed on stage.

When I tallied the number of people in the story, I was amazed when the total reached one hundred and four – and all of this by the end of 1962 when they settled on the final lineup of John, Paul, George and Ringo – The Fab Four. Naturally, along the way, there may have been extra musicians not recorded here. Tony Bramwell recalls them hiring a Salvation Army drummer, and two unnamed members of the Ivy Benson Band who joined them on stage in Hamburg, but without further corroborative evidence they cannot be included. It is my hope that this book will bring forward new stories for the next edition. Not taken into account any number of times the musicians from The Beatles had a jam session with musicians from other groups, like, for example, when members of The Beatles, The Big Three, Gerry and the Pacemakers and Rory Storm and the Hurricanes had an impromptu jam session at the Zodiac Club. This would be a common occurrence and not a formal appearance.

As with *Liddypool*, I was not content to simply read books and repeat the stories. I wanted to track down the people and interview them for their firsthand, eyewitness testimony. I have been overwhelmed by the generosity of so many who have been happy to tell me their stories, some of which have never been divulged before. I'm referring to people like Bill Smith, founding member of The Quarrymen; Ann-Marie Opone, the daughter of Silver Beatles drummer Norman Chapman; Jimmy James and Everett Estridge who were members of the Royal Caribbean Steel Band; and Rod Murray, who vied with his friend Stuart Sutcliffe in a bid to become the bass player with the band.

I was also keen to uncover the eyewitness accounts of the fans who were there as the story unfolded. Many of their memories are shared here for the first time. They give us a different perspective of what it was like to be a fan amid the growing excitement that took place in the years preceding the onset of Beatlemania.

Behind the musicians' tales lies one of the most interesting stories surrounding the music that inspired The Beatles and other Liverpool bands. How were they getting hold of American records so easily? The story is told of the "Cunard Yanks", those Liverpool sailors who crossed the Atlantic to America and came home with bundles of the latest U.S. releases for their grateful families. The story never made sense to me, so I decided to investigate. In the course of my research, a more reliable story emerged that revealed the influence of Radio Luxembourg, the U.S. servicemen of Burtonwood and the incredible record stores in Liverpool. My friend Jimmy Doran was there at the heart of it and unveils the truth about how American music (and, more specifically, rock 'n' roll music) ended up in the hands of the young people of Liverpool.

Having grown up in The Dingle where Ringo was born, I discovered a story that had rarely been told or given much credence. Bill Harry has written about how the journey started in Liverpool 8 and, as I started probing, the story of the influence of the black community in the Toxteth area became essential in learning about the development of The Beatles' sound. The tale begins in Trinidad and was one of those elements of my investigation that proved to be a real revelation to me. Through Jimmy and Everett from the Royal Caribbean Steel Band and Joe Ankrah from The Chants, I discovered where John and Paul used to hang out, the black musicians who inspired them and the clubs owned by Lord Woodbine and Allan Williams that became so influential.

I want to thank Bill Harry for kindly writing the foreword to this book. Bill was my inspiration in starting as a writer, and his support has been invaluable. I also couldn't have completed this book without the incredible historical archive that is *Mersey Beat*, the groundbreaking music paper that chronicled The Beatles' rise to stardom, as well as detailing the whole of the Liverpool music scene.

I also want to thank Pete Frame, whose Rock Family Trees have been an inspiration to me. As with *Liddypool*, I am indebted to The Quarrymen's Rod Davis who has been a constant source of facts, photos and help as I have tried to faithfully present the history of the group. In addition to those whom I have interviewed, I owe a debt of thanks to Mark as my editor and encourager and Kevin Roach who, as well as being the author of *The McCartneys*, works at Liverpool Records Office and has been invaluable as I conducted my research. He helped me locate photographs and old school records to accompany my writing. I also give my thanks to Glyn Morris who had the faith in me to publish *Liddypool* and encouraged me through the publication of this book, too. Without him, this would not have been possible.

Finally, I couldn't have finished this book without the loving support, and patience, of my long-suffering wife Alix and my daughters Philippa, Lauren and Ashleigh.

David Bedford
November 2013

Promotional flyer for Radio Luxembourg.

Foreword

When I received a copy of *Liddypool*, David's first book, I was happy to regard it as something of a tour-de-force, the best book about the Mersey music scene published so far. In addition, it was a superbly designed and produced publication by respected American publishers Dalton Watson. Hundreds of photographs, many never seen before, together with detailed tales covering The Beatles' origins and life in Liverpool, the result of nine years of dedicated research during which David has travelled to all areas of Liverpool, investigating every nook and cranny which had a Beatles association.

'Liddypool' was a familiar phrase to me because John Lennon created it in a *Beatcomber* piece I'd asked him to write for me in *Mersey Beat* in an item I'd entitled 'Around and About', which was basically a spoof on a piece I'd written myself as a round-up of places in Liverpool.

I was also amazed and pleased to note that it was my own *John Lennon Encyclopaedia*, which had inspired David to embark on his first adventure in writing. *Liddypool* proved to be an amazing first-time creation, surpassing previous books on the Mersey music adventure.

Now David has done it again with this incredibly fascinating research into many people associated with The Beatles in Liverpool, albeit people who have rarely, if ever, been written about.

Of course, this is all familiar to me as I've interviewed or been a friend of virtually all of them over the decades and have included lots of them in my own works. However, this volume contains a rich vein of stories from people whose importance I have acknowledged, but many who people are completely unaware of and will be a welcome eye-opener to the thousands of Beatles fans around the world.

This adds a new dimension to The Beatles story because these interviews provide a much-needed insight into the Liverpool lives and the relationships enjoyed by John, Paul, George, Ringo and Pete in those formative years.

A treasure chest of research and a visual delight, this will prove to be a work no Beatles fan should be without.

Bill Harry
Founder of Mersey Beat

Bill Harry.

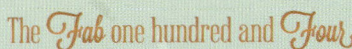

From The Quarrymen to The Fab Four

Below are the members of the Fab one hundred and Four who played in the different group lineups from The Quarrymen to The Fab Four, played with the group, or were backed by them on stage.

Date	Group	John Lennon	Pete Shotton	Eric Griffiths	Bill Smith	Rod Davis	Colin Hanton	Ivan Vaughan	Nigel Walley	Len Garry	Paul McCartney	George Harrison	John Duff Lowe	Les Stewart	Ken Brown	Ray Skinner	Stuart Sutcliffe	Mike McCartney	Tommy Moore	Johnny Hutchinson	Cliff Roberts	Johnny Gentle	Ronnie 'The Ted'	Norman Chapman	Royston Ellis	Pete Best
Summer 1956	The Quarrymen	X	X	X	X	X																				
October 1956	The Quarrymen	X	X	X		X	X	X	X	X																
November 1956	The Quarrymen	X	X	X		X	X			X																
December 1956	The Quarrymen	X	X	X		X	X			X																
Spring 1957	The Quarrymen/The Blackjacks	X	X	X		X	X			X																
6 July 1957	The Quarrymen	X	X	X		X	X			X	X															
7 December 1957	The Quarrymen	X					X			X	X															
Spring 1958	The Quarrymen	X					X			X	X	X														
February 1959	Les Stewart Quartet											X		X	X	X										
2 March 1959	Japage 3	X									X	X														
29 August 1959	The Quarrymen	X									X	X			X											
26 October 1959	Johnny and the Moondogs	X									X	X														
December 1959	The College Band	X									X	X														
January 1960	The Beatals	X									X	X					X									
April 1960	The Beatals	X									X	X					X	X								
23 April 1960	The Nerk Twins	X									X															
May 1960	The Silver Beetles	X									X	X					X									
10 May 1960	The Silver Beetles	X									X	X					X		X	X						
14 May 1960	The Silver Beats	X									X	X					X			X						
20 May 1960	Johnny Gentle and His Group	X									X	X					X		X		X					
14 June 1960	The Silver Beetles	X									X	X					X						X			
18 June 1960	The Silver Beetles	X									X	X					X							X		
24 June 1960	The Beetles	X									X	X					X								X	
12 August 1960	The Beatles	X									X	X					X									X
4 October 1960	The Beatles and Derry and the Seniors	X									X	X					X									X
15 October 1960	Lu Walters, Ringo Starr and The Beatles	X									X	X														
November 1960	The Beatles without George	X									X						X									X
17 December 1960	The Beatles	X									X	X														X
Spring 1961	The Beatles with Steve Calrow	X									X	X					X									X
15 March 1961	Rory Storm and the Wild Ones	X									X	X					X									X
April 1961	The Beatles and Klaus	X									X	X														X
Spring 1961	The Beatles with Tanya and Buddy	X									X	X														X
24 June 1961	Tony Sheridan and the Beat Brothers	X									X	X														X
27 July 1961	The Beatles and Cilla	X									X	X														X
17 August 1961	The Beatles and Johnny Gustafson	X									X	X														X
19 October 1961	The Beatmakers	X									X	X														X
24 November 1961	The Beatles and Davy Jones	X									X	X														X
1 February 1962	The Beatles										X	X														X
5 April 1962	The Beatles with Ray McFall plus The Four Jays	X									X	X														X
April 1962	The Beatles and Gene Vincent	X									X	X														X
April 1962	The Beatles and Roy Young	X									X	X														X
18 August 1962	The Beatles	X									X	X														
11 September 1962	The Beatles	X									X	X														
12 September 1962	The Beatles and Simone	X									X	X														
12 October 1962	The Beatles and The Chants	X									X	X														
28 October 1962	The Beatles and Craig Douglas	X									X	X														
November 1962	John solo	X																								
31 December 1962	The Beatles with Horst and Freddie Fascher	X									X	X														

The Musicians & Performers: 1956-1962

The Fab one hundred and Four
The evolution of The Beatles from The Quarrymen to The Fab Four: 1956-1962

The story of how the group went from being The Quarrymen to The Beatles runs a long and winding road through many different musicians and band members. During this time, they also provided backing for several singers and occasionally had guest musicians join them on stage. Also included in the list are important people who either taught them to play or had a direct influence on their performances. Each one of these one hundred and four people is included in the story.

This is how The Beatles evolved from a group of friends playing skiffle music, calling themselves The Quarrymen (also spelled Quarry Men – there is no definitive way to spell it) to becoming the biggest band in the annals of popular music. The story begins in the summer of 1956 and takes you through to the end of 1962 when the final piece of the jigsaw, the addition of drummer Ringo Starr, saw The Fab Four completed.

To count the members of The Fab one hundred and Four, their name is in italics and there is a number (circled) to show them added to total one hundred and four.

The Fab Four.

Bill Smith, Pete Shotton and John Lennon at Quarry Bank High School.

John Lennon, Julia Lennon, George Smith and *Arthur Pendleton* ④

The story begins with John Winston Lennon. He was taught to play his guitar, in a banjo style, by his mother Julia. After John's Uncle George gave him a harmonica, Julia's neighbour Arthur Pendleton gave him lessons. With his newfound skill, John set about forming his first group.

John, *Pete Shotton, Eric Griffiths, Bill Smith* and *"George" Lee* ④

At Quarry Bank High School, in the summer of 1956, "George Henry" Lee suggested to his friend John Lennon that he should start a skiffle group. The group initially consisted of John on guitar, his best friend Pete Shotton on washboard and school friends Eric Griffiths and Bill Smith on guitar and tea-chest bass, respectively.

John, Pete Shotton, Eric Griffiths, Bill Smith and *Rod Davis* ①

The group was soon enhanced by the addition of Rod Davis, who had acquired a banjo and was quickly recruited.

John, Pete Shotton, Eric Griffiths, Rod Davis and *Colin Hanton* ①

Eric then introduced a friend of his from Woolton, Colin Hanton, who had a set of drums. Colin was quickly added to the lineup and The Quarrymen, for the next few weeks at least, had a settled lineup.

John, Pete Shotton, Eric Griffiths, Rod Davis, Colin Hanton, plus *Ivan Vaughan* or *Nigel Walley* ②

Bill decided to quit, so John called on his friends Ivan Vaughan and Nigel Walley to assume the role of tea-chest bass player. Neither of them saw themselves as the permanent solution, nor did John's friend Michael Hill who was offered the position, so they sought out a more permanent member of the group.

John, Pete Shotton, Eric Griffiths, Rod Davis, Colin Hanton and *Len Garry* ①

Ivan Vaughan may not have wanted to be a musician, but he was instrumental in the group recruiting their new tea-chest bass player. Ivan recommended a schoolmate of his from the Liverpool Institute High School. His name was Len Garry.

John, Eric Griffiths, Colin Hanton, Len Garry and Arthur Davis

Although never added to the group, The Quarrymen would sometimes practise at the home of their friend Arthur Wong and another of their friends, Arthur Davis, would play piano with them. However, as he did not perform with them, he is not included in the one hundred and four.

John, Eric Griffiths, Len Garry, Colin Hanton and *Paul McCartney* ①

The most significant change to the group's configuration occurred on 6 July 1957 when Ivan Vaughan introduced his school friend Paul McCartney to his childhood friend John Lennon at St. Peter's Church. The genesis of The Beatles began on this day and Paul McCartney made his official debut with The Quarrymen on 18 October 1957.

The *Fab* one hundred and *Four*

Paul, *Jim McCartney, Mike McCartney, Ian James* and *Jim Gretty* ③

Paul was influenced and encouraged by his father Jim, an accomplished musician in his own right. However, one of the most important people in Paul's musical journey was his school friend Ian James who taught him to play the guitar and who could have joined The Quarrymen himself. Paul also remembers being shown some great guitar chords by Hessy's employee Jim Gretty.

During a holiday in August 1957, Paul performed with his brother Mike as The McCartney Brothers.

Soon after Paul joined, Rod and Pete left the group. As they were starting to play more rock 'n' roll, the need for a washboard player and a banjo player had diminished.

John, Paul, Colin Hanton and *George Harrison* ①

Len drifted out of the group by the end of 1957 and Paul was keen for his school friend George Harrison to join The Quarrymen, so Eric was forced to leave. By the end of 1957, the core of The Beatles had been formed, with John, Paul and George together, assisted by their drummer, Colin.

George Harrison at the Liverpool Institute.

George, *Harold Harrison, Len Houghton, Geoff Nugent, Peter Harrison, Arthur Kelly, Alan Williams, Colin Manley* and *Don Jefferson* ⑧

George's first group was The Rebels, which consisted of George, his brother Peter, and his best friends Arthur Kelly and Alan Williams.

George was a keen musician who spent hours learning how to play his guitar. He practised with Geoff Nugent who lived nearby, had lessons from Len Houghton, a friend of his father Harold, and took instruction from his school mates Colin Manley and Don Jefferson, both accomplished guitarists.

John, Paul, George and Dennis Littler

While attending parties at Paul's Auntie Jin's house, they would sometimes invite their friend Dennis Littler to rehearse with them.

John, Paul, George, Colin Hanton, and *John Duff Lowe* ①

During 1958, The Quarrymen were able to benefit from the keyboard skills of John Duff Lowe and the five members appeared on the group's first record. On 12 July 1958, they recorded "That'll Be The Day" and "In Spite of All The Danger" at Percy Phillips' studio.

Paul, George, *John Brierley* and *Aneurin Thomas* ②

On a hitchhiking holiday in Wales, Paul and George ended up in the town of Harlech, where they played in a local pub with John and Aneurin, members of local band The Vikings.

John, Paul and George

After a falling out, Colin took his drums and quit the group, with John Duff Lowe also leaving. The Quarrymen were now down to just the three of them.

George, *Les Stewart, Ken Brown* and *Ray Skinner* ③

After John had lost his mother in a tragic road accident in July 1958, The Quarrymen, now with only three guitarists, were no longer able to acquire many bookings. After their final booking in January 1959, the group split up. Wanting to play, George joined the Les Stewart Quartet, which consisted of Les Stewart, Ken Brown and Ray Skinner.

They performed in West Derby, and when George's girlfriend, Ruth Morrison, told them about a new club opening up nearby called The Casbah Coffee Club, they went there to enquire about gigs. The Les Stewart Quartet was soon recruited to be the opening act, but shortly before the club was due to open, the group pulled out.

John, Paul and George

During the early months of 1959, John, Paul and George called themselves Japage 3, though only made one appearance under this name.

Rod Murray and Stuart Sutcliffe. Who would become a Beatle?

George Harrison and Ken Brown

George and Ken Brown quit the group and, after initially offering to play as a duet, Mona Best, owner of The Casbah, asked them to form a new group to open the club.

George, Ken Brown, John and Paul,

George contacted his two former bandmates, John and Paul, and with Ken Brown, re-formed The Quarrymen to open The Casbah on 29 August 1959.

John, Paul, George, *Stuart Sutcliffe* or Rod Murray, plus *Dave May* ②

After a disagreement, Ken left the group and The Quarrymen name was never to be used again. John, Paul and George appeared at a contest using the name Johnny and the Moondogs, but that name was not to last long. To play rock 'n' roll, they needed a bass player and set the challenge to two of John's Art College friends, Stuart Sutcliffe and Rod Murray. Having sold a painting, Stuart won the race and joined the group. He was then given bass guitar lessons by Dave May from Liverpool band The Silhouettes.

Stuart was soon to make a major contribution when he suggested a new name for the group, his homage to The Crickets: The Beatals.

John, Paul, George, Stuart and Mike McCartney

For a short time, before acquiring a full-time drummer, Paul's brother Mike played with the group.

John and Paul

During the school holidays in April 1960, John and Paul travelled to Caversham to see Paul's cousin Bett Robbins and her husband Mike at the pub they ran. The duo appeared as The Nerk Twins.

John, Paul, *Vinnie Ismael, Odie Taylor,* and *Zancs Logie* ③

While hanging out in the clubs of Liverpool 8, John and Paul met several local black musicians from whom they obtained guitar instruction to broaden their musical ability, particularly by playing Chuck Berry songs. These included Vinnie Ismael, Odie Taylor and Zancs Logie.

John, Paul, George, Stuart and *Tommy Moore* ①

In May 1960, now known as The Silver Beetles and managed by Allan Williams, they acquired a new drummer, Tommy Moore. Because they were now a rock 'n' roll band, Williams entered them into the auditions he was holding with promoter Larry Parnes at the Wyvern Club, as Parnes searched for backing bands for his singers.

John, Paul, George, Stuart and *Johnny Hutchinson* ①

On 10 May 1960, with the auditions already underway, The Silver Beetles were still without a drummer, as Moore hadn't yet turned up. They quickly borrowed Johnny Hutchinson from Cass and the Casanovas, who sat in with them until Moore turned up. In spite of this, Parnes decided to book them for a tour of Scotland.

John, Paul, George, Stuart and *Cliff Roberts* ①
On 14 May 1960, the group was playing at Lathom Hall, but Tommy was without his drums. They asked Cliff Roberts from The Dominoes to drum with them. Instead of calling themselves The Silver Beetles, they changed their name to The Silver Beats, for one night only.

John as Johnny Lennon, Paul as Paul Ramon, George as Carl Harrison, Stuart as Stuart de Stael, Tommy Moore and *Johnny Gentle* ①
After the Parnes' audition, John, Paul, George, Stuart and Tommy backed one of Parnes' singers, Johnny Gentle, on a short tour around Scotland. In the promotional newspaper adverts, they were billed as Johnny Gentle and His Group.

John, Paul, George, Stuart and Janice the Stripper
In June 1960, after several arguments, Tommy Moore quit as drummer, and the group was again searching for a replacement. This meant that finding gigs was increasingly difficult for Allan Williams. The only booking he could arrange for them was backing Janice, who was a stripper in one of Williams' men's clubs in Liverpool 8. Embarrassed, but with little option, they reluctantly agreed to provide musical accompaniment for the well-endowed exotic dancer. With Paul on drums, they spent the week on a small stage in a dark, damp cellar, while Janice removed her clothes.

John, Paul, George, Stuart and *Ronnie 'The Ted'* ①
On 14 June 1960, Tommy Moore refused to play with the group despite their pleadings. They therefore turned up at the Grosvenor Ballroom in Wallasey without a drummer. Foolishly, John asked the crowd if anyone could play the drums. Up stepped the physically-intimidating Ronnie 'The Ted' to bash the kit for a bit. When the group members failed to convince him to leave the stage, they called Allan Williams to step in. It's no surprise that this was Ronnie's only appearance with the group.

Norman Chapman, who played with The Silver Beatles.

John, Paul, George, Stuart and *Norman Chapman* ①
Their drumming problem was solved by a chance encounter outside The Jacaranda Club, when they heard the distant sound of drums from the building opposite. On investigation, they discovered their new drummer, Norman Chapman, playing his kit on his own after work. An accomplished drummer, he was soon added to the group.

John, Paul, George, Stuart and *Royston Ellis* ①
On 24 June 1960, when Beat Poet Royston Ellis breezed into town, his new friends, The Silver Beetles, backed him at the University of Liverpool as he performed his poetry.

John, Paul, George, Stuart, *Mona* and *Pete Best* ②
Just as they thought they had a settled lineup, Norman Chapman was called up for National Service and had to spend the next two years in the army. With a booking arranged in Hamburg, they needed a drummer quickly. On 12 August 1960, Paul wrote on behalf of the group to an unknown drummer who had advertised his services in the local newspaper. That same day, Pete Best, drummer with The Blackjacks, was auditioned and given the job. Within days, The Beatles, as they were now known, were heading for Germany.

Pete Best, Ken Brown, *Bill Barlow* and *Chas Newby* ②
Pete's mother Mona bought him his first drum kit when he joined Ken Brown's new group, The Blackjacks, with their friends Bill Barlow and Chas Newby.

Chas Newby.

John, Paul, George, Stuart, Pete Best plus Derry and the Seniors: *Howie Casey, Derry Wilkie, Stan Foster, Brian Griffiths, Billy Hughes, Paul Whitehead* and *Jeff Wallington* ⑦

Now resident in Hamburg, The Beatles often shared the stage with Derry and the Seniors, the first Merseybeat group that went to Hamburg.

Lu Walters, Ringo Starr, John, Paul and George ②

On 15 October 1960, John, Paul, George and Ringo were united for the first time on record when they backed Ringo's bandmate from Rory Storm and the Hurricanes, Lu Walters.

Stuart Sutcliffe, Howie Casey, Stan Foster, Derry Wilkie and a German drummer

Looking to keep the music going at the Kaiserkeller, club owner Bruno Koschmider created new groups by splitting up his bands. Howie Casey and his bandmates were given Stuart Sutcliffe just as his fellow Beatles were heading back to Liverpool in disgrace.

John, Paul, Stuart and Pete

George was deported on 21 November 1960 and the others followed shortly after. However, Uwe Fascher invited the remaining Beatles to play at his club, Studio X, for a couple of nights without George.

John Lennon

Before returning to Liverpool, John made a few solo appearances in Hamburg to earn his passage home.

John, Paul, George, Pete and Chas Newby

With Stuart still in Hamburg, The Beatles were booked at The Casbah, Litherland Town Hall and Grosvenor Ballroom over the Christmas of 1960 and needed a bass player. They quickly asked Pete's former Blackjacks bandmate Chas Newby, who was home from college, to play the bass.

John, Paul, George, Stuart, Pete and *Steve Calrow* ①

Having made their debut at The Cavern, Bob Wooler asked The Beatles to back a young singer called Steve Calrow on stage at The Cavern.

John, Paul, George and Rory Storm and the Hurricanes: *Rory Storm, Johnny Guitar* and *Ty Brian* ③

Promoter Sam Leach ran regular shows at the Liverpool Jazz Society in Liverpool, where, on 15 March 1961, he would get the members of The Beatles and the Hurricanes to join forces and perform as The Wild Ones.

John, Paul, George, Pete and *Klaus Voormann* ①

Stuart quit the group in early 1961, so the group was on the lookout for a new bass player. Their friend Klaus Voormann had often rehearsed with them and put himself in the running for the job. However, it had already been decided that Paul would assume that role.

John, Paul, George, Pete, *Tanya Day* and *Buddy Britten* ②

In the spring of 1961, at the Top Ten Club in Hamburg, The Beatles acted as backing band to singers Tanya Day and Buddy Britten.

John, Paul, George, Pete and *Tony Sheridan* ①

One of the most influential musicians The Beatles encountered was Tony Sheridan, known as the 'teacher'. On 24 June 1961, performing as The Beat Brothers, they backed Sheridan as he recorded "My Bonnie" and several other songs for German producer Bert Kaempfert.

John, Paul, George, Pete and *Cilla Black* ①

At home in Liverpool, on 27 July 1961, The Beatles backed rising star Cilla Black, a future Epstein artist, at St. John's Hall in Tuebrook.

John, Paul, George, Pete and *Johnny Gustafson* ①

A few weeks after backing Cilla, on 17 August 1961, The Beatles invited John Gustafson, better known as Johnny Gus, bass player with The Big Three, to join them on stage at St. John's Hall for a few songs.

Paul McCartney and Pete Best

On 17 October 1961, at a meeting of The Beatles Fan Club, Paul and Pete conducted an unaccompanied performance of a few songs at the David Lewis Theatre.

John, Paul, George, Pete, *Gerry Marsden, Freddie Marsden, Les Chadwick, Les Maguire* and *Karl Terry* ⑤

In a one-off performance, The Beatles teamed up with Gerry and

The Fab one hundred and Four

the Pacemakers and singer Karl Terry as The Beatmakers during an appearance at Litherland Town Hall on 19 October 1961.

John, Paul, George, Pete and *Davy Jones* ①
On 24 November 1961, at the Tower Ballroom in New Brighton, The Beatles backed American singer Davy Jones when he jumped up on stage to join them for an impromptu guest appearance. This was followed by two further appearances backing Jones at The Cavern in December 1961.

Paul, George, Pete and Rory Storm
Their first performance after their new manager Brian Epstein began to represent them was without John, who had a sore throat. Despite the short notice, they quickly recruited Rory Storm to sing with them.

Stuart Sutcliffe, Peter Bosch, Rudiger Neber, Volker Neber and Tony Cavanaugh
Having quit The Beatles, Stuart was not finished with music. In March 1962, only a few weeks before his death, Stu played with a German band The Bats, alongside Peter Bosch, Rudiger and Volker Neber, plus Tony Cavanaugh. As it was after Stuart left The Beatles, these musicians are not included in the one hundred and four.

John, Paul, George, Pete, Ringo Starr, *Ray McFall, Billy Hatton, Dave Lovelady* and *Brian O'Hara* ④
On 5 April 1962, Cavern owner Ray McFall sang on stage with The Beatles, who were joined by Ringo, plus Billy Hatton, Dave Lovelady and Brian O'Hara from The Four Jays.

John, Paul, George, Pete and *Gene Vincent* ①
When one of their musical heroes arrived in Hamburg in April 1962, The Beatles did not need to be asked twice to play. Gene Vincent appeared with them at the Star Club in Hamburg and they backed him on a number of occasions.

John, Paul, George, Pete and *Roy Young* ①
While in Hamburg, The Beatles were now playing at the Star Club. They joined forces with Roy Young, a piano virtuoso with a voice and playing style like Little Richard. So impressed were the group with

The Beatles and Roy Young (left) on stage at the Star Club.

him that Brian Epstein asked Roy to return to Liverpool and join The Beatles. He declined.

Paul McCartney and The Strangers: Joe Fagin, Harry Hutchings and George Harper
On 20 June 1962, the drummer for The Strangers developed a leg cramp, so they recruited Paul McCartney to join them on stage and drum for their set. As this was Paul sitting in with another band, they have not been included in the one hundred and four.

John, Paul, George and Ringo
The final change of personnel came on 18 August 1962, when Ringo Starr was unveiled as The Beatles' new drummer, replacing the sacked Pete Best.

Ringo Starr, *Harry Graves, Marie Maguire, a "Teacher"* and *Red Carter* ④
As Richy Starkey, he was encouraged to play the drums by his childhood friend Marie Maguire as well as an unnamed "Teacher" at the Royal Liverpool Children's Hospital where he was convalescing. His stepfather Harry bought him his first kit. He also learned to play the piano accordion in the Orange Lodge, and spent one day with a Silver Band, though we don't have any names for those involved. One local drummer, Red Carter would have a longer lasting effect on him.

Ringo, *Eddie Myles, Roy Trafford, Peter Healey, John Dougherty* and *Mickey McGrellis* ⑤

Ringo's first group was the Eddie Clayton Skiffle Group, with his work friends Eddie Myles, Roy Trafford, Peter Healey, John Dougherty and Mickey McGrellis.

Ringo, *Alan Robinson, Dave Mckew, Keith Draper, Gladys Jill Martin* and *David Smith* ⑤

Ringo then joined The Darktown Skiffle Group, whose members included Alan Robinson, Dave McKew, Keith Draper, Gladys Jill Martin and David Smith.

Ringo mentioned in one interview that he also played with a group called The Cadillacs, but since no evidence has been uncovered to support this claim, they cannot be counted in the one hundred and four.

Ringo, Rory Storm, Johnny Guitar, Ty Brian, Lu Walters, Tony Sheridan, Roy Young and *Colin Melander* ①

Ringo's music education continued when he joined Al's Raving Texans, with Alan Caldwell, Johnny Byrne, Charles O'Brien and Wally Eymond. They became Rory Storm and the Hurricanes (which had been through several name changes) with Rory Storm (Alan Caldwell), Johnny Guitar (Johnny Byrne), Ty Brian (Charles O'Brien) and Lu Walters (Walter Eymond). Ringo left Rory's group for a short time to join Tony Sheridan's band in Hamburg, with Roy Young and Colin Melander, before re-joining the Hurricanes.

John, Paul, George, Ringo and *Andy White* ①

Having held an unsuccessful first recording session at Abbey Road on 4 September 1962, George Martin brought in session drummer Andy White to record with The Beatles on 11 September 1962. He joined them on "Love Me Do", "P.S. I Love You" and "Please Please Me".

John, Paul, George, Ringo and *Simone Jackson* ①

On 12 September 1962, The Beatles backed teenage singer Simone at The Cavern.

John, Paul, George, Ringo and The Chants: *Joe Ankrah, Edmund Ankrah, Eddie Amoo, Nat Smeda* and *Alan Harding* ⑤

Black vocal harmony group, The Chants, impressed The Beatles so much that they backed the singing group at The Cavern and at two other Merseyside venues.

John, Paul, George, Ringo and *Craig Douglas* ①

When British singing sensation Craig Douglas arrived in Liverpool, The Beatles backed him during his performance at the Liverpool Empire on 28 October 1962.

John, Paul, George, Ringo, with *Horst* and *Freddie Fascher* ②

On 31 December 1962, during their final trip to Hamburg (and their first with Ringo), The Beatles were recorded at the Star Club. At different times, their friends Horst and Freddie Fascher joined The Beatles on stage.

And that is the story of "The Fab one hundred and Four".

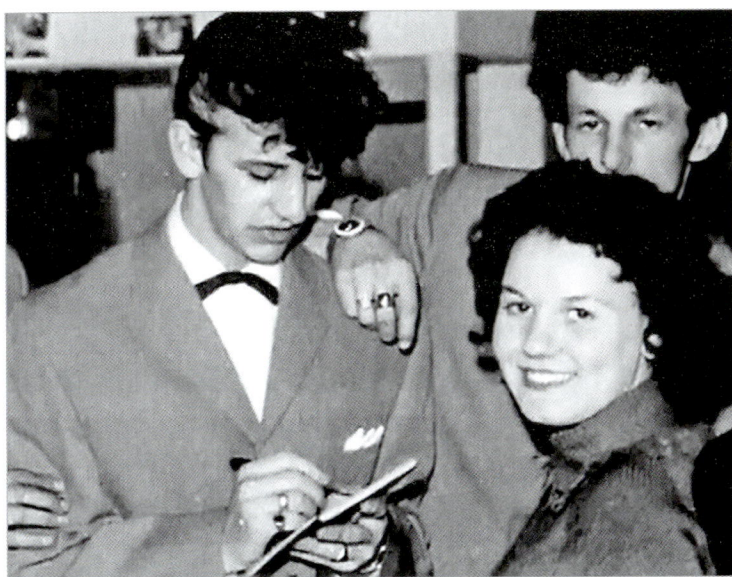

Ringo Starr, drummer with Rory Storm and the Hurricanes, joins The Beatles.

The Story of the Cunard Yanks: how Liverpool groups discovered American records

The influence of American artists on the aspiring musicians of Liverpool was without doubt the most important catalyst in the formation of bands like The Beatles.

Rock 'n' roll came to Britain at a time when the country was struggling for its musical identity. Jazz had dominated the music scene in the 1920s and '30s, but, with the transition of silent movies to "talkies", there was suddenly a large number of musicians who had been playing in the cinemas looking for work.

In a bold step in 1932, the Musicians' Union in the UK placed an embargo on foreign jazz musicians playing in the country. Jazz was booming in Britain after World War II, and although there was a whole host of American Jazz musicians making records, they could not visit the UK because of the embargo. It didn't apply to blues or gospel musicians, and importantly in the late 1950s, to rock 'n' roll musicians from across the Atlantic. The music of the black Americans was available in the UK and becoming increasingly popular. Artists like Huddie William "Lead Belly" Ledbetter and Arthur "Big Boy"

Programme for the Liverpool Jazz Festival held at The Cavern Club in January 1960.

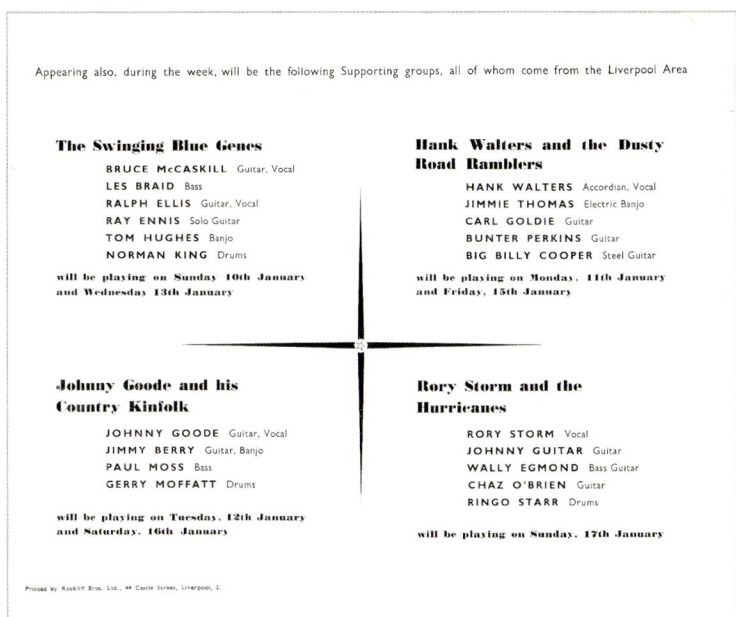

The programme shows Rory Storm and the Hurricanes' appearance at The Cavern Club with Ringo on drums.

Crudup are often cited for their influence on popular music and artists like Elvis Presley.

In Liverpool, Alan Sytner, a 21-year-old jazz enthusiast, opened his first jazz venue, The 21 Club, at 21, Croxteth Road, Liverpool. Having been inspired by visiting Le Caveau de la Huchette in Paris, Sytner wanted to recreate that atmosphere in Liverpool. On 16 January 1957, with Keith Hemmings, an architect friend, he opened the first live music venue in Liverpool – The Cavern Club at 10, Mathew Street. Soon after, a disagreement with Sytner caused a rift and Hemmings left. The Cavern quickly grew its membership to 25,000 and was packed to its capacity of 600 fans regularly.

The Cavern was a member of the National Jazz Federation and one of the largest music venues in the country. In 1958, Sytner sold The Cavern Club lease to Ray McFall and headed to London to manage a new venue owned by Harold Pendleton, a friend of his from Merseyside. Together, they established the now-world-famous Marquee Club. Pendleton was one of the most influential men in the history of British music, a fact that Cavern Director Dave Jones passionately relates. Pendleton created the first National Jazz Festival and, with the help of Chris Barber, a jazz trombonist who was director of the National Federation of Jazz Organisations of Great Britain, The Marquee Club quickly became the country's premier jazz venue.

In Chris Barber's band was Anthony James "Lonnie" Donegan, a guitar and banjo player who entertained audiences with blues and folk songs that became so popular, he recorded an up-tempo version of "Rock Island Line" in 1954, which became a massive hit two years later. Donegan's appearances in Barber's band triggered the skiffle craze that swept Britain between 1956 and 1958. On 6 July 1957, as John and Paul were meeting for the first time, Donegan was at number one in the charts with "Gamblin' Man"/"Putting on The Style", the latter song being in The Quarrymen's repertoire that day.

With the dearth of new jazz musicians in the country, and the absence of the American stars, Donegan's skiffle was a breath of fresh air to young people across the country. Because of Donegan's association with Chris Barber's Jazz Band, skiffle was also acceptable in jazz clubs. Sytner and Pendleton suggested that Donegan take his music north to Liverpool and perform at The Cavern, which he did, on 11 October 1958.

On 29 August 1959, on the outskirts of Liverpool in West Derby, Mona Best opened The Casbah Coffee Club. With a marked absence of jazz music, one of Liverpool's first rock 'n roll clubs was established.

In January 1960, The Cavern hosted the first Liverpool Jazz Festival, though there were appearances by such notable non-jazz groups as The Blue Genes – who became The Swinging Blue Jeans – and Rory Storm and the Hurricanes, featuring Ringo Starr. When Rory Storm's set included some rock 'n roll songs, their fee was halved! However, the seed of beat music was sown, and on 25 May 1960, Rory Storm and the Hurricanes returned for the first advertised beat session at The Cavern. Jazz music was rapidly disappearing and, although the Musicians' Union embargo was lifted in 1958, it was too late for jazz. However, it would be an opportunity for American rock 'n' roll musicians to head for Britain.

At the forefront of this first wave was Bill Haley and His Comets, whose song "Rock Around the Clock", and the film of the same name, are recognised for introducing rock 'n' roll to Britain. Buddy

Holly's March 1958 appearance in Liverpool would be of greater importance to the musicians, but American music and culture were suddenly a la mode.

All Lennon, McCartney and their friends had to do was get their hands on those American records.

The story of the Cunard Yanks is one that has grown to mythical proportions in Liverpool and beyond. The way it has been told is that sailors from the families of Liverpool musicians brought back American records for the groups to learn. The story is partly true, as many Liverpool families had brothers, fathers or uncles at sea who returned home with American records before they were released in the UK. In fact, the record that turned John Lennon on to rock 'n' roll was an imported "Long Tall Sally", brought in from Holland. However, the story has grown to such an extent that many believe that the majority of the American songs played by Liverpool groups were obtained this way. There was always a battle between the groups to get a song that nobody else had, so if a family member brought a record back from America, then you could steal a march on your musical rivals. I spoke to Howie Casey from Derry and the

Popular Radio Luxembourg DJ Pete Murray.

Promotion for Radio Luxembourg by EMI.

Map of Luxembourg.

THURSDAY, 10th NOV.

p.m.
6.30 PETER ALDERSLEY PLAYS MUSIC FOR OPENERS
The first spins of the evening plus Prize Competition.
(Beecham Proprietary Medicines) (Pye Records Ltd.)

7.00 JACK JACKSON'S JUKEBOX SHOW
(Decca Record Co. Ltd.)

7.30 BLAST OFF
Introduced by Colin Nicol

7.45 LET'S TAKE A SPIN
Introduced by Colin Nicol
(E.M.I. Records Ltd.)

8.00 THE ALAN FREEMAN SHOW
(The Decca Record Co. Ltd.

8.15 IT'S POP-PYE TIME
A pick of the top-pops from Pye.
Introduced by Denny Piercy
(Pye Records Ltd.)

8.30 THURSDAY'S REQUESTS
Introduced by Stuart Grundy
(Horace Batchelor)

8.45 MECCA MUSIC PARADE
Introduced by Colin Nicol
(Mecca Ltd.)

9.00 DAVID JACOBS' STARTIME
in which David introduces the stars on record.
(Macleans and Bristows) (E.M.I. Records Ltd.)

9.30 THE CATHY McGOWAN SHOW
Cathy spinning the new selected releases heading for the top.
(Pye Records Ltd.)

9.45 HITS-A-HAPPENING
with Pete Brady
(E.M.I. Records Ltd.)

10.00 THE JIMMY YOUNG HOUR
The YOUNG Sound
The POP Sound
The HIT Sound
All on the E.M.I. Label
(Vitapointe)
(Disky Cosmetics)

10.30 THE JIMMY YOUNG HOUR (Continued)
(Beecham's Powders)
(E.M.I. Records Ltd.)

11.00 BRIAN MATTHEW'S POP PARADE
Introduced by Brian Matthew
(D.D.D. Co. Ltd.)

11.15 JIMMY SAVILE'S "15"
(De Kuyper Advocaat)

11.30 POPS TILL MIDNIGHT
Presented by Alan Freeman
Thirty minutes of late night discs.
(Gordon-Moore Cosmetic Toothpaste)
(Royette)

12.00 HI, MIDNIGHT!
Introduced by Brian Vaughan
(Polydor Records)

12.30 MUSIC FOR SOPHISTICATS
with Alan Dell
(E.M.I. Records Ltd.)

1.00 TONY BRANDON'S MUSIC IN THE NIGHT

2.00 a.m. — Close Down

Typical schedule for Radio Luxembourg programmes.

Promotional flyer for *Charts Tonight At Nine* on Radio Luxembourg.

THE MONDAY SPECTACULAR

INTRODUCED EACH WEEK BY

SHAW TAYLOR — **MURIEL YOUNG** — **RAY ORCHARD**

Advertisement for Radio Luxembourg, from 1964.

COMPLETE SCHEDULE
of the top Radio Luxembourg programmes by the top D-Js!

Sunday	7.00 pm	Jack Jackson The new juke box show
Monday	10.00 pm	Pete Murray's Top pops
Monday	10.30 pm	Jack Jackson's Hit parade
Tuesday	7.15 pm	The Alan Freeman Show
Tuesday	10.30 pm	Jimmy Savile Teen and twenty disc club
Wednesday	10.00 pm	Jimmy Savile Teen and twenty disc club
Wednesday	10.30 pm	The Pete Murray Record show
Thursday	11.15 pm	The Alan Freeman Show
Friday	7.15 pm	The Tony Hall Show
Friday	8.30 pm	The Pete Murray Show
Friday	9.00 pm	The Alan Freeman Show
Friday	9.30 pm	Pat Campbell Chart jumpers
Saturday	10.30 pm	Tony Hall's Hot twenty
Saturday	11.30 pm	Jack Jackson's Record round-up
Saturday	12.00 pm	Jimmy Savile Guys gals and groups

TUNE IN REGULARLY
on 208 metres

Decca-sponsored flyer for Radio Luxembourg.

Seniors, and asked him how they obtained their American records. "Derry became a great source for some of the great, and more obscure, mainly American records. Liverpool has a large black African and Caribbean community and, through Derry, we were introduced to this great music in some of the clubs in Upper Parliament Street, like Joe Bygraves' Club and The Beacon. We also met many American servicemen who were stationed at Burtonwood, the American Air Force Base just outside of Liverpool. They would come into town to these clubs, and there would always be a piano there, so some of these guys would sing the songs and we'd think: 'I like that'. So we were picking up these tremendous influences, which set us apart from the other groups."

I spoke to a friend of mine, Jimmy Doran, and he explained to me how he obtained records by American artists.

"A lot of people say that the Cunard Yanks brought the music over but I would say that my sister and her group of people were listening to Chuck Berry, Buddy Holly, Larry Williams and Little Richard when they came out. Where I lived, the music was all like that, and we did not know anyone on the ships. My sister would get the records from the local record shops."

Not everyone could afford to buy records, so Rod Davis from The Quarrymen explained what they did: "The only way we could learn songs," recalled Rod, "was by listening to the records – often in the NEMS record shop near to Penny Lane or on Radio Luxembourg – and scribbling down the words we thought we were hearing."

Like me, you might have heard of Radio Luxembourg, but not realised how influential it was on post-war British teenagers. The

Radio dial showing the position of Radio Luxembourg on 208 metres, medium wave.

Pat Boone's "Wonderful Time Up There" released on the London-American Recordings label in the UK

Catalogue for the records issued by London-American.

TV Times cover promoting the show, *Cool For Cats*.

Radio Luxembourg DJ Jack Jackson in his studio.

English-speaking commercial radio station started broadcasting as early as 1933 and specifically targeted listeners in the United Kingdom. This was because radio in Britain at the time was controlled by the straight-laced BBC. For many, there was only one source of pop music on the radio and that was form the small Grand Duchy of Luxembourg in Europe.

In 1929, the Luxembourg Society for Radio Studies was formed to persuade the government of Luxembourg to grant them a commercial licence. It was duly approved and, at the end of that year, the Luxembourg Broadcasting Company was established, identifying itself under the name of Radio Luxembourg. It was not long before they were broadcasting across the English Channel. To reach these shores, the programmes were broadcast on Long Wave, but the British Government was not impressed and tried to do everything in its power to stop it. However, in 1934 the European Wavelength Plan came into effect, which allocated spectrum to various countries for radio transmission use. Throughout the 1930s, Radio Luxembourg boasted a huge audience in the UK, the programmes mainly comprising popular dance music and sponsored output.

During World War II, the government of Luxembourg shut down the station. The conquering German army commandeered it as a propaganda tool, broadcasting programmes to the UK featuring the infamous William Joyce, comically named "Lord Haw-Haw" by the British public. After liberation, the U.S. Army commandeered the station, using it for a similar purpose.

For the aspiring musicians of Liverpool in the 1950s, regular English broadcasting began again on the medium wavelength of 208 meters. However, a decent listening experience in the UK could only be achieved after dark. For listeners like young John Lennon, this would necessitate getting an extension speaker installed in the bedroom so that, after bedtime, you could still listen. Thankfully for John, Uncle George was happy to do this.

The most popular shows for eager young ears were:

Sundays: 11:00pm   *Top Twenty* – introduced by Pete Murray.

Mondays: 7:15pm   *The New Adventures of Dan Dare, Pilot of the Future*. Fifteen-minute serial, heard Monday to Friday and featuring the voice of Noel Johnson who also played the part of Dick Barton on BBC radio. This serial began on 2 July 1951 and ran for five years.

           9:30pm   *Perry Mason* serial, heard Monday through Friday.

In November 1959, Roy Mason, a Labour Member of Parliament, raised the question in Parliament about Radio Luxembourg programmes being used by the record companies. "Are you aware that disc jockeys are in many instances responsible for the selection of their records and are, in turn, employed by recording companies such as Pye, Decca, and E.M.I.?" The two disc jockeys named by Mason were Pete Murray and Jack Jackson. "They do Radio Luxembourg programmes for Decca records," he proclaimed.

In the 1960s, a number of disk jockeys began broadcasting live from Luxembourg, with other shows originating from their new London studios at 38, Hertford Street. Interlaced between quiz shows and religious programmes were the pop shows broadcasting the latest hits. Some of Britain's best-known radio presenters started their careers on Radio Luxembourg, such as Pete Murray, David Jacobs, Brian Matthew, Alan Freeman and Hughie Green who would later appear in front of the cameras presenting quiz shows. The biggest name to broadcast was American disk jockey Alan Freed, the man who invented the term rock 'n' roll, the title of his show.

In the 1960s, Luxembourg's commercial monopoly was challenged by the arrival of the pirate radio stations. These were stations broadcasting on ships and structures outside the 3-mile limit of Britain's territorial waters. The most famous was Radio Caroline, which had nationwide coverage operating from two ships, one anchored off the southeast coast of England and the other off the Isle of Man.

Radio Luxembourg needed to compete in this market, so the pre-recorded sponsored shows were dropped in favour of live radio presenters. The UK government stepped in by passing a law making it an offence for any British Citizen to work on a pirate radio station. With the demise of the pirate radio stations, Radio Luxembourg was once again the only provider of popular music. However, in 1967, the BBC launched Radio 1, their first popular music station hosted by many of the disk jockeys who had made their name on Radio Luxembourg or Radio Caroline. It quickly became the station of choice for fans of pop music. Commercial free, it was music and chat without the advertisements. However, in 1973, Independent Local Radio stations were allowed to operate in competition with the BBC and commercial radio was introduced to the UK. This was the death knell for Radio Luxembourg, which finally closed down on 30 December 1992.

Jimmy Doran explained the importance of Radio Luxembourg. "Everyone listened to Radio Luxembourg," he recalled. "My sister, who was a bit older than me, would listen to the show and then have the record in her hand by the following week." I was surprised and enlightened when Jimmy then told me the nature of the shows they heard: "They were sponsored by the record labels. There would be a show by Capitol Records, London-American, Columbia and many others. They would play the latest songs by their artists on their labels, which would be in the shops that week. My sister would listen to them, decide which she wanted, and go and buy them that week. That is how we knew about the American records coming over to the UK."

A look through the schedules of Radio Luxembourg reveals how many labels were involved.

The Capitol Show	Mel Thompson presenting Capitol Records' new releases.
Rockin' To Dreamland	with Keith Fordyce playing the latest British and American hit records.
Record Hop	Benny Lee presents the latest Columbia and Parlophone records.
Philips' Fanfare	records from the Philips label, presented by Guy Standeven.
The Jack Jackson Show	The latest releases from Decca Records and their subsidiary, London-American Records.
The Alan Freeman Show	Freeman played London-American records and would put on an American accent to introduce them.

For the record labels, this was the only way to get airplay in the UK and introduce new releases to the record-buying public. The London label first appeared in America in 1934 representing British Decca's operations in America. Back in Britain, the London label made its debut in 1949 releasing material from its American counterpart, but also from early U.S. independent labels. Some American hit records appeared on EMI's Columbia, Parlophone and HMV labels, but the cream of the crop was usually on London-American. It was on these labels that the fans were able to buy the American songs, promoted on Radio Luxembourg and available in the shops.

"Radio Luxembourg was brilliant," Jimmy continued. "We'd be sitting there on Sunday evening waiting for the programme to start at 7:30pm and there would be a religious programme from Monaco before it. We waited for it to finish and watched the clock, counting down from ten. Then we heard it: 'This is *The Jack Jackson Show*', and he made this noise like a screeching cat, and we would all copy him. He would introduce the records by saying; 'This is a record coming out soon in shops near you.' My mum liked the records, but my dad, sitting in his chair in the corner, would lower the paper and just moan. They would go out to the cinema and pop into the pub for a drink, then to the chippy on the way home. We would listen to the radio shows while they were out, and decide what records we wanted.

"The problem was that sometimes you would lose the radio signal,

The Nigeria Club, Upper Parliament Street, where the U.S. servicemen would bring their American records.

so one of you would have to grab the aerial and find the best spot in the room to get a clear signal and stand there holding this wire until you had to move it again. It would be going in and out. My dad would be sitting there looking over his newspaper, disapproving. 'Will you stop all this noise', and I'd say, 'I know you only want to get up and dance', just to wind him up!

"My brother-in-law lived in Stanhope Street so I was always up there listening to records. NEMS was only one of many record stores because we had a great one on Park Road and one up on Lodge Lane. People say Brian Epstein had this claim that he could get any record, but I could get any record I wanted from the best record stores in the city, so it was not just NEMS. If it was not in, they would get it for us by the next week. Even if it came out in the U.S., we could have it within two weeks in Liverpool, through any of the best record shops.

"I remember when I was eleven, the first record I owned was 'Rave On' by Buddy Holly and I played it to death! My grandma bought it for me, and I remember going home and taunting my sister because I had it and she did not! She took it well. When she brought home

'That'll Be The Day', everything changed. I had listened to it on *The Jack Jackson Show* and, a week later, my sister brought the record in for me. I used to ask her for a record and she would get it for me.

"In 1958, we got our first TV and my sister took the radio into the other room. This was our time with the records, and my dad was happy with that. All we had was the radio and buying records. Every kid came in to watch the telly in our house, but we did not watch a lot. However, there were a few programmes where they played music, so we watched them. On Thursday, Kent Walton hosted *Cool for Cats*, the music of bands, while dancers danced to the latest songs. I remember that was the first time I heard 'Wake Up Little Susie' by the Everly Brothers.

Uncle Mac, presenter of the popular radio show, *Children's Hour*.

"We also watched Uncle Mac on Saturday morning on the *Children's Hour* TV show. It was a request show, so you could hear your name read out. It was a real mixture of songs, but every now and then you would hear a good song. It was worth listening to the whole show in the hope of hearing your favourite being played.

"However, when they came on the telly, the magic was gone. On the radio, we used our imagination to visualise them performing it. There was so much music in our house, whether it was the radio, TV or record player. After school, I would ask my mum if I could put my sister's records on. 'Don't break them!' she would tell me. I was so careful as I placed the record on. I used to turn them over and listen to the B-side too. It would only be a filler on the other side, but I wanted to listen to everything. I always preferred the original recordings, because all of the British stars raced to get a cover version out in the charts first. We had 'Singin' the Blues' by Guy Mitchell and I loved that record. British star Tommy Steele recorded it, but we always got the original from America.

"I used to go to my Auntie Celia's flat in Caryl Gardens, and there would always be music on. She was listening to country music from artists like Hank Williams and Slim Whitman because there was a big country music scene in Liverpool then, so I would listen to them, too. I know that John and George were influenced by the country artists, too, so there was a great variety to listen to.

"I started my record collecting young and I'm still collecting now! My sister was earning money however she could, from sewing and mending clothes and curtains, and then she would spend it on records and clothes. To help pay for records, she was in a record club. The record clubs would go to the record shop and pay a set amount in to save up for the records. There could be ten people in the club and you would pay in your money every week. Then, once every ten weeks, you would spend the club money on the records you wanted that week. That is how she could afford them. She would ask me what I would like, so I would tell her what I heard this week on the radio and she would go and get it for me when it was her turn."

The radio, record shops and television were the obvious outlets for discovering new songs. However, there was another source of American records on the doorstep of Liverpool. Just a few miles outside of Liverpool was RAF Burtonwood, an airfield established in 1941. The United States Army Air Forces (USAAF) took over the base in June 1942 and it became a servicing centre for the United States Eighth, Ninth, Twelfth and Fourteenth Air Forces aircraft. It was the largest airfield in Europe during the war, holding up to 18,000 service personnel.

These servicemen, both black and white, were segregated on the base, but when they went into Liverpool to party, they were, for a short time, together. However, after several incidents of servicemen fighting among themselves, it was decided that black and white shouldn't mix, and were kept apart. The black Americans started to congregate around the Liverpool 8 area where the greatest concentration of Liverpool's black population lived.

"My sister was keen on dancing," said Jimmy, "and the best place to go to was the Rialto Ballroom. It had a great dance hall and there was always a good mixture of locals and the U.S. servicemen. They were bringing their American records down with them and the DJ would

American Mustang planes travel to Burtonwood, along Allerton Road in 1945.

play them. That's another way we got to hear the latest American tunes, like a lot of Motown and black music. Clubs like Dutch Eddie's, The Nigeria Club, Stanley House and the Somali Club were all playing these records, which is where John and Paul would have heard the Isley Brothers' 'Twist and Shout', and songs by The Shirelles, The Chiffons, The Miracles and many more.

"My sister and her husband used to visit all of these clubs and they knew John and Paul because they were regulars. They were forever in the clubs as Lennon lived nearby in Gambier Terrace, which was just down the road. These were his local clubs. It was mainly records being played in the clubs as opposed to bands, and predominantly black artists being played, so the musical influence was huge."

Another witness to these events was Jimmy James, a member of the Royal Caribbean Steel Band. "Just outside of Liverpool was a U.S. base at Burtonwood," explained James, "and the servicemen used to come into Liverpool at the weekend to attend the clubs. I was a DJ in my spare time, and they would bring the records that they had brought from America for me to play. We had access to the latest records from the stores, plus the servicemen bringing their records with them."

Joe Ankrah, singer with Liverpool vocal group The Chants was in an even more advantageous position than most. His three aunties were all dating American GIs from Burtonwood, so they had access to all the records. They brought them back to Joe's grandmother's house and played them over and over again.

Jimmy Doran emphasised this point for me: "There was more influence from Burtonwood than the Cunard Yanks could ever have done. Even if the Cunard Yanks were bringing the records in, and I've thought about this a lot, it wouldn't have made much difference because the records were already here. Even if they brought them back first, they would be available within days here.

"The funniest thing I remember," recalled Jimmy, "was when The Beatles appeared on the TV show *People and Places*, when they were singing 'Love Me Do', and my brother-in-law walked in and said, 'What the hell is he doing on there? He is the biggest bum there is,' pointing to Lennon. 'They're rag-arses! Mary come and have a look at this! Look who is on the telly!' He pointed at the group with this stunned look on his face. 'And that's not the proper drummer!' Ringo had just joined, because they knew Pete as the drummer from when he would hang out with them in the clubs." They couldn't believe that the lads they used to hang out with in the clubs of Liverpool 8 were on the TV. If only they knew what was to come.

Quarry Bank High School magazine, *The Quarry*.

Quarry Bank High School

The story of The Beatles would not be complete without a look at the school where it all began. In spite of the working class image that Brian Epstein tried to craft for The Fab Four, their roots originated within the walls of the middle class grammar schools of Liverpool, like Quarry Bank.

The Quarrymen group was founded here, taking the words of the school song for their name and providing its first members. Started by pupils John Lennon, Pete Shotton, Eric Griffiths and Bill Smith, the group soon added Rod Davis to its ranks. John's friend Michael Hill, who had accompanied him through Dovedale School and into Quarry Bank, was instrumental in turning John onto rock 'n' roll.

Quarry Bank, as with all other grammar schools, could only be accessed by passing the tough Eleven Plus exam – and not all pupils were allowed to take it. Ringo, for instance, was never put forward for the Eleven Plus as there was no expectation of him passing it. He had missed too much school because of illness. Failure to pass the exam would automatically mean that the pupil attended the local secondary modern school. In John's case, that would have meant going to Rose Lane Secondary Modern.

Quarry Bank was very much modelled on the best public schools in England, a point proven by the appointment of its first Headmaster R.F. Bailey. A former housemaster at Shrewsbury School, he was also once a student at Eton, widely considered England's finest public school.

The former Quarry Bank High School, which is now Calderstones School.

Aerial photo of the Quarry Bank High School site, with the school buildings at the top of the picture.

The main house at the centre of the school site was completed in 1867 for a prosperous timber merchant, John Bland. It was acquired by Liverpool Corporation in 1920 with the intention of converting it into a school. It is still very grand inside and has the look and feel of a wealthy merchant's home, with dark wood panelling, ornate ceilings and decorative windows. Quarry Bank High School opened on 11 January 1922, and Bailey's words were recorded for posterity: "Eighty boys sat an entrance examination having assembled in front of the largest looking glass in any school in England." By the end of 1922, Quarry Bank had 225 pupils.

R. F. Bailey wanted to incorporate the ideas he had absorbed at public school into the new school in south Liverpool. He introduced the House System, which survived and was expanded up to 1967. The first ones established were Mersey, Esmeduna, Wavertree and Sefton in 1923, Allerton and Childwall in 1936, with Aigburth and Woolton, where John would be placed, established in 1946. He started the Unity Boy's Club and devoted his life to the boys of Quarry Bank and the development of the school. Those who met him held Bailey in great esteem.

Europe's descent into war affected the school. Evacuation to Wrexham, North Wales took place during January and February of 1940, when there was some slight damage to the site during bombing raids. Lessons were held in air raid shelters and gardening replaced Physical Education on the curriculum. Teachers and Old Boys continued to join the service and sixty-nine of them were killed in action. Their lives have been commemorated on the honours board at the back of the school hall.

Bailey retired in 1947 after 26 years in charge of their schools, and he died on 1 March 1951. Later that year, the Lower School of Quarry Bank High School was renamed Bailey House, with its forms, 1R, 1F and 1B after Bailey's initials.

Mr. E. R. Taylor was Headmaster of Quarry Bank High School from 1947 until 1956 when he moved to Wolverhampton Grammar School. It was during Taylor's time, on 4 September 1952, that a certain John Winston Lennon was admitted to the school.

Taylor was replaced by Mr. William E. Pobjoy, a languages specialist, who was Headmaster from 1956 until 1982. It was Pobjoy who was instrumental in giving John a future at Art College when any further education looked impossible. He saw something in young Lennon and backed it up with a recommendation to the art school. By setting him on this important path, Pobjoy would change the course of John's life. At Art College, he met his future wife Cynthia, his close friend and fellow Beatle Stuart Sutcliffe and Bill Harry, founder of *Mersey Beat* and a well-respected Beatles author.

William Pobjoy, Headmaster of Quarry Bank High School from 1956.

A glimpse of life at Quarry Bank is reflected in the pages of the school magazine, *The Quarry*. "Because of the way that THE QVARRY is spelt on the school magazine," explained Rod Davis, "it was always known as 'The Ovary' by the pupils." One of the most prominent advertisements in the magazine was for the Raleigh Lenton bicycle, which was the preferred present of many of the boys, including John, on passing their Eleven Plus. Pupils were encouraged to submit items for publication and John managed to have his "Tale of Hermit Fred" published in the Easter 1957 edition. The issue also featured one of his drawings, simply signed "JWL, Vc", with Vc standing for his class, year 5, C stream (the bottom set, based on ability).

One amusing entry in the 1957 edition is the opinion poll conducted among staff to discover their favourite songs, with a "trend to 'pops'" encouraging the thought that the staff was comprised of "squares".

The hallowed halls of this grand school – most notably Quarry Hall – were about to echo to the sound of a different form of music; skiffle, played by some of its own students.

Map of the site of Quarry Bank High School.

The Fab one hundred and Four

A cartoon that John drew, which appeared in the school magazine, *The Quarry*, at Easter 1957.

THE TALE OF HERMIT FRED.

The wandering hermit Fred am I
With candlestick and bun,
I knit spaghetti apple pie
And crumbs do I have fun!
I peel the bagpipes for my wife
And cut all negroes' hair
As breathing is my very life
And stop I do not dare.

J.W.L., *V.c.*

"The Tale of Hermit Fred", written by John, which was published in the school magazine, *The Quarry*.

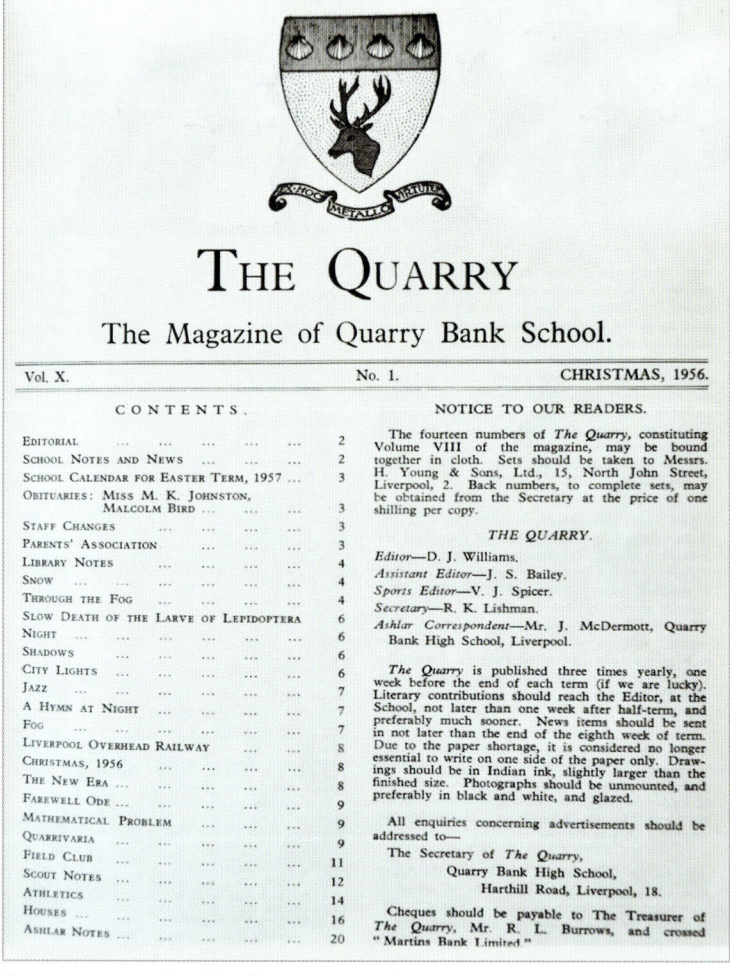

THE QUARRY
The Magazine of Quarry Bank School.

Vol. X.   No. 1.   CHRISTMAS, 1956.

CONTENTS.

Editorial	2
School Notes and News	2
School Calendar for Easter Term, 1957	3
Obituaries: Miss M. K. Johnston, Malcolm Bird	3
Staff Changes	3
Parents' Association	3
Library Notes	4
Snow	4
Through the Fog	4
Slow Death of the Larve of Lepidoptera	6
Night	6
Shadows	6
City Lights	6
Jazz	7
A Hymn at Night	7
Fog	7
Liverpool Overhead Railway	8
Christmas, 1956	8
The New Era	8
Farewell Ode	9
Mathematical Problem	9
Quarrivaria	9
Field Club	11
Scout Notes	12
Athletics	14
Houses	16
Ashlar Notes	20

NOTICE TO OUR READERS.

The fourteen numbers of *The Quarry*, constituting Volume VIII of the magazine, may be bound together in cloth. Sets should be taken to Messrs. H. Young & Sons, Ltd., 15, North John Street, Liverpool, 2. Back numbers, to complete sets, may be obtained from the Secretary at the price of one shilling per copy.

THE QUARRY.

Editor—D. J. Williams.
Assistant Editor—J. S. Bailey.
Sports Editor—V. J. Spicer.
Secretary—R. K. Lishman.
Ashlar Correspondent—Mr. J. McDermott, Quarry Bank High School, Liverpool.

The Quarry is published three times yearly, one week before the end of each term (if we are lucky). Literary contributions should reach the Editor, at the School, not later than one week after half-term, and preferably much sooner. News items should be sent in not later than the end of the eighth week of term. Due to the paper shortage, it is considered no longer essential to write on one side of the paper only. Drawings should be in Indian ink, slightly larger than the finished size. Photographs should be unmounted, and preferably in black and white, and glazed.

All enquiries concerning advertisements should be addressed to—
   The Secretary of *The Quarry*,
      Quarry Bank High School,
         Harthill Road, Liverpool, 18.

Cheques should be payable to The Treasurer of *The Quarry*, Mr. R. L. Burrows, and crossed "Martins Bank Limited."

Contents page for *The Quarry* magazine.

The Quarry Bank High School song, "The Song of The Quarry", written by the school's first Headmaster, R.F. Bailey.

The Liverpool Institute High School "Green Book" given to every pupil.

Liverpool Institute High School for Boys and Liverpool Art College

Though the original lineup of The Quarrymen consisted solely of Quarry Bank pupils, they would soon add friends from the Liverpool Institute such as Ivan Vaughan, Len Garry, Paul McCartney and George Harrison to their ranks. As with Quarry Bank, the Institute, known affectionately as the Inny, was one of Liverpool's premier grammar schools.

After Bill Smith left the group, John tried to recruit his friend Ivan Vaughan who, upon leaving Dovedale School, applied for the Institute instead of following John to Quarry Bank. Ivan played tea-chest bass with The Quarrymen for a short time, but he did not see himself as a musician. After Blue Coat School pupil Nigel Walley temporarily held the position, it was Ivan who recommended one of his new school friends, Len Garry, for the job.

Ivan would soon make the most important introduction of his life when he took his new school friend, Paul McCartney, to meet John Lennon. The Beatles connection would then be enhanced when Paul introduced his school friend George Harrison to John at the end

Liverpool Institute from the air.

of 1957. John Duff Lowe, pianist for The Quarrymen in 1958, was also a contemporary of Paul and George's at the Inny. When the group was looking for a roadie, the first person they turned to was their Inny schoolmate Neil Aspinall, known as Nell, who later became their trusted aide and confidante. Neil eventually became Chief Executive of The Beatles' Apple Corps. Another of their Inny cohorts, Tony Bramwell, would go on to work with Brian Epstein at NEMS before serving as head of Apple Films and, later, as director of Apple Records. However, it was not just The Quarrymen and The Beatles who benefited from an education at the Institute. The school's roster of musicians also included Les Chadwick from Gerry and the Pacemakers, Colin Manley and Don Andrew from the Remo Four, plus Paul's brother Mike McCartney, who became known as Mike McGear during his successful recording career with The Scaffold.

Ivan Vaughan, Len Garry, John Duff Lowe, Neil Aspinall and Mike McCartney's entries in the Liverpool Institute register.

The school had its origins in 1825 but occupied different premises while the money was raised to build a dedicated building on Mount Street. The Institute was first known as the Liverpool Mechanics' School of Art. In 1832, the name was shortened to the Liverpool Mechanics' Institution.

Its initial primary purpose as a Mechanics' Institution was to provide educational opportunities for working men, mainly through evening classes. Lectures for the general public were also provided, general interest topics ranging from Arctic exploration to Shakespeare and philosophy. By 1840, the Institution offered evening classes, lectures, a library and a boys' lower and upper school. In 1844, Victorian author Charles Dickens delivered a talk in the main lecture hall. By the 1850s, a formal art school had begun to evolve from the evening classes and, in 1856, this diversity was acknowledged by yet another name change – this time to The Liverpool Institute and School of Arts, the name which remains on the façade of the building.

In 1905, Liverpool City Council took over the management of secondary schools when the Board of Governors presented the school and assets to the City. From then on, the school was formally known as The Liverpool Institute High School for Boys.

One of the Institute's most famous pupils, Paul McCartney, was presented with a prize for art at the school Speech Day on 15 December 1959.

The Inny went into decline in the mid-1960s with the introduction of comprehensive education in Liverpool. It was closed by the City Council in 1985 after two decades of contention, political dispute and very little upkeep of the building fabric. The building stood empty and neglected, with its roof leaking and walls crumbling until, in 1987, one of its former pupils, Paul McCartney, was granted use of the building and site for a new educational establishment. Having played there with Wings in 1979, Paul returned one night in 1990 to reminisce about his school days, while he was writing his Liverpool Oratorio. This visit is tellingly captured in *Echoes*, a DVD that accompanied the Liverpool Oratorio box set. McCartney was determined to save the building somehow and, during a conversation with Sir George Martin, the idea of a fame school emerged. (Martin was already helping educator Mark Featherstone-Witty start a London

Liverpool Institute Speech Day invitation.

The Liverpool Institute High School

The Governors and the Headmaster request the pleasure of the company of

_____

in the Philharmonic Hall, on Tuesday, 15th December, 1959, at 7.30 p.m.

when the Prizes will be distributed and the Address given by

THE RIGHT HON. THE VISCOUNT LEVERHULME, T.D., B.A., J.P.

A reply to the Headmaster not later than 8th December would be appreciated.

P.T.O.

Kindly bring this invitation card with you

Ticket for the Liverpool Institute Speech Day.

THE LIVERPOOL INSTITUTE HIGH SCHOOL

SPEECH DAY

PHILHARMONIC HALL, HOPE STREET,
TUESDAY, DECEMBER 15th, 1959
7.30 p.m.

ADMIT ONE

The programme for the Liverpool Institute Speech Day.

THE CITY OF LIVERPOOL

LIVERPOOL INSTITUTE HIGH SCHOOL

SPEECH DAY

TUESDAY, DECEMBER 15th, 1959

The PRIZES will be Distributed and the ADDRESS given by

THE RIGHT HONOURABLE THE VISCOUNT LEVERHULME, T.D., B.A., J.P.

Chairman: Professor R. A. MORTON, Ph.D., D.Sc., F.R.I.C., F.R.S.

The programme showing Paul's award.

SPECIAL PRIZES

Prize for Music	D. Norris
Prize for Spanish	J. D. Lunt
Prize for Latin and Greek Verses—given by Mr. Bentliff	R. T. Crofts
Prize for Art	J. P. McCartney
Prize for French—given by the French Consul	F. J. McKie

The façade of Liverpool Institute High School.

The Liverpool Institute for Performing Arts, based in the former school building.

secondary school with an innovative curriculum.) McCartney and Featherstone-Witty joined forces to create The Liverpool Institute for Performing Arts (LIPA). The new company took over the Liverpool Institute Trust, established in 1905.

The building was remodelled behind its old facade and re-opened in 1996 under a new and more appropriate name: the Liverpool Institute for Performing Arts.

For Paul, it was not just the pupils and building that he remembered. One of his teachers, Alan "Dusty" Durband, is cited by Paul as a big influence. "I owe him," said Paul. "I had great respect for Mr. Durband because he managed to get us to read books. He taught Chaucer and, to this day, I know where all the naughty bits are. Teaching literature to us in general was a struggle but he managed it." Paul says that because of Alan's teaching of English Literature, he was encouraged to read more and that, in turn, helped him attain his only scholastic achievement: 'A' Level Literature. "I think after The Beatles' 'Thank You Girl' period," he recalled, "we blossomed with our writing, say, with 'Eleanor Rigby'."

Durband, born in the Dingle, had won a scholarship to the Institute and, after attending Cambridge University, returned to the Institute as a teacher in 1953. He was appointed Head of English in 1956. Durband was one of the driving forces behind the creation and later renovation of the Everyman Theatre in Hope Street, Liverpool, which opened in 1964.

One of the other teachers at the Institute during Paul's time there was Alfred "Cissy" Smith, brother of John's Uncle George.

Alan Durband, teacher at Liverpool Institute.

Liverpool Institute (the white building) from the air, next to the Art College.

Liverpool Art College

John's further education after Quarry Bank was at the Art College in the building adjacent to the Institute, although the Art College had its origins as part of the Liverpool Institute. In 1883, a new building housing the School of Art was opened around the corner on Hope Street, adjacent to the principal building housing the High School on Mount Street. The Art College, by which it was later known, took in talented students often without formal academic credentials, like John Lennon.

It was here that John met Stuart Sutcliffe, Cynthia Powell, Bill Harry and Rod Murray. With the buildings being adjacent, it was easy for Paul and George to walk out of the Institute and into the more relaxed atmosphere of the Art College to practise.

In 1970, the Art College became one of the four constituent parts of the Liverpool Polytechnic. Later, in 1992, it became part of Liverpool John Moores University with the School of Art and Design being housed in the Art and Design Academy. The building was closed in 2013, but has been obtained by LIPA.

Paul's entry in the Liverpool Institute register.

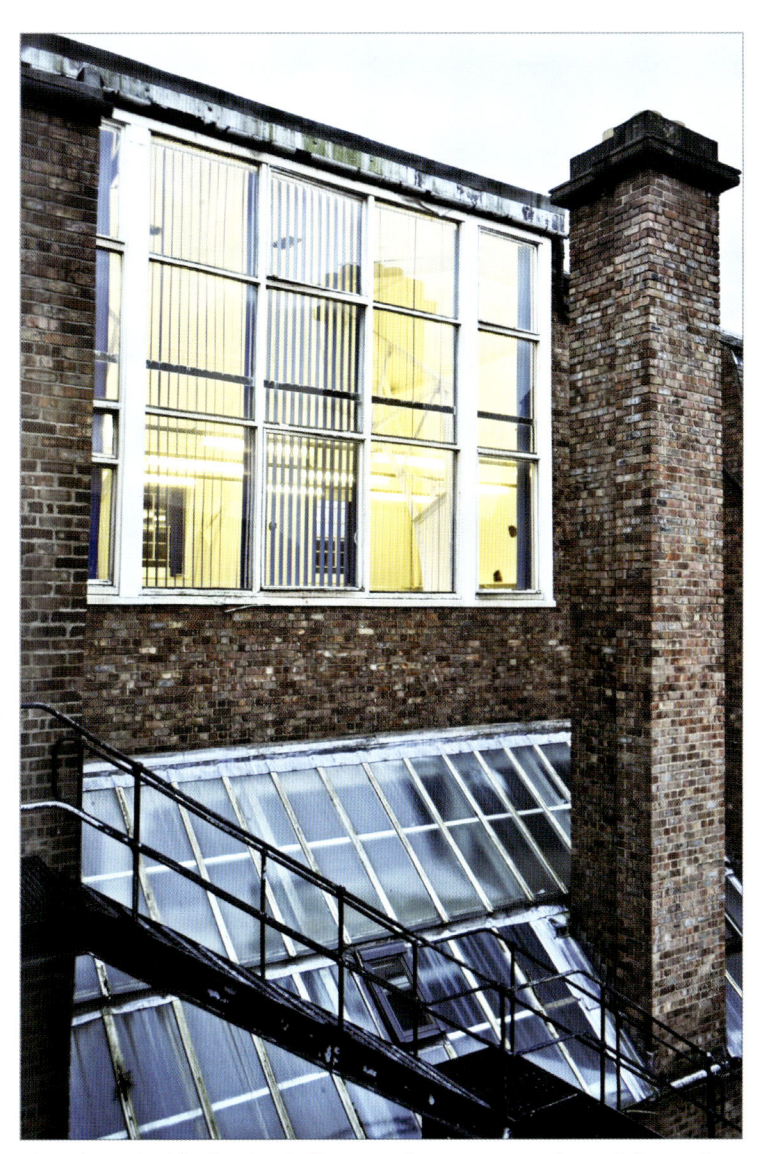

View from inside the Art College to the art room where John and Stuart spent many hours painting.

The *Fab* one hundred and *Four*

JULY 1956 – OCTOBER 1959

The Quarrymen

The Quarrymen were formed at Quarry Bank High School in the summer of 1956 by John Lennon, Pete Shotton, Eric Griffiths and Bill Smith, at the suggestion of Geoff Lee. They used the name until the final lineup of John, Paul, George and Ken Brown played at The Casbah in October 1959. Paul and Mike McCartney played as a duo during this time, too.

One can't take a critical look at The Quarrymen without also acknowledging those who influenced them, like John's mum Julia, an accomplished musician; Paul's dad Jim, who was also in a band and lent his experience to his son; and George's father Harry who, although not a great musician himself, encouraged his son and arranged lessons for him. Outside of their families, there were friends and neighbours who helped them on their musical journey.

During that time, The Quarrymen had thirteen different musicians who drifted in and out of the group:

John Lennon	Pete Shotton	Eric Griffiths
Bill Smith	Rod Davis	Ivan Vaughan
Nigel Walley	Len Garry	Colin Hanton
Paul McCartney	George Harrison	John Duff Lowe
Ken Brown		

The group began as a fun thing for friends to do at school – playing skiffle music as Lonnie Donegan did on the records. A few little performances at their school and local halls meant that they gained experience, without being technically gifted.

The Quarrymen at The Casbah, 29 August 1959: George, Paul, Ken and John.

In the spring of 1957, a school friend of John's witnessed Lennon's group taking part in a talent competition as The Blackjacks, and this name was probably only used for a couple of weeks, according to Rod Davis.

All that changed when John was introduced to Paul at St. Peter's Church on 6 July 1957 and a rock 'n' roll group began to take shape. Paul's friend Ian James had helped Paul learn the chords and lyrics to the songs that he performed for John. By the end of 1957, the nucleus of The Beatles – John, Paul and George – were together.

Still, there were others with whom they played, like Arthur Davis and, in Wales, John and Aneurin. George's first group, The Rebels, was instrumental in helping him fulfil his dream to play in a band. Formed with his brother Peter, his friend Arthur Kelly and Alan Williams, George took inspiration from wherever he could find it. His childhood friend Geoff Nugent remembers playing on street corners with George, and Tony Bramwell recalls George receiving lessons and tips from his school friend Colin Manley, who became one of the greatest guitarists in Liverpool.

In his book *Yesterday Came Suddenly*, author Bob Cepican discovered that in 1959, John, Paul and George, and maybe one other musician, used the name J. Page Four: J for John, pa for Paul and ge for George. However, Mark Lewisohn, in his book *The Beatles – All These Years: Volume One: Tune In* revealed that, at the end of 1958, one of John's Art College friends, Derek Hodkin, became involved with the group.

Hodkin told how, armed with a tape recorder, John, Paul and George appointed him as manager. They needed a new name and after several were discounted, they agreed upon Japage 3 (pronounced jaypage three). The group only made one official appearance at La Scala Ballroom in Runcorn on 2 March 1959. Derek soon gave up his managerial duties too.

At the beginning of 1959, with performances hard to come by, George joined the Les Stewart Quartet with Les Stewart, Ken Brown and Ray Skinner. Fate was to play a part in the story when George and Ken reformed The Quarrymen with John and Paul to open The Casbah Coffee Club on 29 August 1959.

When they fell out with Ken, they were down to just John, Paul and George once more and the name The Quarrymen was never used again by them.

John Duff Lowe, Len Garry, Rod Davis and Colin Hanton (hidden) return to the stage in Quarry Bank Hall, August 2011.

The Fab one hundred and Four

Geoff "George Henry" Lee

He was never in The Quarrymen, but Geoff Lee was to make a suggestion to his friend John Lennon that would have far reaching consequences. "George Henry" Lee's real name was Geoffrey Lee, as he explained to me: "I was given the nickname 'George Henry' by my teachers because of the famous large department store in Liverpool, George Henry Lee. Because the teachers called me 'George Henry', everyone assumed my name was George, so that is what I was called. One day, John Lennon cycled down to my house in Cressington, knocked on the door and asked if George was in. He was told that nobody by the name of George lived there and went back home!

"I was in John's class at Quarry Bank and we shared a desk for a while. There was a gang of us," Geoff explained, "like Eric Griffiths, John Lennon, Norman Bennett and a few others, and we would go out at lunchtime to buy fish and chips, and then eat them behind the bike sheds. John would always be singing, as his ambition was to be like Elvis. I remember him singing 'Blueberry Hill' and thought he had a good voice. When Lonnie Donegan came out with 'Rock Island Line', it was like nothing we'd heard before. Everywhere, skiffle groups were springing up, and when I heard The Vipers Skiffle Group, I thought John had the vocal talent, so one day, I said to him, 'why don't you set up your own skiffle group?'

"Of course, that is what he did, and though I wasn't musical, I had a guitar. At that time, John didn't have a guitar yet, so I gave him the one I had and he carried it with him everywhere on his back. It was battered and didn't sound too good, but at least he had one to start with."

Geoff "George Henry" Lee, wiping his eye, who suggested to John Lennon that he start a skiffle group.

John later remembered Geoff's generosity. "I used to borrow a guitar at first. I couldn't play, but a pal of mine had one and it fascinated me.

Eventually my mother bought me one from one of those mail order firms. I suppose it was a bit crummy, when you think about it. But I played it all the time and I got a lot of practise." Although much has been written about the Gallotone Champion guitar that was bought for him by his mother, until now, nobody knew from whom John had borrowed his first guitar. Unfortunately, Geoff can't recall the make of the guitar he gave to John.

Geoff used to visit Aunt Mimi's house every week to watch the TV show *Son of Fred*, which featured Peter Sellers and Spike Milligan from *The Goon Show*. "We loved The Goons, and this programme was like a TV version of the radio show.

"John's humour was so much like The Goons, and from quite an early age. I can remember sitting next to him and he was so clever with words and so funny, too. We were only twelve or thirteen, yet he was like a comedian with his hilarious stories and cartoon drawings. He used to draw them all the time and pass them to me. If only I'd kept them! They would be funny characters with speech bubbles full of rude words.

"We then drifted into different friend groups as I went down the Sciences route in school, whereas John was doing the Arts. He became best friends with Pete Shotton, the 'White-Headed Carrot' as we called him because he had bright blond hair and a red face. John was desperate to get on to the dances at the school that were held every six months or so, which he eventually did with the group. The sound was raw to start off with and, though I would hang around with the group, I wasn't really involved. I may have contributed a bit of percussion here and there, but it wasn't my thing."

Geoff and John lost touch with each other and it was a few years before Geoff saw his old school friend again, though not in person. "I was walking down the road and was looking in the window of the local newsagents' shop," Geoff continued. "There was a magazine with these four faces on it, and I thought I recognised one of them but couldn't place him. Then I realised, of course, that it was John and The Beatles!"

Geoff left Liverpool and moved with his family to Stafford, where he still lives with his wife, Deryl, and sons Jonathan and Damian.

Maybe he will now realise that he started something really big with a simple suggestion to his school friend, John Lennon: "You should be a singer and start a skiffle group."

Who knew what would happen next?

Geoff Lee with his wife Deryl.

Woolton Quarry, which Pete Shotton admits was a contributory factor in naming the group, The Quarrymen.

John Lennon,
Julia Lennon, Uncle George Smith
and Arthur Pendleton

John Winston Lennon was born in Oxford Street Maternity Hospital on 9 October 1940 to Alfred and Julia Lennon and taken to Julia's family home at 9, Newcastle Road in the Penny Lane area. He was raised from the age of five by his Aunt Mimi Smith at her home, "Mendips", in Woolton, a middle-class area.

Lennon first attended Mosspits Lane Primary School before Mimi moved him to Dovedale School. At the age of eleven, he transferred to Quarry Bank High School where The Quarrymen were formed. After five years at Quarry Bank, he enrolled in the Liverpool Art College where he met Cynthia Powell, Stuart Sutcliffe and Bill Harry.

John started his musical journey on a guitar lent to him by his friend Geoff Lee, before his mother bought a guitar for him. Being somewhat proficient on the banjo, Julia taught John to play his guitar using banjo chords. The other instrument for which he became famous was the harmonica or mouth organ. I always wondered why he chose that instrument, knowing it was partly because he was given one, though there are various stories about who gave it to him.

Julia Baird, John's half-sister, remembers its origins. "Mimi's husband, Uncle George, gave John his first mouth organ, when he was about fourteen years old," she recalled in her book, *Imagine This*. "He loved it. He would carry it in his pocket, or in his mouth and make a noise. He brought it over to show Mum—

John Lennon at Quarry Bank.

The *Fab* one hundred and *Four*

my, who couldn't play it herself, but knew a neighbour who played it well, Arthur Pendleton. He lived two houses away from us at 5, Blomfield Road and our mother sent John there to learn the basics of puffing and blowing. He lived with it as an attachment for some time, even while he was practising the banjo, as he could grip it with his teeth and suck and blow air, creating a din, until something resembling a tune began to emerge."

John, centre back row, at Dovedale School in 1951.

Mosspits Lane Primary School leaving register, showing John's attendance for a short time.

John's entry in the Dovedale Primary School register.

John with his mum, Julia.

BLOMFIELD ROAD, 19

Dykins, John A.—J . . . 1
Dykins, Julia . . . 1
Wood, Elizabeth . . . 3
Wood, Arthur A. . . . 3
Cain, Arthur Leslie . . . 3
Cain, Thelma May . . . 3
Pendleton, Arthur . . . 5

Street directory showing Julia Lennon living as Julia Dykins at 1, Blomfield Road, and Arthur Pendleton at 5, Blomfield Road.

Arthur Pendleton's house (right) and Julia Lennon's house (far left).

The *Fab* one hundred and *Four*

John's photo booth picture from 1960. Image © Mark Naboshek

John has written "ME CROSS EYED".

Alf Lennon's entry in the St. Silas School register.

On his trip to Edinburgh to see his aunt and uncle, he played the mouth organ on the bus. The bus driver later gave John a mouth organ that had been left behind by a passenger and stored in lost property. John was now the owner of an even better harmonica, which he played for years.

One myth surrounding John and his harmonica involves Delbert McClinton, the musician who provided the distinctive harmonica on Bruce Chanel's "Hey! Baby." Some have suggested that McClinton taught John how to play the hit song, but McClinton put the record straight. "We shot the breeze," McClinton said. "He came out to three shows, and we hung out maybe 18 to 24 hours total during two weeks. Then I came back and about a year or two later in an interview he said he was influenced by 'Hey! Baby.' Now, it's morphed into 'I taught John Lennon how to play harmonica!' It's been romanticised a bit," he said.

John used the harmonica to great effect on "Love Me Do" and other early Beatles tunes. A possible reason for his interest in the harmonica could be traced to *The Goon Show*, one of his favourite radio programmes. Every show had two musical interludes. One of them was Max Geldray who would play a different song on the harmonica every week accompanied by his band. He was a versatile performer and could play almost anything. It's quite possible that he inspired a young John Lennon to take to the instrument.

1, Blomfield Road, the home of Julia Lennon.

John's father, Alf Lennon.

John's parents were both musical and they passed that influence and talent down to him. However, with his father it was more inherited than taught, as the time Alf spent with John was limited.

Alf lost his father when he was very young. His mother couldn't afford to bring up all of the children, so he and his sister Edith were sent to the Blue Coat Orphanage (later the Blue Coat School) on Church Road, just up from the Penny Lane roundabout and very near Newcastle Road, where John would first live with his mother. Stunted by rickets at a young age, Alf grew to only 5 foot 4 inches tall. While still at the Blue Coat, he decided to run away. He had auditioned for a children's music hall act, *Will Murray's Gang*, at the Liverpool Empire and, having passed the audition, joined the travelling show. His successful run came to an end in Glasgow where he was discovered and brought back to the Blue Coat for punishment.

Alf left the Blue Coat at the age of fifteen and looked for work, though never settled in any job for long. He preferred to visit the local theatres and cinemas where he was a well-known figure. It was

Bioletti's Barber Shop, to the left of Cousins, made famous in the song "Penny Lane", where Alf and John had their hair cut.

in one of these cinemas, The Trocadero in Camden Street, Liverpool, that he met one of the usherettes, though he did not speak to her.

However, he met her again in Sefton Park while walking one day and introduced himself. Her name was Julia Stanley and they began a lengthy courtship which culminated in their marriage in 1938 at the Liverpool Registrar's Office in Bolton Street.

The *Fab* one hundred and *Four*

Newcastle Road, bottom right, with the shelter in the middle of Penny Lane roundabout to the left of centre.

The F.W. Woolworth store, where Julia Lennon worked.

Alf was a proficient musician, playing the banjo and doing passable impersonations of Al Jolson and Louis Armstrong. During his career in the Merchant Navy, he was considered a natural performer and was well-known for entertaining his shipmates. It is interesting to note that so many of these personality traits were passed on to John despite Alf's absence from his son's life.

Julia was also proficient on the banjo and piano, as her daughter Julia Baird remembers clearly. "As John entered his teens and spent more time with us, she started to teach him music and he loved it. I can see John so clearly, concentrating intently on the mother-of-pearl-backed banjo that had belonged to his grandfather, who had brought it back from a sea trip and then left it to our mother."

John's mother had been inspired by her own parents, as his cousin Stanley Parkes remembered. "My grandfather, George Stanley, played the banjo and ukulele and he taught Julia to play, and Julia taught John. My grandmother, Annie Stanley (née Millward) was also musical and played the piano. She taught Julia to play, who of course taught John. I also remember when my family was living in Fleet-

John Lennon, when he was with The Beatles.

wood, Lancashire, and John would come up to stay with us. I was forced to do piano lessons, which I did not enjoy, as all of my friends were outside playing. We also had a piano accordion, which I tried to play, but to no avail. John picked it up, strapped it over his shoulders and just started playing. I asked him how he knew how to play it and he just said, 'I don't know, I just played it.' He was so natural. He took it back to Liverpool with him and kept it for quite a while.

"I also remember watching him play the piano," Stanley continued, "and I noticed he was not using his thumbs. He just stretched his long fingers as wide as possible and played, so I asked him why he did not use his thumbs too. 'I can't play with them. I can only use my four fingers to play.' I was also amazed because he couldn't read sheet music either."

Stanley was responsible for John reuniting with his mother, Julia. As they became closer, Julia became John's musical tutor. She gave him lessons at 1, Blomfield Road, her home with her partner John Dykins and their two daughters, Julia and Jackie. John spent a lot of time with her and this time was well spent as she kindled John's love for music.

251, Menlove Avenue, known as "Mendips".

"She would stand behind him," recalled Julia Baird, "leaning over his shoulder, and raise the neck of the banjo high. She would place her hands over his, their left hands on the neck of the banjo and right hands in the strumming position over the hole, and notes would happen. Sometimes, to get it right, she would tell him just to concentrate on the left hand and she would strum or finger pluck. Sometimes she would press the strings herself to change the notes and John would strum and pick and pluck as loud as he could, making music."

As John became more proficient on the banjo, they would play along to a record, even slowing the speed down until he could pick up the tune. "Then mummy would take the banjo herself," remembered Julia with a smile, "return the needle dial to normal speed and play along, with John staring at her fingers on the strings, playing air guitar, before he had another go."

In an interview years later, John recalled those days with his mother clearly and fondly: "The very first tune I ever learned to play was 'That'll Be the Day'. My mother taught it to me on the banjo, sit-

Menlove Avenue after the tall hedges had been removed from the central reservation. "Mendips" is the first house on the left (with dark roof).

ting there with endless patience until I managed to work out all the chords. She was a perfectionist. She made me go through it over and over again until I had it right. I remember her slowing down the record so that I could scribble out the words. First hearing Buddy Holly absolutely knocked me for a loop. And to think it was my own mother who was turning me onto it all."

Julia was also proficient on the ukulele, though it is not known if John ever learned this instrument as well. In addition to the stringed instruments, Julia was also an accomplished player of the piano accordion. She would put the straps onto her shoulders and lead the singing and dancing in their house, which her young daughters enjoyed immensely.

It was perhaps the most dominant instrument in the living room at Blomfield Road that would have a significant influence on John's music career. Regarded in many homes as an extra piece of furniture, the piano was used religiously by Julia in teaching music and leading the sing-alongs in their house.

Julia encouraged The Quarrymen to rehearse in her house and often took part herself. Rod Davis remembers those practises well: "When we would go to practise at Julia's, she would say something like,

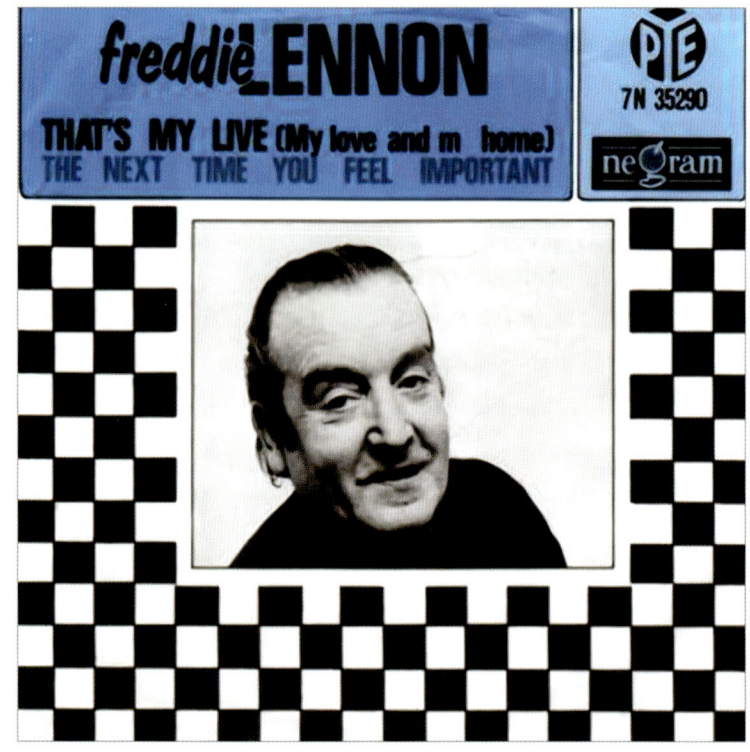

Alf "Freddie" Lennon's 1965 record, "That's My Life (My Love and My Home)".

Rod Davis holding his banjo, with his brother Bernie and sister Rosemary in the foreground with a washboard.

'I don't like those horrible guitars, let me have a go of your banjo,' and I have a clear recollection of her standing with her back to a fireplace playing my banjo. I used a piece of parachute cord as a strap and you can see it clearly in a photo which I think was probably taken on 6 July 1957 as my sister is in her brownie uniform and she was wearing this in the Rose Queen parade. She is playing the washboard held by my brother."

John, of course, lost his mum when he was only seventeen. She was knocked down and killed by an off-duty policeman on Menlove Avenue, close to "Mendips", her sister Mimi's house.

Alf walked back into John's life in 1964 after The Beatles had hit the big time. He stirred up quite a bit of controversy when he was encouraged to release a record. "That's My Life (My Love and My Home)" was released in 1965 and caused a stir in the press, but not in the charts. In 1966, "Freddie Lennon" (the name under which Alf recorded) tried again and issued three singles with the group Loving Kind. These records did not sell well either. It was the subject of increased tension between John and Alf and was seen as an opportunity to cash in on his son's fame.

John and Alf were estranged for many years, but were reconciled in the hospital where Alf was dying from cancer. Alf left John his life story so John would see it from his father's perspective.

The *Fab* one hundred and *Four*

Pete Shotton

Peter Shotton was born on 4 August 1941. His parents hailed from Sunderland in the North East of England. They moved to Liverpool after his father, George, left the Merchant Navy and landed a job in Tate & Lyle as a draughtsman. Bessie, Pete's mother, worked for the marketing company Gallup Poll, stopping people and asking them for their opinions about new products. Pete had an older brother named Ernest, an older sister Joan and a younger brother David.

The Shotton family lived at 83, Vale Road, just behind "Mendips" and very close to Ivan Vaughan and Nigel Walley, who also lived on Vale Road. This semi-detached property also had an air-raid shelter in the back garden, a remnant from the war. These Anderson Shelters had provided protection for British families during the war, but now this particular shelter would soon have new life – as a rehearsal room. Though small, the acoustics in these structures were good as they were constructed from corrugated iron.

Pete Shotton at Quarry Bank, 1956.

The little gang of Pete, Ivan and Nigel kept to the top of Vale Road, near Strawberry Field. This was because Liverpool Council-owned properties stood at the other end of Vale Road and the neighbourhood parents, including Pete's and those of his friends, told them to keep away. "The Council house kids did strike me as being rougher, tattier," Pete said. "We kept to ourselves, our own territory."

However, unlike most of the other families, the Shottons did not own their home. They rented it, making them not all that different from the families down the road. Pete was the undisputed leader of his little gang for a short time, until a new boy named John Lennon moved to the area. John was bigger, older and looked tougher. The boys sized each other up, and it was not long before Pete found John's Achilles' heel: his middle name, Winston. Anytime Pete wanted to tease his friend, he would just call him "Winnie"! This had been revealed in Sunday School when each child had to give their full name.

There was a patch of waste ground between Vale Road and Menlove Avenue known by the boys as The Tip. It was here one day that Pete took a chance and called John "Winnie". This time it backfired. John pounced on Pete and threatened to beat him up if he ever called him "Winnie" again. Pete agreed, and once he was at a safe distance, turned to John and shouted "Winnie! Winnie! Winnie!" and ran for safety.

Pete ceded control of his gang to John without too much fuss and a lifelong friendship was formed. On the first bend of Vale Road was an old disused garage, which John and his friends used as a den. It was here that John and Pete decided to become 'blood-brothers'. John sawed away at his wrist with a knife, but it was blunt and did not draw blood. The two boys improvised and swore allegiance to each other without the blood.

The two boys were soon known as "Shennon and Lotton", a terrible duo who would terrorise Woolton. They were almost inseparable. However, Pete's mother wanted him to stay away from Lennon, and Aunt Mimi considered Pete a bad influence on her precious nephew. As history has proven, they were as bad as each other!

Shotton attended Mosspits Lane Primary School, which John attended briefly before being moved to Dovedale School. Quarrymen Len Garry and Nigel Walley also attended Mosspits.

For Bessie and Mimi, their hopes of keeping their charges away from each other were dashed when they both passed their Eleven Plus exams and were sent to Quarry Bank High School. Here, they got into many scrapes, and headed down the same road to academic failure. They much preferred spending time together and creating mischief than trying to learn.

One of their classic capers took place when they discovered a quantity of unused lunch vouchers that the school was about to toss out and took them back to "Mendips". They hatched a plan to sell the vouchers in school for half price and made a tidy profit until they were discovered! The two boys spent a lot of time in front of the Headmaster for constantly causing trouble in class and, on one occasion, were suspended from school. Not wishing to tell Mimi, John told his mum. He and Pete left for school as usual and headed straight for Julia's house. With her more carefree outlook on life, Julia did not share the same concerns as Mimi and never said a word.

Pete was not musical and was only in the group because he was John's best mate. He wanted to leave, but did not have the heart to tell John. At the same time, John wanted him out, but couldn't sack his best mate. It all happened one day in August 1957 at a wedding reception in Toxteth. They were both drunk and were sitting on the floor laughing and joking. Intoxicated, Pete plucked up the courage to tell John he wanted to leave. With that, John picked up Pete's washboard and smashed it over his friend's head, leaving him with the wooden frame around his neck. "That takes

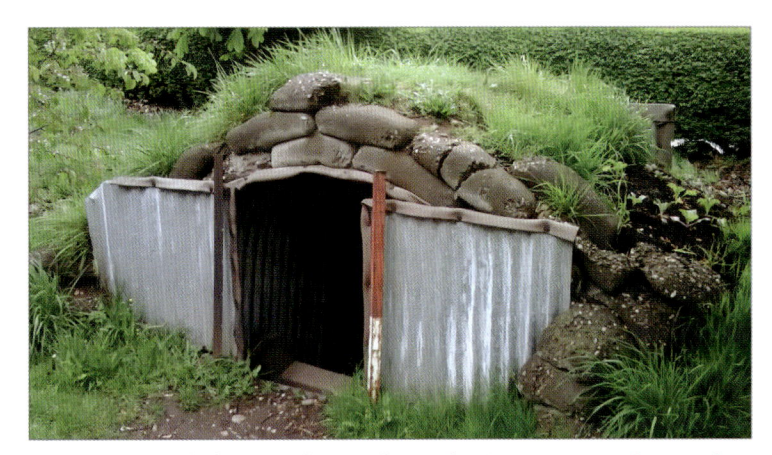

83, Vale Road, the home of Pete Shotton.

An Anderson Shelter, similar to where The Quarrymen rehearsed.

care of that problem, doesn't it?" laughed John.

After school, Pete joined the police and during his passing out parade on the completion of his training at the Police Training School on Mather Avenue, Constable Shotton had an audience. Backing on to the Mather Avenue field was the garden of 20, Forthlin Road. There, on the roof of the outbuilding, were John, Paul and George, marching up and down with broom handles. Pete was nearly thrown out for giggling. He did not last long as a police officer and with The Beatles starting to make some money, John offered to set him up in business.

The Dutch Café, situated on Smithdown Road not far from Penny Lane, became Pete's first venture into the catering business. Because it remained open until the early hours, it was a popular gathering place where bands, taxi drivers and bus drivers could get a late cup of tea and a bacon sandwich. Years later, John helped set up Pete in business at a supermarket on Hayling Island on the south coast of England.

In the late 1960s, Pete was recruited by John to work for Apple and was given the task of overseeing the new Apple Boutique, which opened on 7 December 1967 at the intersection of Baker and Paddington Streets in London. However, the shop was a disaster and closed on 30 June 1968. Pete was then appointed the first Managing Director of Apple Corps. After his career with Apple fizzled out, he returned to Hayling Island and stayed there until the late 1970s. He then began the restaurant chain Fatty Arbuckles, which he later sold for an undisclosed sum.

Liverpool & Bootle Constabulary Training School on Mather Avenue, where Pete Shotton trained to be a policeman.

The Dutch Café (left, with windmill) on Smithdown Road, where Pete became joint owner with John's help.

Mosspits Lane Primary School where Pete Shotton and John Lennon attended.

Bill Smith

William Frederick Smith was born on 12 July 1940 at Sefton General Hospital, and lived at 20, Oulton Road in Childwall. At the age of four, he was enrolled at Mosspits Lane Primary School, the same school attended by Pete Shotton and, for a short time, John Lennon. Even though he was three years older, Bill was in the year above John at school, as the new school year began in September. As a result, Bill did not know that John had even attended Mosspits.

Bill sat the Eleven Plus exam, which he passed, enabling him to go to Quarry Bank. This would lead to his eventual meeting with John Lennon. "As you know," Bill recalled, "when you passed the Eleven Plus, you got a bike or a watch. Well, my father just told me the exams were too easy anyway, and I got nothing!"

Although his first year started with promise, Bill's time in form 1R did not end well. A meeting was held between his father and the school during which Bill was given the option of either heading for the lowest class, 2C, or re-doing his first year with the hope of staying in the 'A' Stream, the top class. The decision was made to re-do his first year. This action meant that he would end up in the same year as John, though they wouldn't be in the same class. In their second year at Quarry Bank, Bill had achieved his ambition and progressed into 2A and John into 2B. However, it was during their third year at Quarry Bank that Smith teamed up with Lennon and Shotton, and the mischief escalated.

"I remember one occasion in class," Bill remembered with a smile, "when each boy took it in turn, with the teacher's back to the class, to let out a sharp whistle. The teacher would keep turning around, but couldn't catch who it was. Then, when the teacher turned around again, John shouted, 'Ah, Shotton, he's caught you out now!' and everybody else started blaming Pete. The teacher marched Pete off to the Headmaster, even though he was innocent!" That was one of John's typical practical jokes at Shotton's expense.

By the summer of 1956, the skiffle craze had hit the UK, and groups sprang up all over the country. Much has been speculated about the beginning of The Quarrymen, and I asked Bill what he remembered.

"We started the group as John, Pete, me and Eric, outside the woodwork room in school. I can't remember ever being called The Blackjacks, but I do remember the discussion about naming the group. I was the one who suggested the name The Quarrymen, because of our school, but John did not like the idea. However, the others sup-

Bill at Quarry Bank.

The Fab one hundred and Four

Smith L, Lennon, Shotton, Jones K, Beattie, Jackson, Jacobs, Walpole, Turner, Hamill, Fazakerley, Fo[...]
Anderson, Williams, Clemson, Brooke, Mr. Burrows, Jones P, Elliott, Rhind, Hillier, Rowley
Callaway, Gooseman, Bolt, MacEvoy, Norbury, Monchar, Jennett, Raiswell

Bill, top left, next to John Lennon and Pete Shotton.

ported my suggestion, and we became The Quarrymen. I know this was during 1956, but I can't remember dates now."

Once the group had been started and named, they had to allocate instruments, with Bill appointed tea-chest bass player. Of course, this meant acquiring a tea-chest, and he knew the place to get one. "I pinched one from the woodwork room! Well, it was not pinching as such, because Cliff Cooke, as well as teaching woodwork, also taught Religious Education and Music, plus he was the leader of the school Scout Troop, the 4th Allerton. There were a few tea-chests in the room, so I took one of them."

The Quarrymen were now formed and, within a short time, Rod Davis was added to the lineup. Bill doesn't remember many performances, just the occasional talent competition. "I remember that we decided to decorate the tea-chest bass. We painted it first, and then John painted cartoons on the sides of it. I kept it at my house, and took it with me whenever we were playing. My time with the group came to an end after we were playing in a talent contest, in West Derby, I think, and had to carry it on the bus. This involved placing it in the luggage compartment under the stairs on the bus, and I just felt that it was so much hassle. I did not want to carry on. I thought that we were messing around, and my father was telling me not to waste my time, and concentrate on my education."

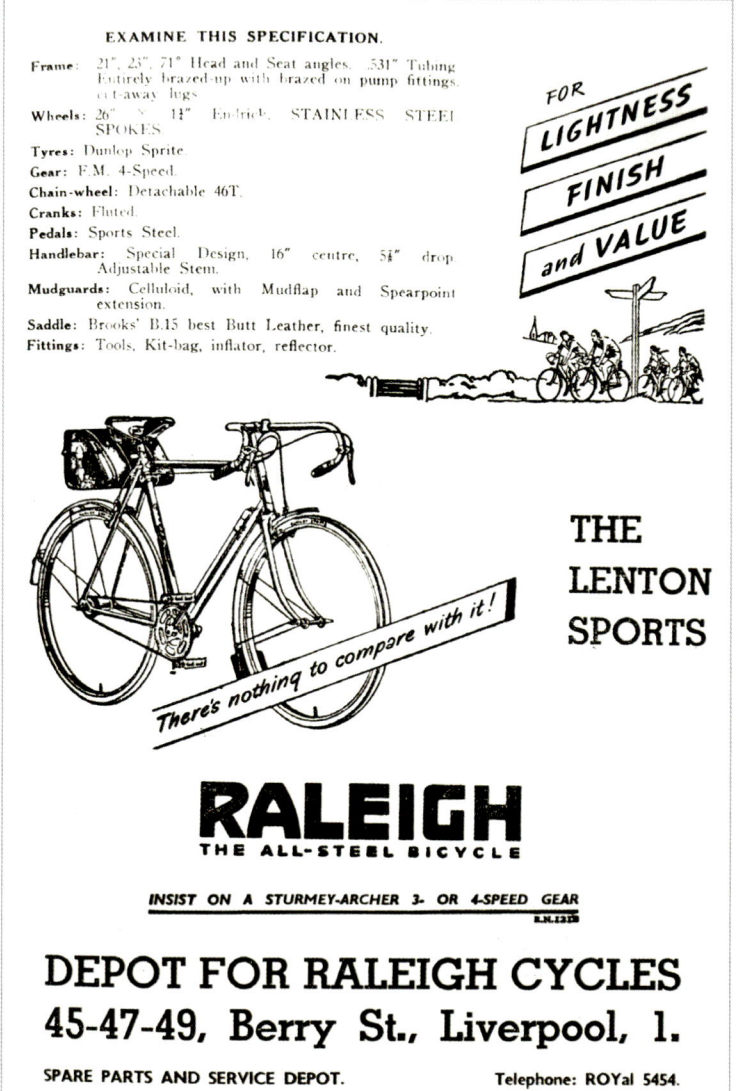

EXAMINE THIS SPECIFICATION.

Frame: 21", 23", 71° Head and Seat angles. .531" Tubing Entirely brazed-up with brazed on pump fittings. cut-away lugs
Wheels: 26" × 1⅜" Endrick, STAINLESS STEEL SPOKES
Tyres: Dunlop Sprite.
Gear: F.M. 4-Speed.
Chain-wheel: Detachable 46T.
Cranks: Fluted.
Pedals: Sports Steel.
Handlebar: Special Design, 16" centre, 5¼" drop. Adjustable Stem.
Mudguards: Celluloid, with Mudflap and Spearpoint extension.
Saddle: Brooks' B.15 best Butt Leather, finest quality.
Fittings: Tools, Kit-bag, inflator, reflector.

FOR LIGHTNESS FINISH and VALUE

There's nothing to compare with it!

THE LENTON SPORTS

RALEIGH
THE ALL-STEEL BICYCLE

INSIST ON A STURMEY-ARCHER 3- OR 4-SPEED GEAR

DEPOT FOR RALEIGH CYCLES
45-47-49, Berry St., Liverpool, 1.

SPARE PARTS AND SERVICE DEPOT.   Telephone: ROYal 5454.

Advertisement in *The Quarry* promoting the Raleigh Lenton, the bike that John and many of his friends received as a reward for passing the Eleven Plus exam.

Bill kept the tea-chest bass in his house, but it was not to stay there for long. While Bill was not at home, Lennon and Shotton headed over to Oulton Road and stole the tea-chest bass from his home.

Pete Shotton remembered it well, and described the story to Len Garry for his book *John, Paul and Me, Before The Beatles*. Pete and John concocted a letter for school so that they could bunk off to retrieve the tea-chest. They stated that Pete and his close relation John Lennon would have to be excused on Friday afternoon to attend the funeral of his fictional Aunt Gertrude. It worked, and so the boys had the time off school to follow through with their plan.

The two lads took the bus to Bill's house, and weren't sure if the house was empty, but John had a plan. As Pete recalled, John told him, "What we'll do is that I'll knock on the door and ask if they have seen my lost cat called Ginger, just in case someone's in. His mum and dad don't know me anyway." Thankfully, for them, the house was empty. However, they had to find a way in. Pete found the kitchen window open, sneaked in and unlocked the kitchen door for John to come in.

They searched around the house for the tea-chest, with no luck so far, when they realised there was somebody coming up the path. It was a door-to-door salesman, who proceeded to knock on the front door. John plucked up the courage to answer the door, and was ready with a story when the salesman asked for his parents.

"Nah, me mum's dead and my father's in the clink," he said in a manner that demanded pity. The salesman was launching a new drink product. He wanted them to try it and then conduct a survey. When asked how many brothers and sisters were there, John promptly replied, "I've got three sisters and four brothers, and my Uncle Herbert looks after us."

The salesman left seven bottles of the drink, which John and Pete duly drank on the spot. Then the search for the tea-chest resumed, with the instrument eventually found in the garage. Lennon and Shotton headed to the bus and took the tea-chest home.

However, that was not the end of it. Bill was not to be outdone. "I decided that I wanted it returned, so I went to Pete's house at 83, Vale Road and pinched it back!"

Bill's family moved to Woolton soon after. "Our family moved from our Childwall home to 298, Menlove Avenue, opposite John's home at "Mendips". I kept the tea-chest bass in the attic of our house for years, though when my father was clearing out the house, he threw it away!" What could that be worth today? Another priceless artifact gone forever!

Although Mimi figured significantly in John's life, Bill only met her

298, Menlove Avenue, Bill Smith's home.

Back row (left to right) Bill Smith, Pete Shotton, John Lennon, Don Beattie and Mike Hill.

When the May 1957 Quarry Bank school photo was taken, Bill was pictured next to Pete Shotton and John. However, before the photograph was shot, Lennon, Shotton and Smith came up with a plan. "We decided we would stand our collars up, and wet our hair so that it looked greased back. As you can see, I am wearing a sports jacket with the collar turned up, and I'm not even wearing a school tie. I don't know how I got passed the school prefects, but I did. At the last minute, John and Pete decided to put their collars down, and adopt an Elvis look, leaving me on my own to see the plan through."

As John was meeting Paul at St. Peter's Church in July 1957, Bill was preparing for life after Quarry Bank. "When I was sixteen, I had the opportunity, through my membership in the Air Training Corps in Speke, to take my glider pilot's licence, but a combination of my father, and Headmaster Mr. Pobjoy put an end to this chance. The following year, when I left school, I could have joined the Royal Air Force, but instead opted for a life at sea. After initially working at Mapletons Nut Food Company Ltd. in Garston, I joined the National Sea Training School in Sharpness, Gloucestershire, aboard the *TS Vindicatrix*. I was there for about six weeks of training."

Bill's Seaman's Record Book shows that he attended from 16 September to 25 October 1957, achieving a Catering Certificate. From there, he spent many years travelling the world and seeing many cities and countries. He even spent a short time in 1961 on board a Swedish vessel, the *Justus Waller*, before joining the Transatlantic liner *Mauretania* that sailed between New York and Naples. He left his life at sea in November 1963. In December 1963, he and his new wife left

a couple of times, as she was not often in the house when John's friends were there. "I remember that John fancied playing a trick on the medical students who were living at "Mendips", so he asked me to rush in from the garden and start running the vacuum around, while the students were studying. I ran in through the French windows from the garden, did as he suggested, and the students did not react at all!

"One of the strangest things we ever did was trying a séance in the front room of "Mendips", with John, Pete, me and maybe a couple of the other lads. We all sat at a table, with the cards laid out, and a glass cup on which we placed our hands. We all admitted that at one time or another, they had deliberately moved the glass, but there were definitely times when none of us moved the glass. That was weird. I also remember taking some of my father's George Formby records down to John's mum's house in Blomfield Road, but I never got them back. Thankfully, they weren't missed!"

The *Vindicatrix* training ship.

Bill's Merchant Navy record.

Liverpool for South Africa, where he lived for nearly 40 years.

The last time Bill saw John was when he was on leave in January 1962. They took the bus into town and headed for the Storyville Jazz Club in Temple Street, where Bill took out a temporary membership, signed in by John. They shared a couple of pints that night, and soon Bill was back at sea, never to see his school friend again.

Bill has now returned to his native Liverpool, though wisely spends the winter in warmer climes.

Bill Smith pictured in Liverpool in 2012.

The *Fab* one hundred and *Four*

Eric Griffiths

Eric Ronald Griffiths was born in Denbigh, North Wales to Welsh parents on 31 October 1940, just a few weeks after John Lennon. Eric's father was a male nurse before World War II and was later called up for duty as a pilot. He was killed in 1941 over the North Sea, leaving a wife and two children – Eric and his older sister Joan.

At the age of three, Eric moved to his grandparent's house in Bootle, North Liverpool, where he attended school. When he turned ten, his family moved into a semi-detached house at 96, Halewood Drive in Woolton, a home purchased by his mother, who worked for the Civil Service in the Employment Exchange. Eric lived there until he was eighteen.

He attended Belle Vale Primary School where he was one of only two students who passed the Eleven Plus exam, though he always claimed he was not very academic. Passing the exam meant that he would attend Quarry Bank High School. On 4 September 1952, he was placed in form 1B. The nucleus of the original Quarrymen was together. Eric's only memory of those first days at school involved being chased around the playground, having his cap stolen and being called a newt.

Eric and John saw an advertisement for guitar lessons in a shop window. "It was a bloke over in Hunts Cross," said Eric. "John and I went to him for two lessons, but then gave up. He was really a classical guitarist. He wanted us to do things like theory and learn music. That was no good to us."

Eric (centre) at Quarry Bank, 1956.

So Eric joined John, who was taking lessons from his mother, Julia. "We used to skive off school, buy ten Woodbines and a bag of chips, then go to Julia's house. She always let us in." As Julia played banjo, and not guitar, John and Eric had to tune the first four strings like Julia's banjo, so the top two strings were left loose. The chords they learned were banjo chords, so when The Quarrymen performed,

Eric's house at 96, Halewood Drive.

John and Eric played their guitars like a banjo and Rod Davis, who joined the group soon after Eric, actually played a banjo.

His time ran out with the group in December 1957 when George Harrison was invited to join The Quarrymen. Eric was given an ultimatum by manager Nigel Walley. "I got a phone call one day from Nigel," recalled Eric. "He made it clear that I either had to change to the bass guitar, or leave the group. John had already asked me about playing the bass guitar. I was pretty angry at the time of the phone call. I said I wanted to speak to John himself, but Nigel said he was not there. I did not quite believe that."

As a founding member, his anger was surely justified. "I suppose my slight feeling of anger was because I thought I'd contributed quite a lot to the group," Eric said. "I had worked with John from the very beginning, when we were learning the guitar together. We helped each other with the chords, worked together on which songs we were going to play, how we would play them. John was better than me on the guitar, but not much. He was not as good as Paul or George, but I always got on with John.

"I decided not to bother arguing with them. I was not going to buy a bass guitar, as it would cost me too much money, money I couldn't see myself getting back. So I just left. I soon got over any anger. It did not bother me, really."

Griffiths did better than Lennon and left school in the summer of 1957 with GCE exam passes in English, Mathematics and History. He soon began a career in engineering. However, Eric decided to abandon engineering, too, and joined the Merchant Navy as a cadet navigating officer. He continued to meet his old friends from the group when he was on leave, but he soon lost contact with John and Paul.

Records indicating when Eric joined the Merchant Navy have helped establish when he left The Quarrymen and George joined. Eric was clearly out of the group by early December 1957 when George replaced him and subsequently joined his first ship in February 1958.

He left the navy in 1964 and married his wife Relda at Woolton Parish Church. He spent the next thirty years working in the prison system, modernising prisoners' working practises. In 1972, he left the English Prison Service to join the Scottish Prison Service and moved to Edinburgh with his wife and three sons.

In 1994, he changed careers, concentrating on the family business, a chain of dry cleaners. When The Quarrymen re-formed in 1997 for the 40th Anniversary of the day John met Paul, Eric rejoined his old bandmates and continued to play with them for several years, including a concert at the author's invitation at Dovedale School in 2004, until his death at the beginning of 2005 after a short battle with cancer.

Eric with The Quarrymen at Dovedale School, 2004.

The Fab one hundred and Four

Rod Davis

Rodney Verso Davis was born in Sefton General Hospital on 7 November 1941. His Dublin-born father James was a cost clerk at Tate & Lyle's sugar refinery in Liverpool. In 1939, his family purchased their house at 129, King's Drive in Woolton for £650. The Davis family was also one of the first in their area to have a car, an Austin A70 Somerset, which was occasionally used to take The Quarrymen to gigs, with the tea-chest bass on the roof, when Rod's father could drive them.

Rod attended Sunday School with John, Pete, Nigel and Ivan at St. Peter's, so he knew them from an early age. It was a tradition for children to be sent to Sunday School in the afternoons, giving parents some peace and quiet.

He was given piano lessons, but did not keep up with them. When he purchased a banjo from a relative, he was quickly added to The Quarrymen lineup at the suggestion of Eric Griffiths. Rod's parents were both violinists, so musical talent was abundant in the family already.

A promising scholar, Rod attended Springwood Primary School in Allerton, where he excelled and skipped a year. He did so well that he was entered for the Margaret Bryce Scholarship at the age of ten, earning him automatic entry to the Liverpool Institute High School. "I went to the Institute to sit the exam and decided I did not want to go anyway," Rod explained. "It seemed like a barracks and the food was horrible. I was a very fussy eater in those days. They gave us stew with beetroot for lunch, so that was it. I did not want to go. So I put down Quarry Bank as my first choice when I came to sit the Eleven Plus."

It was at Quarry Bank, where he was in the same "house" as John and Pete Shotton, that Rod became a Quarryman. He'd just purchased a banjo and, not knowing how to play it, was taught by John and Eric who, in turn, had been tutored on the instrument by Julia Lennon.

Rod Davis (back row centre) at Quarry Bank, May 1957.

129, Kings Drive, the home of Rod Davis.

On 9 June 1957, The Quarrymen played at Liverpool's Empire Theatre for The Carroll Levis Discovery Show, a 1950s talent competition for young people. "The preliminary heat was on a Sunday, and my mother wouldn't let me go," recalled Rod. "The rest of the band went without me and got through the heat. Then there was the show itself where we only played one number: 'Worried Man Blues'. A skiffle group had come from North Wales with a coachload of supporters and they beat us on the applause meter. All credit to them though. They were leaping all over the stage and the bass player was rolling on his back. They gave a real show. We were just standing there, expecting people to appreciate our music."

In addition to the fête at St. Peter's, The Quarrymen appeared at The Cavern on 7 August 1957, though Rod, like Paul McCartney, was away on holiday and missed that gig. Rod remained a member until the summer of 1957, and although he was there on the day John was introduced to Paul, he left The Quarrymen before Paul officially joined.

"I only met Paul on one occasion after the Woolton fête," says Rod Davis, "and it was at Aunt Mimi's a fortnight later. He dropped in to hear us practising. From my point of view, I was the person he was replacing. It's like Pete Best. You're the guy who doesn't know what's going on."

Rod stayed on at Quarry Bank, where he joined the sixth form. He decided to progress from the banjo. "I decided to learn the guitar, so my brother Bernie and I sold our electric train set and bought a Spanish guitar," Rod recalled. "As I knew the principles from the banjo, I soon learnt enough chords and became very interested in folk music. I also played in a jazz trio when I was still at Quarry Bank with Gerald Greenwood (piano) and Les Brough (drums)." He then progressed to Cambridge University where he studied French and Spanish and developed a love for folk music and then bluegrass. This brought him full circle as bluegrass was one of the root musical forms that gave birth to skiffle. He extended his musical prowess by also learning the mandolin and fiddle.

After teaching French and Spanish until 1968, he discovered a love for travel and spent many years leading expedition holidays to places like Russia, Turkey and the Sahara Desert.

"In 1994," recalled Rod, "with John Duff Lowe, who played piano for The Quarrymen in 1958, we formed an electric band under the name of The Quarrymen. We made a CD and played several concerts in a touring show which included Cynthia Lennon, Denny Laine and The Merseybeats."

Rod remains a member of the re-formed Quarrymen and still performs with them as they enjoy renewed notoriety as members of John Lennon's first group.

Rod Davis and Eric Griffiths look at the camera at the Quarry Bank School Fête, July 1954.

The re-formed Quarrymen performing at Quarry Bank School in 2011. John Duff Lowe, Colin Hanton, Len Garry and Rod Davis with Owen Clayton.

Colin Hanton

Colin Hanton.

Colin was born on 12 December 1938 in Bootle, north Liverpool, and so was the eldest of The Quarrymen by a couple of years. His father's family was from County Wexford and his mother's family from Dublin, both in Ireland. His father, John, was a fireman in the Bootle Fire Brigade in Liverpool. During the war, he saw action as Bootle suffered in the May Blitz when the Luftwaffe tried to attack the great Liverpool docks, gateway to America. Colin remembers Liverpool practically being on fire. In 1942, his father's fire crew received a direct hit. John was the only one to survive and spent many months in the hospital.

In 1945, the family moved to a rented house in Woolton – swapping houses with family members who wanted to return to Bootle. Colin briefly attended Springwood School, the same as Rod Davis, but at age nine, he returned to Bootle after his mum died. Unlike his bandmates, he has some memories of the war. "My earliest memory is of standing outside with my grandfather, looking up to him, and he seemed to be all lit up, because in the background, the whole of Liverpool was on fire."

The family soon moved to 4, Heyscroft Road in Woolton. This time, he attended St. Mary's Catholic Primary School in Woolton, followed immediately by the senior school in Horrock's Avenue, Garston. He was, therefore, not a grammar school boy like most of the group. In fact, with all the changing of schools, he was not even put in for the Eleven Plus exam, so there was no chance of attending a grammar school.

Secondary school did not provide many memories for Colin. "I don't remember much about it, except all the buildings seemed to be prefabs. In my last year, we had a nun, Sister Gertrude, who was very strict. She came into our class one Monday and said, 'Did you all go to church on Sunday?' One boy held his hand up and said no, he'd gone fishing with his dad.

"She walked over to him and went slap, slap, slap, right on his face. She hit him with the flat of her hand first, then the back, at least six times. She then asked if anybody else had not been to church. Naturally, we were all shaking, but we managed to say, 'Oh yes, we went to church yesterday, Sister". Like many boys, Colin was caned on a regular basis, but it was not for anything more serious than being late three times a week.

When he was about eleven, Colin's father re-married. "I used to call her Aunty Peggy for the first few years, till my father took me aside one day and asked if I'd call her mum, so I did. We all got on really well".

One day, he met a boy on the bus who lived near to him in Woolton.

St. Mary's School.

His name was Eric Griffiths. Quickly discovering that Colin had a set of drums, Eric recruited him into the group. "I used to listen to jazz records and play the beat on the furniture," explained Colin. "My parents said that if I bought the drums, I could play them in the house. I went to Frank Hessy's Music Centre and bought a drum kit in installments of ten shillings a week. It was £34 in total. Eric asked if he could hear me play. I set up the drums, put on a record and played along to it and he said, 'Come and meet the lads'. That was it. I was a Quarryman."

Unlike his compatriots in the group, Colin was a working-man with a wage. He had left school in 1955 and joined a furniture company called Guy Rogers in Speke. "It was a big place, making all different types of furniture. They had a good reputation. High class. I got taken on more or less as a labourer and then I was told I'd earned the opportunity to become an apprentice upholster, starting on £3 per week rising to £4 per week, which was not bad for a lad of 16 in the mid Fifties, living at home."

The addition of a drummer helped The Quarrymen stand out from most of the other skiffle groups. When the band later made the transition from skiffle to rock 'n' roll, Colin became indispensable. As the other members fell away, he became the last of The Quarrymen who had performed with John at St. Peter's to stay with the group. However, at the point when only John, Paul, George and Colin remained in the lineup, an incident occurred that would result in the drummer quitting.

Colin's home at 4, Heyscroft Road.

We were at the Finch Lane Busmen's Sports & Social Club. We all turned up and George's dad was there. I did not know why we were there, as I did not spend much time with John and Paul. I just received a call to say we were playing somewhere. There was a manager from the "Pivvy" in Lodge Lane there, as they had started bingo and wanted a resident group for thirty minutes in between houses. He came along to see us perform. We were in the dressing room, which was nice, and they had pictures of famous people who played there. We even had proper curtains on the stage.

"As the curtains opened, John started straight into the songs, and then he would introduce us. After our last song – we did about five songs – the curtains were due to close, but they were stuck, so John joked, 'While they get the curtains fixed we'll play another song'. We did 'Lost John' and then the curtains did close this time. We went backstage and the manager came to see us and said, 'That was an excellent show lads, so there's a pint at the bar for you', which was a mistake. We did not just stop at one, and then me, Paul and John were drunk, and there was only poor George who was not drunk.

"I don't remember much, but we went back on stage for the second half, and at one point I said to John, 'What are we doing?' and Paul laughed and John said, 'See, he doesn't even know what we're doing,' – if you weren't drunk, you'd be embarrassed.

Hessy's Music Centre in Stanley Street.

The hall of the Finch Lane Busmen's Sports & Social Club where The Quarrymen played.

The Finch Lane Busmen's Sports & Social Club.

We finished our set and went into the dressing room. Then the manager came in and said, 'You've blown it lads; that was a disaster'. The man from the "Pivvy" who had come to witness the group then came in and he had obviously just come off stage, and up to the venue, as he still had his stage makeup with plenty of rouge, eye make-up and stuff. John was slouched in the corner and he ribbed the poor man unmercifully, as only John could. He was telling us about being professional and how to treat your audience and I was suddenly sobering up quickly as I did not know it was an audition. I remember standing on the tables and singing, and I was wondering what was happening, and then things did not seem that funny anymore.

"We jumped on the bus and Paul had started to do this funny voice. I had some deaf friends, and you know how a deaf person speaks, well he was doing this voice. I'm sure he was not insulting deaf people, as that was not his way, but I was in this drunken state sobering up. Paul kept making these noises and talking in this stupid voice, and I just rounded on him and verbally attacked him. I don't think it would have come to anything, but Pete Shotton was with us and he shouted, 'This is our stop Colin'. So we ran down the stairs, I grabbed my drums and we jumped off. Of course, it was not our stop. We were in the middle of Old Swan or somewhere, so I think that was his way of diffusing things.

"And that was that. So we had to get the bus back to Woolton. I just went back to my house and put my drums away and that was me, finished. I never told them I was quitting but they never contacted me again. I thought, 'I don't need this.' We just had the row, I told Paul to shut up and I think he was shocked. They probably did not want me and I did not want them so that was it."

Does Colin regret his decision? "No regrets," he says. "You can't have regrets. You just have the life you've been given. I could have given up my trade, gone to Hamburg and been sent back with nothing, so I did not, and I'm still working now. Of course, I've had a bit of a life again recently with The Quarrymen, which is great."

Rod Davis and Colin Hanton on stage at Quarry Bank Hall, August 2011.

Ivan Vaughan

Charles Ivan Vaughan was born on 18 June 1942, the same day as Paul McCartney. He attended Lidderdale Infants School before moving to Dovedale School with John Lennon. He was John's neighbour, living behind "Mendips" on Vale Road in a house named "Vega", and their gardens almost backed up to each other. When John attended Quarry Bank, Ivan went to the Liverpool Institute where he met Paul McCartney. The two quickly became friends, placing Ivan in the very unique position of introducing Paul to his old friend John at the St. Peter's Church Garden Fête on 6 July 1957.

Ivan looked back on his childhood in a book he wrote about being diagnosed with Parkinson's Disease. *Ivan: Living With Parkinson's Disease* spends most of the time openly discussing how the disease had taken over his life. But those glimpses into his childhood spent with John and Paul reveal the true character of the man. To those who knew him, Ivan was the clown who inspired John at a very young age with a zany sense of humour.

"Throughout childhood," he recalled, "I used to whip myself into states of euphoria as the class clown, or by inducing excitement through stress: for example, by stealing money. Once I opened a drawer in a teacher's desk containing a box full of two-shilling pieces that had been collected for a school trip. I took the money over a period of a week, thinking that if the amount went down bit by bit no one would notice. Each night I crawled excitedly under my bed to watch the pile of coins growing steadily higher. On the Friday, the teacher announced that the money had been taken and asked whoever had done it to see him.

"A wave of terror passed through me and by the following Monday, I could stand it no longer. I went home at lunchtime, brought back all the money and persuaded the boy who had been left in charge of the remaining funds to let me look after it while he went out to play. As soon as he had gone, I pulled open the drawer and carefully emptied my pockets into the box. They would not all fit in, so I put the surplus loose. Then I left. Two days passed and still nobody noticed that the money had been returned. The following day, I volunteered for dinner-time guard duty. After waiting five minutes, I opened the drawer and, even though nobody was looking, gave a big shout and rushed out of the classroom and down the corridor to the staff-room. 'Sir, the money's back!'

Ivan Vaughan at the Liverpool Institute, 1956.

"I blurted out the story of how I had thought to check if the remains of the fund were still there and had found that all the money had been returned. 'Amazing,' said Mr. Holmes, and the matter was pursued no further. This was not an isolated incident in my childhood and adolescence," Ivan admitted.

Ivan Vaughan's house, "Vega".

View through to the rear of "Mendips", from Ivan's garden.

Ivan had met John when he was only about four years old. "One wet morning," he recalled, "there was a knock at the front door. My mother opened it, and looking down, found a boy a bit older than me, smiling, but preoccupied with the effort of remembering what he had been rehearsed to say. 'I believe a little boy lives here. I wondered if he might like to come out and play.' He stood there in the porch, rain pouring down behind him, with a pair of slippers under his arm."

Ivan invited him in to the house, asking for John's name and noting that he lived round the corner. In fact, their gardens almost backed onto each other. "Next day," said Ivan, "I went round to the house and we played with Dinky cars. I was surprised by his generosity and willingness to share his toys. He was happy even for me to take some of them home. When his Uncle George came home with some sweets, John readily shared them. There was an immediate bond between us. He was older, read books, and his greater intelligence and experience were apparent. I accepted his leadership but I was determined to preserve my independence. From the warm security of Aunt Mimi's control, John accepted me into his life. John was a member of his local library and immersed himself in books so that by the age of five he was already a fluent reader. We played together at weekends and after school. There were numerous parks, a golf course, and fields full of tangled growth and trees – just right for playing cowboys and Indians. In one barren area with large clumps of hard earth we played football and cricket. We spent hours digging out tracks to race our Dinky cars. Our most exciting game, though, was 'fires'. We would go to a large area of waste ground, and simply set fire to the straw and watch the blaze. I have never understood why nobody stopped us."

One man who knew Ivan well was school friend Stan Williams. "I had known Ivan before we arrived at Dovedale School because we had already spent three years together at Lidderdale Road Infants. We were part of the first post-war intake of five-year-olds to toddle through its gates in 1946. I liked Ivan very much. He was a big, strong lad and much more confident than me – always in the thick of harmless mischief which, nevertheless, in those days spelled big trouble if you were caught by one of the strict, spinster schoolmistresses.

"I well remember the two of us legging it home on the morning of a major school break-in. The teachers were out on the pavement, desperately trying to marshal the melee of children, who were arriving in the midst of a chaos of cop cars blocking the street. Running policemen added to the excitement of an unexpected Monday morning crime scene. Now big enough at seven to make our own way to school, Ivan had arrived that morning from beyond Penny Lane on the tram, whereas I lived in the next street. I was a gullible fool who would have obeyed the teacher's death-ray stare and beckoning finger to get into the gate, even though kids with parents were being allowed to turn back and go home. Ivan looked at me and said something like, "Fuck this for a game of soldiers… Come on, Stan… We're off!"

"We dived up the nearest back jigger (alley), chased all the way by two sharp-eyed women who were clearly determined to keep us at school. We were well ahead of our pursuers, but the buggers kept up the chase. Once around the top of the long lane, Ivan suddenly leapt onto a bin, hauled himself up over the wall and within seconds had unbolted a backyard gate to let me in. Crouched down and safe, we waited until the women's gasping conversation in the lane had ceased. Once they had gone, we let ourselves out for a day of freedom, fashioned by Ivan's quick thinking. That was the big difference between Ivan and me. He was the bold, streetwise risk-taker, which made him such a suitable sidekick and accomplice for his Woolton neighbour, the daredevil John Lennon.

"Ivan and I loved Dovedale School. We sat alongside one another in the top seats of Mr. Bell's Eleven Plus class and played together in all the school football, baseball and cricket teams. Ivan was not the most skillful sportsman, but he was fearless. Once or twice, in an emergency, he was put in goal by Mr. Bell, who knew a brave bugger when he saw one. Ivan was afraid of nothing and this quality endeared him to John Lennon. I'm certain of that.

"After Dovedale, we went to separate secondary schools," continued Stan, "and then on to different universities. When we were Sixth Formers, I met him on several occasions in town, and we chatted about life, school… and music. While I travelled up to Scotland in 1964 to begin a 40-year career in teaching, Ivan was sharing in the spectacular success of his pal John and enjoying the excitement of being present at some of the most iconic studio recording work in the history of popular music.

Ivan Vaughan's entry in the Dovedale Primary School register.

"That he was dearly loved by John there can be no doubt. Have a look through Lennon's book of poems, *In His Own Write*. Sprinkled throughout the verses can be found references to his pal, such as 'My Ivan's are getting cold'… 'We must strive the Ivan while it is hot'… and 'Treasure Ivan'. Clearly 'Ivy', as John and Paul liked to call him, is very much a part of the Lennon psyche.

"My last memory of Ivan was sad and tragic," recalled Stan. "It was Christmas 1984, and I happened to switch on to a controversial BBC 2 Horizon programme about Parkinson's disease. It was simply called *Ivan*. I had no idea that the university lecturer, engaged in a brave, moral and scientific struggle to find out more about the illness that was ravaging both his mind and body, was the Ivan of my childhood. I wrote to him and he typed a letter back, although his illness must have made the task difficult. He invited me to visit him, but he was gone soon afterwards and the world was a poorer place for his passing.

"I know that he will always be remembered in Beatles folklore as the person who got the Lennon-McCartney partnership going, when he introduced John to Paul at the Woolton Parish Church Garden Fête. He was, however, someone far more significant than that to his close family and those he taught and influenced, as well as the extended family group known as The Beatles."

Young Ivan was quickly admitted into John's gang, which consisted of John as leader, along with Pete Shotton and Nigel Walley. He was not sent to Quarry Bank like John. Instead, he attended the Liverpool Institute. Because of this one turn of fate, Ivan became possibly the most important person in the story of The Beatles.

When he arrived at the Liverpool Institute, he became classmates with another boy who, coincidentally, was born on exactly the same day as him – Paul McCartney. A friendship developed between the two, which resulted in Paul's invitation to join him at the Woolton Village Fête. Here, of course, Ivan would introduce Paul to his childhood friend John. In this single act, The Beatles were born, and we have Ivan to thank for it.

When he went to University after school, Ivan lost touch with John and did not see him for several years. Then, while playing with his son just outside his London house, a white Rolls-Royce pulled up.

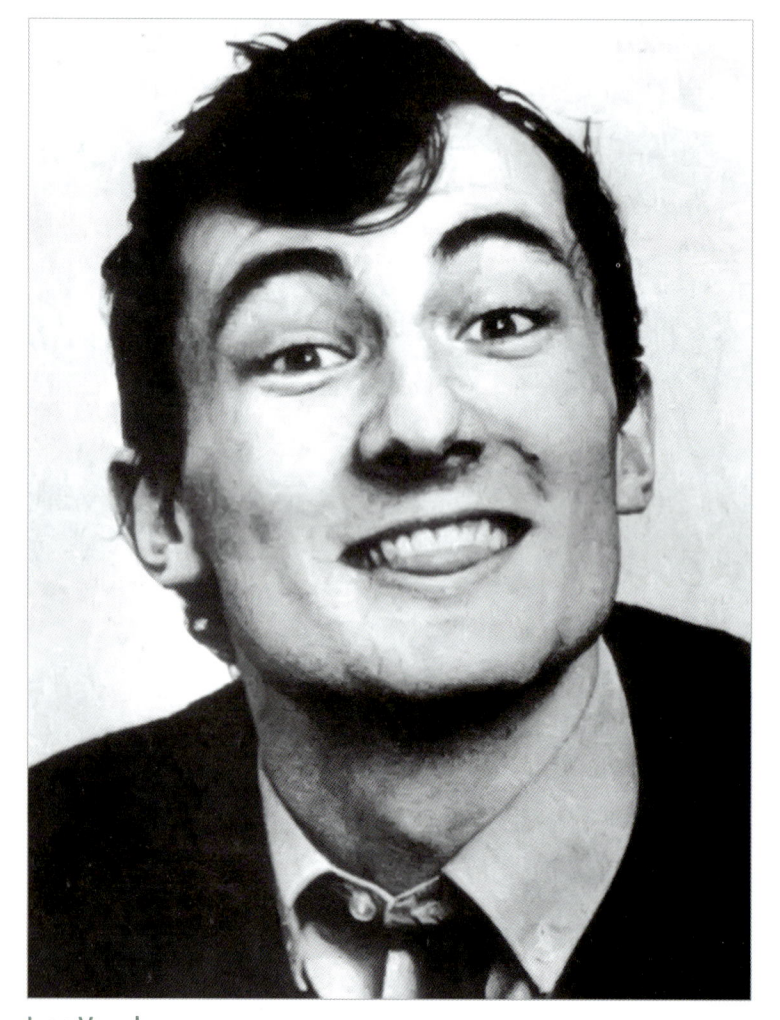

Ivan Vaughan.

John popped out with a woman Ivan did not know.

"Hello Ivy! This is Yoko," John said excitedly. "Yoko who made the *Bottoms* film?" replied Ivan, who had been to see it with his wife Jan just a few months earlier. "We sat round the table," explained Ivan, "and John took a biro, drew a diagram and said: 'This is what Apple's all about.' The word Apple appeared in the centre with various divisions, including records, shops, electronics, films and foundation, radiating out. 'This is where you come in,' he said, pointing to the word 'foundation'. 'I want you to set up a school.' Trying to keep calm," explained Ivan, "I asked him to explain what he had in mind. He hadn't thought beyond the broad idea of a school embracing the most child-centred of regimes which his children and those of his friends could attend."

Ivan agreed to join Apple and set about putting a plan together, looking for the most appropriate building. However, the financial viability of the plan meant that it did not receive the backing from the board. Nothing ever came of it. Ivan kept in touch with Paul more than John, though even that eventually tailed off.

When Ivan was diagnosed with Parkinson's, he decided to call John. He tried different phone numbers, eventually hearing a familiar voice on the other end of the line say 'Yeh?' As Ivan recalled: "I automatically dropped into a Liverpool accent. "'Ello, John, ow ya doin', this is Ivan.' John immediately responded with skepticism. 'Just a minute. 'Ow do I know you're Ivan? What did you have painted on your teachest?'" I told him 'Jive with Ive, the ace on the bass.'"

John explained why he had to ask that question. "Okay. I have to do that 'cos people keep gettin' your name from books about The Beatles and ring up pretendin' to be you. So, 'ow are you? 'ow's Jan?" They talked with each other for a while about family and then Ivan revealed what was really happening in his life. "I let out that I had Parkinson's Disease", Ivan said. "He had heard of it and volunteered to get me some books to help. I was impressed as ever by the warmth he could generate in just a few words and by his sharp intuition when he said, 'You'll have more time to devote to the things that really interest you, like archaeology.' Before we spoke, I had been thinking that I would be able to read more about travel and archaeology."

Although it had been three years since they had spoken, it sparked

John and Ivan with the Dovedale Junior School boys in the Isle of Man 1951, taken by teacher Fred Bolt. John Lennon is centre left with arms outstretched. Jimmy Tarbuck is on John's left in a boxing stance. At Jimmy's left is Ivan Vaughan, and behind them is Michael Hill.

The Fab one hundred and Four

Ivan Vaughan, centre row, second from right, at Dovedale Road School in 1950.

Stan Williams (top left) and his school friend, Ivan Vaughan (top right).

many childhood memories for Ivan. He thought about how strong their friendship remained. More was to follow when, a few weeks later, a parcel arrived at Ivan's home. It contained several books, courtesy of John and Yoko. "There was *How to Get Well*," remarked Ivan, "which had on the flyleaf a message from John, which read 'to start looking'. *The Snow Leopard* had a note saying 'to relax'. This last book gave me the greatest pleasure and I frequently re-read passages from it.

John's accompanying letter urged me, in punning language, to keep my spirits high and strongly suggested that it was up to me whether I sank or swam. I must not lose faith in myself.

"Ten weeks later, he was shot dead. Paul and I did not contact each other about it. In fact, we never brought it up in conversation. I hardly reacted outwardly at all. The day after John's death, however, a colleague said that he supposed I was very upset at what had happened. I heard myself say: 'I don't know what I feel. I don't know that I feel much at all.' As soon as he had gone, I instinctively made my way to a room where I knew I could be alone, and I wept profusely."

When Ivan's book was published, Paul wrote the notes for the back cover. "Ivan was born on exactly the same day as me in 1942. We grew up together and were good mates at school, so it naturally came as a shock to learn he had developed Parkinson's Disease. It is no surprise, however, to see the courageous and vital way in which he is confronting the problem and, by reading this enlightening book, I am sure you will come to the same conclusion."

Ivan lost his battle with Parkinson's on 16 August 1993. Paul was so moved by his death that it prompted him to start writing poetry again. In his anthology of poetry, *Blackbird Singing*, Paul wrote a poem simply called "Ivan". "After having written many song lyrics with and without John Lennon," explained Paul, "I wrote a poem on hearing of the death of my dear friend Ivan Vaughan. It seemed to me that a poem, rather than a song, could perhaps best express what I was feeling. This poem "Ivan" led on to others".

Nigel Walley

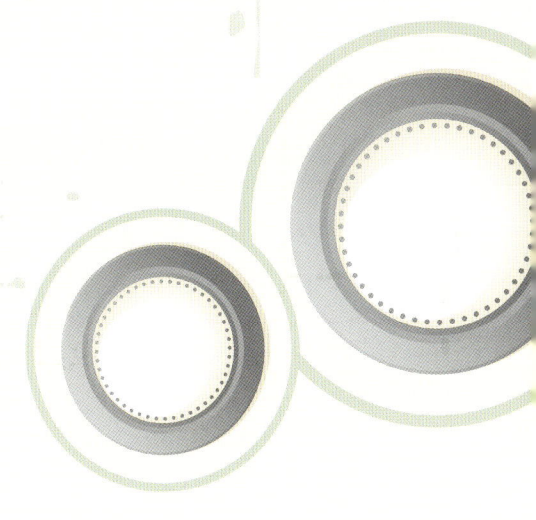

Christopher Nigel Walley, known as Nigel, or "Wallogs" as John referred to him, was born on 30 June 1941. He lived on Vale Road behind John's home "Mendips" in a house called "Leosdene", which was just down the road from Ivan Vaughan and Pete Shotton. Walley was part of John's gang and went to Mosspits Lane Primary School with Lennon and Shotton. However, John was only there for a short time, as Nigel recalled in an interview with the *Liverpool Echo*:

"We knocked around together from the age of four. We then went to Mosspits Primary but John was expelled for being disruptive when he was just five or six years old. I remember he bullied a girl called Polly Hipshaw. He then went to Dovedale School and, later, Quarry Bank High School while I went to the Blue Coat, but we remained friends as we lived so close to each other. I'd say Pete Shotton was John's closest friend, with me next.

"John always had a mouth organ in his inside coat pocket and then his mum taught him how to play the guitar, although at no time back then did I think he would go on to become famous. The Quarrymen must have been one of a hundred skiffle groups in Merseyside and we went into loads of competitions and did not win one."

After leaving Mosspits, Nigel attended Blue Coat Grammar School on Church Road near Penny Lane. John was keen to have all of his friends in The Quarrymen, so Nigel was invited to play the tea-chest bass. He was not that keen on playing skiffle music, and after being jumped by a couple of lads following a gig one night, he decided to quit dragging the wooden crate around with him. Ivan Vaughan then assumed the duties of tea-chest bass player in the group.

However, Nigel was to take on a far more important role in The Quarrymen as the group's manager. They needed someone to promote the group and secure bookings. His first task was to place a business card in the local sweetshop window at 2d per week, and in the *Liverpool Daily Post* and the *Liverpool Echo*.

When The Quarrymen were deciding on their repertoire, Nigel says, "they picked out records by Buddy Holly, Bill Haley and popular rock 'n' roll numbers of the time. Elvis Presley's 'Heartbreak Hotel' was a number John was particularly struck on. We saw Buddy Holly live with the Crickets when he appeared at the Philharmonic Hall in Liverpool in March 1958. It was one of the highlights of my life. We just picked the tunes from records that were readily available in the shops."

Nigel was now working as a golf professional at the local

Nigel Walley.

Lee Park Golf Club, which was an exclusive Jewish golf club. By coincidence, one of the members of the club was Dr. Joseph Sytner, whose son Alan ran the popular jazz venue, The Cavern Club. In an effort to book The Quarrymen at The Cavern, Nigel asked Dr. Sytner if he could recommend the group to Alan. Although it was a jazz club, they also permitted skiffle groups to play there.

Sytner spoke to his son, and although he was interested in booking them, he would have to see them perform elsewhere first. To that end, Nigel arranged for the group to play at Lee Park Golf Club. As this was considered to be an audition, they would not be paid for the appearance. However, they could expect to receive free drinks, a meal and, if they did well, the hat would be passed around so patrons could show their appreciation. They were most appreciative indeed, and the group earned more money than they had ever received for a performance, with the added bonus of passing the audition. Alan Sytner duly booked them to appear at The Cavern on 7 August 1957. Although Paul had joined by then, he was on holiday and did not appear with them. All went well at the gig until John decided they should play some Elvis Presley. After "Hound Dog" and "Blue Suede Shoes", a note was quickly passed by Sytner to the stage: "Cut out the bloody rock 'n' roll". With The Cavern's strict jazz-only policy, the group had overstepped the mark, and would not be invited to return.

At the beginning of July 1957, "Wallogs" and Lennon decided that they should enlist in the Merchant Navy, so they headed into Liverpool to join up. However, due to their age, the recruitment office telephoned their parents and that was the end of the matter. This was very fortunate as only a few days later, John had a meeting with destiny – and Paul McCartney – at the Woolton Village Fête.

However, there would be a tragic twist to the friendship between Nigel and John when, on 15 July 1958, Nigel had called to John's home to see if he was there. He was, in fact, at his mother Julia's house. Julia was with Mimi at "Mendips" and about to leave, so Nigel offered to walk with her to the corner where Menlove Avenue crossed Vale Road. Nigel, haunted by what happened next, recalled the incident years later:

"I went to call for John that evening but his Aunt Mimi told me he was out. Mimi was at the gate with John's mum, who was about to leave. We stood chatting and John's mum said 'Well, you have the privilege of escorting me to the bus stop!' I said, 'That will do me fine. I'll be happy to do that.'

We walked down Menlove Avenue and I turned off to go up Vale Road, where I lived. I must have been about 15 yards up the road when I heard a car skidding. I turned round to see John's mum going through the air. I rushed over but she had been killed instantly.

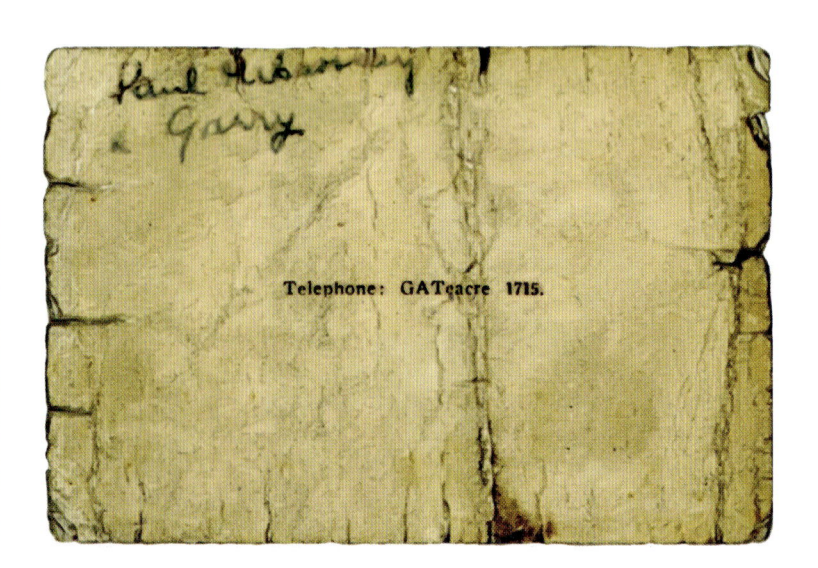

Nigel's business card for The Quarry Men.

Blue Coat School, where Nigel Walley attended.

Nigel Walley's house, "Leosdene."

I had nightmares about it for years. I can see it today – Julia lying there with her hair fluttering over her face.

"I did not see John much after that because he became a bit of a recluse. It worried me because, deep down, I wondered whether he blamed me for the accident and was thinking, 'If only Nigel Walley had stayed a minute longer talking to my mum'. But hindsight is a wonderful thing."

Nigel continued to obtain some bookings for the group, though Paul suggested he receive a lesser fee, as he was not playing. John, however, was keen to stand up for his friend. "Paul and I did not get on very well in those days," recalled Nigel. "I was receiving the same money as the band when I was manager but Paul thought I should be getting just ten percent. But John supported me saying 'You've

The Fab one hundred and Four

got to look at it this way, Paul – if we did not have Nigel, we wouldn't be getting half the engagements we are getting'." Paul was not to be thwarted and won his argument.

At the end of 1958, Nigel and his family moved to New Brighton on The Wirral. With the increased distance, and reduced fee, he decided that his time in music management was over, and he quit the group.

Nigel's skill with a golf club resulted in him being the youngest golf professional in England. He has had a long career as a golf professional in Austria and has played in countries like Peru and the Bahamas.

Nigel has fond memories of John: "We were just very good friends. He was a very funny person. We used to get into the usual scrapes. John was always a bit wild, wanting to stand out. The thing with John, though, was that he was as blind as a bat. He had glasses but he would never wear them. He was very vain about that.

"So if we were in a shop or out somewhere, John was always walking into things like shop counters or walking into lampposts. In a shop you'd hear "CRASH" and you'd know that was John. He was a great cartoonist and could have made a living out of that. He was very witty, always deliberately getting people's names wrong. I think he always believed he would make it and become famous one day.

"John and I always stayed in touch after he was a Beatle. I would go round to his flat or house and we'd talk. He never forgot any of the old gang. In fact towards the end of his life, he was becoming more and more nostalgic.

"John was just a lovely guy really – a really lovely man who we all still miss very much."

Receipt for the interment of Julia Lennon at Allerton Cemetery, paid for by her brother-in-law, Norman Birch.

Julia was walking towards the bus stop when she was knocked down by a car on 15 July 1958.

Michael Hill

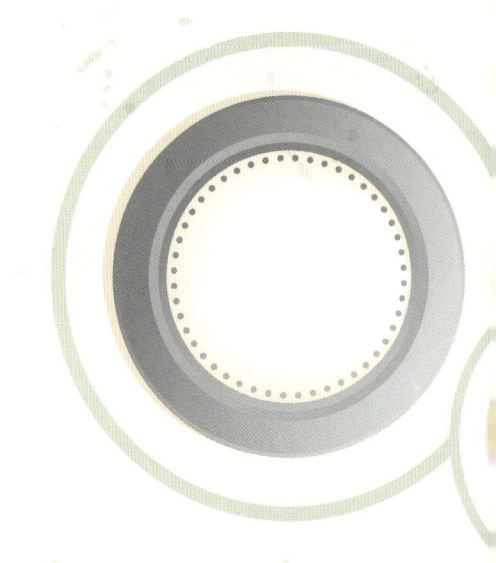

Michael Hill was a school friend of John Lennon, attending Dovedale School and Quarry Bank with him. Michael had a massive influence on John's eventual career, though of course they never realised it at the time. He lived at 69, Dovedale Road, a short distance from Quarry Bank and, earning money delivering newspapers, he was able to build what was considered the largest record collection of anyone at school. Because both his parents worked, Michael's house was empty during the day, and was therefore the perfect place for schoolboys to escape to and listen to records. For a period of 18 months in 1956-57, several days a week during school lunch breaks, Michael and his best friend Don Beattie plus John and his mate Pete Shotton would cycle to Michael's house for record-listening sessions.

In his book, *John Lennon: The Boy Who Became a Legend*, Michael recalls how it happened: "In 1955, I had bought a record by the Lonnie Donegan Skiffle Group called 'Rock Island Line' with 'John Henry' on the B-side," explained Michael. "These two U.S. railroad songs had been recorded and issued a year before as part of a band album, when Lonnie Donegan was a guitar player with Chris Barber's Jazz Band, before he formed his own group. The two songs had only just been released as a single. This took a while to take off, but by January 1956 Donegan's 'Rock Island Line' had climbed to number 1 in the British hit parade.

"This hit record, and Lonnie Donegan's appearances on television and in theatres around the UK, created a teenage fad in 1956 and 1957, by popularising a form of music known as skiffle. All over the country, would-be musicians, most of them teenage boys, were motivated to buy guitars, intent on learning to make their own music. They got together to form skiffle groups so as to have a go at this 'do-it-yourself' type of music.

"John enjoyed listening to 'Rock Island Line' at my house, so much that he went out and bought his own copy that he played at his mother's house. It was the first record he had ever bought, but it did not inspire him to think of becoming a musician himself. It took a few more months and a more dynamic performer than Lonnie Donegan to do that."

Although skiffle was great for getting young people to take up their guitars, washboards and tea-chests, it was only ever going to be a stop-gap for John because rock 'n' roll was his dream, his real passion. That passion was ignited at one of those lunchtime sessions at Michael's house in the spring of 1956 when he played John a new record he had just brought

Michael Hill at Quarry Bank, 1956.

back from a school trip to Amsterdam. It was by an American artist called Little Richard.

John acknowledged the influence of Little Richard on his life when he said, "Little Richard was one of the all-time greats. I still love Little Richard. That's the music that brought me from the provinces of England to the world. That's what made me what I am. I had no idea of doing music as a way of life until rock 'n' roll hit me. That's the music that inspired me to play music."

However, John also acknowledged the source of that inspiration. "This boy at school (Michael Hill) had been to Holland," recalled Lennon. "He said he'd got this record by someone who was better than Elvis. Elvis was bigger than religion in my life. We used to go to Michael's house and listen to Elvis on 78s. We'd buy five Se-

69, Dovedale Road, where Michael Hill turned John Lennon on to rock 'n' roll.

Michael and John in the Dovedale School register, leaving for Quarry Bank.

John Lennon's copy of "Rock Island Line", which he sold to Rod Davis.

Michael's copy of "Long Tall Sally".

The *Fab* one hundred and *Four*

nior Service cigarettes loose in the shop and some chips and we'd go along. The new record was 'Long Tall Sally' (B-side 'Slippin' and Slidin''). When I heard it, it was so great I couldn't speak."

And so Lennon, inspired by Lonnie Donegan, but turned on to rock 'n' roll by Little Richard, was ready to make his mark on the music world.

"By the summer of 1956," Michael recalled, "approaching the age of sixteen, John was intently practising at playing his new guitar. So too was our friend and classmate, Eric Griffiths. Rod Davis, another Quarry Bank boy but in a higher academic grade than us, had acquired a second-hand banjo soon after John and Eric got their guitars. Rod was a serious student and not a close friend of theirs or mine, although John had known him since they had attended Sunday school together ten years before."

Finding a tea-chest bass player proved to be more problematic and several people came and went in this role, such as Bill Smith, Nigel Walley and Ivan Vaughan. However, Michael was nearly one of The Quarrymen.

"In October 1956," remembered Michael, "during rehearsals on the stage of the Quarry Bank High School assembly hall in preparation for the group to play in the intermission of a sixth form Quarry Bank/Calder High School dance – their first public performance – I even had a go myself. That was the nearest I ever got to playing with The Beatles! John had asked me earlier to fill this role but at the time, I was totally focused on studying and trying to make up for a lot of lost time as school-end exams approached. So I turned the offer down."

Michael deserves his place in history, not as a member of The Quarrymen, but for turning John on to rock 'n' roll. For this, we should be eternally grateful.

The stage in Quarry Bank Hall, where The Quarrymen performed.

Len Garry

Leonard Charles Garry was born in Liverpool on 6 January 1942. His father Harry, who had served in the Merchant Navy in the war, was then a printer with the *Liverpool Echo*. Len's mother Phyllis was a hairdresser and continued to work at home. Len had an older brother Walter, born in 1939.

They lived at 77, Lance Lane, just off Woolton Road, and Len went to nearby Mosspits Lane Primary School, the same school Pete Shotton had attended the year before (though they did not know each other at the time). Len's musical career began when he took piano lessons but, like his friends, soon gave up. Len did well at Mosspits and successfully passed the Eleven Plus exam, enabling him to progress to the Liverpool Institute. There, he quickly made friends with a lad from Woolton named Ivan Vaughan.

Len Garry at the Liverpool Institute, 1956.

One of his earliest musical influences was a teacher at school. "I can recall sitting in assembly every morning listening to the pianist, Miss 'Fatty' Forester. We would have to sing some stupid songs with lyrics such as 'Come lasses and lads, get leave of your dads, let's off to the Maypole high' etc. The songs were awful and I judged them to be very sissy-like. This was probably my first real experience of what music was and I was not very interested in it."

A more important musical influence was his grandfather's records, which he listened to at their Baby Linen Shop at 113, Woolton Road. "I would listen to the Ink Spots, Bing Crosby and Frank Sinatra on Grandfather Cartwright's wind up gramophone," Len said. "I must admit that I preferred Sinatra, as his voice seemed to have a lot more life in it. I also liked the Ink Spots for their harmonies and soft tones."

"My mother was musical," explained Len. "She was an accomplished pianist, could read music well and had a good singing voice. Quite often there would be a sing-song on a Sunday evening when my Uncle Jack would sing duets with my mother around the piano. Jack and mum would sing mainly Ivor Novello songs, such as 'We'll Gather Lilacs in the Spring Again'. We had inherited an upright piano from Grandfather Cartwright, as he had recently passed away. I struggled on the piano, although I found the theory of music very boring and the exercises I was given to do even more boring."

Miss 'Fatty' Forester, as Len describes her, was a large, domineering woman, and Len remembers those weekly piano lessons very well. "She would stand immediately behind me as I sat at the piano. She would say, 'keep those wrists up Leonard and watch the metronome.' I did slowly manage to reach the standard of playing the 'Blue Danube'. Eventually, I gave up the classes.

Len's house at 77, Lance Lane.

Len Garry's entry in the Liverpool Institute register.

"I was given a combined radio/record player for Christmas one year. I would listen to Radio Luxembourg's *Top Twenty* late on Saturday nights with artists such as Pat Boone, Guy Mitchell and Frankie Laine, who all made an impression on me. I was more aware now that I really did have the gift of a good singing voice and my interest in popular music grew.

In the summer of 1955, Ivan brought Len to meet his friend John Lennon and their gang in Vale Road, which included Nigel Walley and Pete Shotton. Shotton recognised Len from Mosspits and then he glanced over at John. "I looked at him, his expression. It was that of a rather shy, tousle-haired youth," remarked Len, "smaller than me and a little stockier in build. He had a quizzical expression, as though he was assessing my credentials as a person. I could almost feel his gaze penetrating me. 'Hi I'm John', he said in a rather sarcastic tone' and the ice was broken."

It was not long before the fledgling Quarrymen were looking for a permanent tea-chest bass player, having experimented with several others, though Len cannot remember precisely when it was. "I estimate I joined in late 1956, possibly September, because I know I was fourteen and I did not turn fifteen till January 1957," recalled Len. "I did not actually want to play the tea-chest. I really wanted to sing, but John was the singer, so in order to play with them, I had to be content with the tea-chest."

Len became a regular with the group and played the tea-chest bass at the photographed 22 June 1957 performance on Rosebery Street and at St. Peter's Church on the famous day when John met Paul. As they both attended the Liverpool Institute, Paul and Len became friendly and would often take the same bus home. Len would hop off at Penny Lane to head home. He soon noticed that Paul had become friends with another Inny lad, George Harrison. The discussions on the bus soon turned to guitars and music and it is clear that on a number of occasions, George tried his best to join The Quarrymen.

Len remembers one particular day when they all took the bus to Speke to listen to this new wonder kid. "We went round to George's house and were duly impressed with his expert rendition of instrumentals such as 'Raunchy' and 'Guitar Boogie'. George must have been encouraged by our favourable reaction as he became an avid follower and admirer of John Lennon, much to John's annoyance, as he regarded George as 'only a young lad.'"

As 1957 ended with a gig at Wilson Hall on 7 December, the tea-chest bass was still evident in The Quarrymen, but the repertoire was changing. Len could see that rock 'n' roll was here to stay. What could he do? Colin Hanton says that Len left before Eric, and Len has never claimed that he played in The Quarrymen with George. Therefore, what we are left with is the fact that Len must have drifted out of The Quarrymen sometime after October 1957 when he is photographed playing at the New Clubmoor Hall, and before December 1957 when Eric left. As tea-chest bass player, his position was tenuous, as the group was evolving into a true rock 'n' roll band, and so there was no need for the skiffle instruments or musicians, which is why Rod and Pete, on banjo and washboard respectively, had already left. Of course, Len could have stayed if he had purchased a bass guitar, but that did not happen, so Len was gone, just before George Harrison joined.

His concern over his role in the group became a moot point in the summer of 1958 when he was rushed to hospital, unconscious. "I can remember waking up a few days later," Len remembered, "and asking for a cigarette. Eventually, I was transferred to Fazakerley Hospital, which was about six miles away, to the north end of Liverpool.

"I was diagnosed as suffering from tubercular meningitis. I was placed in an isolation cubicle and told that I was very fortunate to be alive with all my faculties intact. I realised that I was lucky to be alive."

The Quarrymen carried on without Len, but still came to visit their friend in the hospital while his health improved. However, his part in their story was finished.

Len Garry performing at the 50th anniversary of John meeting Paul at St. Peter's, Woolton in 2007.

Paul makes his debut with The Quarrymen at New Clubmoor Hall. Len is playing tea-chest bass (behind Paul).

The *Fab* one hundred and *Four*

SPRING 1957

The Blackjacks

There has been much speculation as to whether John Lennon ever played in a group called The Blackjacks. Stan Williams, a friend of John's from Dovedale School, was in a group called The Satellites, taking part in a talent competition at The Pavillion Theatre, known locally as the "Pivvy", in Lodge Lane, Liverpool. Stan has a clear recollection of seeing his former school friend fronting a skiffle group and calling themselves The Blackjacks.

"John had no guitar then," recalled Stan, "but had bravado, nevertheless, to sing and play a tea-chest bass wearing a natty pair of leather gloves. I can see him to the left of the stage, leg perched up on the tea-chest bass, and plucking away singing 'Maggie May'. John only managed a verse and chorus before they were stopped by the judges and asked to leave the stage. There were about four or five in Lennon's group, and I remember them wearing matching outfits: black jeans and a white shirts." The Quarrymen still used this look when Paul made his official debut in October 1957 at New Clubmoor Hall.

I asked Stan to try and confirm when this took place, and he remembers it clearly. "At the time we formed our skiffle group, my grandfather was very ill, and he used to interrupt our rehearsals if we were too noisy. He died in the summer of 1957, and this event was not long before he died. I am sure, therefore, that this event was in the spring of 1957, maybe February or March at the latest."

When I asked Bill Smith, founding member of The Quarrymen about this, he couldn't ever recall using the name The Blackjacks, so it must have been after he left. However, Bill told me that they often played the card game, blackjack, so it would explain where the name could have come from. As Stan was a childhood friend of Ivan Vaughan, and Ivan wasn't in the lineup that day, it was after Ivan had left the group too.

I asked The Quarrymen's former banjo player Rod Davis what he remembered. "We were The Blackjacks for a time," observed Rod, "but I think we got rather fed up with that. I seem to be the only person who remembers this," he said. "It was, I think, before the time Len and Colin joined. Pete and Eric said they had no recollection of it at all either. Our uniform was black jeans and white shirts, and I think that's where it came from, but the name The Blackjacks didn't last long, maybe a couple of weeks at most. Someone recently suggested that maybe I had got confused with Pete Best's band called The Blackjacks, however by the time that band was functioning I was out of The Quarrymen by a couple of years." The group that featured future Beatles Pete Best and Chas Newby was also called The Blackjacks, formed in 1959, but there is no connection.

Stan's suggestion that this event was in the spring of 1957 is most likely. This would certainly fit, as the lineup of The Quarrymen was still fluctuating before they had a settled lineup just weeks before John met Paul at St. Peter's Church on 6 July 1957. The Quarrymen's first appearance was in October 1956 at the Quarry Bank School dance, and they also later appeared as The Quarrymen in the *Carroll Levis TV*

Search for Stars at the Liverpool Empire on 9 June 1957. Little is recorded about what happened in between these dates, as they were mainly rehearsing in each other's houses.

The fact that John was playing tea-chest bass would also fit at this time, because he was still learning to play guitar on the instrument lent to him by Geoff Lee. He wouldn't be quite ready to play it in public yet. They also only got part way through "Maggie May" so it wasn't a memorable event either: in fact, it is one they would wish to forget! In helping to date it, The Vipers Skiffle Group released "Maggie May" in January 1957, so The Blackjacks' appearance must have been after this, fitting Stan's timing of the event in spring 1957.

It is almost impossible therefore to know what the lineup was for this appearance. What we do know, however, is that for a short period of time, John's group was called The Blackjacks.

The Pavilion Theatre, Lodge Lane, where The Blackjacks performed.

22 JUNE 1957

Charlie Roberts photographs The Quarrymen

Charles Roberts was born in Blackpool, after his mum was evacuated there as were so many of Liverpool's expectant mothers. He was immediately brought back to the family home at 84, Rosebery Street. Through mutual friends Arthur Wong and Kevin Hanson, Charlie became friends with Quarrymen drummer Colin Hanton. It was through this friendship that, on behalf of the residents of Rosebery Street, Charlie invited The Quarrymen to play at their street party. The event, one of many being held across Liverpool, was organised to celebrate 750 years since Liverpool became a town by virtue of the Charter King John signed in 1207.

"At that time," remarked Charlie, "The Quarrymen would play anywhere for free, because they were doing it for fun. They became more serious after Paul joined, and maybe John was taking it serious, but it was really just friends having some fun. They all turned up, and set themselves up on the back of a wagon that Fred Tyler had brought along. He also wired up a speaker system so that they had something for the microphones, so they made quite a loud noise, which was good."

I wanted to know what The Quarrymen were like, and Charlie recalled some fond memories. "I thought they were great, playing good music and entertaining. When you compare them to other bands, I suppose they weren't that good, but I enjoyed listening to them, and so did the crowd.

Charlie Roberts with one of his famous photographs.

"I can't remember what songs they played, but it was good fun. The street was decorated with bunting, and we had sandwiches and drinks, and had a good time. There was an incident involving John, who seemed to upset some of the lads in the crowd. I think he had been winking at some of the girls, and it became obvious that there could be trouble, so as soon as they finished, they grabbed their instruments, and ran into my mum's house. Some reports have said that the police came and escorted them to the bus stop, but The Quarrymen just stayed in our house for about an hour, and then after everyone had gone, they went home.

Charlie Roberts by his house, displaying the poster for The Quarrymen's appearance in Rosebery Street, 22 June 1957.

Charlie Roberts by the ladder, putting up the bunting for the street party.

The Quarrymen in Rosebery Street, 22 June 1957, photographed by Charlie Roberts.

STREET PARTY COMM 4 PM SAT JUNE 22

RACES*
RECORDS * SONGS
FANCY DRESS * LUCKY DIP
DANCING * PRIZES
GAMES ETC.

SPECIAL ATTRACTION 5PM

QUARRYMEN Skiffle Group!

Reproduction of the original poster displayed in Charlie Robert's window.

The Fab one hundred and Four

Rosebery Street in 1974, shortly before the houses were demolished.

"The party was such a success," said Charlie, "that the City Council awarded us a prize for the best decorated street, and so the following week we had a second party, with entertainment provided by The Merseysippi Jazz Band, all paid for by the City Council, which was great."

Charlie followed The Quarrymen to many of the venues they played, like Wilson Hall in Garston, where one particular incident sticks in his memory. "I remember Wilson Hall, when we all had to suddenly run away after the performance. I don't know who started it or what it was about, but everyone legged it! I was okay, because I hadn't been performing, so nobody knew me, but the others had to run. The first thing to discard was the tea-chest bass, which was too big and heavy to run with."

The Quarrymen often went to "Barneys", the club at St. Barnabas Church Hall. But, like most venues, alcohol was not available. "We used to meet in the Rose of Mossley pub on Rose Lane," recalled Charlie, "and then we would go on to "Barneys". We all had to wear proper suits and ties to get in there. After "Barneys" closed, we would then go to the Dutch Café on Smithdown Road, which was open late, one of the few places still open into the early hours of the morning."

One of Charlie's funniest memories takes place in an area called Ford to the north of Liverpool: "The Quarrymen had been booked to play at a party, and so we all travelled up there on the bus as usual. However, the party was in a house, and so there was not much room for the boys to play. By the time they had realised what time it was, the last bus had gone, and so they all decided to stay the night in the house. At some point, John and Paul went out for cigarettes, and there were obviously road works nearby, because they returned with a warning lamp they'd picked up. Everything went quiet, but when we tried to go home, we went to open the door, but somebody had put cement into the door lock! Nobody admitted doing it, but we all had our suspicions, because only John and Paul had been out. So, we all just left through the back door and said nothing."

One of their friends, Arthur Wong, had a great car and they all used to ride in it. "Arthur's dad had a very good business," Charlie recalled, "and so Arthur had a Vauxhall Cresta PA, a great car with fins, two-tone paint, very much like the American cars. We used to drive around, and I clearly remember John and Paul on the back seat of the car, with Paul trying to master 'Raunchy'. We had a great time driving around in it with Arthur and we would often end up at Arthur's home at 42, Heydale Road, in Mossley Hill.

"As well as the car, Arthur possessed a Grundig Tape Recorder, and when The Quarrymen went to Arthur Wong's house, they would rehearse in the front room and he would record them. If only he had kept those tapes!" This reminded Charlie of those sessions, and his boss from work. "My boss at Littlewoods, Arthur Davis, was a good pianist, and he would often come down and play the piano with The Quarrymen in Arthur's house. But one day he decided he did not have the time, and stopped coming down. Just think, he could have been a Beatle!"

Although Charlie was not present at the studio when The Quarrymen made their first record, "That'll Be the Day" and "In Spite of All the Danger", he ended up with the record for a while. "The record was passed around," Charlie recollected, "and I don't know who gave it to me, but I ended up with it in my possession for ages. I took it to work with me, and played it over the music system in Littlewoods, mainly 'That'll Be the Day', because we were all Buddy Holly fans, and it went down well. Nobody seemed interested in where it was, but I did not want to keep hold of it, as it was not mine, so I gave it back to one of them."

One of the other gigs that Charlie remembers well took place in Woolton Village, above the pet store. "It was one of those small rooms," he recalled, "and they were playing at a 21st birthday party. I don't know who was drunk, but I remember a few of them leaning out of the window and being sick. We never used to drink that much and I don't remember John ever drinking much. Colin drank more than the rest of us, but he was a bit older and working by then, so he could afford to drink."

Charlie ended up at Junior Art College at Gambier Terrace when John was across the road at the Art College, where Charlie eventually worked. He never encountered John at College, but knew his reputation through the staff.

He lost touch with the lads after he went to work and they went on to fame and fortune as The Beatles. But Charlie continues to play an important part in the story with those historic photos, capturing The Quarrymen for the first time on film.

42, Heydale Road (right) where The Quarrymen rehearsed, and the author's present house (far left).

The *Fab* one hundred and *Four*

PROGRAMME

STALLS — SIDESHOWS — ICE CREAM — LEMONADE

Teas and Refreshments in large Marquee situated behind the hut.

2-00 p.m. PROCESSION leaves Church Road, via Allerton Road, Kings Drive, Hunt's Cross Avenue; returning to the Church Field. Led by the Band of the Cheshire Yeomanry. Street Collection by the Youth Club during the procession.

3-00 p.m. CROWNING OF THE ROSE QUEEN (Miss Sally Wright) by Mrs. THELWALL JONES.

3-10 p.m. FANCY DRESS PARADE.
Class 1. Under 7 years.
Class 2. 7 to 12 years.
Class 3. Over 12 years.
Entrants to report to Miss P. Fuller at the Church Hall before the procession.

3-30 p.m. to 5-00 p.m. MUSICAL SELECTIONS by the Band of the Cheshire (Earl of Chester) Yeomanry. Bandmaster: H. Abraham. (By permission of Lt.-Col. G. C. V. Churton, M.C., M.B.E.).

4-15 p.m. THE QUARRY MEN SKIFFLE GROUP.

5-15 p.m. DISPLAY by the City of Liverpool Police Dogs. By kind permission of the Chief Constable and Watch Committee.

5-45 p.m. THE QUARRY MEN SKIFFLE GROUP.

8-0 p.m. GRAND DANCE in the CHURCH HALL

GEORGE EDWARDS BAND also The Quarry Men Skiffle Group

TICKETS 2/-

REFRESHMENTS AT MODERATE PRICES.

The programme from the Garden Fête at St. Peter's Church, 6th July 1957.

6 JULY 1957

John Lennon meets Paul McCartney

If ever there was a pivotal moment in the history of The Beatles, then Saturday, 6 July 1957 has to be that moment. Without John and Paul meeting, becoming friends and forming their legendary musical partnership, then what we see today as The Beatles' legacy would never have even started. There are many versions of what happened that day, and as most of it is from memory, there is no definitive account. However, I have spoken to members of The Quarrymen and eyewitnesses who were there to compile what I feel is the closest account of what happened.

Quarrymen drummer Colin Hanton has clear memories of that day. "Pete Shotton's mum was on the church committee I think, so she got us the gig. It was a brave decision by the church committee because, of course, we were the first generation of teenagers, skiffle was just in, it was the early days of rock 'n' roll, and the music was frowned upon as the devil's music. It was like a grey world before and suddenly it was Technicolor. I remember being bold and going down to town and buying two pairs of luminous socks – shocking green and orange. Such was rock 'n' roll. It was my little rebellion.

"The church took a gamble and it paid off. Everyone in the village came, as there was no sitting in watching the television as not many people had one. Back in 1957, Woolton was out in 'the sticks'. The trams used to stop at the top of Kings Drive and the conductor would unhook the wiring and then go back to town. After that, you

The Quarrymen on stage at the Woolton Parish Church Garden Fête on 6 July 1957.

had to walk. Woolton was an isolated village and it has still maintained a village mentality. A lot of building went on, but back then, below the bottom of Kings Drive where I lived was all fields.

"If anything big was coming up in the village, everyone turned out to march or to watch. The summer fête was the biggest event of the year. There was a marching band and everyone would be marching along with them. The local coal wagons and potato wagons were dressed up and decorated with banners and streamers. It was an important day for Woolton."

As the village got ready for the big event, one young man was inside "Mendips", preparing himself for a momentous day. That morning, John had spent hours arranging his hair and squeezing into his skin-tight, leg-hugging drainpipe trousers. John stormed out of the house. This was his day and Mimi was not going to ruin it for him.

The biggest coincidence, or twist of fate, was the friendship that one boy had with both John and Paul, though the two future Beatles did not know each other yet. Ivan Vaughan lived in the house behind John and had attended Dovedale Junior School with him. However, instead of following John and their friends to Quarry Bank, Ivan's parents sent their son to the Liverpool Institute, where he ended up in the same class as the boy born on exactly the same day as him – 18 June 1942. That boy was Paul McCartney. Knowing his new friend's love of music, Ivan decided that he should bring Paul to meet his childhood friend John. If it was not for this coincidence, it is highly unlikely that John and Paul would have met.

Ivan had to convince Paul to come and see The Quarrymen. Ivan's clinching argument was that it was "a good place to meet girls". With his best jacket on, Paul set off to meet Ivan for what turned out to be a momentous day.

Every year, the church celebrated on the first Saturday on or after 29 June, which is the Feast of St. Peter. This was the highlight of the calendar for the village of Woolton. The festivities included a parade around the village on the back of lorries. There were usually five vehicles and, in 1957, the last of these carried The Quarrymen. The parade also included children's organizations like Brownies, Scouts, Sunday School and Youth Club members. In between, there were Morris Dancers and the highlight for one young lady was to be crowned as the Rose Queen.

At exactly 2 p.m., the bells of St. Peter's Church chimed. The parade route headed down Church Road, left on to Allerton Road, right on to Woolton Street, and left down King's Drive toward where Rod Davis, Colin Hanton and Eric Griffiths lived. It snaked along Hunts Cross Avenue and up Manor Road, turning right on to Speke Road and back along Woolton Street, turning left into Allerton Road.

Rod Davis, banjo player with The Quarrymen, remembers the parade well. "We were on the back of a lorry for the parade around Woolton, much to John's disgust – how could we play and sing while moving? The acoustics were appalling. All John remembered was thrashing his guitar as loudly as possible as there were no amplifiers. Thrashing the guitars was the only way. Some skiffle groups had four guitarists. As a rule, we had to keep telling Colin to play the drums with his brushes so he did not drown us out. Now we have to urge him to 'give it some welly'."

In 2009, Rod was looking through some of his father's photographs. There, to his amazement, was a series of photos that captured the parade and, to his delight, two photographs of The Quarrymen on the back of the lorry. As the procession came to its end, the lorries drove up Church Road and back to the St. Peter's, where they stopped.

Everyone paraded along the path that passed through the graveyard, and into the field at the rear of the church. Several years before, a small stage had been erected for this annual event, which was po-

St. Peter's Church, Woolton.

The Rose Queen and her attendants, with the retiring Rose Queen from 1956.

sitioned at the bottom of the field. The Scout hut, which housed The Quarrymen's instruments, was up the hill where the school currently sits. There were tents for refreshments and first aid facilities.

The Rose Queen, 13-year-old Sally Wright, was crowned and, following a fancy-dress parade for the children, Dr. Thelwall-Jones formally opened the summer fête.

Len Garry remembers how they entered the Scout hut with their equipment and then walked around the stalls. John smashed a few plates at one of the game stalls (after putting his glasses on) and that made him feel better. When they heard the brass band finishing, they made their way to the stage and set up. They played at 4:15 p.m. after the Police Dog display team, which was the main attraction.

As they took to the stage, Reverend Pryce Jones introduced The Quarrymen and John took over. "John Lennon was at the microphone", Len said. "He was centre stage and positioned in the front, saying before we started, 'Len, get a bit closer'. I replied, 'I can't. Not with this thing,' referring to the tea-chest with frustration." John quickly introduced himself and the band members. Nervously, he asked, "Is this thing on?" When the crowd replied "yes", he decided against a long introduction and launched into "All Shook Up" followed by "Blue Suede Shoes". Then the moment he had been waiting for was upon him. He stepped up closely to the microphone and, for the first time, performed "Be-Bop-A-Lula".

In the audience were his mum Julia and her two daughters Julia and Jackie, plus his good friend Ivan Vaughan. Ivan was standing next to someone John did not know: Paul McCartney, whom Ivan had invited there to see this group. Also standing in the crowd was one of their friends, Geoff Rhind, who had the foresight to bring his camera with him. He stood by the stage and took the famous photo of the young group of upstarts.

Paul remembered arriving at St. Peter's. "I'd been invited over by Ivan, and he took us along. I remember coming in to the village fête, like you do, sort of enter the field, it's all on, there's all sideshows. The music came from this little tannoy system. It was John and the band. I remember that I was amazed. I mean, I saw the band and I thought, oh great, I'll listen to the band 'cos I was into the music, and Ivan said, 'I know a couple of lads in the band, and these are my mates.'"

John launched into "Maggie May", the famous song about a Liverpool prostitute. They played many popular skiffle numbers like "Cumberland Gap" and "Railroad Bill", plus "Come Go With Me". "We were in the audience watching," recalled Paul, "and I remember John singing his own words to the song called 'Come and Go With Me',

The Brownies on parade.

The young people carry out an operation.

because we'd heard it on the radio. I had, too, in my house but I did not know he knew it yet. It was a lovely song by the Del Vikings. John did not know the verses, but he knew the "come, come, come, come, come, come and go with me'. Now he did his own little words, which were good. They were from the blues; 'down to the penitentiary', all this stuff, which weren't on the real record."

Rod Davis said that John was not making up the words. "They were the words that we always sang," Rod explained, "as the only way we could learn words was by listening to the records – often in the NEMS record shop near to Penny Lane – or on Radio Luxembourg, and scribbling down the words we thought we were listening to. So, when we performed these songs, these were the words we sang. What we couldn't recognise we improvised and 'penitentiary' sounded bluesy so it went in. The problem was that we couldn't afford to buy all the records we wanted, so you had to get the words off the radio or in record booths." However it happened, Paul was impressed by John's performance, though he noticed John was playing some strange looking guitar chords. "I remember at the time," said Paul, "that he was playing banjo chords on his guitar, 'cos as fellas look at other fellas' fingers, and kinda thinking 'what's he playing there?'

"John's mum Julia had taught him to play these banjo chords, and he'd got a guitar, 'cos it was more fashionable, it was more modern than a banjo, but he still played with the banjo tuning, and I think he only had four strings at the time, which was like a banjo. So, he had his banjo chords and he was playing the song, and I thought well

Overleaf: The Marching Band leads the parade down Kings Drive in Woolton.

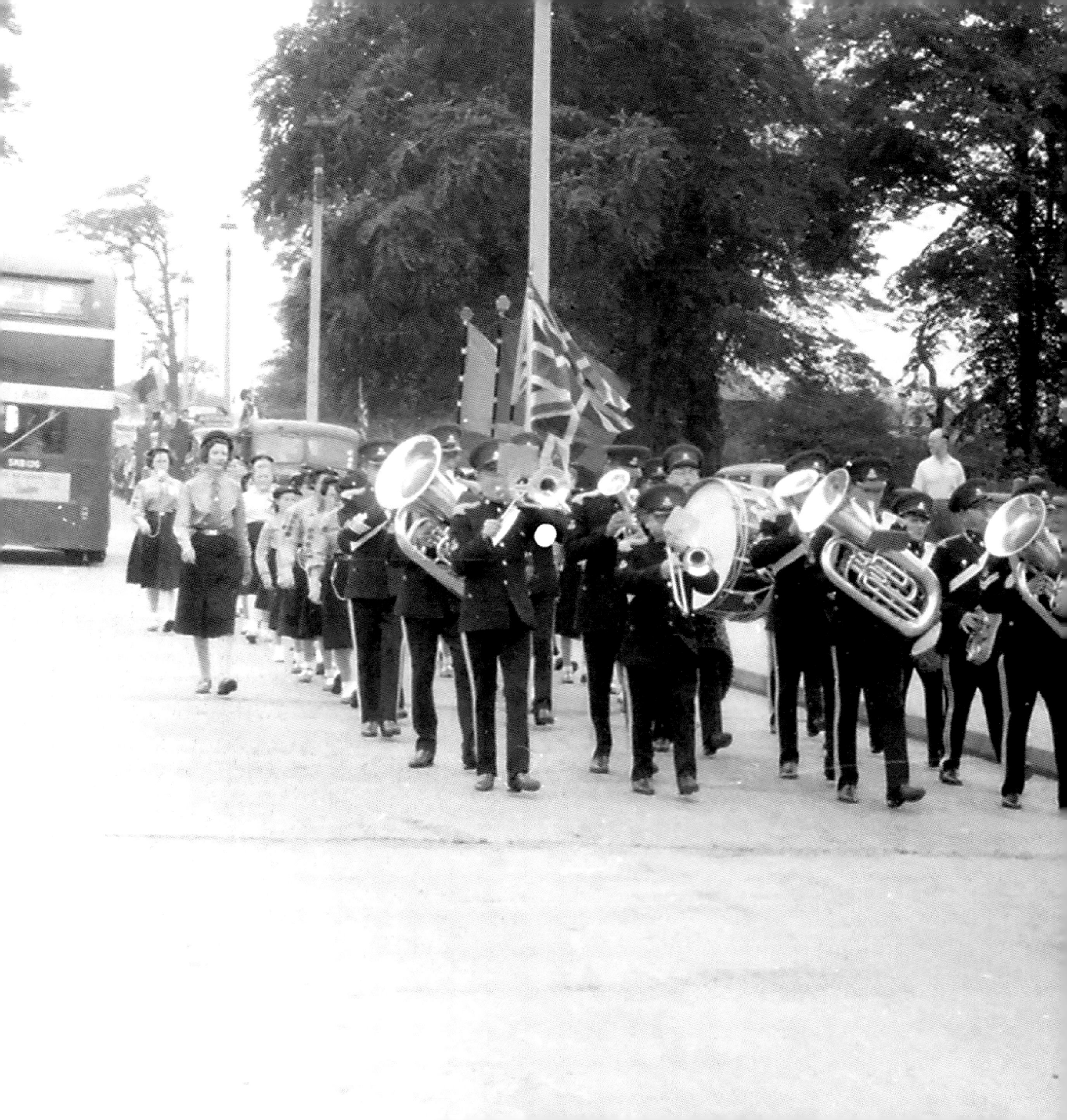

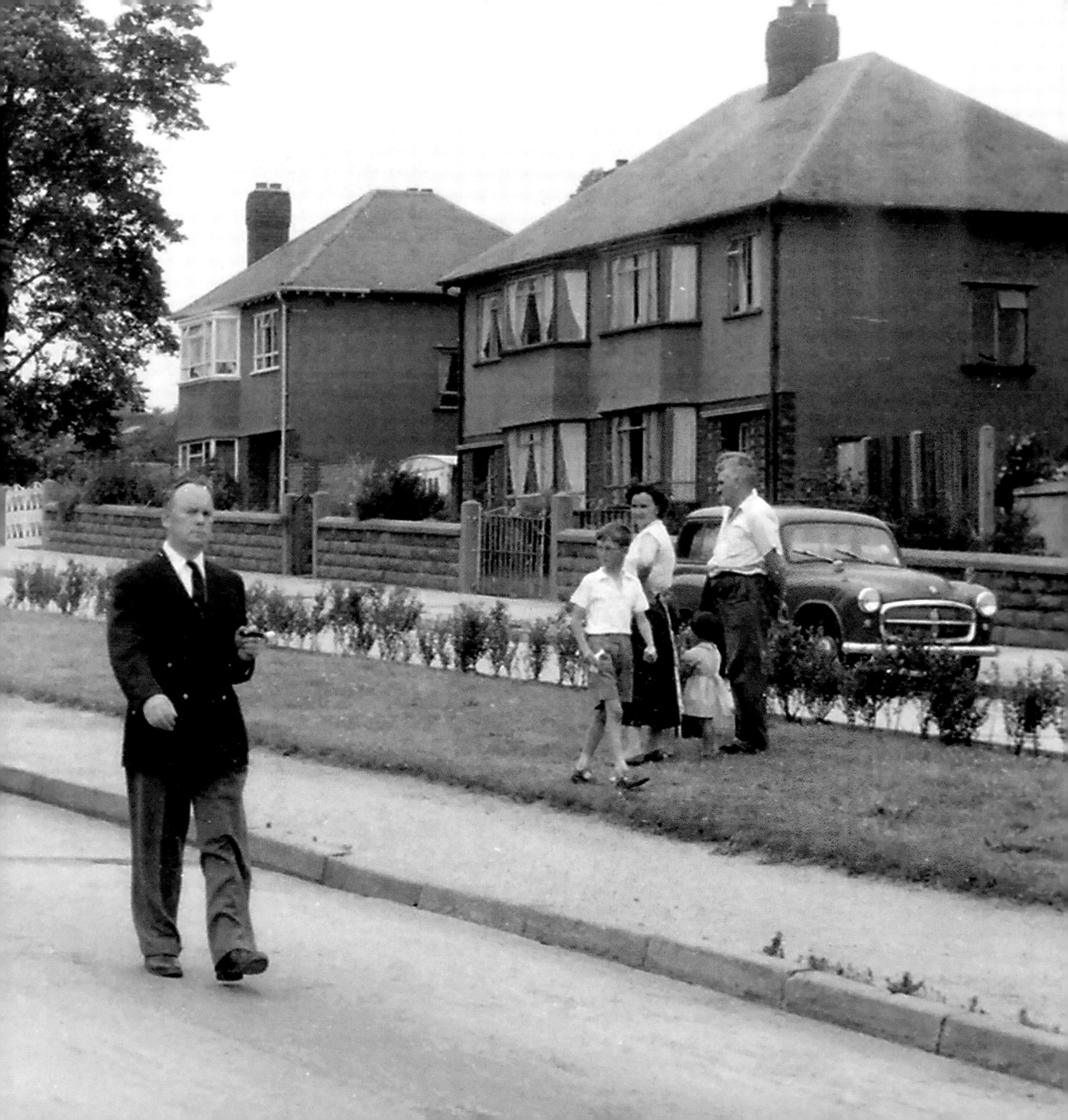

great, you know, he looked good, and he's singing good, you know, he looks like a good lead singer, and all that. He had his glasses off, so he looked suave, without the glasses."

Colin Hanton looked back to the day and although the programme indicates that The Quarrymen played twice, he doesn't think they did. "People say we played two sets in the afternoon," recalled Colin, "but I don't remember playing two sets. The way these events go, we were programed to go on twice, but things overrun and it knocks everything out, so I only remember playing once in the afternoon.

"At some time in the afternoon after playing, we had stored our equipment in the big Scout hut. We went in, and I was messing with my drums and there was a lad on his trumpet and then there was John, Ivan, and this other lad, who of course turned out to be Paul McCartney. Now, everyone says that the first meeting of John and Paul took place in the church hall later on that day, but I was not in the hall then, so it must have been in the Scout hut. I couldn't confuse the two. I reckon the first introduction happened in the Scout hut in the afternoon."

This makes sense, because why wait until the evening to meet when they were there in the field in the afternoon? Why wait another few hours before making the introduction? "I am adamant

The Quarrymen on the lorry: Pete, Eric, Len, John, Colin and Rod.

The Quarrymen (Eric, Pete, Len, John (hidden), Colin and Rod) turn to look at photographer James Davis.

that the introduction took place in the afternoon in that hut," said Colin emphatically.

Paul recalled: "After they'd finished playing, Ive took us to the church hall just behind the church, that was up the hill a bit from where the fête was. We went up there and, by now, they'd finished their set so they were kind of, you know, having a beer. It was not crazy drinking or anything, but it was just like, social, a bit of fun. I remember John looking at me, we used to really think John looked pretty cool 'cos he was a bit older than us, and he would do a little bit more greased-back hair than us, than we were allowed, you know our parents would really, well, I just did not dare do it, the way my dad was. So John was kind of, you know, quite groovy, you know he looked a bit of a 'Ted' (Teddy Boy) then and he did have a drape."

"Paul suggested John was drinking a lot," observed Colin, "but you couldn't get hold of booze. There were no off-licences (shops where you could purchase alcohol) or places to buy booze, and if you looked under eighteen there was no chance at all, so he couldn't have been drunk. He maybe had obtained a bottle off someone, but that would have been all."

At the end of the afternoon performance, Len recalls a conversation between Ivan and John, where Ivan mentioned that Paul had promised to bring his guitar. John suggested to Paul that he go home and bring it back. Len is the only one to mention this and recalls Paul cycling home and returning later with his guitar over his shoulder. However, having spoken to the other Quarrymen as well as Paul's friend Ian James who was also there that day, no one remembers Paul going home for his guitar. In fact, it becomes obvious that Paul

The field where The Quarrymen played.

did not have his guitar when we examine what happened in the church hall.

Ivan and Paul discussed times and agreed to meet in the hall about teatime where food was being served. Paul mentioned that he couldn't stay for the evening performance. So, what did happen when Paul met John? We have to examine the different accounts from each person present, take the bits they agree on and come up with the best guesstimate.

What we can deduce is that the meeting lasted for about twenty minutes by the steps of the stage in the church hall. Ivan introduced Paul to John, who nodded an acknowledgement, probably without lifting his head, and grunted as teenage boys do. Paul did not stay long as he had to leave early because he was planning his dad's birthday party for the next day. The problem is that those present were teenagers preparing for a gig. They would not have had any idea that what they had witnessed was the most important meeting in music history.

John was sitting on the steps by the stage, next to the radiator, strumming his guitar, looking as if he knew what he was doing. Rod explains what happened next: "We had been playing together for something around a year and we could play the correct chords for all the tunes in our repertoire, except that Eric and John had theirs tuned like banjos and played banjo chords, as opposed to tuning their guitars normally and using guitar chords. Funnily enough, Lonnie Donegan did the opposite and played guitar chords on a banjo. Banjo tuning is an open G chord and many guitarists nowadays experiment with open tunings. We could tune our guitars like banjos, as we hadn't learnt guitar chords. I played a banjo anyway, so I had no problems."

GARDEN FETE
ST. PETER'S CHURCH FIELD

WOOLTON PARISH CHURCH   Rector: M. Pryce Jones

Saturday, 6th July, 1957
at 3 p.m.

ADMISSION BY PROGRAMME:
CHILDREN 3d.

PROCEEDS IN AID OF CHURCH FUNDS.

Programme for the Garden Fête on 6 July 1957.

At that time, John tuned the top four strings of his guitar as a banjo. I asked Rod Davis about John's prowess on the guitar. "John and Eric went to a guitar teacher in Hunts Cross to learn the guitar," Rod said. "This was before the group even started, according to Eric. After two lessons or so, they realised that it would take forever as he was trying to teach them from the music and all they wanted was a few chords to accompany songs. So John's mother, Julia, offered to teach them some banjo chords. This involved tun-

Eric, John and Len performing with The Quarrymen on 6 July 1957.

The stage erected in the field at St. Peters in 1953.

The stage in the early 1960s playing host to the Woolton Follies.

The stage in the hall of St. Peter's Church, photographed in 1956.

ing their guitars to four-string banjo tuning. I can't remember what they did with the fifth and sixth string. I asked Eric some time ago and I think he said that they just tuned them to the G chord. As I recall, we played almost everything in C or G."

St. Peter's Church Hall, where Paul met John.

John and Paul talked by the steps at the edge of the stage, on the right.

Paul was asked to play something, so he had to re-tune John's guitar from banjo tuning to guitar tuning. Paul offered to show John how to tune it, which was a good start, and certainly impressed John. "John, you know, was pretty cool, he had nice big sideburns or, as we called them, sideboards," said Paul. "I remember him just leaning over me, and we were round a piano in the church hall, and there was a couple of guitars, and on the guitar, which I think must have been backwards, because I had a mate from the Dingle (Ian James) who played the guitar, so I was used to turning the guitar upside down. I played a bit of 'Twenty Flight Rock', and I knew a lot of the words, and that was like very good currency in those days." Ian had taught Paul to play "Twenty Flight Rock", which Paul played to John, which got Paul into The Quarrymen.

Paul played John's guitar upside-down, a feat he had conquered while learning with his friend Ian James, on whose guitar Paul had practised. Ian's guitar was right-handed, so he is a witness to the fact that Paul learned to play a right-handed guitar upside down. Paul also not only knew all of the words to the songs, but could play all of the proper guitar chords, too, as well as tune a guitar. Paul remembered his father Jim's advice not to be too pushy. John Lennon was most impressed. No wonder.

"They just really wanted to be getting the words to that song," recalled Paul. "Like, they hadn't got them to 'Come Go With Me'. That was one of the big things then, how d'ya get the words man? Yeah well, I know a fella who lives in Bootle, and he knows B7. We'd all pile on a bus to go and learn a chord. The words were the same, so it was a great thing if anyone knew the full words to 'Twenty Flight Rock' and I'd learnt them all, because I'd got the record. It was one of the first records I'd ever got, from Curry's in Liverpool. So that was it. I went up to the church hall, and I remember thinking John smelt a bit beery and a bit older than I was used to, 'cos I was only 15. I hadn't quite seen the grown up world just yet, because I was younger than them."

As if that was not enough, on prompting from John, and at Ivan's suggestion, Paul sang "Long Tall Sally". Paul had a greater vocal range than John and could do an excellent Little Richard impression. Little did Paul realise that "Long Tall Sally" was the song that had turned John onto rock 'n' roll at his friend Michael Hill's house. He couldn't have chosen a better song. Paul also performed Gene Vincent's "Be-Bop-A-Lula", one of John's favourites.

Paul's friend Ian James recalled how he nearly joined The Quarrymen that day, too. Ian was an important part of the famous day of 6 July 1957 when John met Paul for the first time, so I asked him what he remembered. "Paul had invited me to come along to the fête, and told me to bring my guitar, too. I was not there for the afternoon performance, but I promised to come up in the evening. I came over to the church hall, where Paul and Ivan were with John and the other Quarrymen. We started talking about the possibility of playing together that evening for their last performance. We discussed who would play which song, and who would sing which song, but in the middle of our discussion, the vicar walked in and said he was sorry but we wouldn't be able to play. So John suggested that we all go down to the milk bar in Woolton Village, where they knew the lady who owned it, who would let them play. I became a bit fed up at that point, and decided to go home. I suppose that was my chance to join The Quarrymen. I know that The Quarrymen did perform again in the evening, but Paul had also gone home by that point."

After the boys had finished their short meeting, Paul remembered what happened next. "After that, we just went to the pub, and had a couple of drinks. I had to kid on I was 18. I must have been awkward trying to look older than that. You had a sports jacket, you tried to look all that. I remember there was a bit of a panic on, 'cos one of these fights that used to come up, suddenly went round the pub. We're needed, all the lads are needed, there's like a mob somewhere, and I thought, 'Jesus Christ, what have I got myself into here?' I'm gonna go and suddenly I'm with this rampaging mob. It did not come off anyway, so I remember that particularly being one of my boyhood fears of that day, thinking I've come for a day out and suddenly I'm with all these men, you know, and we're gonna be hurling machetes at each other. That blew over and we had a nice evening."

After Paul left a good impression, John had a big decision to make. Could he, as the group's leader, welcome another person into the band who was a better guitarist and a good singer? Thankfully, John allowed his brain and not his ego make the decision. He invited Paul to join. That is where, as the plaque on St. Peter's Church Hall says, "it all started moving". In later interviews, John recalled that he asked Paul that day to join the group. However, a couple of weeks after the Woolton meeting, Paul was heading up to see Ivan. As he cycled along Vale Road near Ivan's home, he saw Pete Shotton on the corner of Linkstor Road. Pete called Paul over and said that he and John had been talking and would like him to join The Quarrymen. What did Paul think? He simply said, 'Okay', and that was it. The importance of that conversation would soon become evident as the genesis of the greatest musical partnership of all time began.

Plaque erected on the church hall commemorating the historic meeting.

The *Fab* one hundred and *Four*

Paul McCartney and Jim McCartney

The biggest influence in Paul's musical journey was undoubtedly his father, Jim.

Jim McCartney was born to Joe and Florrie at 8, Fishguard Street in Everton and was the third eldest of seven children. The McCartneys moved shortly after Jim's birth to 3, Solva Street in Everton, which was a rundown terraced house near Liverpool city centre. Here, Jim attended the Steers Street Primary School off Everton Road. He left school at fourteen and found work at A. Hanney & Co., a cotton broker in Liverpool. The job entailed running up and down Old Hall Street with large bundles of cotton that had to be delivered to cotton brokers or merchants in various sales rooms. He worked ten-hour days, five days a week and received a bonus at Christmas that was almost double his annual salary.

Jim met his future wife Mary in June 1940 at 11 Scargreen Avenue, the McCartney family home. Mary was staying with Jim's sister, Jin, because of the lack of accommodation in Liverpool at the time. As Mary sat quietly in an armchair, the air-raid sirens sounded, so the group moved to the Anderson shelter in the back garden to wait for the all-clear. Because of an intense bombing raid, the signal did not come and their vigil in the cellar lasted until dawn. Mary talked long enough with Jim to become romantically interested in him and thought that he was "utterly charming and uncomplicated" and possessed "considerable good humour."

They took out a marriage licence at Liverpool Town Hall on 8 April 1941 and were married a week later (15 April 1941) at St. Swithin's Roman Catholic Church in Gillmoss, Liverpool. They first lived at 10, Sunbury Road, Liverpool, and then resided for a short time during November 1942 at 92, Broadway, Wallasey. Jim's job at Napier's was classified as war work, so the McCartneys were given a small, but temporary, pre-fab house at 3, Roach Avenue in Knowsley.

Mary's job as a nurse enabled them to move to 75, Sir Thomas White Gardens, off St. Domingo Road in Everton, where they lived in a rent-free, ground-floor flat supplied by her employers.

Paul at the Liverpool Institute, 1956.

Paul, second from left on the front row on a Scout trip in 1950.

Shortly after, in February 1946, they moved to 72, Western Avenue in Speke. Two years later, the family moved once again, this time to 12, Ardwick Road, still on the Speke Estate. This last move was because Mary resigned from her job as a District Nurse.

In 1955, Jim and Mary moved their family for the seventh and final time to 20, Forthlin Road in Allerton, a further step up the social ladder.

James Paul McCartney was born on 18 June 1942 at Walton General Hospital in Rice Lane, Walton, during the time they lived on Sunbury Road. Mary had previously worked at the hospital as a nursing sister in charge of the maternity ward.

Jim came from a musical family, and, with both Paul and Mike, this tradition continued. Jim's father, Joe McCartney, was a traditionalist who liked opera and played an E-flat tuba in the local Territorial Army band that played in Stanley Park. Joe played with the brass band at Copes' Tobacco factory where he worked. He was also proficient on the double bass and sang.

Jim learned how to play the trumpet and piano by ear and, at the age of seventeen, started playing ragtime music. His first public appearance was at St. Catherine's Hall, Vine Street, Liverpool with the Masked Melody Makers, a band that wore black masks as a gimmick. In the 1920s, he led Jim Mac's Jazz Band with his brother Jack on trombone and composed his first tune, "Eloise". Paul would record the song as "Walking in the Park with Eloise" in 1974.

By coincidence, Jim had an upright piano in the Forthlin Road front room that he had bought from North End Music Store (NEMS) owned by the Epstein family. Jim had a collection of old 78 rpm records that he would often play. On occasion, he would perform his musical "party-pieces" – the hits of the time – on the piano. One of the most important things that Jim did for the young Paul and his brother Michael was point out the different instruments in songs on the radio. He also took his sons to brass band concerts and taught them the basics of harmony, melody and the relationship between

Paul's entry in the Liverpool Institute register.

Next to Paul's name in the Liverpool Institute register, the school has written "The Beatles". You can also see John Charles Duff Lowe and Colin Manley.

The Fab one hundred and Four

121

the instruments. Paul credits Jim's tuition as being helpful when later singing harmonies with John Lennon.

When Paul was looking back at those days with his dad and the family parties came straight to mind. "My dad used to play piano on New Year's Eve," he recalled, "and all the ladies would sit around sipping their rum and blackcurrant. After half an hour, they would be singing, and I grew up associating those songs with family and good times. I thought these songs were so well-structured. So did John. We loved the craftsmanship." Paul would pen his own tributes to the old style songs with "Honey Pie", "Your Mother Should Know" and "When I'm Sixty-Four".

Paul wrote the tune to "When I'm Sixty-Four" when he was 16. The lyrics came much later. "It was about myself, looking to the future. Retirement age of 65 felt too obvious, so I made it a year earlier. 'Will you still need me, will you still feed me', he sings – I was a bit tongue-in-cheek there. I could have said, 'will you still love me'. Feed was funnier."

Tragedy struck the McCartney family when Paul's mother Mary died from breast cancer at the end of October 1956. For Paul, who was only fourteen, music was his comfort. Jim encouraged his son by purchasing a nickel-plated trumpet as a present for Paul's next birthday. Paul didn't enjoy playing the trumpet, so he swapped it for a £15 Zenith model 17 acoustic guitar, which he played every day. Paul also played his father's Framus Spanish guitar when writing early songs with John.

Paul started playing the family piano by ear in the front room of Forthlin Road. Although Jim advised his son to take music lessons, he preferred to learn 'by ear', just as his father had done. After Paul

72, Western Avenue, the McCartney's first house in Speke.

Walton Hospital with tower (top), where Paul and Mike McCartney were born.

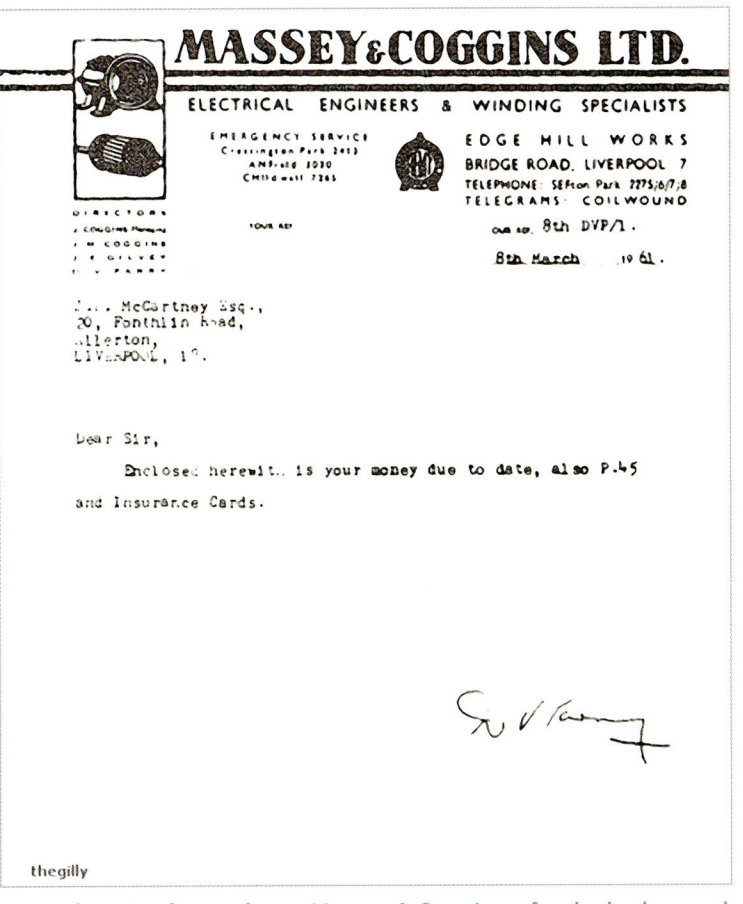

Letter from Paul's employer, Massey & Coggins, after he had ceased his employment there.

Paul often played the piano during The Beatles' early days in Hamburg.

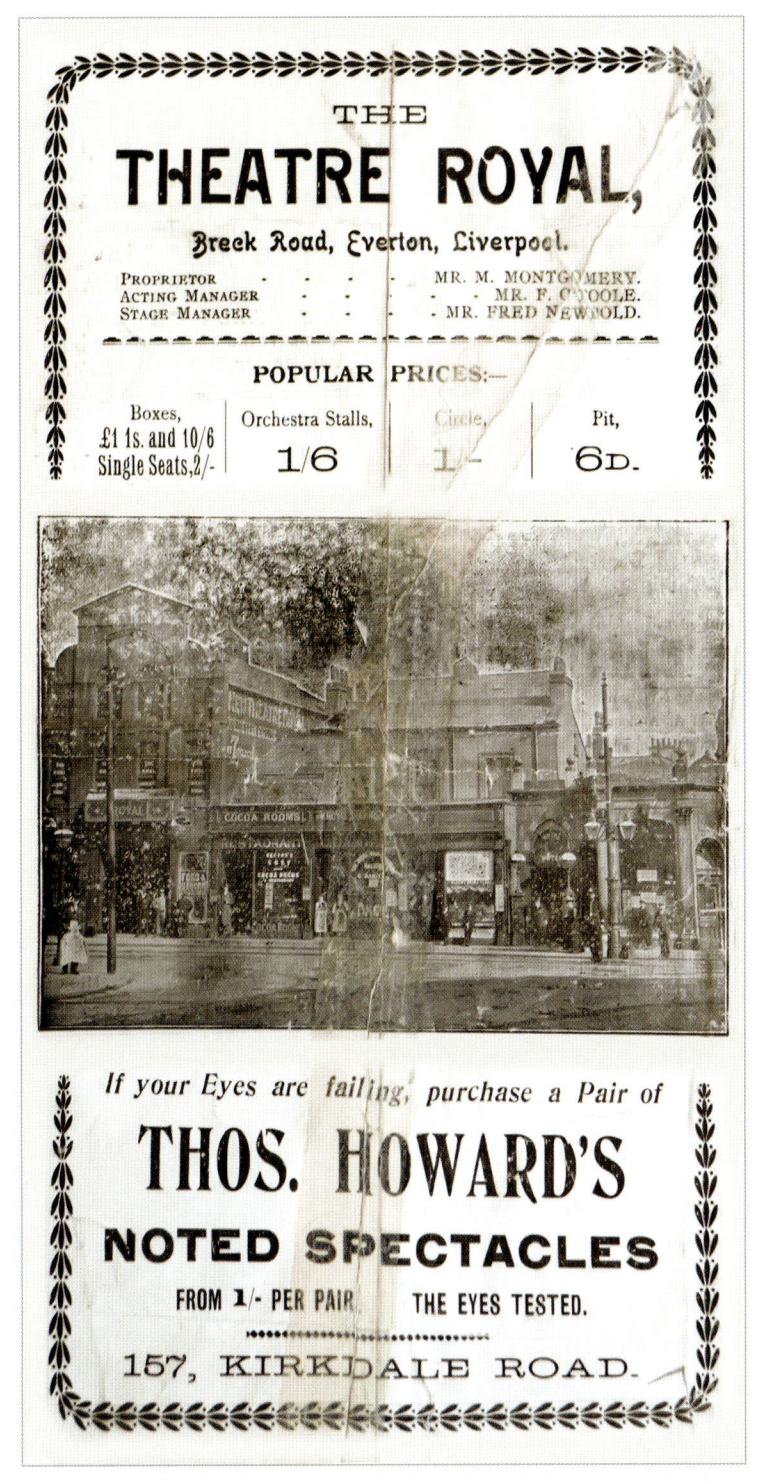

Programme for the Theatre Royal, where Jim McCartney worked.

The Fab one hundred and Four

and Michael became interested in music, Jim connected the radio in the living room to the boys' bedrooms using extension cords connected to two pairs of Bakelite headphones. In doing so, they were able to listen to Radio Luxembourg at night when they were in bed. This would be key in Paul's musical education as he listened carefully and learned the words to the songs.

Jim warned Paul that John would get him into trouble, although he did allow The Quarrymen to rehearse at Forthlin Road in the evenings. One of Jim's biggest decisions was to allow Paul to go with The Beatles to Hamburg. He was against it at first, but after Allan Williams dropped by to reassure him about the trip, he agreed to it.

One interested observer to the influence of Jim McCartney over his sons was Angie McCartney, Jim's second wife, who married Jim in November 1964. "Jimmy Mac, Paul's dad, always used to say that music was a big influence not only in his own young life, but in the lives of his sons Michael and Paul," recalled Angie. "Jim's father was an opera lover and used to play records of many classic arias to all

20, Forthlin Road, home of the McCartneys from 1955.

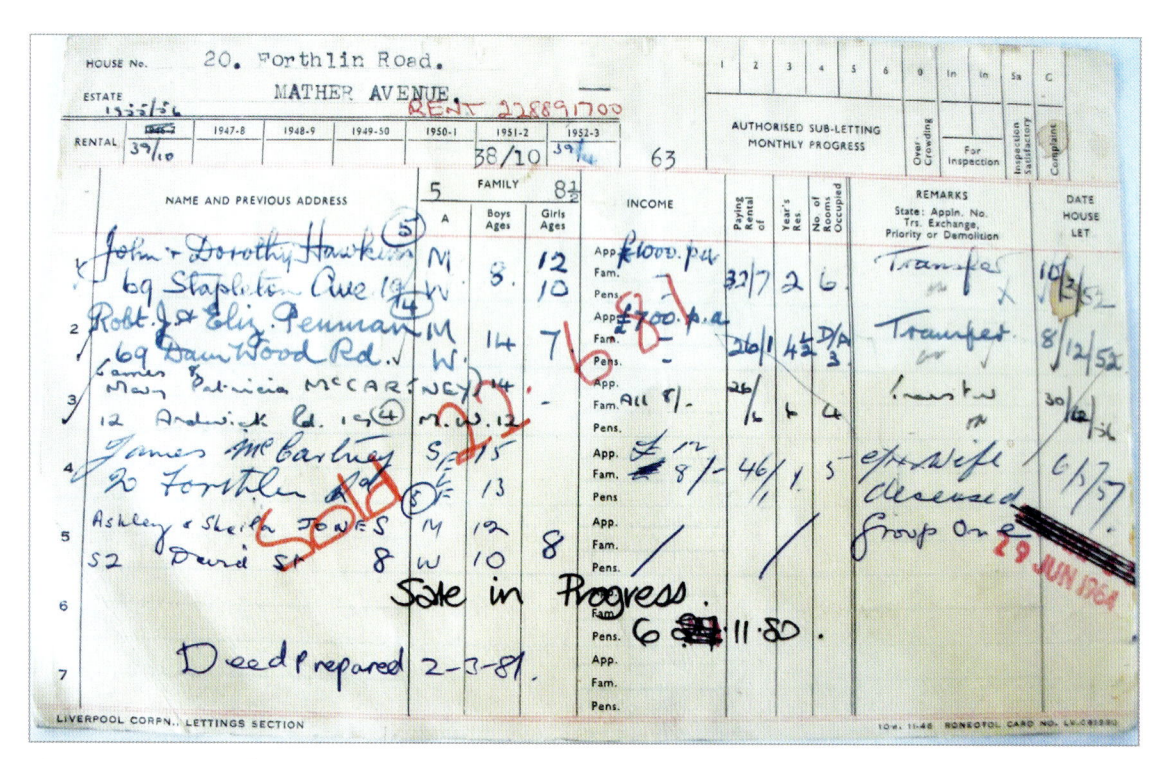

The rent agreement for 20, Forthlin Road.

Jim with his second wife Angie in the garden of their home, "Rembrandt".

Opposite: Paul, Jim and Michael McCartney in their back garden at 20, Forthlin Road.

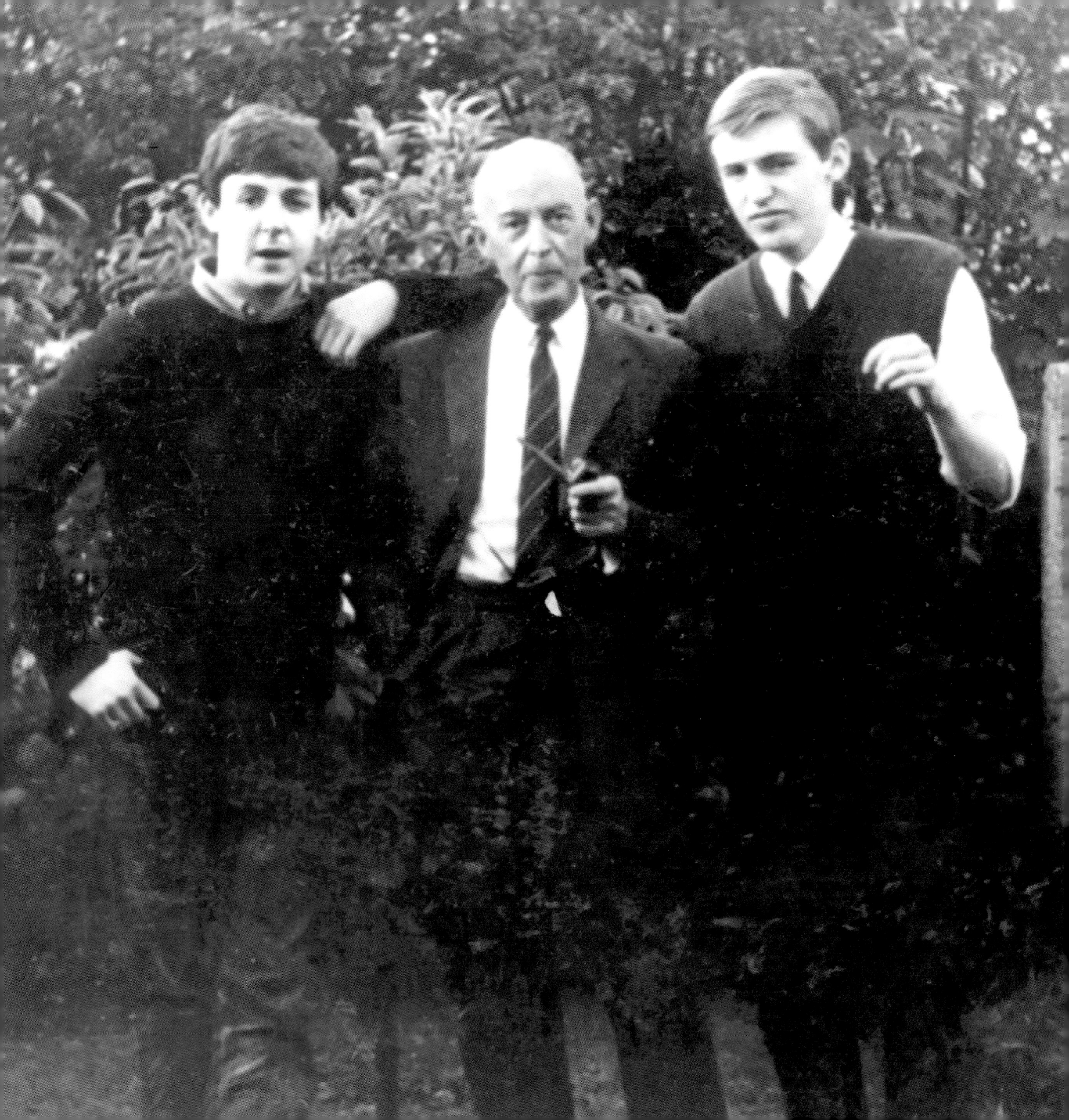

of his generation of McCartney kids growing up. This instilled in Jim an awareness of music, then his interests expanded into songs from the shows, then jazz, and led him to form his own Jim Mac's Band, which has been well documented in Mike McCartney's book *Thank U Very Much*.

"Jim's first love was the trumpet, and he even tried to get Paul interested, but without a great deal of success. The piano always figured largely in the boys' young lives, and he knew it influenced Paul, maybe a little more than Mike, whose main interests leaned more towards writing, humorous stuff, drawing, photography, and all of the many talents, which we know he still pursues today.

"The McCartney family parties always focused on the sing-alongs around the piano, keeping many of the "oldies but goodies" alive through generations, and during my years of being married to Jim, this certainly held true. Old favourites like 'Carolina Moon' would always be featured, and in fact, when ITV filmed their James Paul McCartney special at a New Brighton pub, that song was included."

In the early days of Paul's partnership with John, the two budding composers predicted that they might end up writing a musical. "I've sort of gone off the idea," Paul has said. "It used to be because the old musicals, 'Oklahoma', 'West Side Story' and 'Carousel', were too good, too well-crafted for us to better.

"When John and I first met, one of our conversations was, 'What do you do? Oh, you've written a couple of songs. Oh, I've written a couple too.' So, we showed our songs to each other and agreed they weren't very good and maybe we could do better. And that was the start of our thing. We did not know how to do this. We did not know how to make a record. We had to rely on grownups, so it did give us this lovely innocence that now seems really very sweet. I'm so glad we had an innocent period."

It was that innocence in their partnership that proved instrumental in transforming Lennon and McCartney into the greatest songwriters of the twentieth century – and possibly of all time.

Paul with his famous Hofner violin bass in The Cavern.

Paul McCartney and Ian James

Paul is rightly acknowledged as the best all-round musician in The Beatles.

Paul enjoyed playing the piano in the front room of their Forthlin Road home, which had been purchased from the Epstein family's North End Music Store (NEMS) in Walton. Jim was an accomplished pianist and would often play the piano at home. As Paul recalled in *The Beatles Anthology*, "I have some lovely childhood memories of lying on the floor and listening to my dad play 'Lullaby of the Leaves' (still a big favourite of mine), and music of the Paul Whiteman era, old songs like 'Stairway to Paradise'. To this day, I still have a deep love for the piano, maybe from my dad. It must be in the genes. He played the piano from when I was born well into The Beatles."

Jim refused to teach his son how to play the piano, as he couldn't play it properly. Instead, he sent Paul for piano lessons, but he did not stick to it. "I was not very good at going into an old lady's house," Paul recalled. "It smelled of old people, so I was uncomfortable. I was just a kid and she started setting me homework. I thought it was bad enough coming for lessons, but homework! That was sheer torture. I stuck it for four or five weeks, so I gave up. To this day, I have never learned to read or write music."

At the Liverpool Institute, Paul had met classmate Ian James in 1954 and they became good friends. Ian would soon play an important, but often-overlooked part, in the story of The Beatles.

Ian was born in Oxford Street Maternity Hospital, the same place as John Lennon, and lived for his first couple of years in a flat in Alexandra Drive on the edge of Princes Park. He soon went to live with his grandparents in The Dingle at 28, Dingle Lane, before moving to 5, Alder Street, also in The Dingle. Sadly, his father died when he was only 15, giving him something in common with Paul, who had lost his mum. The family later moved to a house near Heathfield Road, which is just off the Penny Lane roundabout. When he attended the Liverpool Institute, the family had moved to 43, Elswick Street. Ian went to St. Silas School in the Dingle, the same school attended by Ringo Starr and Billy Fury. Ian recalled his remarkable story: "I came from a musical family, and there were many instruments in the house: a banjo, a zither and a cornet among others. My grandfather had seven brothers who all played in the local Salvation Army band, so music was always an important part of family life. I was given a Spanish classical guitar, with nylon strings, and I taught myself to play it. This was a couple of years before the skiffle craze

Ian James at the Liverpool Institute, 1956.

The Fab one hundred and Four

hit the UK in 1956." When Lonnie Donegan's "Rock Island Line" made the charts on both sides of the Atlantic in 1956, teenagers started forming their own skiffle groups, and the sales of guitars rapidly increased. If you already knew how to play a guitar, your services were sought out by many friends. One of Ian's friends and guitar pupils was Paul McCartney.

"After leaving St. Silas, I moved to the Liverpool Institute in 1953," recalled Ian. "For the first year, we were split into six forms, and then at the end of the first year, we were put into 'streams', according to ability. It was in the second year that I was put into the same form as Paul, and we therefore sat close to each other, as our surnames are close alphabetically. We soon discovered a mutual interest in music and became friends."

Ian told the author what the young McCartney was like at school. "We did tend to talk a lot in class, and in those days, teachers could throw anything they liked at you. It was usually the blackboard duster, which had one soft side, and the other made of wood. That was often aimed in our direction. If you were really bad, then you would get a whack from a gym shoe, which could have the board duster inside it, or you would be sent to the Headmaster, The 'Baz', for the cane! There were some teachers, like E.R. Jones, who had nicknames. Jones' nickname was 'Lizzy', as his initials were E.R., as in our Queen, Elizabeth Regina.

Alder Street, Dingle, where Ian James lived when he was young.

Ian's entry in the Liverpool Institute register.

"In our form, you would start the day with ten good conduct points, and then one would be taken away for misbehaving. It normally did not take Paul and me long to lose them. If I was caught chatting, I would lose a point, so Paul would put his hand up and complain, so he would lose a point, so I would complain again, and this went on and on until we had lost all our points. This was usually achieved by the end of the first day!

"Paul was always good company, and very funny, too. He was a great mimic and would tell funny stories from our favourite television show, or *The Goons* from the radio. He also showed his early talent for art, though there was one funny incident when he and I went up to the art room during a free lesson, and we decided to take the brooms from the cupboard, dip them in paint, and then create an original painting. What a mess it was! One painting I remember him doing had a face like Edvard Munch's "The Scream". He was a talented artist.

"Paul and I became good friends, and, as my house was in the Dingle, we would often walk from school at lunchtime to the house. By now, I had moved from the classical guitar to a Rex cello-shaped acoustic guitar, which was bought by my grandparents from Hessy's at 18-20 Manchester Street, near the Birkenhead Tunnel entrance.

"I had been learning some local folk songs and the like, and was becoming quite proficient on the guitar. I became quite popular in school because, in 1956, skiffle had arrived and I was the one who could already play the guitar. Paul's dad bought him a trumpet, but he did not really take to it, plus he wanted to sing, which is difficult with a trumpet in your mouth!

"With our mutual love of rock 'n' roll, Paul and I would frequent all the record shops in Liverpool. I remember the first record I bought very clearly. The two of us went to the local record shop, Park Music & Radio Company, which was a gramophone dealer, as they were called back then, at 271 Park Road in the Dingle. It was Elvis Presley's 'Hound Dog', and we just loved Elvis. I recall playing it on my new Dansette record player. I was given an old 78 rpm record with it and did not want to be playing that all the time! We would then go into Liverpool and became regulars in all of the record stores, like the one in the basement of Blacklers' Department Store, where I bought the Carl Perkins record 'Lend Me Your Comb', and Cranes in Hanover Street."

One famous record shop was in Great Charlotte Street and was called NEMS, the very shop where Brian Epstein first ran a record department. After his success here, the business opened another NEMS store, the more famous one, in Whitechapel. One of the most important records that they bought was in a record store in Elliott Street – Eddie Cochran's "Twenty Flight Rock", which Ian showed Paul how to play and which Paul later played for John at the summer fête at St. Peter's Church. The boys soon became familiar faces in those shops, as Ian remembers with a smile. "When we went in, the shop assistants would call us over and tell us about the latest releases. However, like many others, we would listen in the shop, try and remember the lyrics, then leave without buying anything!

"Paul and I would spend hours working out the lyrics to the songs so that we would have them exactly right. It was not just our house where we played. I would often go to Forthlin Road and practise. If we were there, I would bring my guitar, Paul would play their piano and we would be joined by Paul's brother Mike on drums. We had a great time, though Paul's dad Jim would be in the next room trying to place his bets on the horses over the phone, and if we were too loud, he would come and tell us to be quieter!

"Paul became very keen to learn to play the guitar, so on those nice summer days when we would walk to my house, I would grab my

The row of shops where Leo Gallagher's tailor's shop was situated at the end, at 272A Mill Street.

Former site of the tailor that Ian and Paul visited.

Opposite: NEMS, Great Charlotte Street, where Paul and Ian bought records.

guitar and we would take our shirts off and get a sun tan, while I taught Paul to play his first guitar chords. With many of the American rock 'n' roll songs, you only needed to know a few chords and you could play them."

One aspect that has always intrigued me as a right-handed guitarist is whether Paul would need to re-string the guitar, or did he learn to play them upside down? Ian was happy to explain:

"I may have changed the strings on a couple of occasions, but it is a big job, and there did not seem much point, so I showed Paul the chords, and he learned to play them upside down. It became clear that Paul wanted his own guitar, and so Jim let his son take his trumpet back to Rushworth and Dreaper in Whitechapel, Liverpool, and exchange his trumpet for a Zenith model 17 arch-top acoustic. After a few alterations so that he could play it left-handed, Paul had his own guitar. This was around the time that Paul's mother died, and his guitar became his therapy. As Mike McCartney said, "It was just after mother's death that it started. It became an obsession. It took over his whole life. You lose a mother and you find a guitar.'"

As Paul and Ian became more proficient on the guitar, they decided that they should take their musical talents out onto the streets of Liverpool. Since they thought they should become the British equivalent of the Everly Brothers, they needed to dress the same. They got matching D.A. (Duck's Arse) haircuts, plus jackets to make them look smart. Paul had a white sports jacket, while Ian had one, which was powder blue, with sparkles in the material. To complete the look, they would have to wear the latest trend in trousers, which was drain-pipes. However, most parents would not want their sons to be wearing trousers that thin, so Ian used to visit a tailor, Leo Gallagher, who had a shop at 272a Mill Street, and he would have his trousers taken in as tight as possible.

The Fab one hundred and Four

"Paul wanted his school trousers to be the same as mine," said Ian, "but there is no way that his father would let him alter them. Therefore, during a lunch break, Paul and I would walk to the tailor, have the trousers taken in a little bit at a time, and then return to school. If Jim asked why his son's trousers looked thinner, Paul could honestly tell him that they couldn't be, as they were the trousers that he had bought. The tailor even gave me one of the tools of his trade, which was a leg-shaped piece of wood. This enabled you to put the trouser leg over it, and then chalk in exactly where you needed to narrow the trousers.

"We would then head off to the local park, where we would look for the fairground. This was usually in Sefton Park, and we would have our guitars on our backs as we strolled around looking cool, and trying to pick up girls." As Paul recalled in *Anthology*: "Me and my teenage mate Ian James both had fleck jackets with a little flap on the breast pocket, and would go around the fairgrounds and places." Paul also told official Beatles biographer Hunter Davies that, "We used to go around the fairs, listening to the latest tunes on the Waltzer trying to pick tunes up. We also tried to pick up birds. But it never worked. I haven't got the flair picking up like that. We used to go around everywhere together dressed the same thinking we were really flash. We both had Tony Curtis haircuts. It took us hours to get it right."

Funnily enough, they were never that successful in attracting the opposite sex. To make them feel better, they would go to Ian's house and put on an Elvis record, his first UK number one hit, "All Shook Up". Paul remembered: "We thought the girls would come flooding to us, us being in these jackets. But, of course, they never took any notice of us. We could not get arrested. That got us down, we got depressed, got the teenage blues, so much so that it gave me a headache. So we went back to his (Ian's) granny's house in the Dingle, round by where Ringo lived, and we put 'All Shook Up' on

Ian's record, "All Shook Up".

the record player. And I swear that hearing that song got rid of the blues, my headache went and we were lifted out of that depression."

Paul also shared his first ever composition with Ian. As Ian recalls, "It was during one of my visits to Forthlin Road that Paul played me the first song he ever wrote, 'I Lost My Little Girl'. I was so impressed that he had written a song."

Paul did give credit to Ian and his important role in joining The Quarrymen. Paul remembers his meeting with John: "He was 16 and I was only 14, so he was a big man. I showed him a few more chords that he did not know. Ian James had taught me them really. Then I left. I felt I'd made an impression, showed them how good I was." For the record, Paul had turned 15 a few weeks earlier. He also said in *Anthology*, "I did 'Twenty Flight Rock' and knew all the words. The Quarrymen were so knocked out that I actually knew and could sing 'Twenty Flight Rock'. That's what got me into The Beatles. I knew all the words because me and my mate Ian James had just got them. He and I used to get into all the record shops and write down the words. 'Twenty Flight Rock' was a hard record to get. I remember ordering it and having to wait weeks for it to come in. We would buy them from Cranes in Hanover Street or NEMS in Great Charlotte Street. We used to go around the shops, listen to the record, and then not buy it. The shops were very annoyed, but we did not care because now we knew all the words."

With having such an influence on Paul, I wanted to know if the two of them had ever discussed forming a group. The simple answer was no. Apart from playing together in each other's houses, or at the fairgrounds of Liverpool, the only other public appearance of Paul McCartney and Ian James was on the last day of the school term before Christmas in 1956. At the end of term, you were allowed to bring in whatever you wanted, like toys or games. So Paul and Ian decided to take their guitars in. This was witnessed by the tea-chest bass player of The Quarrymen, Len Garry. "I can recall that a certain Paul McCartney had brought in his guitar and that together with his friend Ian James, who taught him many chords, they entertained some of their classmates."

Paul decided that Ian should meet another of his school friends, George Harrison. As Paul knew from his long journeys on the bus to

Paul with his Zenith Guitar, 1957.

school every day, George had purchased a guitar and was starting to learn. It therefore made sense for George to learn from Ian as well, so, on several trips to the Harrison's Speke home at 25, Upton Green, Ian helped advance George's musical education.

This would be the end of their musical collaborations, as that September, Ian moved into the sixth form, while Paul had to stay behind for a year and redo his exams, and so did not see as much of each other. Paul was invited to join The Quarrymen and the rest is history. Ian formed a skiffle group, The Mateys, and played several gigs around Liverpool over the next couple of years.

After Ian left school, he spent 12 months working for the Liverpool Education Authority, before joining the Army for the next three years. On one visit home in 1962, he met Paul who told him about playing with The Beatles in Hamburg, and so, as he was based in northern Germany, he decided that it would be great fun to drive down to Hamburg to see Paul and The Beatles. He bought a really cheap car and set off for the Star Club with the intentions of meeting up with Paul. However, he only got as far as Hanover before the engine blew up. He abandoned the car and headed back to his base, and never made it to Hamburg.

Ian did not meet Paul again until 1990, while Paul was on his world tour. As McCartney was due to play in Liverpool, the *Liverpool Echo* newspaper decided to plan a backstage reunion of Paul with some of his school friends from the Liverpool Institute. Ian remembers it well. "There were six or seven former pupils together, who were waiting their turn to go and see Paul." When Paul saw Ian, he put his arms round him and gave him a massive hug, and Mike McCartney took a couple of pictures of the two school friends together. Paul was determined that they would stay in touch, and he and Linda kept that promise to Ian and his wife Liz.

The following year, Ian and Liz were invited to attend the world premiere of the *Liverpool Oratorio*, Paul's classical work, in the Anglican Cathedral in Liverpool. Ian had a surprise part way through the performance, when he recognised some of the words, spoken in Spanish, which was one of the languages Ian and Paul studied at school. In the oratorio, the words were spoken by the Headmaster and their Spanish teacher, Miss Inkley, who was trying to teach the boys a song in Spanish. "Tres conejos, En un arbol, Tocando, El tambor. Que si, Que no, Que si. Lo he visto yo". Ian also remembered the words exactly from school, and couldn't wait to tell Paul, so he dropped him a line after the performance. Paul immediately wrote back to him. "You and I are probably the only living idiots who can recite 'Tres Conejos' word perfect. On my travels to Spain, I couldn't find anyone who had even remotely heard of it, but recently in America I met a South American woman from Colombia who remembered it from her childhood – so God knows where we got it from (Dickie Moore, I suspect)." Paul was correct, as it was from their teacher Dickie Moore, and it is the story of three rabbits in a tree. No wonder it was never very popular!

Paul was to make a return to Elswick Street, the street where Ian grew up. The hit BBC series *Bread* was filmed there, and Paul and Linda made an appearance in the show. When interviewed by the *Liverpool Echo*, Paul recalled his times with his friend Ian. McCartney even suggested that, should he form another band, he would call it "Paul Goes to the Dingle". Ian also laughs that Paul always refers to him as "Ian James from the Dingle".

Ian James, photographed by Paul McCartney.

Sadly, the next time that Ian was to see Paul was to attend the memorial service for Linda after she died. "Linda was a lovely lady," recalled Ian, "who kept her promise to stay in touch, and was always kind and considerate."

In 2001, Ian struck up a friendship with Beatles collector and writer Mark Naboshek during Mark's research for an article he was writing about Paul and Ian for *Beatlology* magazine. In late 2005, Ian contacted Mark saying that he was thinking of auctioning his guitar to fund his retirement. After all, this was the guitar Paul had learned to play on – in fact, probably the first guitar that Paul played.

I asked Mark to tell me what happened next. "The first step for Ian was finding an auction house. He'd looked into Cooper-Owen because it was in England. I told him I'd check with an American rock auction company to see what kind of perks they'd offer to secure the guitar for their sale. In the end, Ian chose to go with Cooper-Owen because he felt more comfortable with a British company, if only for the convenience.

"Being a longtime collector, I knew the importance of good provenance when you're trying to auction an item. In Ian's case, his word alone on the authenticity of the guitar would have only gone so far.

I was aware that he was still friends with Paul and that they'd see each other every so often. In fact, Ian had mentioned that he might contact Paul to see what he might remember about the old Rex. This was a start, but in doing so, he'd need to get Paul's confirmation in writing.

"I told Ian that if Paul would sign some kind of letter of authenticity stating that his (Ian's) guitar was the one on which he learned to play, then there would be no telling how high the bidding would go. Better yet, if Ian could take a photo of Paul with the guitar, then the sky would be the limit."

Ian contacted Paul and, several weeks later, Paul invited Ian to his offices at MPL (MPL Communications, the holding company for the business interests of Sir Paul McCartney) in London. With the old Rex in hand, the two friends reminisced about the guitar and the good times they shared. Ian wanted Paul to provide some authentication so that he could sell it, and Paul was only too happy to help. Ian laughs now at an awkward moment. "I had done a draft of what I thought needed to be said, which I showed to Paul. He looked at it and quite happily signed it. However, I really needed it to be on MPL headed paper, but felt embarrassed having to ask again, but I struck up the courage and asked him if it was possible to have it typed up. Paul immediately said that would be fine and disappeared for a couple of minutes. He walked back in with the letter already typed up, and signed it there and then. I couldn't believe it. I knew he was busy and had another meeting coming up, but instead of throwing me out, he introduced me to his graphic designer, and went on to tell him about our trips to the tailor in Mill Street and getting our trousers narrowed."

Paul also agreed to pose with the guitar and was happy for the photo to be shown. "After all," he said, "it's history".

Paul's letter stated:

"The above guitar, belonging to my old school pal Ian James, was the first guitar I ever held. It was also the guitar on which I learned my first chords in his house at 43 Elswich (sic) Street, Liverpool 8."

Mark continued: "I was thrilled when Ian later informed me that he'd gotten his meeting with Paul. He sent me all the savory details, including images of the letter Paul signed and the photo of him posed with the guitar. Now we'd wait to see what Cooper Owen could deliver.

"In the meantime, I was writing an article for *Beatlology* magazine about the Ian-Paul friendship and, though it was as yet unpublished, passages from my narrative were used in the worldwide press for the guitar. That made me proud.

"Before the auction took place, Ian sent me a token of his appreciation for my help. It arrived from England in a package so tightly secured, it could have survived a disaster of any proportion. It took me what seemed like forever to carefully extract the contents, but when I did, I held an unfathomable treasure – the original 78 rpm record of Elvis' 'All Shook Up' – the very record that Ian and Paul had played as young teens and which had impressed Paul so much, he still speaks about it today. I couldn't thank Ian enough for giving me this priceless gem.

The Mateys, Ian's skiffle group.

"A month and a half later, on 28 July 2006, the guitar auction took place and I almost fell out of my chair when I saw the hammer price of over $600,000! When Ian had first contacted me, I remember telling him that I wanted the guitar. He told me that he'd like that more than anything, but he was counting on a hefty sum for his retirement. Without Paul's provenance, we were thinking it might bring $50,000 tops – if he was lucky. But with Paul's backing, well, who knew? I certainly couldn't have foreseen the final tally! It gave Ian a comfortable retirement and I couldn't have been happier for him! I thought it was wonderful that he was able to reap the rewards of having been such an important influence on his old friend Paul. Like the adage says, 'What goes around comes around'! Ian did something positive for Paul and, 50 years later, that positivity came back to Ian a hundredfold."

Ian remembers it well. "The whole day was quite strange. We had to attend a funeral on the way down, and then had to battle with the London traffic. By the time I got there, there were only a few items left. The guitar was one of them, and I was really nervous. The bidding started going up, and there were obviously a few bidders in the room, but two telephone bidders, too. The price reached £120,000 quite quickly, and then seemed to stall, but I was happy with that. Then it was obviously down to the telephone bidders to fight it out to the bitter end. The price kept creeping up and up, and eventually reached a total, including fees and commission, of £330,000! I couldn't believe it. It turned out that the telephone bidders were an American, Chuck Jackson who was successful, and a bidder from Russia. Chuck spoke to me afterward and told me that he was buying that guitar, whatever it cost."

Elswick Street, where Ian lived in The Dingle.

So Ian's guitar, on which Paul McCartney learned to play the chords that he taught John, and on which Ian also showed George Harrison how to play chords, was no longer in Ian's possession. He had relinquished one of the most important guitars in musical history, but his story should be told to every Beatles fan.

Ian James, the man who taught The Beatles to play guitar.

Ian with his guitar at home.

Ian's famous guitar that Paul McCartney learned to play on.

The Fab one hundred and Four

Paul holding Ian's guitar at MPL, London, on 24 March 2006.

AUGUST 1957

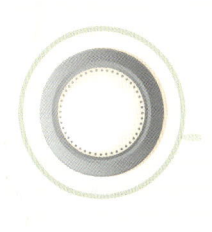

The McCartney Brothers – Paul and Mike

Now that Paul had taken up the guitar seriously, musician-dad Jim was keen for his youngest son Mike to learn to play a musical instrument, too. Not wishing to have anything quiet, Mike chose the drums, which he would bash to his heart's content at their home in Forthlin Road. And so, the McCartney household was augmented by a drum kit, which Paul would spend some time getting to know better while his brother was in the hospital.

Just weeks after Paul and John met, Jim McCartney sent his two sons off to Scout Camp at Callow Farm in Derbyshire. Boys will be boys, and on the first day of camp, they strung up a rope with a piece of drainpipe to lift logs up a cliff. They pondered, if it could hold some wood, surely it could hold a boy scout. After being volunteered, one guinea pig stepped forward: Mike McCartney.

They lowered Mike over the cliff. As he headed down a bit quicker than expected, the strong men at the top holding the rope decided to pull up sharply. Not a good idea, as it turned out. Mike slammed into a tree and fell into a heap at the bottom. After being rushed to the Royal Hospital in Sheffield, the X-rays revealed multiple fractures of his left arm. Mike spent the next four weeks with his arm in plaster, marooned on the wrong side of the Pennines, with occasional visits from Liverpool by his dad.

At the end of August, the plaster came off, and although the breaks were healed, Mike was left with nerve damage to his left arm. Jim decided Mike needed a holiday, so he booked some time at Butlin's Holiday Camp in Filey, Yorkshire. An extra incentive for going to that camp was that the McCartney's cousin Bett and her husband Mike were working there as Red Coat entertainers. Mike Robbins, as well as being a Red Coat, was also in charge of the national talent contest with a prize of £5,000. Since Paul and Mike had been singing together at home and working on a passable version of the Everly Brothers' "Bye Bye Love", Paul suggested that they perform it on the stage. The 15-year-old Paul was confident in his ability, but 13-year-old brother Mike was not, and refused to go up on stage.

Paul was not to be outdone by a simple refusal from his brother. As he walked onto the stage, he whispered something to Mike Robbins, who quickly announced, "We have with us in the audience today Paul's younger brother Michael who only yesterday came out of Sheffield Hospital with ninety-seven fractures after breaking his arm up a mountain, and the two brothers are going to give us a little number, will you welcome please... Mike McCartney."

Mike climbed onto the stage, obviously wishing he could break his brother's arm in re-

Mike McCartney at the Liverpool Institute, 1956.

Mike McCartney's entry in the Liverpool Institute register.

In 1974, Mike released his album *McGear*, a collaboration with his brother, who, with his band, Wings, provided the music. Paul was still under a contract dispute with Apple, so even though he played on the album and produced it, he was not originally credited. Mike provided the vocals for the album.

As well as being a talented writer and performer, he showed from an early age an aptitude for photography. Thankfully for Beatles fans, he photographed several iconic pictures, including Paul and John working together.

As a result of seeing Mike's photographs, the National Trust restored and opened his old 20, Forthlin Road home. He has published several books of his photographs and has exhibited these around the world. He is a great ambassador for Liverpool and the Wirral, where he has lived for many years.

venge! However, cousin compère Mike stepped in, proclaiming, "Ladies and gentlemen, for the first time on any stage, a really warm welcome for... the McCartney Brothers!" So, for the first and last time, the brothers performed together on a stage, and after "Bye Bye Love", Paul did his party piece, "Long Tall Sally", which he had performed a few weeks earlier for John Lennon at St. Peter's Church.

Peter Michael McCartney was born on 7 January 1944 and was educated at the Liverpool Institute High School. He wanted to get into the Art School, but ended up as a ladies' hairdresser.

As well as performing with Paul, he made an appearance with The Beatals as drummer, though no date has been recorded.

Mike's show business career began as a member of the Liverpool group of performance artists, The Scaffold, which he joined with Roger McGough and John Gorman. Not wanting to capitalise on his brother's fame, Mike changed his last name to 'McGear' and was an integral part of the 1960s Merseybeat era, with a mixture of songs and poetry, laced with satirical comedy.

In 1967, Mike McGear wrote the Top 5 hit record "Thank U Very Much", performed with the Scaffold. The following year, he managed to top the UK charts with their hit song "Lily the Pink", which stayed at number 1 for five weeks. The Scaffold had hit records around the world and toured many countries performing their shows.

Mike McCartney with Geoff Nugent from The Undertakers.

140

André Bernard, where Mike McCartney worked as a hairdresser.

Paul McCartney and Jim Gretty

One man who possibly had a most significant influence on the musicians of Liverpool was Jim Gretty, resident guitar salesman at Hessy's Music Shop in Liverpool. Hessy's was famous for selling their instruments on finance, which made it particularly attractive to most of the musicians who were starting groups on Merseyside. A popular man, James Gretty was born in 1914 in Liverpool, and lived at 7, Reckesmith Street.

Gretty had worked as a local entertainer on Liverpool's clubland circuit since the 1930s. He obtained a job as a demonstrator at Hessy's after he suggested to owner Frank Hessy that a good way of selling guitars would be for him to give free lessons to anyone who bought a guitar. This proved to be very popular and it is fair to say that with Gretty, many of the Liverpool musicians received their only guitar lessons. Frank Hessy opened a second shop in Stanley Street and each Monday night, Gretty offered tuition to a group of up to 40 aspiring musicians.

Gretty was interviewed by David Pritchard for his book, *The Beatles: An Oral History*. "When the rock 'n' roll craze started after skiffle," Gretty said, "all the kids wanted to learn how to play guitar. I used to teach every Monday night in a little shop just along the road in Whitechapel between 6pm and 7:30pm. When you bought a guitar at Hessy's, you got free lessons, and I was the teacher. There were between 50 and 70 people in one night, learning the basic chords of the guitar. I used to have a big blackboard with six lines that were the strings, and big dots, and I'd say, 'that's the key of so-and-so.' I would sing a song, and we had a right good time. We had all sorts of kids in for lessons from many bands. We had Gerry Marsden of Gerry and the Pacemakers and people from The Fourmost. Everybody in the Liverpool groups who made the top came for lessons. It got very, very popular."

Gretty was also a variety agent who advertised in *Mersey Beat* and booked The Beatles on a number of occasions around Liverpool,

Jim Gretty in Hessy's.

Hessy's Music Centre, Stanley St.

though they were not rock 'n' roll evenings. The events tended to be variety shows at venues like the Albany Cinema in Maghull and the Pavilion Theatre in Lodge Lane (where The Beatles were billed with the Royal Waterford Showband). For the Pavilion Theatre show on 2 April 1962, the Royal Waterford Showband was billed as "Ireland's Pride" and The Beatles proclaimed "Merseyside's Joy".

Before Brian saw The Beatles at The Cavern in November 1961, he had a conversation with Gretty. "Brian Epstein came to me once," he said, "since his store was in Whitechapel a few doors away, and said, 'Jim, I'd like to get hold of a few groups because I think I'd like to manage a couple. You know them all. What's your favourite?' I said, 'There's Gerry Marsden, The Fourmost, The Beatles and Rory Storm. They're the best so far.' Brian then asked me where he could see The Beatles, and I said, 'I tell you what, Brian. I've got a show in a theatre called The Albany Cinema at Maghull in a couple of week's time. If you want, I'll get you a ticket.' He came to the show, on 15 October 1961, and sat in the audience, next to our Member of Parliament, Bessie Braddock, and all those invited guests. The Beatles were supporting Ken Dodd and some others, and it was a proper show act like the Palladium shows. It was really a tip-top lineup. Brian came back to me on Monday morning and said, 'Jim, I like those Beatles. I'd like to manage them.'"

However, that three-hour charity show at the Albany Cinema did not go that well for The Beatles. Liverpool comedian Ken Dodd, the show's headliner, complained about the group. One of the group members entered Dodd's dressing room and said they'd been told that if they gave him their card he might be able to secure some bookings for them. Dodd threw the card away. Paul McCartney reminded him of it a few years later and Dodd said, "No, you've never worked with me, lad." When Paul mentioned that it had been on the Albany show, Dodd said, "That noise was not you, was it?" Paul said, "Yeah, we were rubbish, weren't we?" "You certainly were," said Dodd. "I had you thrown off." Dodd later appeared on a television special with The Beatles, where they joked together.

If they were that bad, would Brian really have been impressed with them, and want to manage them? This is before Raymond Jones came into NEMS and asked about "My Bonnie", and before Brian saw them at The Cavern. However, Bill Harry had been discussing The Beatles with Brian as they featured so heavily in *Mersey Beat*, so he obviously did have knowledge about them at this time.

TIP TOP VARIETY
JIM GRETTY
V.A.F., M.A.A.
also **THE JIM GRETTY VARIETY AGENCY**
Artistes and Bands supplied for all occasions
Telephone : SEFton Park 3482

Jim Gretty's advertisement for his agency.

Hessy's Music Centre, Manchester Street.

FRANK HESSY
Limited

62 STANLEY STREET
(Corner of Whitechapel)

LIVERPOOL 1

FOR ALL MUSICAL INSTRUMENTS
OUR EASY TERMS ARE "EASIER"

Business card from Hessy's. Image © Bill Harry.

JIM GRETTY, the jovial Merseyside entertainer and agent has recently been producing cabaret at the Sambar Rooms, London Road, and intends to make it one of the foremost venues for dancing and entertainment on Merseyside.

Jim, who has a big agency and many clubs to look after, knows a good artiste when he sees one and maintains that if he could play a guitar like BOB HOBBS, there would be no-one to touch him as an entertainer. To Jim's mind, Bob Hobbs is the best guitar player in the North beyond any doubt.

He turned down an offer last year to appear in Germany for ten weeks, as he did not want to jeopardise his agency. However the offer has been modified and Jim has decided to appear there for a fortnight during the summer.

Jim Gretty's feature in *Mersey Beat*. Image © Bill Harry.

Billy Kinsley from The Merseybeats recalled a funny story in Bill Harry's *Mersey Beat* about Gretty: "One story I fondly remember of Jim is way back when Hessy's was in Manchester Street. Tony Crane and I were chatting to him when who should walk in but John Lennon. John had lost the spring off his Rickenbacker's Bigsby unit and in those days there was no way to get hold of another one. So, Jim told us to carry on talking while he found one. He just happened to see one on a brand new Gibson and duly gave it to John. If that guitar was sold the next day he would have had to find one for that model and so on. The point I'm trying to make is – what on earth would we have done without him! Jim was a great help to all of us in those days. I recall that years later while Jackie Lomax and I were recording with George Harrison, one of the people George asked me about was Jim."

The Beatles, like many of the musicians, would pop into Hessy's when they had spare time. "You know," recalled Gretty, "they used to come in for a visit, just everyday chaps. They'd just go, 'aye, give me a hello, Jim.' They'd sit and we'd have a chat and I'd ask, 'Do you want anything?' They'd say, 'No, we'll just look around, Jim. Then they'd pick a guitar up and away they'd go, you know, just having fun. George Harrison would come in often, as did John Lennon. The Cavern Club was just two minutes away from the shop, so on the way to play The Cavern, they could drop in and have a little go on the guitars. We never used to chase them out, because we knew that they were good customers. They used to watch my fingers as I played. But, by Jove, I could watch their fingers now!"

Having played a part in the lives of John and George, he was also to have an impact on Paul and one of his most famous songs.

The second chord played in the verse section of The Beatles' 1965 hit "Michelle" is the F7#9 chord. In a 2004 interview, McCartney said, "I learned that chord from Jim Gretty, a salesman at Hessy's music shop in Liverpool. All the guys who worked in that store when we were kids were jazz guys. They had to play jazz well if they wanted to hold down their jobs. Gretty showed us jazz chords. I remember George and I were in the guitar shop when Gretty played it, and we said, 'Wow, what was that, man?' And he answered, 'It's just basically an "F", but you barre (cover) the top two strings at the fourth fret with your little finger.' So, Jim Gretty showed us this one great ham-fisted jazz chord, bloody hell! George and I learned it off him." In Dominic Pedler's book, *The Songwriting Secrets of The Beatles,* he refers to this chord as the "Gretty Chord".

This again demonstrates that the young Beatles were taking inspiration from everywhere as they began to expand their repertoire, and were never too young to learn. Gretty, who was also a well-known country music performer around Merseyside, continued to offer advice to all the local groups and budding musicians, including one aspiring guitarist – yours truly! He died in 1992 at the age of 78 and remains one of the unsung heroes of the Liverpool music scene.

"Michelle" by The Beatles, featuring the Jim Gretty chord.

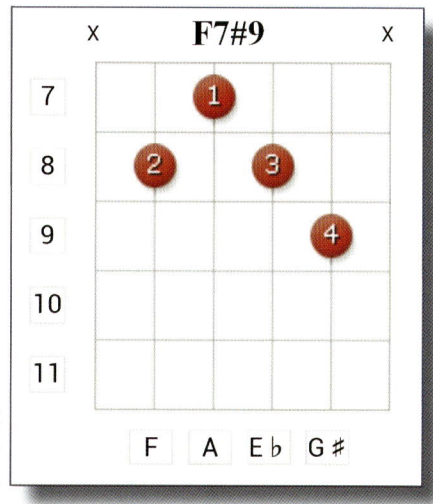

The F7#9 chord that Jim Gretty showed to Paul McCartney.

The original sign from Hessy's Music Centre.

7 DECEMBER 1957

George Harrison,
Harold Harrison and Len Houghton

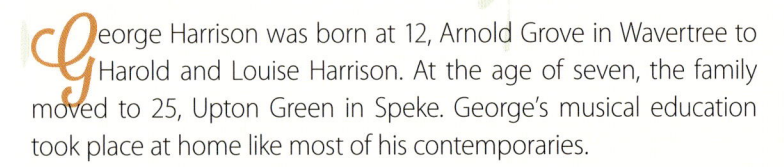

George Harrison was born at 12, Arnold Grove in Wavertree to Harold and Louise Harrison. At the age of seven, the family moved to 25, Upton Green in Speke. George's musical education took place at home like most of his contemporaries.

He attended Dovedale School, the same as John, though they did not know each other there, being two school years apart.

There would be music in the house, such as Josef Locke, dance-bands and Bing Crosby. In *The Beatles Anthology*, George remembered listening to his parents' records: "All the old English music-hall music. We had one record called 'Shenanaggy Da', but the hole in the middle was off centre so it sounded weird. Brilliant." Rod Davis explained what George was talking about. "For some reason, there was a fashion for making a second hole in a shellac record an inch or so away from the proper hole. On a wind-up gramophone, when you placed it on the turntable, you had to put the old steel needle pickup on it and start the record from stationary, otherwise there was no way you could put the needle on the moving record. The wiggling movement of the record on the turntable made the music oscillate and the voices and instruments sounded totally weird.

The words of George's record went:
    'Oh, shenaniggy da, he plays a guitar
    And laughs ah ah ah.
    Sunday and Monday, Tuesday, Wednesday
    Thursday, Friday
    Saturday Sunday Monday…'

"I think we must have had a copy of this at home for the words and tune to stick in my memory. We certainly had a good half dozen records with extra holes, maybe from my grandparents. It was fun playing them as kids."

George was critical of those who said they only listened to rock 'n' roll, as he remembered all of the different influences, like Josh White's "One Meatball" or Hoagy Carmichael songs. George's older brother Harry had a record player, which he treasured, and that nobody else was supposed to touch. However, as soon as Harry was out, George and his other brother Peter would sneak into his room and play the records. They would listen to anything and everything they could.

George Harrison at the Liverpool Institute, 1956.

George's father, Harold, had been a seaman on the White Star shipping line and brought records back with him from America, like the 'Singing Brakeman' Jimmie Rodgers, the first country singer George remembers. Rodgers had hits like "Waiting For a Train", a record that George's dad possessed. As George recalled, "that was the one that led me to the guitar. Later, there were people like Big Bill Broonzy and Slim Whitman, the first person I ever saw playing a guitar."

When George entered Alder Hey Hospital with tonsillitis and nephritis, he decided that he really wanted a guitar. An old Dovedale School friend, Raymond Hughes, was selling a guitar. "I was now at the Institute" recalled Harrison, "and hadn't seen him for about a year, and he had a guitar he wanted to sell. £3 10 shillings, it cost. It was a lot of money then, but my mum gave me the money, and I went to Raymond's house and bought it.

"It was a real cheapo horrible little guitar, but it was ok at the time. I saw that it had a bolt in the back of the neck. Being inquisitive, I got

25, Upton Green, home of George Harrison.

George Harrison (second from left, centre) at Dovedale School.

a screwdriver and unscrewed it and the whole neck fell off. I couldn't get it back on properly, so I put it in the cupboard in two pieces and left it there. Finally, my brother Peter fixed it back together for me.

"My father had played a guitar when he was in the Merchant Navy. However, when there was no work, he gave up being a seaman and sold it. When I started playing, he said, 'I had a friend who plays and somehow he still knew him, and he phoned him up. His name was Len Houghton, and he had an off-licence that he lived above. On

The Fab one hundred and Four

Speke from the air, where the Harrison family moved in 1950.

Arnold Grove, 1972. George's house is the sixth door on the right.

Thursdays, he would be closed, so my dad arranged for me to go down there each week on that night for two or three hours. He'd show me new chords and play songs to me like 'Dinah' and 'Sweet Sue', and songs of the Twenties and Thirties. It was very good of him." However, in spite of George's fond recollection, there is no listing for a Len Houghton, or variation on that name, in Speke, or an off-licence owned by anybody with that name in the Liverpool area at that time. Arthur Kelly mentioned he and George having lessons at The Cat pub, though whether this was with Len Houghton is not clear.

The first rock 'n' roll record George ever heard was Fats Domino's "I'm In Love Again" and then Elvis' "Heartbreak Hotel". Of the latter, George said, "that just came out of someone's radio one day and lodged itself permanently in the back of my brain."

That first guitar that George owned was a Dutch Egmond acoustic, which was put up for auction in November 2003 and sold for £276,000. Not a bad return on £3 10 shillings!

The register showing George joining Dovedale School.

George's first guitar was an Egmond.

The Egmond guitar that belonged to George Harrison.

George with his father Harold.

George Harrison and Geoff Nugent

Geoff Nugent is a legend on Merseyside for being part of one of the best Merseybeat bands of the 1960s, The Undertakers. He told me how his musical education began in Speke, with his good friend, George Harrison.

Geoff lived at 29, Marton Green, just five minutes from Upton Green, where George Harrison lived. The two became friends around the age of thirteen, not only because they lived near each other, but because they were the same age, separated only by a day or two – depending whether you believe George's birthday was 24 February or 25 February. At the time, George was celebrating his birthday on 24 February though, in later years, it was always 25 February!

They spent many hours in each other's houses, learning songs together like "Guitar Boogie" – the song that, ironically, Paul tried to play at the New Clubmoor Hall and messed up, proving the dire need for a lead guitarist in The Quarrymen.

Geoff and George had the same guitars – no-name cheap models worth about 50 shillings. They soon got Hofner Presidents, though Geoff's had an electric pick-up. Geoff was always more of a rhythm guitarist and George showed from a very early age his prowess as a lead guitarist. "I was a bit jealous", Geoff told me, "because George had a quick mind and quick fingers.

"George often came to our house, and he loved my mum's fry-up and her bread-and-butter pudding, but his favourite was her 'wet

The Undertakers, with Geoff Nugent (far right).

The Fab one hundred and Four

Nelly', which was bread that was going a bit stale, soaked in water, with raisins added, and then cooked in the oven. It was fantastic. We would then practise in the house or, if the weather was nice, we would go and sit on the street corner with our friends, including George's brother Peter, and play songs together. George was really good at the instrumentals, like 'Raunchy', which was the piece he played as his audition to join The Quarrymen. We used to play that on the street corners in Speke. We would sometimes go to other friends' houses, or to houses of some of the local girls, and we would just play and sing. That is how we learned."

Geoff provided new information about George's audition for The Quarrymen. We know that George auditioned for the group in December 1957 and joined after impressing John. However, it seems that George had already tried to join the group before then.

Geoff Nugent with his Maton guitar in the Isle of Man, aged 15.

When George had the opportunity to audition for The Quarrymen, he turned to Geoff for some help. "George came round to my house and told me that he was going to audition for this group called The Quarrymen, and could he borrow my amp. I said, 'No! My mum will kill me!', so I never lent it to him. It was only a little thing, about the size of a transistor radio, and cost my mother about sixteen guineas, so I daren't lend it to him. One of my biggest mistakes!

"George was going to the local girl's school, Speke Secondary Modern, on Central Avenue, just up the road from his house. I don't know the day or the date, but it was a dark night, and that was where he told me he was going." This audition was obviously unsuccessful, but he never gave up, and tried again on the bus outside Wilson Hall in Garston, where John finally accepted George into the group.

"As we know," recalls Geoff, "George joined The Quarrymen, and I was in a group called Bob Evans and The Five Shillings, and we had started as a skiffle group and moved onto rock 'n' roll. One of my early guitars, before I got the Hofner, was when my mother went to a woman's house in Western Avenue and bought it off her. It was a Broadway guitar, and had been used by the lad who owned it, but it was a good guitar. I have since learned that Paul McCartney remembers owning a Broadway guitar, and he lived on Western Avenue, so I wonder if my mother bought the guitar from Paul's mother. I could

29, Marton Green, home of Geoff Nugent.

have played one of Paul's early guitars. After that guitar, my brother gave me his Hofner President, which was a blond colour, as opposed to George's Hofner, which was a brunette colour. They were great guitars."

After joining The Quarrymen, Geoff and George did not see as much of each other as their musical paths took different directions. However, they would still see each other at the various venues when The Beatles and The Undertakers were making their way around the city. Geoff remembers his other Beatles-related mistake. "It was 1961 and we were playing on the same bill as Rory Storm and the Hurricanes, whose drummer at the time was Ringo. I was playing the only song I ever wrote, called "It's You I Love", and Ringo came over to me and told me he liked the song and could he sing it. I said no! Another good move from me!"

The next time Geoff would almost cross paths with The Beatles was in August 1962 when, walking along Whitechapel in Liverpool, Geoff spotted Johnny Byrne from Rory Storm and the Hurricanes. "Hello Johnny, what are you doing here?" he asked. "Aren't you supposed to be playing at Butlin's?" Byrne looked back at him and was obviously not happy. "We were, but Ringo has quit the band and came back to join The Beatles as a replacement for Pete Best." Like most people in Liverpool at the time, he couldn't believe what was happening.

Geoff still plays with The Undertakers around Merseyside and has raised a lot of money for local charities by supporting Merseycats, the rock 'n' roll children's charity.

Geoff Nugent (right) with original Undertakers' lead singer (and Apple Recording artist) Jackie Lomax at The Casbah in 2009.

Geoff performing in 2012.

The Fab one hundred and Four

The Rebels –
George and Peter Harrison, Arthur Kelly and Alan Williams

The first group George ever played with also included his older brother Peter, his school friend Arthur Kelly and another friend from Speke called Alan Williams. Peter had been the first of the Harrisons to own a guitar and when George suggested forming a group, he was happy to join his kid brother.

Called The Rebels, they made their debut in a British Legion Club in Dam Wood Road, Speke. "I remember The Rebels had a tea-chest with a lot of gnomes around it," George recalled. "One of my brothers had a five-shilling guitar which had the back off it. Apart from that, it was all fine. Just my brother, some mates and me. I tried to lay down the law a bit, but they weren't having any of that. We thought we made a pretty good sound but so did about four million other groups."

George's brother Peter remembered that cheap guitar. "I fixed one that had literally bent into the middle," he said. "There was a strap inside that was shorter than the guitar, so when I screwed it up, it pulled it straight. We used that on stage because we had a skiffle group go-

Louise, George, Harold, Peter and Harry Harrison.

The British Legion Club where The Rebels played.

ing." Peter recalled their limited time together as a skiffle group. "We used to do the working men's clubs, like the British Legion and all that, for five bob (shillings) a night and all you could drink."

One of the lesser-known members of The Rebels is Alan Williams. Esther Shefer met Williams in Kalamazoo, Michigan and discovered the amazing fact that not only was he in a group with George Harrison, but he was a near neighbour of Paul McCartney in Speke. The McCartneys lived at 12, Ardwick Road, and the Williams family at 22, Ardwick Road. Alan was two years Paul's senior, being ten when they first met. They were part of the same gang that included Paul's brother Mike.

Alan met George at the youth club in the Congregational Church in Ardwick Road, and found out that George wanted to form a skiffle group. George approached Alan and asked him if he could play the tea-chest bass. At first, Alan said that he had no musical talent, but George persisted. Alan was a bit surprised that George asked him to join the group since they were acquaintances from riding the bus to school. Alan joined Peter and Arthur Kelly in completing the lineup. Alan recalls that Peter and Arthur also took turns at playing the harmonica, while he played either washboard or tea-chest bass only: that was the extent of his musicianship.

Alan's memories of the one and only appearance of The Rebels

Arthur Kelly at the Liverpool Institute, 1956.

are sketchy, though he does remember that they could not have practised for more than a few weeks before the performance. The engagement was secured through the Harrison family, which, as we know, was only supposed to be the support act. They therefore did a lot of improvising and had some fun too. There was much excitement among the band as they carried their instruments to the hall and as they ran back to the Harrisons' to recount their experiences that night. Alan was the boy Louise Harrison was to write about whose fingers were red-raw and almost bleeding from playing that night.

It was hard for Alan to understand why, with the success of the night, that they never played again or even practised after that night. In Alan's mind, George already had an idea about the band he wanted to be in, and it was not playing skiffle music. Alan lost contact with George after The Rebels broke up, though he did see Paul and George years later when he watched The Beatles play at The Cavern.

The next morning on the bus to school, George told Paul McCartney about the gig. After that, Paul began to join George in the Harrison's front room, where they played their way through his chord books. "Paul was very good with the harder chords. I must admit that. After a time though, we actually began playing real songs together, like 'Don't You Rock Me Daddy-O' and 'Besame Mucho'. Paul knocked me out with his singing, especially, although I remember him being a little embarrassed to really sing loud, seeing as we were stuck right in the middle of my parents' place with the whole family walking about. He said he felt funny singing about love and such around my dad. We must have both been really a sight. I bet the others were just about pissing themselves trying not to laugh."

For George, it was all about the music. The first rock 'n' roll record he remembered was Fats Domino's "I'm In Love Again". But the first guitar-oriented music he heard was Jimmy Rodgers singing "The Brakeman's Blues".

The remaining member of The Rebels, Arthur Kelly, was a close friend of George's from the Liverpool Institute and they spent many hours learning and playing the guitar together. Arthur lived at 9, Botanic Street in Wavertree, much closer to the Institute than George. It was Arthur who suggested the group call themselves The Rebels: "We were trying to think of a name and I had just seen *Rebel Without a Cause*, so I said. 'What about The Rebels?'

"We got Peter, George's older brother, to teach us bass, and we went to the local British Legion Club, which was an ex-servicemen's club. I think there were about six people in there standing at the bar drinking, but it was a gig for us. When we got to the end of our repertoire, we just sang them all again. By the time we got back, we were really excited. Poor old Pete's fingers were bleeding because he'd been thumping away at this piece of string for the last hour and a half. That was really the start of it. However, that was our one and only gig."

Elvis had a big impact on Arthur, too. So much so that when he first listened to Elvis, he rushed to see George and tell him of his discovery. "Have you heard this guy Elvis Presley?" he said excitedly to George. "He's phenomenal!" Arthur says that at that point, skiffle was dead and rock 'n' roll was the only music that mattered.

Paul, Arthur Kelly, George and John.

Buddy Holly was also a musical hero to them. Once Arthur had the record "That'll Be the Day", he took it to George to hear, and the impact was immediate. "That's really good. Can I borrow it?" George replied when the record ended. Kelly loaned it to his friend, and when he returned to George's house the following week, it was clear what he'd been doing with his time. "He had learnt the intro, all the chords, and the guitar break – the lot," Arthur remembered. "This is what amazed me about George. He had this ability to memorise things."

George wrote to Arthur from Hamburg over several days in September 1960, during The Beatles' first trip, and is an interesting glimpse into the life of the young Beatle:

"Dear Archibald lad, I am playing a rolling rock in Germany-ingdaleboroughland". He mentions his bandmates, "John, Paul and Stuart Deane" (a reference to Stuart's image as their own James Dean). George also comments on The Beatles' new drummer. "We have Pete Best, Mrs. Best's little lad with us from Kasbah (sic) fame and he is drumming good."

Interestingly, George reveals the future plans which, after spending Christmas in Hamburg: "We are going with a man to Berlin. I want to be home for many a dying nig (sic) and will miss Santa on the 25th. We will earn 60 marks a night (£30 a week). Tony Sheridan and his two are here also but he got the sack tonight." George then reveals his passion for guitars, talking in detail about the Fenders owned by fellow musicians, but his desire was for a Gretsch, a dream that came true and is the guitar make for which he became known.

Possibly the most telling observation that would have far-reaching consequences for The Beatles, was about a group that had recently joined them in Hamburg.

"Rory Storm and the Hurricanes came out here the other week, and they are crumby. He (Rory Storm) does a bit of dancing around but it still doesn't make up for his phoney group. The only person who is any good in the group is the drummer."

The drummer, of course, was Ringo Starr.

Arthur's entry in the Liverpool Institute register.

Peter Harrison's entry in the Dovedale School register.

The Fab one hundred and Four

George Harrison, Colin Manley and Don Jefferson

According to Tony Bramwell, George Harrison's childhood friend and later director of Apple Records, one of George's greatest teachers and influences was Colin Manley, a fellow pupil at the Institute. Manley, who was regarded as an exceptional guitarist, was born in Liverpool on 16 April 1942. Together with fellow Institute pupil Don Andrew, he formed the Remo Quartet in 1958. Colin was on lead guitar and vocals, Don was on bass and vocals, Keith Stokes provided guitar and vocals and Harry Prytherch played drums. They later changed the name to The Remo Four and were one of the top bands in Liverpool.

Colin said, "At the time, we were very influenced by an Italian chap called Marino Marini who had appeared at the London Palladium. That's where the name came from. We thought Remo sounded like it ought to be in Italy." As a musician, his personal influences included some of the greatest guitarists of the day, like Duane Eddy, Chet Atkins, Barney Kessel, the Ventures, Les Montgomery and Albert Lee.

As Colin attended the Institute with both Paul McCartney and George Harrison, he could often be seen with them in empty classrooms. "Colin Manley was brilliant," Paul McCartney said during an interview on BBC Radio Merseyside in 1988. "He was the finest guitarist around Liverpool in the early 1960s and he could do all that Chet Atkins stuff with two fingers. A lot of the lads tried to play like that, but only Colin could do it really well." George learned a lot of his solo guitar work from Colin as they practised at school.

Colin's musicianship came to the fore when The Cavern was host in 1961 to The Remo Four and The Shadows. The audience witnessed as The Shadows, one of the top British groups of the sixties, were outclassed. "I can't dispute that," says Shadows' lead guitarist Hank Marvin. "We had a bad night. The Remo Four were excellent and a far better proposition than us."

George could hardly have wished for a better tutor than Colin who was regarded as possibly the best guitarist in Liverpool by his fellow musicians. Years later, in the autumn of 1964, The Remo Four toured

Don Andrew and Colin Manley at the Liverpool Institute, 1956.

with The Beatles, Mary Wells and Tommy Quickly. During one of the numbers, Colin would borrow John Lennon's Rickenbacker.

Another successful Liverpool musician, Mal Jefferson, was at the Liverpool Institute with Colin Manley from 1955-59. "Colin was two years above me and was in my brother Don's class," explained Jefferson. "They were best friends, crazy about music and loved Lonnie Donegan, Skeeter Davis and the American folk singers. They formed a skiffle group with Don on tea-chest bass and Colin on guitar. They performed in our front garden at 6, Davidson Road, Old Swan in Liverpool, with one or two other friends, on occasional weekend afternoons. I remember them playing 'Worried Man', 'Freight Train' and 'Rock Island Line'. Kids gathered around the gate and they collected small change from grateful onlookers.

"In 1959," said Mal, "they got Hofner guitars – a President Bass and a blond guitar – and small amplifiers. They teamed up with Harry Prytherch and Keith Stokes and called themselves The Remo Quartet. They entered competitions at The Pavilion Theatre, Lodge Lane, and The Empire Theatre in the Liverpool city centre. At The Empire, their guitar amp caught fire during 'Charlie Brown', a song which they later recorded at Phillips' studio in Kensington. I've still got it on disc.

"Around this time, they rehearsed in our kitchen at weekends. Sometimes on a Sunday afternoon, George Harrison came round to work out songs with Don. They locked themselves in the upstairs bedroom and I could hear them working out chords and writing out lyrics. One weekend, George became stuck on a chord. I think it was Ray Charles' 'Hallelujah'. They took a break and Don went downstairs to make tea. I popped in on George, and said 'E diminished'. George looked at me: 'Never heard of it'. I taught him the chord and he used it much later on his Beatles' song, 'Something'. I used to study and memorise chord shapes and names from a chord book and was fascinated by compound chords like 13ths, 11ths and 7ths with flattened 5ths.

"In 1961, I was in the Civil Service," Mal continued, "and went on day release to Childwall Hall County College in Liverpool. Colin was also there and we used to eat together. Colin would start with two plates of chips and half a loaf of bread. I never saw anyone eat like him!

When The Remo Four got their Fenders, Colin was becoming a real virtuoso and would attempt any type of music from the charts.

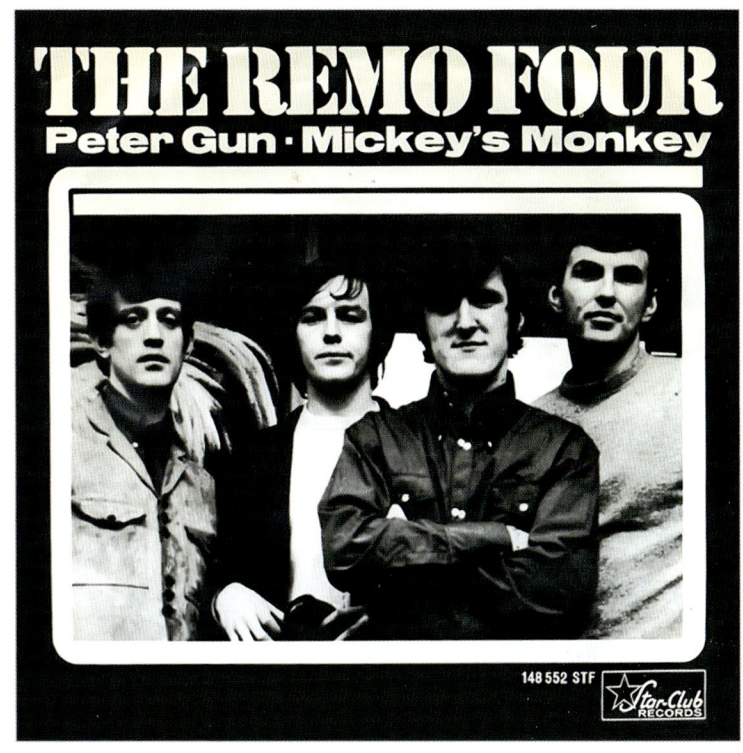

The Remo Four's single, "Peter Gun".

'Petite Fleur', 'The James Bond Theme', and 'Take Five' – he learned them all by heart and taught them to the band members, who were all excellent musicians. The one that impressed me most was 'Desafinado'. They purchased the record at midday from NEMS, practised it in the afternoon, then did it that night at The Cavern, and it was note perfect. It's about the most difficult piece you could ever copy.

"When I started playing guitar with show bands in the middle 1970s, Colin would deputise for me when I was on solo gigs. We could both read music and I can't remember any other guitar players who did. Colin was an extraordinary talent, who spent every hour of the day practising. I always tried to get him in my studio to record the Remo instrumentals, but he was always busy or away with the Swinging Blue Jeans. Colin was the apex of Merseyside guitarists, and everyone revered him. George learned so much from him, and would watch him on stage at every opportunity."

I spoke to Harry Prytherch, the original drummer with The Remo Four about his memories of his bandmate. "Colin Manley was not

MERSEYBEAT LEGENDS

THE REMO FOUR

Merseyside's all-time greatest instrumental group. Our picture shows the original line-up: (left to right) Don Andrew (bass), Harry Prytherch (drums), Keith Stokes (vocals/rhythm guitar) and Colin Manley (lead guitar). With their all-Fender guitar line-up and the special Ajax professional drum kit, they were admired by every other group on Merseyside. In an interview, Paul McCartney was asked what he did on his night off - he replied that he went to the Cavern Club to watch the Remo Four!

just a great guitar player, but a wonderful person," said Harry. "We spent many hours together practising in the early years, between 1958-1962, when The Remo Quartet started and in 1961 when we became The Remo Four. Paul McCartney was once asked what he did on his night off, and he replied that he goes to The Cavern to watch The Remo Four. I think he meant that he went to The Cavern to watch Colin Manley with The Remo Four. Colin was a great guitar player and a lovely man."

Colin Manley died on 9 April 1999.

The Remo Four in 1961:
Don Andrew, Harry Prytherch, Keith Stokes and Colin Manley.

The Remo Four

The original Remo Four were reunited in 1992: Harry Prytherch, Keith Stokes, Colin Manley and Don Andrew.

The original 1961 line-up was recreated by the Liverpool Echo in 1992 for Don Andrews' birthday party at the Beatles Story, Albert Dock, Liverpool. The original line-up consisted of Harry Prytherch on drums, Keith Stokes on guitar and vocals, Don Andrews on bass and Colin Manley on lead guitar.

7 DECEMBER 1957

George Harrison joins The Quarrymen

Paul had become friendly with George Harrison, as they both lived in Speke on the outskirts of Liverpool and attended the Liverpool Institute. It was because of these coincidences that while taking the same bus to school, they discovered a mutual interest in guitars and music. "It took from four o'clock to five to get home in the evening to the outskirts of the Speke estate", recalled George, "and it was on that bus journey that I met Paul McCartney, because he, being at the same school, had the same uniform and was going the same way as I was. So I started hanging out with him. His mother was a midwife and he had a trumpet."

Paul remembered how he came to know Harrison. "I knew George long before John and any of the others. They were all from Woolton, the posh district, and we hailed from the Allerton set, which was more working class. George and I had got together to learn the guitar and we were chums, despite his tender years as it seemed to me then. In fact George was only nine months younger than I was but to me George was always my little mate. But he could really play the guitar, particularly a piece called 'Raunchy' which we all loved. If anyone could do something as good as that, it was generally good enough to get them in the group."

Paul was eager for George to join The Quarrymen. At first, John was not keen because he was a mature seventeen-year-old and George was only fourteen. From independent and corroborative accounts, It is known that George watched the group at Wilson Hall in Garston

George with his Egmond guitar.

The Fab one hundred and Four

and, on the bus that evening, played the instrumental hit "Raunchy" for John and Paul. That was enough to convince John that George would make a decent lead guitarist. In the past, it has been accepted that the date of that audition was 6 February 1958.

They did not need four guitars, so Eric was given the ultimatum of either buying a bass guitar or leaving. He left.

However, doubts have been cast on the date of George's audition by Quarryman Rod Davis. I asked him what his investigations had revealed.

"In June 2010, I was glancing at Hunter Davies' book *The Quarrymen*, said Rod, "and, on page 89, I noticed the following which came from an interview by Hunter with Eric Griffiths: 'Aged sixteen, just about to be seventeen, he got a job as an apprentice engineer at Napier's on £3 a week. For the first few weeks, all he seemed to do was file down a metal cube, hour after hour, which bored him stiff. Once a week he went on day release to a local college and hated it. Eric managed to survive five months at Napier's, then he did what many fed up and frustrated Liverpool youths have done over the centuries. He went off to sea… Eric sat some tests and was accepted as an officer cadet in the Merchant Navy. In January 1958 he reported for duty at Liverpool docks to join the *MV Debrett*, one of the ships in the Lamport and Holt Line.' "

Rod started thinking about this and the dates did not add up. "Although Hunter's book had been published in 2001 and I had read it several times," he said, "I was not aware of the significance of this piece of information, particularly as it affected the date of Eric's leaving The Quarrymen as a result of George being asked to join. Eric's story, which he had frequently told during Quarrymen interviews, was that John and Paul wanted George to join as he was such a good guitarist. However, this would have meant four guitarists in the group, which was fine for a skiffle group, but too many for the rock 'n' roll group that they had now developed into. They suggested that Eric buy an electric bass, but he said he could not afford it on the meager earnings from The Quarrymen or his wages as an apprentice, and besides he was a guitarist and not a bass player. So he was asked to leave.

"If Eric had indeed joined his first ship in January 1958, then this would have helped date George's joining. So I spoke to Eric's widow Relda on 24 June 2010 and she checked his seaman's papers which showed that he joined his first ship, in Liverpool on 11 February 1958. The ship sailed on 14 February and did not return until 18 April. His next ship left on 3 May.

Rod continued: "Something else whose significance had escaped me. On page 102 of Hunter's book, there is a photograph of Eric's Seaman's Discharge Papers and the stamp on the very top of the page shows very clearly the date of 11 February 1958 and the signature of the Superintendent at the Mercantile Marine Office in Liverpool who issued the document is also dated 11 February 1958. This correlates perfectly with the date for Eric joining his ship in Liverpool, quoted to me by his widow."

This is where the conflict with the dates given arises. If George auditioned on the previously assumed date of 6 February 1958, Eric couldn't then suddenly join the Merchant Navy as an Officer Cadet and join his first ship on 11 February. And, as he reported for duty on 11 January, his departure must have been before then.

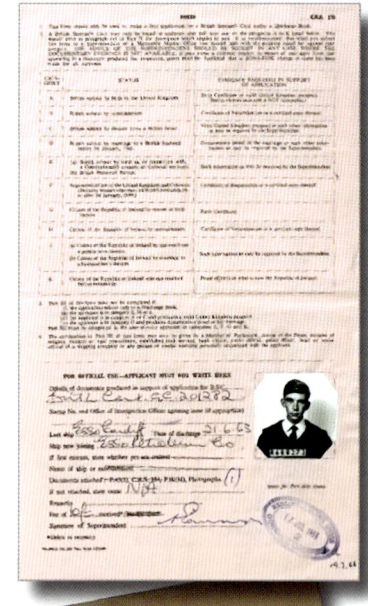

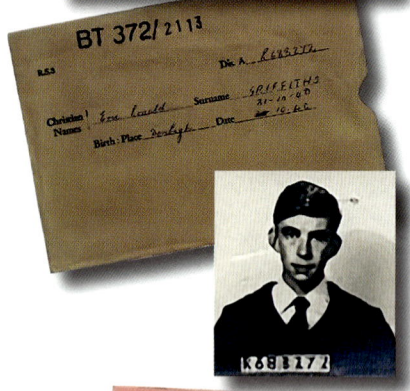

Eric Griffiths' Merchant Navy application form (top) and records.

"Surely", muses Rod, "if Eric had known he was going to sea then he would not have been so angry at being thrown out of The Quarrymen in favour of George."

After obtaining a copy of Eric's Merchant Navy records, I learned that the standard method of joining the Merchant Navy was to enroll, undertake a medical and sit the entrance exam. Then, at the end of this process, there was a role assigned on your first ship. This process typically took three to four weeks. Eric had obviously shown enough ability to be made an Officer Cadet, which enabled him to enjoy a good career in the Merchant Navy. After leaving, he went on to join the Prison Service in Scotland.

George Harrison remembers seeing The Quarrymen for the first time at Wilson Hall, Garston, and The Quarrymen played there on Thursday 7 November 1957, Saturday 7 December 1957 and Thursday 6 February 1958. 6 February 1958 could not have been the date that George joined.

If the 7 December 1957 appearance of The Quarrymen at Wilson Hall is the most likely time that George was introduced to the group, Eric was presumably sacked from The Quarrymen somewhere between that date and mid-January 1958, to give him enough time to become an officer cadet by 11 February 1958 and join his ship.

This date certainly makes more sense, but why was there a need for a change of guitarist? Eric was a founding member with John and they had learned together. One possible reason became evident on 18 October 1957 at New Clubmoor Hall, where Paul made his official debut with The Quarrymen. Part way through performing "Guitar Boogie", an instrumental tune, Paul made a mistake and John had to make a joke about the "new boy" to get him out of an embarrassing situation. Paul knew that he couldn't be a lead guitarist, and nor could Eric or John. With rock 'n' roll now becoming more prominent in their repertoire, and skiffle on the way out as fast as it had appeared, the only way for the group to improve was to drop the tea-chest bass and get a better guitarist. John knew the group needed a lead guitarist and Paul knew whom to call.

George had tried on a couple of occasions to impress John, who, soon to turn seventeen, did not want the 14-year-old Harrison hanging around. However, after Paul's mishap at the New Clubmoor Hall, George was invited again to audition for The Quarrymen.

Rod Davis spoke to drummer Colin Hanton who, of course, was still a member of the group at the time though, like the others, did not keep a diary or realise the importance of these events. "Colin certainly knew about John and Paul wanting George in and Eric out. He has told me many times of how he realised that, as he was only the drummer, his opinion as to whether Eric should be sacked or not was of little account as John and Paul were now in charge. This was despite the fact that Eric had originally got him (Colin) into The Quarrymen."

So, just five months after Paul had joined The Quarrymen, there were only John and Colin remaining from the original group. But, just as Colin thought he had survived the cull, there was a shock in store for him. His days were numbered, too.

Former site of Wilson Hall, Garston, shortly after demolition. It stood on the right, just before the houses.

8 MARCH 1958

John Lennon, Paul McCartney, George Harrison and Dennis Littler

Dennis Littler has many Beatles connections. As well as knowing John Lennon, Paul McCartney and George Harrison well, his family were friends with the Flannerys, who included Joe, future Beatles promoter and Peter, better known as Lee Curtis, whose band Pete Best joined after he was dismissed from The Beatles.

Dennis was born in 1938 and grew up in Roby at 92, Dinas Lane, just a short walk from his friend Ian Harris' home. A frequent visitor to 147, Dinas Lane, Dennis came to know Ian's parents, Paul's Auntie Jin and Uncle Harry, plus his cousins, Paul and Mike McCartney, who stayed at Auntie Jin's house for around two years after their mother died. Jim McCartney, Auntie Jin's brother, would often stay at his sister's house too. In a nice coincidence, Paul's Uncle Harry and cousin Ian were responsible for installing the stage at The Cavern Club.

Dennis attended Park View Primary School, where Stuart Sutcliffe would later study. As an apprentice electrician, he was working at Times Furnishings in Lord Street, Liverpool, while Brian Epstein was working there. However, it is for his connection with The Quarrymen, and the famous photograph with John, Paul and George for which he is best known.

I talked to Dennis and asked him about his friendship with the future Beatles.

"Ian Harris and I had formed a group, The Four Lads, which consisted of me on guitar, Ian on trumpet,

Dennis Littler.

Brian 'Yosser' Hughes on drums and Bobby Parr who played saxophone. It was a strange mix for a group! I had paid £19 on hire purchase (about £800 in today's money) for an Antoria Cello acoustic guitar, which was about two week's wages then: I was working as an apprentice electrician at the time. I bought it from Hessy's, as everybody did in those days.

"Paul, George and John would often come to my house and play on my guitar, because it was a lot more expensive than the guitars they had, and obviously was a much better guitar too. I never performed with The Quarrymen, but rehearsed with them. I remember Paul coming to me one day and saying that he had worked out how to play 'Butterfly' by Charlie Gracie and he played it perfectly. He had that knack of being able to pick a song up so quickly and it was obvious how good he was. He could pick up songs like 'Long Tall Sally' by ear, and sing like Little Richard too because he had such a great voice.

"When Ian got married, John, Paul and George were asked to provide some music, which is when the photo was taken by Mike McCartney, the first colour photograph featuring The Beatles. I am seen next to the wall with my glass of Guinness. I don't remember much about the day I'm afraid." The wedding took place on 8th March 1958 at St. Aloysius Roman Catholic Church, near the end of Dinas Lane.

"At the age of 21, I was called up for National Service in the RAF so I lost touch with them. However, when Paul had his 21st birthday party at Auntie Jin's, Ian invited me to come along. I wasn't sure, but I decided to go. By then, June 1963, The Beatles were enjoying a bit of fame after their first hit singles, so there was quite a crowd outside the house. I walked through the crowd and was welcomed into the house. I saw George and John to say hello, and then Paul came over to see me and we had a good chat. He told me he had somebody special for me to meet and to follow him. At the party were Gerry and the Pacemakers, Billy J Kramer, Brian Epstein and many other stars, but I'm not one for celebrity. However, Paul opened the door and there was my guitar hero Hank Marvin and Bruce Welch, from The Shadows. I was lost for words for a moment, which doesn't often happen!

"Paul and I lost touch after that, but I was working in The Every-

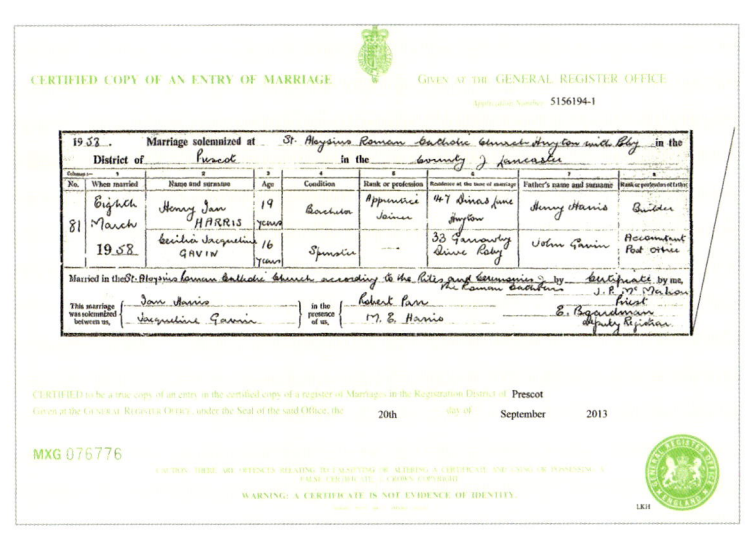

Marriage certificate for Ian Harris showing the date The Quarrymen played at his wedding.

man Theatre one day and the manager wanted to introduce me to the people rehearsing there. It was The Scaffold with Mike McGear (Mike McCartney's adopted pseudonym for his music career), about to make one of their first performances. He recognised me straight away and said, 'Is that you, Dennis?' and we had a lovely chat. We have kept in touch over the years.

"When it came to selling my guitar, my wife Jacqui suggested we should sell it as it had been laying in the loft. She contacted Mike, who told Paul, who kindly sent me a letter, which she then gave to Bonhams, the auctioneers."

The letter, dated 28 June 2012, said:

"I well remember the parties at my Auntie Jin's house where we would often bring our guitars and play. Dennis would often join in and on the occasions when we forgot to bring our guitars, Dennis would kindly lend us his to play on."

"When the guitar went to the auction," said Dennis, "they put a reserve of £20,000 on it, which amazed me. My son rang me to tell me it eventually sold for £35,000 plus tax! I was stunned!"

Dennis never pursued a career in music, and lives with his wife Jacqui in Formby, just to the north of Liverpool.

Dennis Littler, Brian Hughes and B. Davies.

Dennis Littler with his famous guitar, plus bandmate Bobby Parr.

Dennis' Antoria acoustic guitar, played by John, Paul and George.

SPRING 1958

John Duff Lowe joins The Quarrymen

One of the musicians who became a member of The Quarrymen after Paul and George had joined was John Duff Lowe, a friend of Paul's from the Liverpool Institute. The group had changed personnel once again, with only John and Colin Hanton remaining from the early line-up.

John Charles Duff Lowe was born on 13 April 1942 in Liverpool, and lived at 1, Halsey Avenue in West Derby.

Duff, as his friends knew him, recalled how he joined the group in the spring of 1958, while walking across the playground at the Inny, heading for the bike sheds to grab a sly cigarette. Paul approached him and they chatted about music, as they often did. Paul and Duff shared many of the same lessons, especially Music and languages.

The reason for the conversation that day involved Paul seeking Duff's help with moving from the key of C to E, and what to play in between. Duff explained that a B-minor 7th was the best progression, which obviously impressed the eager McCartney. The next time they met up, Paul invited his school friend to attend a Quarrymen rehearsal at Forthlin Road the following Sunday.

What was so unique about John Duff Lowe? He was a talented pianist who could emulate Jerry Lee Lewis. He would be able to help with The Quarrymen's transition from skiffle to rock 'n' roll while giving their sound an added dimension. However, one problem faced Duff and The Quarrymen. Not every venue had a piano and it clearly was not possible to take a piano with you. This meant he could only play with the group when the venue provided its own piano.

Duff had started piano lessons at the tender age of six. Because he was the only member of the group with any knowledge of music theory, he was a considerable asset. In *The Beatles Anthology*, Paul revealed why Duff was invited to join the group. "Duff was a friend of mine from school who could play the piano. He could play the arpeggio at the beginning of Jerry Lee's 'Mean Woman Blues'. That was the reason he was in. No one else we knew could play arpeggios right up the piano key-

John Duff Lowe at the Liverpool Institute, 1956.

The Fab one hundred and Four

John Duff Lowe's entry in the Liverpool Institute register.

board. We could do one broken chord and pause again. He could go right through with the correct fingering."

As well as being an accomplished pianist, Duff was a trained chorister, having famously auditioned for the choir at Liverpool Anglican Cathedral with Paul McCartney in February 1953. Both failed that audition, though Duff attended a second audition in October of that year with the encouragement of his parents. This time, he passed.

In many ways, it was fortunate that Paul failed his audition, as the weekly routine was intense, involving rehearsals, voice training, lessons and services. This would occupy a couple of evenings each week, not to mention every weekend. As each Saturday would be taken up, then this could have included 6 July 1957: the day Paul met John.

Duff did not know John Lennon. Their first meeting occurred at Paul's home, and a nervous Duff was waiting expectantly for the leader of the group to arrive. It was not long before he spotted John walking up to Paul's front door, collar turned up, strumming away on his guitar. Although Paul had invited Duff into the group, John must have given approval as the undisputed kingpin of The Quarrymen. Therefore, the group now had a pianist who would enable them to expand their repertoire. Rehearsals were always on Sundays and usually at Paul's Forthlin Road home. The majority of the gigs were on Saturday evenings.

Because he could only play when the club had a piano, Duff was in and out of the group, depending on the venue. Some of the clubs stand out in his memory, like the notorious Wilson Hall in Garston where the local Teddy Boy gang would make their requests clear. Duff recalled one evening when John was suffering with a sore throat and Paul was doing most of the vocals. However, the gang leader decided John should sing "Whole Lotta Shakin'" and wouldn't take no for an answer! Duff was beginning to earn accolades for his piano skills even though some of the instruments were in a poor state of repair.

Duff did not want to tell his parents that he was in a group, so he would sneak out of the house under false pretences. He would wear his stage shirt under his normal clothes and did not even have his own pair of denim jeans. John let him have an old pair of his and, while waiting to change buses at the Penny Lane roundabout, he would slip off his trousers put on his jeans. Such was the life of the covert rock 'n' roller!

Distance was a problem for Duff. He lived in West Derby very near The Casbah Coffee Club and about five miles from John and Paul. This meant that travelling to and from rehearsals and gigs was a time-consuming affair. However, for rock 'n' roll, it was worth it.

The Quarrymen's record, "In Spite of all the Danger", recorded on 12 July 1958.

One of the most significant events in the early days of The Quarrymen was the making of their first record at Percy Phillips' studio on 12 July 1958. Paul had introduced "In Spite of all the Danger" to the group at one of their regular rehearsals. They practised it until they were confident enough to perform it for their most critical of judges: Jim McCartney. They were excited about the prospect of recording an original song.

They all pitched in to raise the money to make the record, though they couldn't afford to record it to tape. After a couple of rehearsals in the studio, they cut the song straight to disk. In the days that followed, they passed it along from member to member and, somehow, it ended up in Duff's possession permanently. It was stored away for years.

When Duff decided to sell the record in the early 1980s, the *Times* newspaper ran the story and, before the disc made it to Sotheby's to be auctioned, Paul McCartney had called, looking for his former band mate. Duff did not return the call. When a letter from Paul's solicitor arrived threatening legal action if he sold the record, Duff decided it was time to contact him. As it contained an unpublished song of Paul's, he was advised that if he tried to sell it, he could face action through the courts.

Paul wanted to buy the record and Duff wanted to sell it, so an agreement was reached, with McCartney purchasing the historic disk. In 1995, the song appeared on *The Beatles Anthology 1* CD.

In spite of the record and having three future Beatles in the group, performances were harder to come by. With drummer Colin Hanton quitting soon, Duff's appearances dwindled. By the end of 1958, The Quarrymen were reduced to just John, Paul and George. Duff joined another Liverpool group, Hobo Rick and the City Slickers, fronted by Liverpool actor Ricky Tomlinson. With The Casbah close to home, he would often attend the club with his near neighbour and school friend, Neil Aspinall.

After leaving the Liverpool Institute, Duff began work at a Liverpool stockbroker's office. Being based in the Liverpool city centre, he would often go to The Cavern at lunchtime to see The Beatles. He recalled the time he went to talk to John and, on saying hello, Lennon, quick as a flash, introduced him to his friend, saying, "This is Duff. He breaks stock", a joke referring to Duff's occupation as a stockbroker.

Duff contacted former Quarrymen Rod Davis and Len Garry in 1992, and they recorded a couple of unreleased albums. He now performs at events all over the world with Rod, Len and Colin as a member of the re-formed Quarrymen.

John Duff Lowe with the record and plaque outside Percy Phillips' house.

12 JULY 1958

Percy Phillips records
The Quarrymen

Although neither a member of the group nor a musician, a special place in the story of The Quarrymen belongs to Percy Phillips, who enabled them to cut their first record on 12 July 1958.

Percy Francis Phillips was born in March 1896 in Warrington, Lancashire. Having been injured in World War I, he returned to Liverpool and soon set up shop in Brunswick Street in the Liverpool city centre selling bicycles and motorbikes. In 1925, Phillips moved to a home at 38, Kensington. He converted the front of the structure and started selling and charging batteries from there. The business did well for many years, but when it tailed off in the 1950s, he looked for another way to earn a living.

He began selling electrical goods and, by the end of the decade, was mainly stocking records and record players. The records Phillips sold reflected his taste in music: American Big Band and Country and Western hits by people like Hank Williams. The shop became popular with young people, but they weren't really looking for the records he was selling. They wanted rock 'n' roll, especially "Rock Around the Clock".

Some of the local musicians started asking if he could make demo discs and that inspired his next business idea: a home studio. Phillips' son Frank was taking a sound recording course at EMI in London, so he paid a visit to him and, while there, spent £400 on a portable recording set-up and disc-cutting machine made by Master Sound Systems. He brought the equipment back to his Kensington home, initially setting it up in the damp cellar. Because this was not the ideal location, he soon moved the studio to the back room of the house.

The studio consisted of three large metal boxes with leather handles. The first contained an amplifier, the second a quarter-inch tape recorder and the third the disc cutting lathe. Accompanying this was a heater for the lathe, an HMV ribbon microphone, a Reslo microphone, a four-way mixer unit, some ten-inch EMI acetate blanks (aluminium

Percy Phillips (right) in his studio.

discs coated in acetate lacquer) and three pairs of headphones. Phillips was a stickler for details and kept extensive notes.

He soundproofed the small twelve square foot room by installing carpeting and placing blankets over the door and windows. He even designed his own reverb unit located in the cellar. This chamber consisted of a microphone in a tin bath. Phillips was truly a man of vision, as there was no comparable facility for recording anywhere in Liverpool. Consequently, he was responsible for recording many of the city's greatest bands and singers. However, he reserved his first official session for himself – recording his own version of "Bonnie Marie of Argyle".

He named the studio Phillips' Sound Recording Services and advertised it as P. F. Phillips' Professional Tape and Disc Recording Service. His business cards read: "PF Phillips, 38 Kensington, Liverpool, 7. Television and Battery Service. Gramophone Record Dealer. Professional Tape and Disc Recording Studio."

Phillips Sound Recording Services was now open for business. He cut his first disc on the machine on 7 August 1955, and went on to make numerous discs over the years, with considerable sound quality. By 1957, skiffle groups were lining up to make records. He also made spoken word discs for actors and performers. One local lad called Ronnie Wycherley – later renamed Billy Fury by Larry Parnes – recorded a double-sided 78 rpm shellac disc at the studio. With this recording, Wycherley was signed by Parnes and went on to be one of the UK's most successful stars.

Phillips kept a log detailing each recording session, though this usually noted what was done rather than who had made the recording. We can see from his entry on 12 July 1958 that it states: 'Skiffle. 10 inch double sided. Direct. 11/3'. This is The Quarrymen's recording, indicating that a double-sided acetate was to be cut direct to the machine and not to tape first. Though the cost was stated as 11 shillings and 3 pence, Phillips remembered charging 17 shillings and 6 pence. "The charge was 17s 6d to do both side of a demo disc," Phillips recalled in an interview with the *Liverpool Echo*, "but they only had 15s (15 shillings), so I hung on to it until they came back with the rest. I think it was John who turned up a couple of days later with the final half crown. John was always the gaffer."

The Quarrymen recorded "That'll Be the Day", a Buddy Holly favourite of theirs, and an original song credited to McCartney/Harrison called "In Spite of all the Danger". Despite the writing credit, Harrison's only contribution was the guitar solo.

The boys waited in the front parlour and recorded in the back room studio. The studio consisted of two tape-recorders, a microphone

Percy Phillips' studio at 38, Kensington.

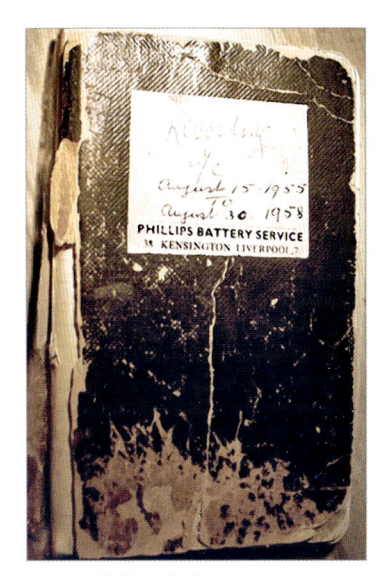

Percy Phillips' diary.

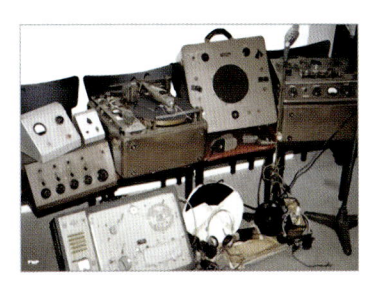

Percy's equipment.

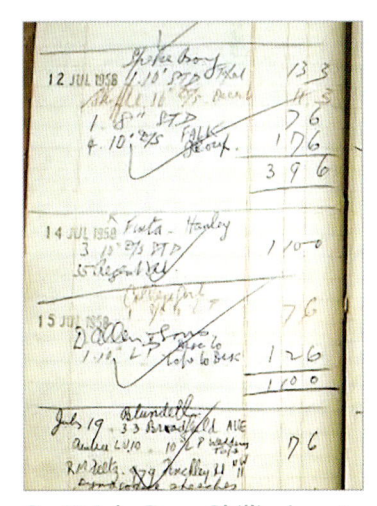

On 12 July, Percy Phillips' wrote Skiffle in his diary – it was for The Quarrymen.

The Fab one hundred and Four

Percy Phillips reveals to the *Liverpool Echo* how he wiped over the original tape of The Quarrymen (although no tape was actually made!).

hanging from the ceiling, a piano and disc-cutter. Colin Hanton spoke about that famous first recording. "We met at a theatre and walked up there. All I remember was this back room with electronic equipment in the corner. We set up our equipment with me in the corner and the lads with their guitars. There were no amps. It was all-acoustic. John Lowe was over by the wall on the piano. I was hitting the drums and he said that they were too loud, so I tried again but there was still the same problem which was finally fixed by putting a scarf over the snare to soften it and keep it as quiet as possible.

"John Duff Lowe reckons there was one microphone hanging down from the ceiling, which picked everything up. Phillips was complaining because he said we should get the tape, which was a pound, but we just had enough each. I always felt that was one of the reasons to invite John Lowe along – to split it five ways. John and Paul went white at the thought of a pound.

"Percy was fed up because we were taking too much time, and starting to look at the clock. 'In Spite of all the Danger' was quite long, and he said to chop a verse off. John said no. John Lowe could see Phillips from where he was sitting and he was apparently telling John to finish. We kept going, so the record ended with the song going almost to the centre of the disc, right to the hole in the middle.

"He gave us the disc and off we went. It was a big thing. How many people had records like popular crooner Matt Monro? So we had a record, too, and could listen to ourselves. It was a momentous day for us. I can still remember it so clearly".

The record was sold in 1981 by Duff Lowe to Paul McCartney for an undisclosed sum and appeared on *The Beatles Anthology 1* in 1995.

This was not the last time that Percy played a part in The Beatles' story. Bob Wooler, the legendary compere from The Cavern, was a frequent visitor to Phillips' shop and they would often talk about their love of music. Percy would create compilation discs for Wooler to use at the various venues where he was the MC. Phillips also sold Bill Harry's music paper, *Mersey Beat*, so could keep in touch with the local music scene.

Another frequent visitor was a fellow record store owner from Liverpool, Brian Epstein. They would often listen to some of the rarer records from the U.S. that Percy could get hold of, and sit and talk about the latest music releases. One of the services that Percy provided for Brian was to record The Beatles' radio appearances on his reel-to-reel machine. Most of these tapes were recorded over or lost, but one was discovered when searching through the studio back in 1977. It is hoped that this will be released one day. It contains one of the recordings of the BBC *Saturday Club* from 1963. The Beatles performed "Some Other Guy", "Beautiful Dreamer" and "Keep Your Hands Off My Baby", which Phillips then transferred to a 7-inch 45 rpm acetate. It was sold at auction in 1990.

The Beatles were frequent visitors too, because, as previously stated, Phillips sold records and sheet music, making his shop a popular destination for most of the groups. He closed the studio in 1969 and the record shop in 1974. He passed away in 1984.

Percy Phillips should be remembered not just as the man who launched the recording career of The Quarrymen, but the man who helped numerous local groups and artists record themselves and set many bands on the road to success.

In August 2005, Colin Hanton returned to Kensington for the unveiling of a plaque to commemorate this first recording and celebrate Percy Phillips' important contribution to The Beatles' story. John Duff Lowe was in attendance as well as Julia Baird, John's half-sister. Local radio presenter and former Cavern DJ Billy Butler was also on hand for the festivities.

The plaque erected at the site of Percy Phillips' studio.

JULY 1958

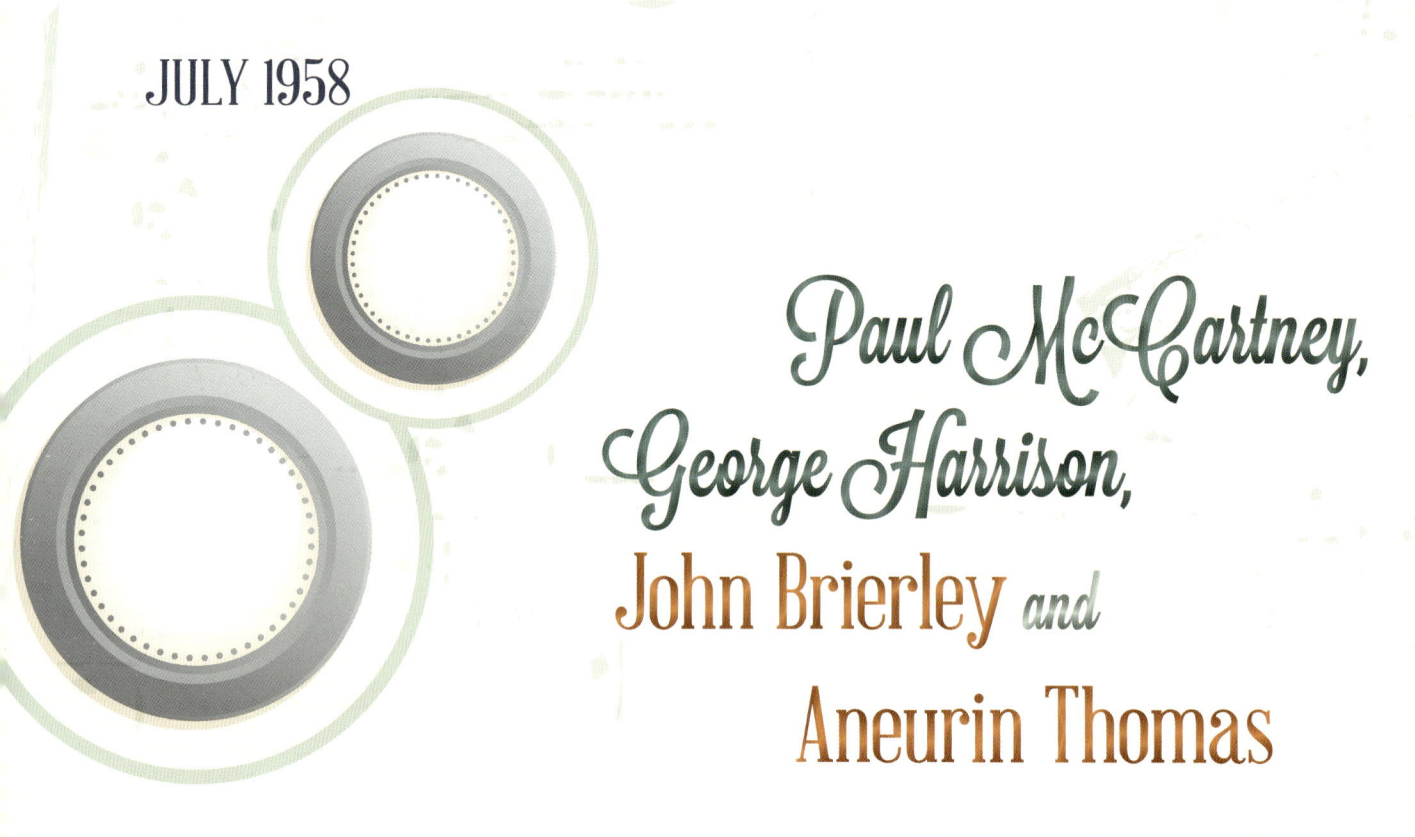

Paul McCartney, George Harrison, John Brierley and Aneurin Thomas

In the summer of 1958, Paul and George decided to hitchhike to Wales. They set off with their guitars, of course, and spotted a sign for Harlech, made famous in the Welsh anthem, "Men of Harlech", that they both knew well. Harlech, an ancient town famous for its castle, was welcoming to the Liverpool wanderers, and they settled into a local cafe, listening to the jukebox in the corner.

Paul and George rehearsed with local group The Vikings in the basement of a barbershop, and Gerry Brookes, who owns the Seasons and Reasons General Store on the site of the barbershop, told me about the famous visit to the town. The two visiting Liverpool musicians decided to camp in a field belonging to John Brierley's family and, as Brierley was in a local group, the talk soon turned to music. Paul and George moved from their tent into the Brierley's house and so, in return for bed and breakfast, they agreed to play with the group. John Brierley and his friend Aneurin Thomas were members of The Vikings, and they were performing regularly at the Queens Hotel, which was run by Thomas' dad. The group often played on Saturday nights, and so one evening, Paul and George stepped up and performed with John and Aneurin as a quartet in Harlech. According to Brookes, the lady who lived in the flat above the barbershop remembers the group rehearsing and making a terrible noise, and local man Bill Crews had kept hold of the tea-chest bass that George played, though eventually he ripped it apart and used it for firewood!

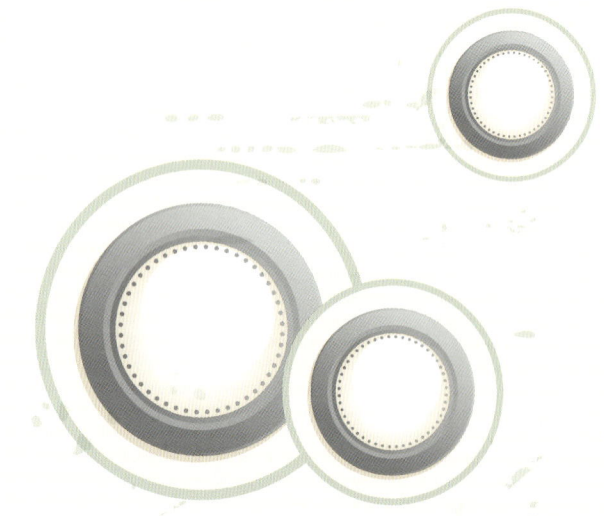

FEBRUARY 1959

The Les Stewart Quartet – Les Stewart, Ray Skinner, George Harrison and Ken Brown

By the beginning of 1959, bookings for The Quarrymen had dried up, and they stopped performing. John had struggled for enthusiasm since his mother's death the previous July. Wanting to perform, George went looking for a band to join and found one in the Les Stewart Quartet. They were playing in West Derby, at the local British Legion, and more often at the Pillar Club in the basement of Lowlands, a community hall on Haymans Green. Dave Bamber was a regular at the Pillar Club, but wouldn't go to The Casbah in the same road when it opened, as he felt it was too rough. Bamber saw George at the Pillar Club performing with the Les Stewart Quartet. The Pillar Club opened in 1959, before The Casbah, and saw bands like The Searchers, Gerry and the Pacemakers, Billy J. Kramer plus Manchester group, The Hollies. Allegedly, The Beatles failed an audition here too. The club could hold up to 400 people and groups like The Searchers also played in the over-21s Club on the ground floor. By now, George had a girlfriend, Ruth Morrison, who was friendly with the Best family, owners of a large house at the other end of Haymans Green.

When Mona Best decided she wanted to open a rock 'n' roll club in the basement of her home in the same road as Lowlands, Ruth told George, and he told the group. The Les Stewart Quartet, who had a good local reputation, were approached by Mona Best to see if they wanted the residency at her new club. All the group members decided to get their hands dirty and help get the club ready for opening. Ken Brown in particular was very impressed with the new club and its owner, Mona Best.

"We hit it off straight away", Ken recalled of his first meeting with a lady for whom he always had great affection. "Mo was very warm and friendly and took everyone as they were. She was shrewd, mind you, and she could read people well. Unlike the other mothers, she was so full of enthusiasm and had the energy of a teenager. I was so

Ken Brown.

The Fab one hundred and Four

drawn in with the excitement that I would go to work, come home and go to The Casbah, and then work there until 3 a.m., when I'd slip home, go to bed, get up and do it all again. It was a special place".

Ken's constant presence at The Casbah and his desire to help prepare for its opening caused friction in the band. The Les Stewart Quartet had played at Lowlands at the bottom of Haymans Green, but was now without any gigs. They would still meet once a week or so to rehearse at Les' place, but there were no prospects on the horizon. "I thought that if we worked with Mo to get the residency I was doing well for the group," said Ken. "So I worked hard there, helping as much as I could so that our band would have a regular place to play, because there were so few opportunities to have a residency anywhere. Anyway, I started missing rehearsals because I was spending time at The Casbah getting it ready for the opening night. So one night at Les' place, he tells us that we weren't going to play at The Casbah.

"In fact, Les was quiet, and it was his girlfriend Sheila who spoke up, telling me how I'd missed rehearsals and was not committed to the band. I thought, hang on, I'm doing this for the band. I said to Sheila, 'Why don't you let Les speak for himself?' But he did not. She was adamant, so that was it. I said I'd very clearly promised Mrs. Best that if she would give us the residency, I would bring the band and I would help in whatever way I could. I couldn't go back on that. I promised I wouldn't let her down.

The Pillar Club was in the basement of Lowlands Community Centre, where George Harrison played with the Les Stewart Quartet.

"They wouldn't change their minds, so I said, 'Right, I'm going, who's coming with me?' George stood up and out we went and left the group".

After they left the group, George and Ken began playing as a duo in local clubs. This was all a few weeks before The Casbah was due to open. Rory Best accompanied the duo to a few local bookings and realised they weren't the finished article.

29 AUGUST 1959

The Quarrymen – George Harrison, Ken Brown, John Lennon and Paul McCartney

Mona Best was expecting a group to open her club, so Ken Brown was left with a dilemma. "I had promised to have a band for the opening night, and here I was with only George. It's a start but we needed to do something. It was not unusual then to have a group and no drummer, so that was all right. It was then that George told me about his two friends who he had played with before, and gave them a ring. That, of course, was John Lennon and Paul McCartney. I went to see Mo and told her what had happened and that George had a couple of friends who could help us out. So they came down and we had a few practises in The Casbah to be ready to open in a couple of weeks' time."

On 29 August 1959, George, Ken, John and Paul opened The Casbah Coffee Club and decided to use the name three of them had used before: The Quarrymen.

The Quarrymen performed for the next few weeks until one night when Ken was not well and couldn't play. He had stomach cramps and, though he was desperate to be there, he obviously couldn't play in his condition. John, Paul and George offered to play as a threesome. Mo put Ken in charge of collecting the money. At the end of the night, a row broke out over money. Mo would hand out

Come on down to The Casbah Coffee Club.

The Fab one hundred and Four

the fee to them, splitting the £3 evenly: fifteen shillings (75 pence) each. After Mo had given John, Paul and George their fifteen shillings, they asked her for Ken's share of the money. She was adamant that they were a group and would be paid as a group. She refused to give them Ken's share.

The others, led by John, protested.

The first I knew was when George came up to me and told me what the others had told Mo", said Ken. "As far as I was concerned, if I did not play, I did not get paid. But then I was not the boss, Mo was. Whatever she had decided was the most important. Therefore, I told George what I thought and that they should speak to Mo about it. It was up to her. Anyway, George went back and there was a row with Mo, and they picked up their stuff and left. I did not know what had happened as I was upstairs and did not even know they'd left. I only found out later. They never said anything more to me."

Ken, Chas, Bill and Pete

Ken continued: "So there I was again, this time on my own. I thought, start again and get a group together. I asked Rory (Best), because he had a great personality and would have been ideal, but he said

Ken Brown's piano, that was played by Paul and many other pianists.

no. I then spoke to Pete (Best) and suggested we form a group – me on guitar and him on drums. 'Great,' he says, 'but I haven't got any drums'. So we saw Mo and she bought Pete his set of drums. We then added Pete's friends Chas Newby and Bill Barlow and The Blackjacks were formed."

The Quarrymen at The Casbah Club, with Paul looking at Cynthia Powell.

OCTOBER 1959 – AUGUST 1960

Johnny and the Moondogs to The Silver Beatles

When John, Paul and George fell out with Mona Best at The Casbah, it meant that Ken Brown was no longer with the group. It seems that was the final straw and The Quarrymen name was never used again by them.

John, Paul and George decided to enter the local finals of Carroll Levis' *TV Star Search*. The auditions were held at the Liverpool Empire from 26-31 October 1959 and, for this competition only, they called themselves Johnny and the Moondogs. Although they did not win, they were placed high enough to qualify for the regional final in Manchester.

The final was held at Manchester's Hippodrome Theatre on Sunday 15 November. The group gave a decent performance, but since the decision was based on audience applause, three Liverpool lads playing in Manchester had little to no chance of winning. If that was not bad enough, any finalists would have to make a brief re-appearance at the end of the night. Unfortunately, the boys had to return home on the last train, so they couldn't stay for the end. That was the end of Johnny and the Moondogs. The name of the group was probably inspired by the American DJ Alan Freed, whose pioneering *Moondog Radio Show* premiered some of the best rock 'n' roll music in the U.S., and his Saturday *Moondog House Rock 'n' Roll Party Show* was the highlight of the week on Radio Luxembourg.

The group needed a bass player, so they approached Stuart Sutcliffe and Rod Murray, John's friends from Art College to see if either of them wanted the job. Rod set about making a bass guitar, but Stuart managed to sell a painting to John Moores, enabling him to purchase one. With some tutelage from Dave May, Stuart joined the group. As a foursome, they appeared at the Art College as The College Band, but decided they needed a new name for the group. After a discussion, Stuart suggested they should name the group The Beatals, in homage to their hero Buddy Holly's group, The Crickets. Over the first few months of 1960, they called themselves The Beatals, The Silver Beetles, The Silver Beats and The Silver Beatles, and toured Scotland with Johnny Gentle as His Group. There doesn't seem to be a consistent use of the spelling of Silver Beetles/Silver Beatles, though the latter appeared more from around June 1960.

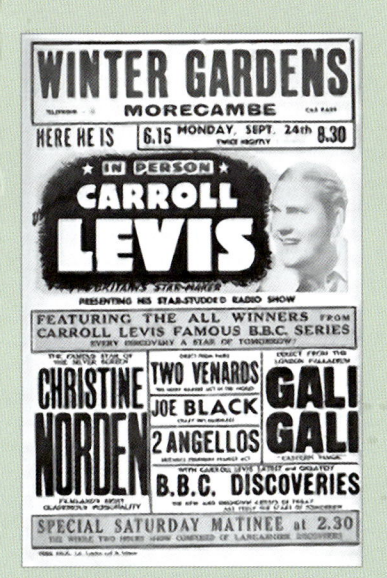

Poster for Carroll Levis, who held shows to discover new talent.

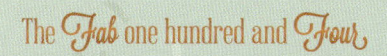

The Fab one hundred and Four

The Empire Theatre, where Johnny and the Moondogs performed.

Advertisement for the Carroll Levis show in Manchester, where Johnny and the Moondogs performed on 15 November 1959.

Poster for Alan Freed's *Moondog Coronation Ball*.

They also made appearances backing Janice the Stripper in a strip club owned by Allan Williams and Lord Woodbine, much to their shame. While hanging out in the clubs in the postal district of Liverpool 8, they met some of the musicians, like Vinnie Ismael, Odie Taylor and Zancs Logie, who, over the next twelve months, would pass on some of their skills to John and Paul. They performed with beat poet Royston Ellis, who convinced John that he should spell the group's name as BEATLES.

They had a few drummers in this period, with both Mike and Paul McCartney stepping in, as well as Cliff Roberts from The Dominoes and Johnny Hutchinson from The Big Three. They found a permanent drummer in Tommy Moore, a one-night-only drummer in Ronnie 'The Ted' and Moore's replacement in Norman Chapman. They also approached an unknown drummer through an advertisement in the *Liverpool Echo* before asking Pete Best to join them on their first trip to Hamburg. Pete had learned his trade with The Blackjacks alongside Ken Brown, Bill Barlow and Chas Newby.

Now they were finally a rock 'n' roll band, and on the road to Germany.

DECEMBER 1959

Stuart Sutcliffe and Rod Murray are invited to join John Lennon, Paul McCartney and George Harrison

When John and Paul realised that they needed a bass player in their group, they approached two of John's friends, Stu Sutcliffe and Rod Murray, and offered them the position. The first one to accept would get the job, provided they had their own bass guitar. They both welcomed the challenge, and Stuart Sutcliffe won. However, Stu has probably had more criticism than any other member of The Beatles over his talent, or perceived lack of musical ability.

For decades, the memory of Stuart Sutcliffe has been tainted by those who claim that, even though he was a brilliant painter, he was not much of a musician.

How many times have you heard it said?

'He was only in the group because he was John's friend'.

'He used to stand with his back to the audience'.

'He used to play unplugged so that they couldn't hear how bad he was playing'.

'He looked great on stage, but he couldn't really play'.

Stuart's talent as a painter has never been in doubt, with a long career as an artist assured, if only he hadn't died at the tender age of only 21.

Rod and Stuart playing it cool next to the Ford Prefect they had borrowed for their trip to Stratford-Upon-Avon in the summer of 1959.

The Fab one hundred and Four

Many art experts have said that, had he lived, Stuart would have been one of the pre-eminent painters of the 1960s.

On the other hand, there have been many authors and commentators who have told us repeatedly that Stuart couldn't play the bass. I decided to speak to the people who knew him best: his sister Pauline; Art College friend and flatmate Rod Murray; friend and fellow musician Klaus Voormann; and other musicians who were there at the time. What evidence can we find to support the claim that Stuart was a good bass player? Or will we find evidence to substantiate the opposing view that he really couldn't play?

Stuart's musical skills began when he started playing the piano as a young boy. "Stuart had previously been learning the piano," said Millie Sutcliffe, Stuart's mum. "Stuart's father was a wonderful pianist, a classical musician, though not commercial or anything like that. He played just for his own pleasure. Stuart's knowledge of music helped him, and he was a pretty good singer, too. He could see the potential of the group and enjoyed playing with them. I heard that they were playing down at The Jacaranda in return for their supper, and the music was good. Even then, the girls were tearing buttons from their coats. One girl kissed him and then fainted! I have been to The Cavern and they were great. I went very prejudiced and prepared to be disappointed but must admit that I was thoroughly delighted."

As Stuart was learning the piano, his father Charles bought him a Spanish guitar, which he played a little, but not to any great level. This alone was not enough to give him an edge in joining the group. As his mum Millie had said, Stuart was also a good singer. He was, in fact, the head chorister at his local church of St. Gabriel's, Huyton.

John and Paul challenged Stuart and Rod to get a bass guitar and join them. All was going well for Rod as he started to make his own bass, but then Stuart's painting was purchased by John Moores at the art exhibition in the Walker Art Gallery. The exhibition ran from 19 November 1959 to 17 January 1960 and, contrary to some reports, Stuart did not win the competition. However, John Moores, who sponsored the competition, purchased Stuart's painting, giving him the money to buy the bass guitar.

Buying the bass and joining the group was neither a quick nor automatic decision. Paul McCartney later remembered how and where the

Stuart with sisters Pauline and Joyce, and mum Milly.

Stuart's portrait of one of his girlfriends, in the style of Modigliani, in the Percy Street flat.

Dot Jones, Stuart Sutcliffe and Chris Jones, who is playing Stuart's guitar.

Dave May, who gave Stuart bass guitar lessons.

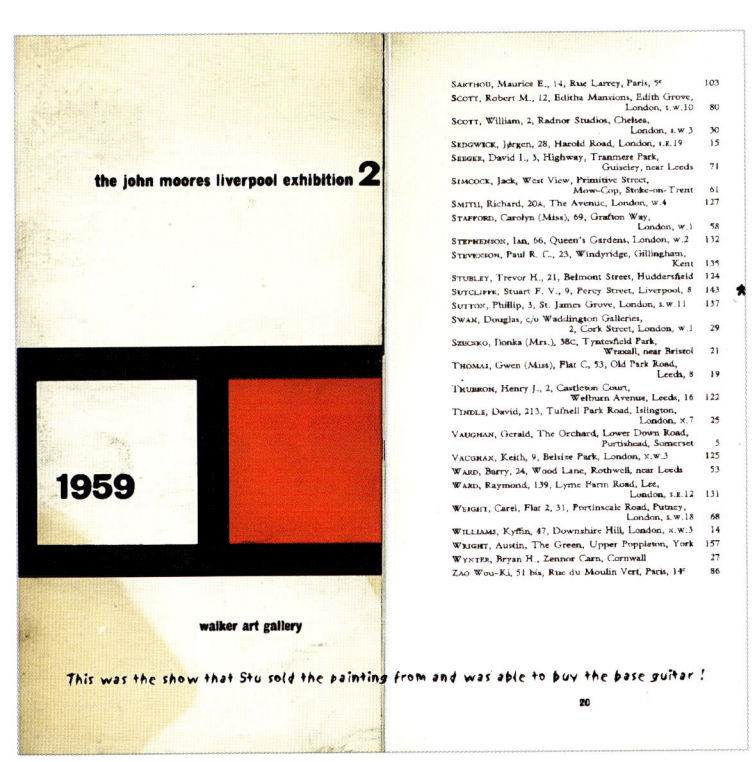

Programme for the John Moores Exhibition where Stuart entered his painting.

decision was made: "We were sitting with a cup of coffee – John, Stuart and I, the two of us trying to persuade Stuart that he should get this bass, and he said, 'No, this is a painting prize. I'm supposed to get canvases.' That was where we talked him into it – at The Casbah."

Rory Best witnessed Stuart Sutcliffe's entry into the group. Sitting in the corner of this coffee bar, up against the wall, was Stuart. Pinning him in were Paul McCartney and John Lennon, trying to convince Stuart to spend his art money on a bass guitar. "Stuart was not keen as he wanted to buy art supplies," said Rory. "The club was closed and I was clearing up, waiting to go up to the party that was starting upstairs.

"These parties were the stuff of legends and everyone wanted to be there, though not everyone was allowed in. I saw what was happening, and that Stu was explaining that he and his dad were adamant he had to buy paints, brushes and canvases."

Exasperated, Rory finally took action. "I went over to him and said, 'For God's sake, Stu, just buy the guitar and let's get up to the party.' And so he said 'okay' and that was it."

Stuart went to Hessy's and purchased a bass guitar. He paid a deposit in cash, but financed the rest of it, enabling him to spend some of the

The Fab one hundred and Four

183

Stuart's cheque showing a payment to Paul in respect of his guitar purchase from Hessy's.

One of the Art College students on the left with Chris Jones, Stuart Sutcliffe and Rod Murray, in Ye Cracke.

money on his art supplies. At that time, Stuart couldn't play the bass guitar. As George Harrison said, it was "better to have a bass player that couldn't play than to not have a bass player at all." However, Stuart had to do something about it, and straightaway recruited Dave May of the local group, The Silhouettes. May was a fellow Art College student of John and Stuart. "I had a homemade guitar which wasn't very good," said May, "because I don't know anything about the technical side. The Students' Union bought The Beatles equipment and Stuart had a Hofner bass guitar, which was the bees' knees, but he couldn't play a note. I always remember going over to John and Stuart's flat in Gambier Terrace. I said, 'I'll teach you to play 'C'mon Everybody' if you let me measure your guitar.' That was the bargain. I taught him to play the song – it's only three notes – and then measured his guitar. I then made my own guitar and Stu Sutcliffe played with The Beatles."

I spoke to Rod Murray about Stuart and how he nearly joined The Beatles. John, Paul and George started to frequent the rented Percy Street flat that Stuart and Rod Murray shared and began rehearsing. Rod even lent his tape recorder to Stuart for the occasional rehearsals that took place at Paul's house at 20, Forthlin Road. "Stu would borrow the recorder and go to Paul's house to record," said Rod, "but he had to buy his own tapes as they were so expensive." The audio quality was poor, but if you listen to these tapes, you can understand why not many people rated the group at that time. Some of these recordings appeared on *The Beatles Anthology 1*, released in 1995.

The suggestion that Stuart played with his back to the audience mainly originated with Allan Williams and his 1975 book, *The Man Who Gave The Beatles Away,* when he referenced the photographs taken at the Larry Parnes audition at the Wyvern Club on 10 May 1960. In the photos, taken by Cheniston Roland, Stuart can be seen standing side-on to the rest of the group. Paul McCartney said, "If anyone had been taking notice, they would have seen that when we were all in A, Stu would be in another key. But he soon caught up and we passed that audition to go on tour."

At that stage, Stuart had only been playing a few weeks, so he was still trying to get up to speed with the rest of the group, who had been playing together for a couple of years. The photos, Williams suggested, showed Stuart standing with his back to the audience, so the myth began and was perpetuated.

It has also been suggested that Parnes objected to Stuart and would not use The Silver Beatles if he was still in the group, an assertion which has never been proven. In fact, Parnes' objection was to their drummer, Tommy Moore, who turned up late and looked uninterested. Even this did not prevent The Silver Beatles from being chosen to back Johnny Gentle on a tour of Scotland, so they couldn't have been that bad. But, tell a story often enough and it becomes 'fact'.

By May 1960, Stuart had been playing with the group for several months and had been steadily improving. As The College Band, John, Paul, George and Stuart had performed at regular Saturday night dances, and Stuart had even begun taking on responsibilities as the group's manager, working to secure bookings for them.

The Silver Beatles' tour with Johnny Gentle has been written off as a disaster, but that was far from the truth. They learned a lot on the road and Stuart was obviously enjoying the experience.

After the group returned home from their tour, Allan Williams, now acting as their manager, obtained several engagements for them around Merseyside. While the group received better reviews the more they played and developed, they were far from being one of Liverpool's top bands. Derry and the Seniors, then considered one of the area's best groups, did not have a very high opinion of them. Howie Casey, the Seniors' saxophonist, said: "They were a nothing little band." When Casey heard that The Silver Beetles might follow the Seniors over to Hamburg, his verbal assault on the group escalated. "They might destroy the scene," Casey recalled saying. "I said send a band like Rory Storm or The Big Three. When they (The Beatles) did turn up, they were vastly improved. The improvement was like night and day."

When they arrived in Hamburg, The Beatles suddenly realised that they were expected to play up to eight hours every night. They had to expand their repertoire and do it quickly. As George would recall: "We had to learn millions of songs. We'd be on for hours. Saturday would start at three or four in the afternoon and go on until five or six in the morning." Necessity is the mother of invention they say – and so it

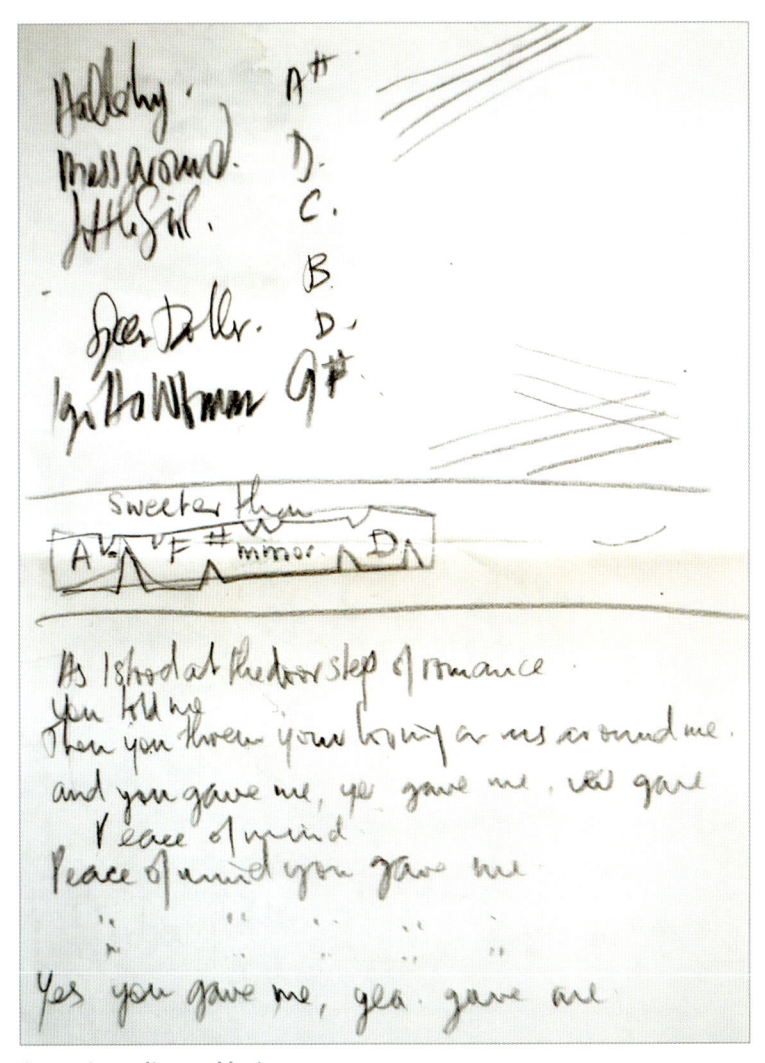

Stuart's set list and lyrics.

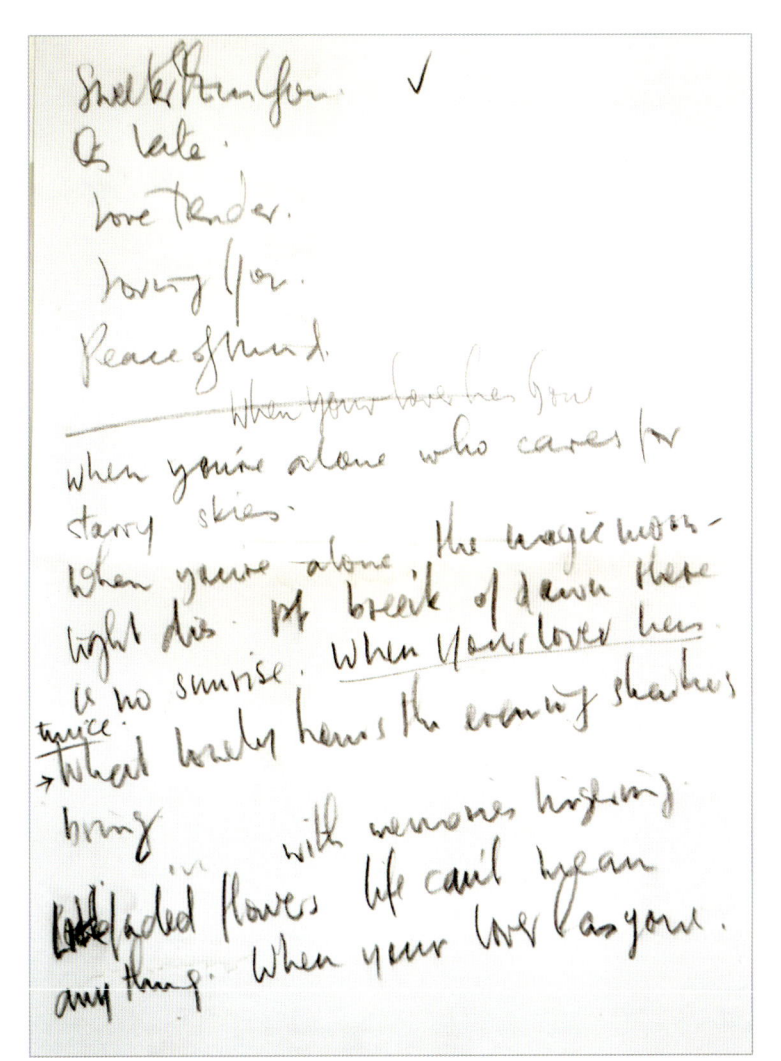

transpired for The Beatles. "We got better and got more confidence," recalled Lennon. "We couldn't help it, with all the experience, playing all night long." Paul also recognised that the more they played together, the more they improved. "We got better and better," observed McCartney, "and other groups started coming to watch us."

If Lennon, McCartney and Harrison could see an improvement in the band, then surely Stuart's playing must have progressed as well. "We have improved a thousand-fold since our arrival," wrote Sutcliffe in one of his many letters home. Within a short span of time, with Pete Best supplying a thumping beat on the drums, The Beatles were quickly becoming the band to see in Hamburg. Suddenly, admirers were flocking to see them. One of them was Bruno Koschmider, who owned The Indra Club (where The Beatles were playing) as well as the larger, more popular Kaiserkeller. Because he felt the group was ready for a step up, he decided to move them to his more popular club.

In order to provide continuous music, Koschmider split up The Beatles and The Seniors, giving Howie Casey the chance to assess Stuart's competence as a bass player up close. "I was given Stuart Sutcliffe along with Derry and Stan Foster from the Seniors, and we had a German drummer. Stu had a great live style," he recalled.

Rick Hardy of The Jets also witnessed Sutcliffe at close hand in Hamburg. "Stu never turned his back on stage," he said emphatically. "Stu certainly played to the audience and he certainly played bass. If you have someone who can't play the instrument properly, you have no bass sound. There were two rhythm guitarists with The Beatles and if one of them couldn't play, you wouldn't have noticed it – but it's different with a bass guitar. I was there and I can say quite definitely that Stuart never did a show in which he was not facing the audience."

One of those who became very close to Stuart in Hamburg was Klaus Voormann, who himself became a great bassist respected the world over. "Stu was a really good rock and roll bass player," said Voormann, "a very basic bass player. He was, at the time, my favourite bass player, and he had that cool look. The Beatles were best when Stuart was still in the band. To me it had more balls. It was even more rock and roll when

Set list showing the songs that The Beatles were playing, including "Winston's Walk".

John, George, Pete, Paul and Stuart at The Indra Club, 1960.

George, John and Paul at the microphone in The Indra Club, while Stuart looks on.

Stuart was playing the bass and Paul was playing piano or another guitar. The band was, somehow, as a rock and roll band, more complete."

In a rock 'n' roll band, the rhythm is driven by the drums and bass guitar working closely together, so the opinion of The Beatles' drummer, Pete Best, is an important contribution to this debate. "Stu was a good bass player," Pete said. "I've read so many people putting him down for his bass playing. I'd like to set that one straight. His bass playing was a lot better than people give him credit for. He knew what his limits were. What he did was accept that and he gave 200%. He was the smallest Beatle with the biggest heart."

When The Beatles returned from Hamburg at the end of 1960, Stuart stayed with Astrid in Germany. This meant that, for the Christmas period, the group needed a bass player. They recruited Chas Newby, Pete's former band mate, for the job. Once Chas left, it became Paul's responsibility. George made an interesting observation in a letter he wrote to Stuart: "Come home sooner, as if we get a new bass player for the time being, it will be crumby [sic] as he will have to learn everything. It's no good with Paul playing bass, we'd decided, that is, if he had some kind of bass to play on!"

After he'd left The Beatles, not long before his death, Stuart was asked to play with a German group, The Bats. He borrowed his old bass guitar from Klaus Voormann (who had recently purchased it from Stuart) and played with The Bats at the Hamburg Art School Carnival and the Kaiserkeller.

Stuart's copy of the photograph taken in Harold's Bar in Hamburg on 28 September 1960.

German group The Bats, with whom Stuart played in 1962.

Stuart wrote the names of The Beatles and their friend, Helmut.

The Fab one hundred and Four

Over the years, Paul McCartney has been routinely accused of wanting Stuart out of the group because he was not a good bass player, but this simply was not the case. In 1964, Paul said in a *Beat Instrumental* interview: "Not that I'm suggesting that every bass player should learn on an ordinary guitar. Stuart Sutcliffe certainly did not, and he was a great bass man." Paul has admitted being hard on Stuart, but this was part jealousy over his relationship with John as well as his reputation as a perfectionist who argued with most of The Beatles during their time.

So was Paul responsible for Stuart leaving? He has certainly been blamed by many fans. While it's known that they fought on stage, Stu was not dismissed by The Beatles, even if he was eased out. The final decision was Stuart's alone. "Stuart played with The Beatles," explained Astrid, "because John has persuaded him, but Stuart's heart was set on painting. He really enjoyed posing on stage, but he did not practise at all, which made Paul very angry. 'It doesn't matter, he looks good', was John's response."

Klaus Voormann confirmed the circumstances of Stuart's exit from The Beatles: "Stuart really decided to stop playing in the band. He was not

Letter from Stuart explaining about his time in Hamburg, and how they were locked up in the cells.

thrown out of the band. He said, 'I don't want to do it anymore. I want to study art.' And that was it." Stuart sold his bass to Klaus, who wanted to join The Beatles, but by that time McCartney had already been pegged as Stu's replacement.

Still, Stuart was not finished with music and, in March 1962 joined The Bats. The group arose from the music scene in Hamburg-Bramfeld in the early 1960s. Towards the end of the 1950s, skiffle groups evolved into amateur rock 'n' roll groups in Hamburg. An Indonesian by birth, Peter Bosch (a.k.a. Pit Kooy) came to Hamburg in 1947 when he still was a young boy. He grew up in Bramfeld where he played bass for Long Erwin and His House Rockers. From spring to autumn 1962, The Bats had their first month-long engagements in Berlin where they appeared in various clubs.

Along with Bosch, the group consisted of two brothers, Rudiger (guitar) and Volker (bass) Neber, and the black drummer Tony Cavanaugh, who came from Tony Sheridan's group of musicians. To distinguish him from the other Tony, the people of St. Pauli called him "Neger-Tony" ("Black Tony").

The Bats became a great success in Berlin. "When we had our last gig at the Grüne Hölle on the Potsdamer Strasse," recalled Bosch, "the whole place was decorated with little black paper bats. The guests and us lay in each other's arms to say goodbye."

In Frankfurt, their next stop, the group fell apart. Rudiger and Bosch joined the Hurricanes from the Netherlands for a short while, playing with them in Heilbronn. Tony Cavanaugh went back to his friends and played the drums for Sheridan's Beat Brothers/Star Combo. Still, The Bats persevered. Volker Neber switched from guitar to drums and guitarist Waldemar Kropp joined the group. Until bass player Helmut Hackbart appeared, they worked with guitarist Colin Crowley, who was also known as Colin Melander, from the Beat Brothers. Occasionally, ex-Beatle Stuart Sutcliffe, who was now living in Hamburg, joined in.

The Bats knew The Beatles from their time at the Kaiserkeller. "They were pretty average musicians," recalled Bosch, "but they were all good singers. For example, Paul McCartney, whenever he did his Little Richard act, you really thought it was Little Richard standing there. John was more of a Chuck Berry, and George did Eddie Cochran quite well".

Stuart, Paul, George, John and Pete at the Top Ten Club, 1961.

The Bats learned quite early to pay attention to their image, which set them apart from most of the other German bands. Like The Silver Beetles did for their tour of Scotland, Volker and his friends chose stage names for themselves. Waldemar Kropp called himself "Croppy Dean" and Barthold Dunker was "Jerry Lion", most probably hinting at the name Jerry Lee Lewis. Helmut Hackbart called himself "Robby Casino" and Neber chose "Rodger Star", a name that seemed to allude to Ringo. Peter Bosch became "Pit Kooy". They soon gave up those stage names, but kept their spectacular stage clothing, consisting of Dracula-like capes that resembled bat wings.

Manfred Weissleder, who had opened the famous Star Club in April 1962, became the manager of The Bats, a position he assumed from 1 December 1963 to 31 March 1964. Weissleder managed to get them a gig at the Ostseehalle in Kiel as the only German band playing with the Roadrunners, Kingsize Taylor and the Dominoes, Fats and His Cats, and Tony Sheridan and the Tornados. Weissleder intended to send The Bats on the Star Club tour to Liverpool together with the Giants, the Phantom Brothers and the German Bonds, but it was cancelled.

Now comprised of four musicians, The Bats continued making music on a semi-professional basis. Although they appeared regularly on stage after the split with Weissleder and made records under the supervision of the famous Polydor producer Paul Murphy, The Bats never made it to the top.

The Fab one hundred and Four

By the end of July 1961, Stu had sold his bass guitar to Klaus Voormann and his music career was over. He had already enrolled in Eduardo Paolozzi's art class on 31 May 1961. His last brief stint with The Bats took place only a couple of weeks before his premature death on 10 April 1962.

Rod Murray

One of those who knew Stuart Sutcliffe well, and was almost a Beatle, was Rod Murray, a friend from the Liverpool Art College.

Rodney Christopher Guy Murray was educated by the Christian Brothers at St. Edwards College in West Derby, though when he contracted tuberculosis, missed three years of schooling. "While in the hospital," Rod recalled, "I learned to play cards, gamble, and play snooker, so all of life's important lessons. When I returned to school, the only way I could study art was in my free time because I was studying the sciences. I always enjoyed art so, in September 1956, having been interviewed by Arthur Ballard, I stood in line with Stuart to sign up for a two-year Intermediate Certificate in Art and Craft. We were put into the same class and quickly became friends."

There was quite a structure to the week at the Art College, with several different classes. "They took us from the very basics," said Rod, "like learning to mix and make our own colours, and the properties of working with canvasses and paper. We studied topics like life drawing and anatomy, structure in nature, perspective drawing, the basics of sculpture and modelling, plus weekly composition exercises in drawing and painting set either in the area close to college or in the local parks and docks. Arthur Ballard, our tutor, would then critique our work, before inviting us to Ye Cracke for a drink.

Rod continued: "The Art College itself was a superb building where we had massive open rooms with lots of natural light coming in. This made it perfect for the art students. One day for a laugh, Stuart, me and June Furlong, our life model, decided to play a trick on the teacher, so we climbed inside a little cupboard to the side of the room, with the idea of jumping out and surprising everyone. Well, we got ourselves in there, but the teacher who came in was a bit of a stickler, so we did not think he would appreciate it. We decided to wait until he had left, and then make our exit. Unfortunately, he stayed for over an

Rod Murray with June Furlong, former life model at the Art College.

hour, so we were stuck in there until he had gone. We couldn't exactly walk out in the middle of the lesson, so that sort of backfired badly.

"We were friendly with a number of the tutors from the Art College," Rod remembered, "and we helped one of them, Austin Davies, to move a really heavy printing press from his flat in Catherine Street to 22, Huskisson Street, where he and his wife Beryl had taken the ground floor and first floor apartments. We were then, with most of the tutors from the Art College, invited to the house warming party, where John, Paul, George and Stuart provided the music.

"We frequented many of the local pubs, but Ye Cracke was our home base really. We were thrown out of the Belvedere, but were okay in most of the others. We then started to go the new Jacaranda Club that Allan Williams had opened in Slater Street, as a lot of the tutors and students from the Art College were going there. Allan asked us to paint the walls downstairs, and a few of us were involved. I know that I painted the shutters by the window, and maybe a few other bits, but the main murals and paintings were done by Stuart and Rod Jones. I don't remember John being involved in that process.

"We did a lot of events for the Student's Union," according to Rod, "where there was always one of us on the committee. Stu and Bill Har-

The Junior Art College on Hope Street.

ry were voted onto the committee in 1957-58, with Bill standing again in 1958-59, and then Rod Jones and me in 1959-60. That's because we needed the cloakroom concessions and benefits for the parties that we held. With the cloakroom, you did not get paid, but kept all of the proceeds from looking after the coats. The group of John, Paul, George and Stuart used to play at the Saturday dances and, as a committee, the Student's Union purchased the amplifier that they used, which was on permanent loan!"

Within a short time, Stu and Rod decided that they should find a flat to-gether, near the Art College. At the beginning of 1957, they rented their first flat at 83, Canning Street. "There's a story to that flat," Rod laughs. "We would only stay there occasionally because when you went down those steps into the basement flat, there were only a couple of rooms. We had set up the little back room with easels from the Art College. We had enough room for a few parties, but we had to keep it quiet so that the landlady couldn't hear us. However, one day, we walked down the steps to the flat and were in the front room, when we were suddenly aware of some noise coming from the back room. We opened

The *Fab* one hundred and *Four*

the door, and there was an Irish family who had moved in. When we asked the landlady what was going on, she told us that as we did not really use the back room, she had let it out to another family!"

This did not appear to be a fair arrangement, so they decided to look elsewhere. "Stuart wrote to me to tell me that he had taken a flat at 12, Canning Street," Rod recalled, "but it was awkward because it was right at the top of the building, in the roof. We constantly had to sneak me in and out of there, because it was only in Stuart's name, and paying for one person, but we shared it. We had to hide from the landlady. I was the invisible tenant. Thankfully, she never worked it out, and only ever thought there was one of us staying there. From there, we could visit the Rialto on the corner of Princes Road, which had a great cinema showing foreign films, which we loved. We would travel to the best cinemas to watch these foreign-language art films, like going across the Mersey to the Continental in Wallasey. And just down Berkley Street, along from the Rialto, was the little Chinese laundry we used. We would take our bag of washing, knock on the door, and then walk into the little entrance hall. There was a plank of wood across it, where you rang the bell, and then waited for this little Chinese woman to come out. We handed her the bag, she tagged everything and then we called back later when it was done.

The Art College (top left) and Gambier Terrace (bottom right).

22, Huskisson Street, where The Silver Beetles played at a house warming party.

"We weren't as unclean as some people thought," Rod said. "One of our biggest problems was getting a hot shower. The facilities in the flat were no good, and nor were the ones in the Art College, which only had cold water. What we would do is walk down to the University of Liverpool Student Union Building and just walk in with our towels and head for their hot showers."

The steps down to the basement flat at 83, Canning Street.

Ye Cracke, where Stuart, Rod, John and Bill Harry met with their friends from the Art College.

9, Percy Street, where Stuart and Rod moved into a flat.

The attic flat at 12, Canning Street.

The boys once again found themselves in need of accommodations more suited to their student lives, which required space for painting and entertaining.

We moved into Percy Street in the autumn of 1958," Rod recalled. "We painted the furniture in black and white stripes, which Mrs. Plant later sent round to Gambier Terrace for us to clean. We took a disliking to the downstairs tenants and decided to vent our anger (and bladders) by opening the kitchen window and pissing on their motor scooter that was parked under it. However, the reason that they eventually moved out arose because the girlfriend of the student on our floor used to sit on the kitchen sink to pee because the loo was so disgusting. Can't blame her, as nobody wanted to clean it. The sink cracked and developed a leak that formed a pool on the floor. The only answer seemed to be to make a hole in the floor and pass the 'water' on to our favourite ground floor tenants. As we did not have a drill we made use of the new fireplace to heat up a poker to burn a hole in the floorboard under the sink. When they moved out, we went down to view the flat and found the kitchen ceiling festooned with green slime.

"By this time, Stu was up painting most of the night and I would get no sleep or Stu would have a girl over and I would get lost to the pub or Rod Jones' flat, or I would have somebody back and Stu would go out.

The Fab one hundred and Four

This worked for a while until John Lennon started to come to the flat regularly to listen to records or just talk. Stu would read a lot, so with Bill Harry and Rod Jones also there, we would get into arty discussions.

Paul and George had started to come round with John for the occasional jam sessions, and John mentioned that the latest thing was to have a bass guitar, so they asked Stuart and me if either of us wanted to buy a bass guitar and join the group. As neither of us had any money, I decided that I would start to make one. One of the modules you could do at the college was Interior Design and Cabinet Making, so as I had always enjoyed making things, I did that lesson. Bill Bateson, the tutor, taught me all the important tips on how to use the tools, so I had access to the saws and sanding machines, and set about cutting out and making the bass guitar."

As history played out, it was Stuart who became the bass guitarist for the group because of the sale of the painting he entered into the John Moores Exhibition at the Walker Art Gallery. Rod explained how it happened: "The John Moores Exhibition started in 1958, and it was for the second exhibition in 1959 that Stuart and I entered. John Moores, a

Artwork in The Jacaranda, leading down to the cellar where the groups performed.

The remnant of Stuart's painting in The Jacaranda.

Re-creation of the original artwork in The Jacaranda cellar.

Stuart's painting that was purchased by John Moores.

member of the wealthy Moores family who ran the Littlewoods business, was always interested in art. William Stevenson, the Principal of the Art College, used to visit his house, at Moores' invitation, to teach him how to paint. Moores also set up a scholarship for the Art College and was a great benefactor.

"To enter the competition, we had to go down to Jackson's in Slater Street, who was the agent, and pay to take part. It was open to everybody, so it was not just the Art College students, and it included sculpture as well as painting. We went down, filled the forms in, and then had to take the paintings down to the Walker Art Gallery. Stuart's was in two parts, so we went down with the first half of his, plus my entry. Unfortunately, we dropped in at Ye Cracke for a drink, and never took the other half down. I think it just lay in the back yard until it rotted and fell apart. We then got the news that mine was rejected and Stuart's had been accepted.

"Of course, not only did I not get my painting into the John Moores exhibition, I did not get to finish my guitar and join The Beatles because Stuart's painting was purchased by John Moores, which gave him the money to buy the bass. I couldn't have done much musically anyway because I'd been sent for piano lessons when I was young and could only concentrate on what one hand was doing. I never pursued a career in music, or even learned to play." Rod's career with The Beatles was so near, and yet so far.

Rod added: "Early in 1960, I purchased a tape recorder from Lewis', and it was on HP, which meant that I needed a guarantor. I stepped outside the store, filled in Arthur Ballard's details and forged his signature. All was fine, until I forgot to pay the installment one month. Arthur came up to me in college, pinned me up against the wall and told me that he had been contacted as the guarantor! Stu, Rod Jones and I held an emergency Student's Union meeting and voted that the Union purchase the tape recorder." What a wonderful thing democracy is! Rod made good use of it and enjoyed recording the lads rehearsing in Percy Street. "How I wished I had saved those tapes," Rod mused.

"The mystery of the burning furniture has been told in many ways, with different versions circulating about what was burned and where it was burned. Rod wanted to put the record straight: "The burning of the furniture took place at 9, Percy Street, not at Gambier Terrace. Our

Art lesson in Sefton Park, with A.K. Wiffen, Lyn Cheetham, Chris Jones, Brian Nicholson, Stuart Sutcliffe, an unknown student, Rod Murray, Alan Waddington, Dot Jones and Brenda Powell.

Rod Murray with the bass guitar he started to make to join the group.

Percy Street flat was a funny place. We had two doors upstairs, which meant that if we heard Mrs. Plant, our landlady, coming up the stairs for the rent, we locked one of the doors from the inside, and then hid quietly so she couldn't hear us. We would then go down to her flat later and pay the rent. We never let her come into the flat, for several reasons.

"One of the first things we did was to remove the fireplace, which made a great improvement to the room. We were doing room makeovers long before they were on television! It was like one of those old war films where we were walking out of the house with bits of the fireplace hidden in our coats for us to dispose of it elsewhere. We would then have to sneak coal back in to keep the other fireplace warm. There was a lovely lady, Molly, who was one of the cleaners at the Art College, and she had taken a shine to Stuart and me, so, as the college was heated by a coal boiler, she would leave the door open by the stores, with a cardboard box, and we would fill it with coal and head back to the flat. Otherwise, the only way to get coal was to walk to the coal-yard in Falkner Square and buy a quarter of fuel.

"When we couldn't get the coal, we searched for wood to burn. Some people seem to be under the misapprehension that we took the furniture from our rooms and burned that. What we actually did was to go down to the basement, where we found old bits of broken furniture lying around. It was dark, and why would somebody leave pieces of

Stuart and his friends in the art room above the lecture theatre. Chris Jones, Tiba, Brian Nicholson (at the back), Stuart Sutcliffe, "Diz" Morris, Rod Murray, Dot Jones with Meg Rimmer (seated) at the front.

The friends from Art College. Back row: Brenda Powell, Chris Jones, Alan Waddington. Middle row: unknown/Brian Nicholson, "Diz" Morris, Ann, Fay, Dot Jones. Front row: Rod Murray, Stuart Sutcliffe, Lyn Cheetham.

antique furniture lying around? We just saw it as recycling, and used those broken bits for firewood. One of the other tenants had decided that, because there were no wooden door frames, he would take a few of the bricks from the doorways so that he could put his car up on bricks over the winter. We thought that was a great idea and used some of the other bricks to brick up the fireplace."

Mrs. Plant was obviously not aware of what they were doing, and the lads seemed to spend a lot of time trying to avoid her. "If somebody heard her," said Rod, "we could also run up to the top flat where, at the top of the stairs, was a cupboard. At the back of the cupboard was a trapdoor which led through to the next-door flat. That flat in 11, Percy Street was occupied by our Art College friend Stan Iverson, so we would knock on the trapdoor and make sure it was okay to come

The art room on the top floor of the Art College. The room had almost floor to ceiling windows. The curved wall was built to demonstrate mosaic work.

Stuart by the fireplace in 9, Percy Street, with his painting on the wall.

On the way to Wales from Stratford, Stu decided to climb a monument in New Radnor, Powys, dedicated to Sir George Cornewall Lewis.

Stuart by the car with his friends "Diz" (Margaret Morris) and "Ducky" (Margaret Duxbury).

Gambier Terrace in 1942.

through. Then we would sit in his flat until Mrs. Plant had gone. Stan once climbed out onto the balcony and chiselled a face into the brickwork, which I have seen attributed to John Lennon in some places – but then, what hasn't?"

"After we had been thrown out of Percy Street in early 1960, I managed to get us a new place at Flat 3, Hillary Mansions, in Gambier Terrace on Hope Street, which was rented in my name this time. We paid just over £3 10 pence per week. We had the whole of the first floor, with Stuart and John in the back room and studio," said Rod, "and I had one of the front rooms. I managed to persuade our friends "Diz" and "Ducky" to move from their flat and take the other front room.

The rear of the Gambier Terrace flat.

"I remember one episode where we had acquired a gas stove. I'm not sure if we had bought it or not. Anyway, we weren't using it, so Sam Welsh, who lived in the bottom flat, decided he needed a cooker. We took it apart in the flat and opened the window. Sam had gone downstairs and put a bed mattress below the window. We dropped the cooker, and it bounced! It fell apart as we looked on, but somehow Sam managed to put it back together again. He then spotted a gas draining pipe in the basement, so he hooked up a hose and had free gas supplied!

"As it was such a big flat, The Beatles used to practise here, which was fine for most of the time, because they weren't disturbing anyone. However, after one particularly loud rehearsal, the downstairs tenants complained to the agents, and we were asked to explain the noise. We told them we were 'repairing loose floorboards' which took a long time. "Ducky" soon moved out, but "Diz" moved in with me, and her place was given to Rod Jones, another friend from the college."

In May 1960, Stuart headed off with The Silver Beetles on the Scottish tour with Johnny Gentle, followed by the August trip to Hamburg that would change his life. He wrote an interesting letter from Hamburg to

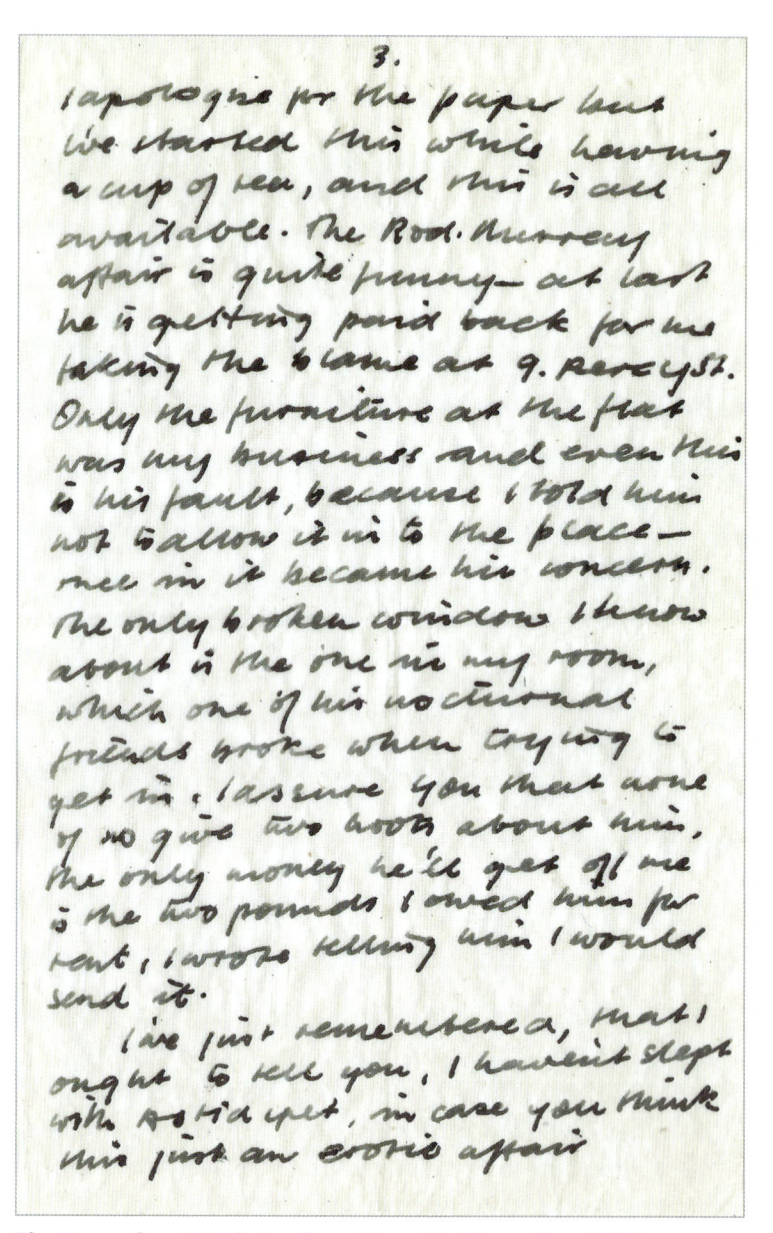

The November 1960 letter from Stuart to his mother, Millie.

his mother in Liverpool, which mentions Rod, so I showed it to him and asked him what he remembered. Stuart wrote:

"The Rod Murray affair is quite funny – at last he is getting paid back for me taking the blame at 9, Percy Street. Only the furniture at the flat was my business and even then this is his fault, because I told him not

Stuart's I.D. card for the art school in Hamburg.

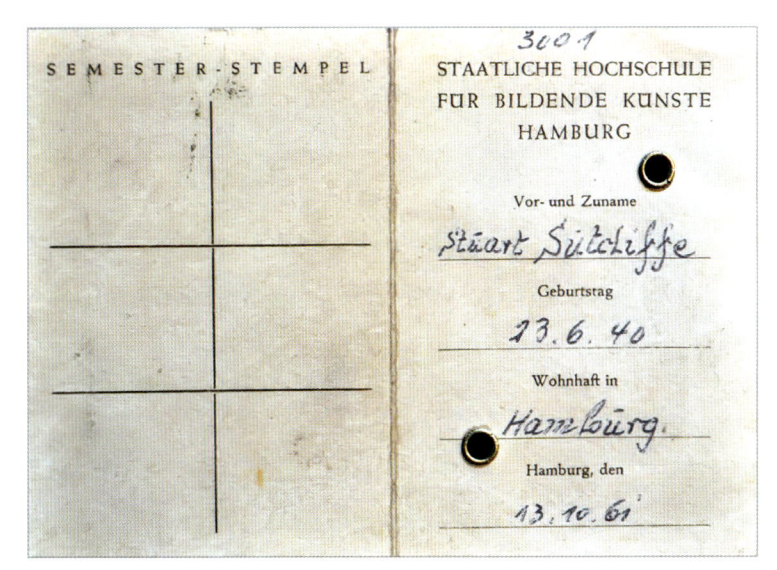

Back of Stuart's I.D. card.

Stuart in his studio in Hamburg.

to allow it in to the place – once in it became his concern. The only broken window I know about is the one in my room, which one of his nocturnal friends broke when trying to get in. The only money he'll get off me is the two pounds I owed him for rent. I wrote telling him I would send it."

"When I saw that letter, I was bemused by what Stuart had written to his mother, because there was never any animosity," said Rod. "I think it is probably Stuart trying to tell his mother not to blame him because it was my fault, which would make sense, because that is what I told my mother! I definitely don't remember any broken window, and I can only assume he is talking about the furniture that Mrs. Plant sent round to us to clean."

Stuart's life could have been quite different, because he did not want to stay in Hamburg. Rod explains about a career change Stuart was looking to make after leaving The Beatles: "Stuart was talking about coming back to Liverpool to do his ATD, the Art Teaching Diploma. When he visited Liverpool with Astrid, they stayed with Allan Williams in his flat in Huskisson Street, and Stuart made his application to come back to the Art College. Unfortunately, they blanked him, because he had walked out on his college work to go to Hamburg. Stuart's mother tried everything to get them to change their minds, but as they were a separate, autonomous body, not even the intervention of Arthur Ballard, the tutor who gave us both so much support, could change their minds. Stuart was quite upset about it, because it was something he really wanted to do.

"He had to go back to Hamburg and was accepted onto the course taught by Eduardo Paolozzi, who recognised the talent that Stuart had. Many years later, I went to work for the Royal College of Art, and one of the first people I was introduced to was Eduardo. The first thing I said to him was, 'you taught a friend of mine.' He remembered Stuart well, and thought very highly of him. Paolozzi was a really nice man, and at his 70th birthday party, he gave me one of his paintings. It is amazing how life goes in circles.

"Stuart did some great work for Paolozzi, but of course he fell ill and died so suddenly. He was going to be the best man at my wedding. When he died, his father was the other side of the world with his ship, so in lieu of Stuart and Charles, I walked Stuart's sister Joyce down the

"The Cronies", a painting by Stuart that he sold to Rod.

aisle and gave her away at her wedding, which was a great honour.

"It came as a great shock when the message came through that Stuart had died. He was, to me, family and friend in one. He had a rare talent and a potential to be a major artist."

Rod concluded: "I still have a few pieces of Stuart's art, like the painting "The Cronies", for which I gave him ten bob (50 pence). I have some of his cartoons, and even some of the script we put together for the pantomime we wrote, based on *Cinderella*, which involved Stuart as Fairy Snow, John Lennon and Jeff Mohammed as the Ugly Sisters, and me as Dandini. It was nonsense verse like you would find in John's *Daily Howl* paper. It was a great time of my life."

Rod went on to have a career, which involved working at the Liverpool College of Art, as well as with the Royal Academy and Imperial College, London. His love of science and art resulted in him developing the art of holography, creating art with lasers and images to make holograms.

JANUARY 1960

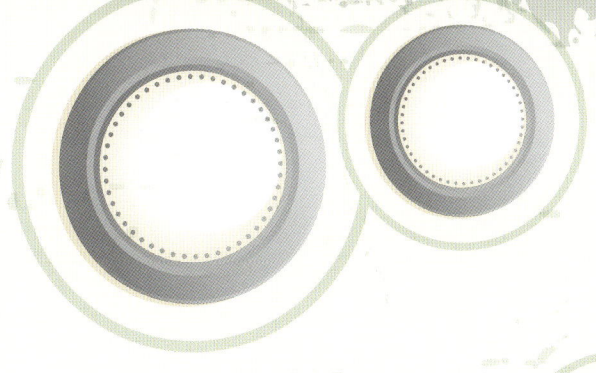

The Beatals

In January 1960, after their brief flirtation with the names Johnny and the Moondogs and The College Band, the group became The Beatals. The evidence was found in a letter that Stuart wrote, citing himself as manager.

There have been different theories about who gave the group its name. In July 1961, John wrote a piece for the *Mersey Beat* paper under the heading: "Being a Short Diversion on the Origins of Beatles". Lennon claimed that "It came in a vision – a man appeared on a Flaming Pie and said unto them 'From this day on you are Beatles with an A'. 'Thank you, Mister Man,' they said, thanking him".

It was a wonderful piece of prose from Lennon, but Beat Poet Royston Ellis claimed to have been the inspiration. The origin of the name was from Stuart's suggestion, in honour of Buddy Holly and The Crickets. It's an insect thing: crickets and beetles. Interestingly, Niki Sullivan, a member of Buddy Holly's Crickets, told in his autobiography how they were inspired by The Spiders, one of Buddy's favourite groups. However, they also considered another name. "We were at Jerry's house, and everything we thought of had been used or did not fit. So Jerry got an encyclopedia, and somehow we got started on insects. There was a whole page of bugs. We thought about grasshopper and quickly passed over that. And we did consider the name Beetles, but Jerry said, 'Aw, that's just a bug you'd want to step on,' so we immediately dropped that. Then Jerry came up with the idea of The Crickets."

One often quoted myth can be debunked. The name was not inspired by the 1953 Marlon Brando film *The Wild One*, which refers to the rival gang led by Lee Marvin as "The Beetles". It was banned in England by the British Board of Film Censors until 1968.

Bill Harry can testify to the fact that it was Stuart who came up with the name, as he was with John and Stu in their flat at Gambier Terrace when he suggested it. John then took delight in changing the second "e" to an "a" for the play on beat music. That was it. However, they initially spelled the name "Beatals". When "Silver" was added, they used it in combination with both "Beetles" and "Beatles" until settling on "The Silver Beatles" and, finally, "The Beatles". If they'd only known that The Crickets, their inspiration for the name Beetles had originally considered using the name they had decided upon.

John, Paul, George, Stuart and Mike

At this point, an interesting temporary addition to the lineup was Mike McCartney, Paul's younger brother. He has intimated that he drummed for both The Quarrymen and for The Beatles. Mike with The Quarrymen? Apparently so. There is a photo of Mike playing The Quarrymen drum kit.

The Fab one hundred and Four

Clientelle

Dear Sir, As it is your policy to present entertainment to the habitues of your establishment, I would like to draw your attention to a band to the "Beatals". This is a promising group of young musicians who play all music for all tastes, preferably rock and roll. They have won many competitions, including Carroll Levis' and auditions for A.T.V. Unfortunately pedagogical activities have hindered them from devoting themselves full time to the world of entertainment.

If necessary the group is prepared for an audition, I hope you will be able to engage them.

Yours sincerely,
STU Sutcliffe (Manager).

Letter written by Stuart, trying to secure bookings for "The Beatals".

However, Colin Hanton doesn't remember Mike being involved with The Quarrymen at all – at least while he was with them. Colin had joined The Quarrymen months before John and Paul met in July 1957. Also, while at scout camp, Mike had broken his arm in several places, also damaging the nerves. This had required a hospital stay of several weeks, followed by months of physiotherapy. By his own admission, any hope of playing drums had vanished. Colin and Mike have conversed on the subject and they have agreed that most likely Mike stood in as drummer for The Beatals on a couple of occasions in April 1960.

Autographs obtained in Scotland in May 1960, showing their pseudonyms, and the group name "Beatals".

23 APRIL 1960

The Nerk Twins – John Lennon and Paul McCartney

The Fox and Hounds pub in Caversham, Berkshire was the venue for an unlikely pairing of two of The Beatles. John and Paul played on consecutive nights at this little village pub as The Nerk Twins, to only a handful of people. So how did they end up in the south of England in a tiny village pub?

They were in the Fox and Hounds because it was run by Paul's cousin Bett and her husband Mike. The couple had both worked as Butlin's Redcoats before taking on the pub and the teenage Lennon and McCartney were keen to get their advice. The Nerk Twins perched themselves on bar stools and, with their acoustic guitars and no microphones, played a set of songs together.

"It was the Easter school holidays and John and I had hitchhiked down from Liverpool to help out in the pub," Paul recalled. "We generally dossed around for a week and worked behind the bar. Then Mike said that me and John should play there on the Saturday night. So we made our own posters and put them up in the pub: 'Saturday Night – Live Appearance – The Nerk Twins'. It was the smallest gig I've ever done. We were only playing to a small roomful."

They sang songs like the Les Paul and Mary Ford hit, "The World Is Waiting for the Sunrise", as well as "Be-Bop-A-Lula" plus other rock 'n' roll and country standards. They reprised the concert the following lunchtime to the same resounding apathy from the locals. "At first, nobody went into the tap room to watch them," recalled Mike Robbins, then landlord of the pub. "My regulars were in the other bar, saying 'Who are these Nerk Twins, then?'"

Although the gig seemed destined to be just a couple of lads with guitars singing to little reaction, Paul McCartney credits the pub session for teaching him and John a crucial lesson in developing the stage act that would soon send girls around the world into a frenzy. "My cousin used to tread the boards. He was a bit show-bizzy," Paul recalled. "He'd been an entertainments manager hosting talent contests at Butlin's and he'd been on the radio. He asked us what song we were going to open with and we said, 'Be-Bop-A-Lula'. He told us, 'No, it's too slow. This is a pub on a Saturday night. You need to open with something fast and instrumental. What else have you got?' We said, 'Well, we do 'The World Is Waiting for the Sunrise' – I played the melody and John did the rhythm – so we played him

The Fox and Hounds Pub, where The Nerk Twins played.

that and he said, 'Perfect, start with that, then do 'Be-Bop-A-Lula'.

"This was our introduction to showbiz wisdom here and I would remember his advice years later when we were organising The Beatles' shows," recalled Paul. However, the locals weren't inspired at all. "When Paul and John had gone," said Mike Robbins, "one of the locals said to me, 'When are you having them Nerk Twins on again, then? They were a load of bloody rubbish but they brought a bit of life into the pub.'"

Hitchhiking was not unusual for the lads, as Paul recalled years later: "John and I used to hitchhike places together. It was something that we did together quite a lot – cementing our friendship, getting to know our feelings, our dreams, our ambitions together. It was a very wonderful period. I look back on it with great fondness. I particularly remember John and I would be squeezed in our little single bed and Mike Robbins, who was a real nice guy, would come in late at night to say good night to us, switching off the lights as we were all going to bed. And I'd ask, 'Mike, what was it like when you were on with the Jones Boys?' – a group that I knew he'd appeared with because I'd got a cutting. And he'd say, 'Oh, it was really good...' and he'd tell stories of showbiz. He was the only person we had to give us any information. I think for John and I, our show-business dreams were formed by this guy and his wife. Mike Robbins has an awful lot to answer for!"

The pair performed for the second and last time on Sunday during the pub's busy lunchtime period, between 12 and 2pm. Afterwards, Lennon and McCartney hitchhiked back to Liverpool, never to be Nerk Twins again. If Paul hadn't admitted in later years that "Two of Us" was about him and Linda, it would makes you wonder if the song was about days like these.

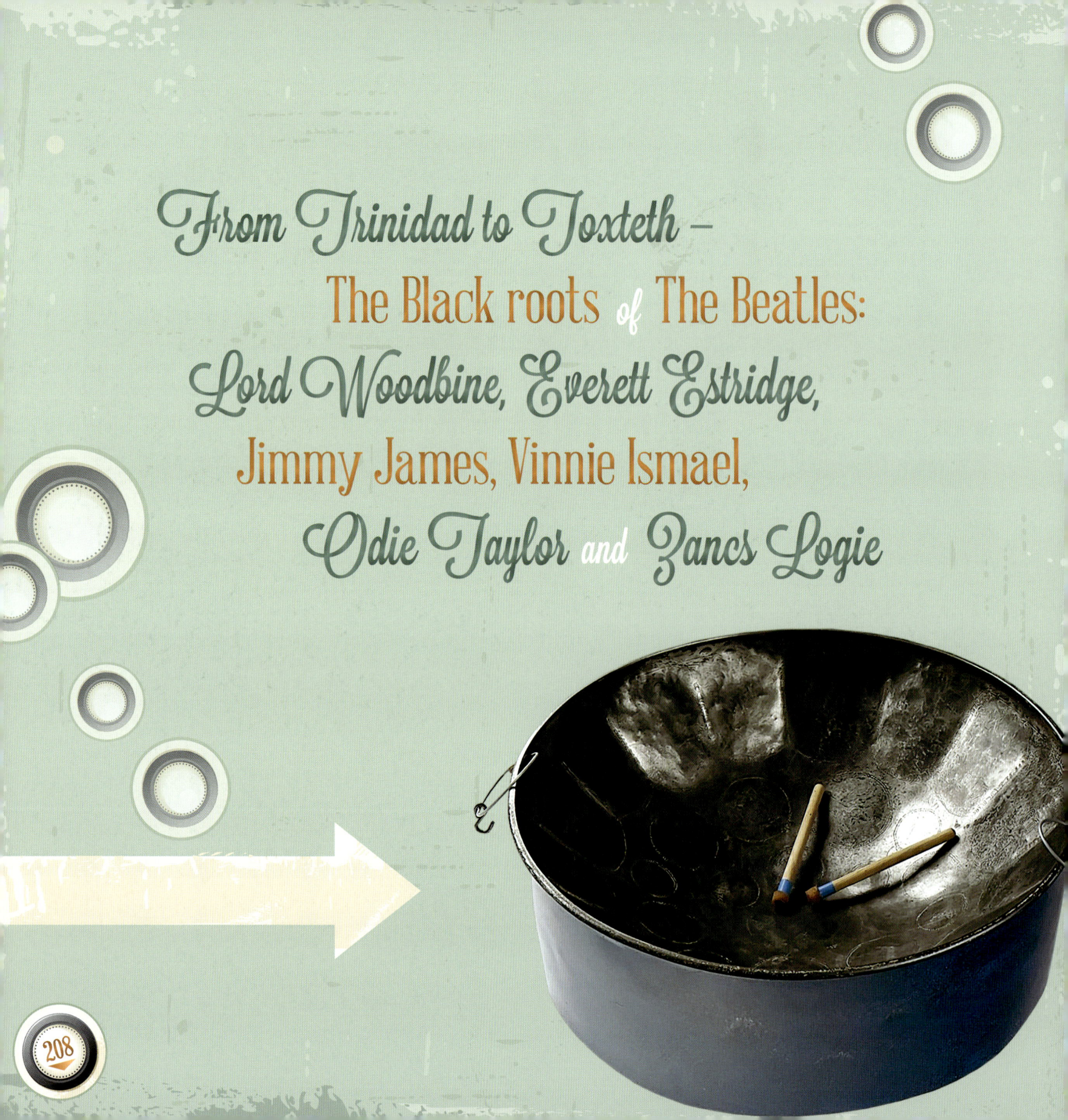

From Trinidad to Toxteth –
The Black roots of The Beatles:
Lord Woodbine, Everett Estridge,
Jimmy James, Vinnie Ismael,
Odie Taylor and Zancs Logie

Fitzroy "Jimmy" James in The Jacaranda.

The Jacaranda Club, pictured in the 1980s.

The story of the influence of Liverpool's black population on The Beatles is one that hasn't often been told. But for those who lived in the area at the time, it's been common knowledge for years. John and Paul used to frequent the clubs in Toxteth which were primarily populated with members and musicians from the local black community, plus visiting sailors and American servicemen. Why were John and Paul there and what did they learn? Did their experiences have any influence on them, and why don't we know much about this portion of Beatles history?

One of the few Beatles authors to mention this period of their history is Bill Harry, who interviewed George Roberts, a band manager and witness to many of these events in Toxteth. Bill also wrote a chapter, "It Started in Toxteth", for his 2009 book, *Bigger Than The Beatles*, where he explained the importance of the black musicians and clubs in that district.

When Liverpool entrepreneur Allan Williams opened The Jacaranda Club (known as The Jac) in Slater Street, Liverpool in September 1958, he needed unique entertainment for his clientele. The club became a hangout for students and tutors from the Art College, and was also popular with nurses and professional businessmen. Alongside this more exclusive crowd were the pseudo-arty Lennon, McCartney, Harrison and Sutcliffe. Stuart and fellow art student Rod Murray had painted the murals on the wall of the downstairs club, so were there on merit as artists. John, Paul and George had added their own paintwork, though that was only in the toilets.

Allan was visiting a drinking club in Liverpool 8, Toxteth, where he saw the All Steel Caribbean Band (later the Royal Caribbean Steel Band) playing a style of music he'd never heard before. He was captivated, and knew that this was the band to establish The Jacaranda as one of the best clubs in Liverpool. "When I saw them," recalled Allan, "I immediately offered them a two-month contract, which lasted for ten years!"

This was the start of a part of The Beatles' musical education that is rarely talked about – that of the local black musicians and their music. Williams began a working partnership with a Trinidadian Calypso singer, Harold Phillips, better known as Lord "Woody" Woodbine. Together, in a time of racial segregation in Liverpool, Williams and Woodbine ran clubs in the Toxteth area that would influence Lennon and McCartney for years to come.

In 2008, McCartney recalled those times in *Mojo* magazine: "Liverpool, being the first Caribbean settlement in the UK, we were very friendly with a lot of black guys – Lord Woodbine, Derry Wilkie (lead singer with Derry and the Seniors), they were mates we hung out with." In 1980, Paul told interviewer Vic Garbarini: "*New Musical Express* was talking about calypso, and how Latin-rock was going to be the next big thing. The minute we stopped trying to find that new beat, the newspapers started saying it was us – and we found we'd discovered the new sound without ever trying." Where better to find it than in Liverpool.

Lord Woodbine

Lord Woodbine is a famous character in Beatles folklore, but his role in the early Beatles' history has often been either ignored or played down. Who was this enigmatic figure and what was his real role in the story of The Beatles?

Harold Phillips, better known as Lord Woodbine.

I spoke to Allan Williams about Lord Woodbine and asked him how they met. "I was in an afternoon drinking club in Liverpool 8, and Woody was singing Calypsos. He couldn't play anything more than the maracas, but he was a great singer and entertainer, and we became friends and business partners."

Together, they ran illegal drinking and strip clubs, called "shebeens", in the Toxteth area. Among these was the Cabaret Artists Social Club in Parliament Street, which was a strip club and drinking den in the basement of a house where The Silver Beatles had backed Janice the stripper. Williams operated from his flat at 58, Huskisson Street, just around the corner from John and Stuart's flat in Gambier Terrace. The flat also happened to be situated on the edge of Liverpool's red-light area and close to Upper Parliament Street, where many of the black clubs were located. Lord Woodbine, a daily visitor to Williams' flat, had another club in Berkley Street called The Colony Club. The Beatles played there in the afternoons.

Harold Adolphus Phillips was born on 15 January 1929 in Laventille, Trinidad and, lying about his age, he joined the Royal Air Force at the age of fourteen, training in Burtonwood, just a few miles outside Liverpool. He returned to Trinidad in 1947.

In Laventille, he began performing calypso on street corners, with his songs commenting on topical events. Phillips returned to England on the first voyage of the *Empire Windrush* in 1948. He was among the many Caribbean citizens on board hoping to start a new life in England. Two older Trinidadians on the voyage with him were also calypsonians: Egbert Moore, later known as Lord Beginner and Phillips' friend Aldwyn Roberts, who became known as Lord Kitchener. Lord Woodbine's sobriquet similarly marks his distinction as a calypsonian.

The moniker Lord Woodbine was not given because of his fondness for Woodbine cigarettes. "No, actually I did not smoke them," recalled Phillips. "The Woodbine came in when I was composing a song about different types of cigarettes. I sang about Woodbines and they changed my name to Lord Woodbine."

After staying with fellow Windrush migrants in Clapham Common's former air-raid shelters, Woodbine worked as a machinist at Shropshire's Wellington Industrial Hostel. He formed a band, The Cream of Trinidad, which became Lord Woodbine and His Trinidadians. The group was among the first calypsonians to tour England. At a talent show, he met a Liverpool jazz musician named Helen 'Ena' Agoro. Helen began accompanying the band on maracas and, after a short romance, she married Phillips in 1949.

It was through this marriage that Phillips made Liverpool his home, and the couple went on to have eight children. To provide for his growing family, he took on a number of jobs, including railway engi-

Allan Williams' flat at 58, Huskisson Street.

Berkley Street in 1962, the former site of the New Colony Club.

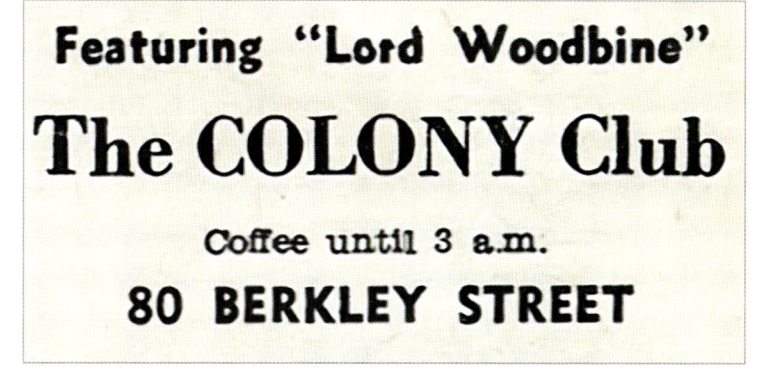

Lord Woodbine's advertisement in *Mersey Beat* for his Colony Club.

The Fab one hundred and Four

neer, carpenter, decorator, gardener, builder, electrician and lorry driver. In the evenings, he sang calypso and played guitar in local clubs.

Woodbine, also known as 'Woody', opened a Liverpool drinking venue on Berkley Street called The Colony Club. In 1958, the pannists took up nightly residence at The Jacaranda Coffee Bar, opened by Allan Williams. A witness to the scene in The Jacaranda, Candy Smith, noticed two white boys in the audience who were always hanging around with Lord Woodbine. She wouldn't have known their names: John Lennon and Paul McCartney. "Where are they coming from, always trying to horn in on the black scene?" she wanted to know. What were they doing and why were they always there? Smith remembered quite clearly. "They would be standing by the stage while the steel band was playing, overwhelmed by the music. Then they'd jump up to a pan player and say, 'Hey, giz a go with that', and promptly join the steel band on stage."

Woodbine had first noticed Lennon and McCartney paying close attention to the steel band at the Joker's Club in Edge Lane, Liverpool, back in 1958. They'd followed him and the music around the clubs in Toxteth, which were mainly frequented by the local black population of the area. But it was during Woodbine's tenure at The Jacaranda when their close friendship began. It's been noted that Woodbine was the first singer/songwriter that they'd encountered and he became a mentor to them. As George Harrison and Stuart Sutcliffe joined them at The Jacaranda, Woodbine became even more of an influence on the group. "I made them get a drummer when they played in my club," he recalled. "Before then, Paul sometimes used to be a drummer. Usually they just came without one."

In an interview with journalist Tony Henry, Woodbine did not claim to have spotted a unique talent, or know they were going to be superstars. "They were just boys wanting to play music," he observed, "living off their dole money which they pooled. John Lennon did all the singing. As a singer myself, I did not think he sounded that good then."

Herbie Higgins was a local musician who used to pay John and Paul to wash his car. He had noticed that his car washers were spending a lot of time with their new friend. "For months and months, they were there with Woodbine," he remembered. "They seemed to live in that place with his band." Higgins, who died in 2011, last saw McCartney in

At the Arnhem War Memorial in Oosterbeek, Holland (from left to right): Allan Williams, Beryl Williams, Lord Woodbine, Stuart, Paul, George and Pete.

1997 when Paul received his knighthood. Higgins was being awarded an MBE. The first question Paul asked him was, "How's my old friend Lord Woodbine? Have you seen him lately?"

For many of the musicians and residents of the Toxteth area, the feeling has always been the same: "Lord Woodbine was behind The Beatles", and they were often referred to as 'Woody's boys'. Is this justified or just wishful thinking? The evidence is clear from those who were there that the influence of Lord Woodbine and the black musicians in the clubs around Parliament Street in Liverpool 8 had a profound and lasting effect on Lennon and McCartney. The two young musicians studied the steel bands and wanted to learn their rhythm and style. John was observed to have picked up his guitar and jammed with Woodbine's steel band, and, when they were supposedly tidying up The Jac, John and Paul would have a quick go on the steel pans.

Woodbine was about to contribute another significant part in Beatles folklore. Working in partnership with Allan Williams, Woodbine promoted The Silver Beatles and helped them get some bookings around Liverpool. However, when some of the steel pannists from the Royal Caribbean Steel Band left for Hamburg, one of the members, Gerry Gobin, immediately made an interesting observation to Woodbine back in Liverpool. "Hamburg has this fab scene," Gerry told Woodbine. "You can play the clubs every night. Come on over, there's money to be made."

It was clear to Woodbine what he should do next. He explained: "I said to Allan, 'Let's go and have a look, there's nothing to lose.'" The two men boarded a plane to Amsterdam and, after a train ride, arrived in Hamburg with only £22.00 in their pockets. Then Williams suddenly turned up with 500 German Marks. "When I asked him about it," recalled Woodbine, "he said he'd found it in the club after everybody else had left." Woodbine said that Williams wanted to blow it on a night out, but he had different ideas. "No!" Woodbine told him. "Let's use it to bring over The Beatles. I knew they'd be ready for this. If it hadn't been for some German dropping his money in that club, The Beatles would never have gone to Hamburg. That was the start of The Beatles."

Derry and the Seniors, featuring the black singer Derry Wilkie, was the first of the Liverpool bands to go to Hamburg, closely followed by The Beatles. Williams and Woodbine drove their group across England and took the ferry to the Hook of Holland. Then, outside the Dutch city of Arnhem in the war cemetery at Oosterbeek, the group recorded their visit with a now-famous photograph. Woodbine, Williams and Williams' wife Beryl Chang posed at the war memorial with Paul, George, Stuart and their new drummer Pete Best for a photo taken by Beryl's brother Barry Chang. John stayed in the van, dumbstruck by the view of hundreds of graves. The prophetic words on the memorial simply stated: "Their Name Liveth For Evermore".

Now driving the van, Woodbine had a scare outside Hamburg when the wheels became stuck in the tramlines on the road. "As I looked up," recalled Woodbine, "this tram was approaching, very fast, bell dinging, and it just was not slowing down. Everyone was screaming, "Woodbine, Woodbine! Get us out! All I could think about was my family back home and these poor boys who shouldn't really have been here but for me. By rights, we should really all have died that day." Mercifully, the tram moved onto a parallel track and whooshed by the terrified passengers in the van.

On that first night in Hamburg, it was Lord Woodbine who climbed onto The Indra stage first, performing a few calypso numbers before the newly-named Beatles came on to make their German debut. Williams and Woodbine had taken The Beatles to Hamburg and set them up in the club, but when the band later negotiated a new contract at the Kaiserkeller, they cut Williams and Woodbine out of the deal and refused to pay them their commission. Although it was only £14, Williams did not pursue them. He did threaten to never let them play again in Liverpool, but it did little good. The Beatles went on to greater things. Williams' and Woodbine's role in The Beatles' story was over.

Did The Beatles remember them? In a later interview, when playing the drums, Paul McCartney made an interesting observation. "This reminds me of my Lord Woodbine days," making one of the few references to 'Woody' by any of the band. Woodbine has largely been erased from Beatles' history, something that obviously disappointed him. "I was portrayed as some dumb black man with nothing to do with The Beatles," Woodbine observed. It is clear that Lord Woodbine should be remembered as an important man who played a critical role in the group's early history. Sadly, he and his wife died in a house fire in Liverpool in 2000.

There was a massive increase in the Afro-Caribbean population of Liverpool in the 1940s and 1950s, when the British Government invited people to come to Britain to fill the country's many job vacancies. However, the offer was not as promising as it sounded. Many arrived in Liverpool looking for the streets paved with gold, but instead found unemployment, segregation and poor living conditions. However, what they brought with them was more important: new music and culture. In the Liverpool 8 area, they opened their own clubs – around thirty of them. Establishments like The Nigerian Club, The West Indian,

The Somali Club in Liverpool 8.

The Somali Club, The Yoruba and Dutch Eddie's began to populate the neighbourhoods of Toxteth.

Steel pan music started on the island of Trinidad in the Caribbean, so to find out more about the music and the important influence of Allan Williams, Lord Woodbine and the black musicians from Toxteth, I spoke to some of the people who were there. These included Fitzroy "Jimmy" James and Everett Estridge, both from the Royal Caribbean Steel Band; Joey Ankrah, a member of The Chants, one of the most successful black groups from Liverpool; and Dr. James McGrath, who wrote a dissertation on the influence of these black musicians on the music of Lennon and McCartney.

Everett Estridge

The story of the Royal Caribbean Steel Band begins with Everett Estridge and a group of friends in London. Having left Trinidad, Everett arrived in London and found work with British Rail. Back in Trinidad, Everett had not only learned to play the steel pans, but how to make them – a rare skill in those days. Even though he was now in London, his desire to play was as strong as ever. I met him in his Liverpool home and, after joking about his bad memory, he promised to tell me what he could remember. He made it clear that he wouldn't fabricate the stories or tell lies because there were so many people doing that already. He told me how he got his group together, and how he ended up in Liverpool.

"I always loved the music," explained Everett with a smile, "and still do now. I was never bothered about group names, or stage costumes or anything else. I just loved the music. So, I got a group together in London with my friends, and I don't even think we had a name. I don't remember one. Somebody lent us a basement, and we worked during the week and rehearsed on weekends. We then started gigging around London. I made the pans and played the lead pan, which I also call the alto pan. There was Gerry Gobin who could play anything, but mainly played the double tenor – and then there was Clinton, plus Ashton and Reggie Dutton, who were brothers."

Suddenly, the whole group moved north to Liverpool, with no accommodation lined up and no known friends in the city, which begs the question: why move from London to Liverpool? "To be honest", said Everett with his infectious laugh, "they wanted to send us for national service! I did not want to join the army and go to another country and either kill or be killed. So, we all decided to take our annual leave from work at the same time and just got on the train with our pans, our clothes, and went to Liverpool.

"We chose Liverpool, because it was a port and we thought that there would be other guys from the Caribbean there, so it seemed as good a place as any to go to. We arrived there with all of our stuff, and we just found some good people in Toxteth who gave us food and lodgings. We had somewhere to stay and found some work to do, but all I wanted to do was play music."

Everett Estridge, a member of the Royal Caribbean Steel Band.

Everett Estridge, Clive Warner and Jimmy James, members of the Royal Caribbean Steel Band in Bedford Street, Liverpool.

When they settled in Liverpool in 1958, the group started to play in some of the local clubs, where they were spotted by Lord Woodbine and Allan Williams, who quickly booked them for an initial two-week period at The Jacaranda. The gig lasted for several years. But where did they acquire the group name?

"I don't know who came up with the name," exclaimed Everett. "I never liked the name Royal Caribbean Steel Band and don't know where it came from. It did not seem right with what we were doing, but I was never worried about that. I was never interested in the band name or costumes or any of that, I just wanted to play." Although the basics of the group were there, other musicians came and went, including Liverpool steel-pannists, like Karl "Slim" John. "'Slim' was our drummer," explained Everett, "but not in a conventional way. He just had a bass drum and a snare drum, no cymbals, but he would make the rhythm on the drum with maracas in his hands! He had these huge hands. I don't know how he did it, and I have never seen anyone else do it, but it was great.

"There were other guys like "Bones" who joined us, and a guy called Victor who played as a substitute musician sometimes. Reggie wanted to leave, and so "Bones" came on the scene. Then there was Clive Warner, and he started with us and we taught him to play, so he was on the bass pan, which is the easiest one to start on. Then in 1960, Jimmy James joined us on the double-second pan."

Everett's role in the group was more than just the lead pan and the

Clive Warner, a member of the Royal Caribbean Steel Band.

person who got the group together. He was also the music arranger, a task he obviously enjoyed. "We would play all of the songs of the day," recalled Everett. I would listen to the songs and think how we could do it differently. I would think of the song and just put a different beat to it and that was that. Everybody loved it."

When I brought up the subject of Lord Woodbine, Everett's response was not what I expected. "I knew Woodbine," recalled Everett, "but we did not have a lot to do with him. He was involved with Allan Williams with their clubs, but we did not see him much. We became good friends. He was not a musician, but he would sing the calypso songs."

Everett was not among the group members who went to Hamburg, and he can't remember who did go. "The only place I ever went to was Holland," he said, laughing. There was obviously a story coming. "I had come to Liverpool to escape the draft into the army and thought I had evaded them, but they caught up with me, so I decided I would go to Holland. I don't why I chose there, but I took my pans and my bags and got the ferry, but as soon as I landed there, the customs people took me to one side and sent me straight back home!" There was a happy ending, as far as Everett was concerned. "I never did join up with the army after all."

Regarding the subject of this book, and the story of The Beatles, I wanted to know what he remembered about them. "To be honest," he said, "I may have bumped into them or seen them around, but I couldn't say that I knew them or we were friends, or have any great stories like that about them. We were always in The Jacaranda where we rehearsed and worked. It was a dark place, with dim lighting, and a smoocher's paradise where they could kiss in the shadows. We had our little stage and there was the coffee bar, but you could hardly see anything. I remember the mural on the wall being painted, but we were concentrating on our music and not paying close attention to what was going on. There were always lots of students hanging around and a lot of them were from the Art College, so we must have talked with them, but I don't remember anything special.

"We were playing seven nights a week a lot of the time and so many people came and went in the crowd. If we weren't playing at The Jac, then we would play anywhere. If somebody asked us to play, I just said 'yes'. I did not care where it was, we just played. We would rehearse most days, so that meant getting down there at about 10am. "Bones" lived near me, but he did not like getting out of bed. He wouldn't answer the door, so I always asked the landlord to let me in, so I could wake him up. He would go to sleep fully clothed, including coat and scarf. He would just look for his hat, and off we went into town."

Some have suggested that there were plenty of drugs and girls around at the time. "I did not even know about drugs, pot, or whatever," said Everett. "All I was interested in was the music, and if there were drugs around, I certainly did not know anything. We just came to The Jac, played our music, and then went home to sleep! Some people have suggested there was more going on, but I did not see it!"

Everett's focus was just on the music, which took up nearly all his spare time. "We would be learning new songs, and practising others, too. The evening performance started around 8pm, and we would play on until about 2am, so we had to learn a lot of songs. It is hard to think of my favourite songs, as we played so many, but I was using classical music, jazz and pop music. I remember we did 'Melody in F', 'There's Always Tomorrow' and 'Inchworm' and I enjoyed playing those. These tunes and melodies were great, but once I had listened to them a couple of times, I could do more with them, and put a rhythm behind them. After that, it was improvisation and arranging the song the way I wanted to play it. But I'll tell you this. If I ever hear 'Banana Boat Song' or 'Yellow Bird' again I will go crazy! Everybody wanted us to play those songs, but I hated them!"

The members of the Royal Caribbean Steel Band in Liverpool between 1957 and 1960 were "Spree" Simon (leader and inventor), Everett Estridge (arranger, tuner and pan maker), Gerry Gobin, "Slim", "Bones" and Victor. Estridge may be from Trinidad, but Liverpool is his town. "You have to come to Liverpool for the experience. There is nowhere like it, so I think of myself as from Trinidad, but secondly from Liverpool. I love this place."

After his career with the Royal Caribbean Steel Band was finished, Everett played with other bands but ended up working for many years at Cammell Laird's shipbuilding. To this day, he has never lost his love for life or for music.

Fitzroy "Jimmy" James

"Jimmy" James joined the Royal Caribbean Steel Band in 1960 when some of the members went to Hamburg. After Everett left, James was asked by Allan Williams to become leader of the band. He visited Liverpool in October 2012 and took time to explain to me how the influence of Trinidad on Liverpool and The Beatles started for him – and how he ended up in Liverpool with no money, no job and no place to stay.

"The steel pan was the last instrument to be invented," said James, "by Winston 'Spree' Simon in the early 1940s. He came over to Liverpool in the 1950s, and with others like Bertie Marshall, pioneered the development of the steel pan as an instrument." James grew up in Trinidad and when he first heard a steel band on the way to school, something stirred within him. "I heard this music coming from behind a fence. I wanted to know more about it, so I decided I wouldn't go to school. However, when I went to speak to the musicians, some of them chased me away, telling me I was too young, and that I should go to school.

"I went back the next day and Lloyd Matthews, who became my mentor, came up with a proposition. As I was only about 9 or 10 years old, he told me to go to school, and then come down after school or at recess. I couldn't go after school as my mother would know, so I told him I would get permission to come early from school. I went back to Matthews and told him that I had been given permission from the teacher to take some time off to study the steel pans with them. Of course," laughed James, "I had no such permission. I spent a week with them and Matthews told me to just observe, which I did."

James then explained about the gang culture at the time in Trinidad, where every area had its own gang with a Captain, Vice-Captain and officers. The young men in these groups had often been to prison for violent crimes. Each gang ruled its own area, but often went to other areas where, inevitably, fights broke out. For this reason, James knew he shouldn't be hanging around with them. "The steel pan at that time was not considered a proper instrument, so the musicians had no respect at that time either. The groups were also associated with the nightclubs, which also meant that there was fighting most nights. That is why I did not want my mother to know what I was doing."

Fitzroy "Jimmy" James playing the steel pans.

The inevitable happened when it was noticed that he had been missing from school for a week. "My teacher came to my house and saw my mother," explained James, "and told her that I had not been to school for a week. To help convince my mother that I had been to school, I rubbed dirt on my face. I came home, and she said nothing. I did my chores, had dinner and went to bed. That is when it started! My mother came in and battered me with a stick, calling me a liar and screaming at me. My stepfather stayed out of it and left it to my mother. I told her I had been at the river with my friends. I did not dare mention the music. I went back to school, but the music was calling me, so after a week, I went back to the group and continued my tuition.

"Well, my mother came looking for me and so, when she was spotted, the guys shouted, 'Your mother is coming, your mother is coming!' So they hid me, but she came marching in demanding to know where I was. 'I hear you have my son,' she shouted, 'and you are criminals. Where is he?' I stayed hidden, but I knew I had to stay away for a while.

"My mother would walk me to school every day, and when I walked past the gang, they laughed at me. About six months went by and I wandered down to the market where I saw the guys, and they were shouting for me to come back. They told me to come and practise in my own time, and of course I wanted to. Well, coming up soon was the big carnival and every band had a mascot. Being only about ten years old, I was perfect for it but, because of the trouble in the past, they said they had to ask my mother. So, they sent a contingent to meet my mother and ask for her permission to let me take part.

"Because my mother knew the reputation of these gangs, and though they were involved in the music, she did not want me hanging around with these kinds of guys. So, of course, she said no! But that did not stop me. I told them she had changed her mind and agreed to let me play. So that my mother wouldn't guess, I took the uniform in a bag and changed into it when I got there. It was a fantastic experience and I got the bug – the fame, the crowds, the cheering and, of course, the music. I was the little guy at the front of the parade and everybody loved me! I was the gopher for the gang. I had to go for this, and go for that, running errands for them. I was in the gang. Of course, as I got older, this meant hanging out in the nightclubs, which had their own orchestras."

Orchestras are generally known to be filled with classical instruments like violins and cellos, but not to the musicians of Trinidad. "An orchestra is a group of more than four steel pans," explained James, "and a band has only four pans. The standard band consists of a Tenor (Lead) Pan, a Double Second, a Guitar Pan and a Bass Pan. Every club and every gang had their own band or orchestra who competed with each other. I looked forward to my life playing in a steel band."

James continued: "The clubs at that time were often filled with Ameri-

The carnival in Woodford Square, Trinidad, 1956.

can servicemen, as we had two U.S. bases on the island. There was an aircraft carrier base and a submarine base, so the servicemen would come looking for the best nightclubs, and of course there would be fighting! As I was so young and hanging around these clubs, as soon as my mother found out, she had to take action.

"She sent me away to another part of the island to live with family. But I got into trouble up there too! I joined a gang, who were considered to be a bad influence, so I was sent back to my mother again.

"At this point, I was introduced to another man who was to have a profound influence on my life. Bertie Marshall was known as "The Scientist" and he took the basic design of the steel pan designed by "Spree" Simon and worked out how to sink the drum deeper, which produced sweeter tones, known as 'water tones'. Although I was still with my gang, I would sneak away to watch Bertie making and playing the pans. However, each gang had their own secret, which couldn't be shared with the opposition. I picked up a type of jazz playing, with different runs and phrases on the pans that I'd never been shown before.

"So, when I went back to my gang, and we were practising, they started asking me where I had learned these new styles from. They did not like them, but my mentor Lloyd just told them to let me play. One of the biggest problems I had was that I was small, and the pan was big. I had to wear it around my neck, hanging from a piece of string, but I almost disappeared behind it. Thankfully, Bertie Marshall came up with the idea of a rack, which was on wheels, so that the player could walk along with the pans, while playing. It was a real skill and I had to practise for ages, with my friends walking up and down pushing the rack while I played the pan."

The violence on the island started to escalate as some of the islanders gained work on the ships going to and from America to pick up fruit. However, while there, they picked up guns and brought them back to Trinidad. Until then, gang fights were settled with machetes and there were many young men walking around the island with only one arm. James was lucky. "Thankfully, I was quick," he said, "because when the fight started, the gang members would open their suit jackets, where they had hidden their machete, and start wielding it about. As one machete headed towards me, I ran and it cut into my shoulder, so I still have a deep scar, but I also have my arm.

"However, when the guns arrived, it started to get serious. I was also shot in the head, but again I was lucky, as it bounced off my skull. I had a bad headache for a long time, but it knocked some sense into me and I decided I had to leave the island, or I would die. My mother went ballistic!"

Getting out of Trinidad was not easy at the time, and most of those who arrived in Liverpool did it the same way – by sea. "You had to give a good reason to the authorities before they would grant you a passport," explained James. "You either had to be a student, or have family overseas, but neither of those applied to me. So, it had to be on a ship, something I had never considered before. I would watch the ships on the horizon, coming in and out of the port, but instead of sharing my dream, I kept this one to myself.

"The first thing I needed to get was a passport, which I thought would be a problem. When I went to the office, there, behind the desk, was a school friend of mine. I had to have medical papers and a portfolio of what I could do for the ship's captain, so I asked him for advice. He told me to go away, come back in 30 minutes, and he would sort it out, and he did. I began to hang out at the shore and wait in the Union Hall, where you could wait for up to two years to get a ship.

"Again, I had a friend who suggested I meet his father, who went out to the ships in the bay and worked with the captains. He told me to wait by the phone, and one day he would call me. Well, at 2am, the

The *MS Octavia*, with "Jimmy" James on board, sails into Liverpool, March 1960.

phone rang and he told me to come down to the shore. He took me out, in the pitch black of night, to a ship. We moored up alongside side it and he headed up The Jacob's ladder on the side. After a few minutes, I got the call to climb up the ladder, bashing myself against the side of the ship. I was taken to meet the captain. He took one look at me and was unsure. 'You're too young,' he said, 'but shouldn't you be at school? What about your mother? Won't you be scared?'

"So, I had to think on my feet quickly. I told him how I needed to help my poor mother, and this was my chance. I used the old blarney! He thought about it, and then said he would take a chance on me, would need a letter from my mother normally, but he did not need one this time. Suddenly, this was the start of a new life and it was starting in two days' time. I was frightened, but I was leaving. I had no clothes for the cold. This was Trinidad. I had to pack what I could. I did not even have a bag. I had so much to do.

The next afternoon, I told the gang I was leaving and they were mad. But then, very quickly, they told me what they wanted me to bring back, like bottles of wine, cigarettes and other duty-free items. However, I still hadn't told my mother I was leaving, and they were coming for me in a few hours. When she went to bed, about 10:30pm, I eventually told her, and she nearly collapsed. She started crying, 'Oh, you hate me. What if the ship sinks?' I was only seventeen and my life was about to change for good.

"The agent arrived and took me to the ship. I'll never forget watching Trinidad disappear as we pulled further out to sea and, suddenly, I was surrounded by darkness. My first trip took me to America and, in all, I was away for six months. I bought a radio and listened to that on the ship, but that is where I first encountered racism. This was a German ship and all of the crew, apart from me and the cook, were white. It was tough, but I survived."

The connection between Liverpool and Trinidad would become very important, but the connection with Hamburg would prove to be vital in the story of The Beatles. The link was created because the ships like those that James and many other Trinidadians had sailed visited the German port of Hamburg. "We all went ashore," recalled James, "and into the town centre. The nightlife was incredible, and nothing like I had seen before. Our next port of call was up the River Mersey to Liverpool. We got off at Birkenhead, across the river, and headed into Liverpool. I knew that "Spree" Simon was there, and I was told that there were plenty of guys from Trinidad in Liverpool, so I went to find them. I had heard that there was a steel band playing at The Jacaranda, but I did not get the chance to see them on that visit.

"We headed across the Atlantic to Canada and dropped anchor in Halifax, Nova Scotia, where it was so cold. I heard a rumour that we were about to lose our jobs, so I decided to stay there with a friend, even though I did not even have a coat. I had to decide what to do next and, for some reason, my music kept calling me. I remembered that Spree had settled in Liverpool and they were playing steel pan music in Liverpool, so my decision was made. I had to find a ship to get to Liverpool."

James arrived in Liverpool, but he did not know anyone or have anywhere to stay. He headed for the one place where he knew he'd find his fellow countrymen: The Jacaranda. "Spree" Simon had already returned to Trinidad, but the Royal Caribbean Steel Band was firmly established at The Jac. He found accommodation in Liverpool 8, in a flat that had no heating and had icicles on the ceiling. "I was close to going home," admitted James, "but as we say in Trinidad, 'let's suck some salt', which means to endure a hard time. I had to prove myself because my pride wouldn't let me go home.

"I went down to The Jac," recalled James, "and there was Everett, who

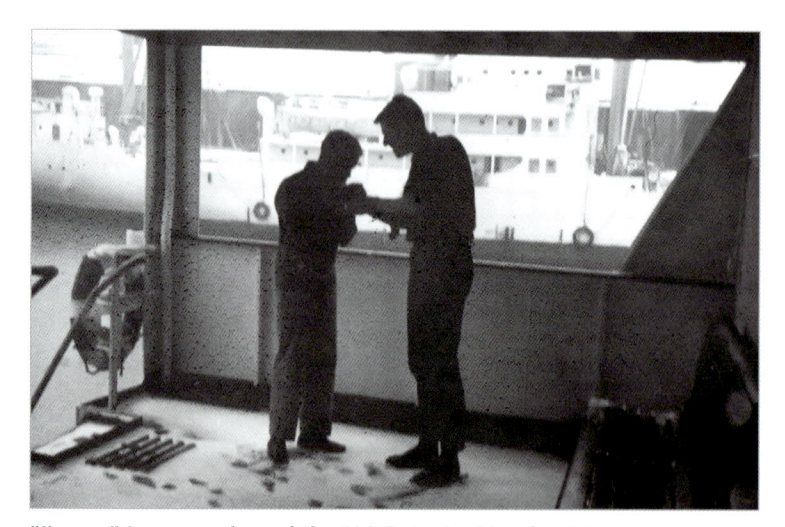

"Jimmy" James on board the MS Octavia, March 1960.

"Jimmy" James' first flat in Liverpool.

was now leading the band. I offered my services, and I was soon part of the band. I became the substitute musician, meaning that I played every night and never had a day off! I actually earned more than the other band members! Lord Woodbine was there with Allan Williams and, not long after I arrived, Woodbine took some of the band to Hamburg."

At this point, I asked James about this episode in Beatles history. We know that members of the Royal Caribbean Steel Band went to Hamburg, which led to the club owner, Bruno Koschmider, looking to find more bands for his nightclubs. But how and why did they end up in Hamburg?

"It was because of the German sailors who were stopping over in Liverpool," explained James. "They came to The Jac, saw the Royal Caribbean Steel Band playing, and then went back to the club owner in Hamburg and told him about this great steel band they had seen in Liverpool. He (the club owner) made contact with Lord Woodbine, who arranged for them to go over there."

Allan Williams and Lord Woodbine took them over to Hamburg and tried to settle them into a club, though Williams remembers a few problems. "When we were there," Williams recalled, "they stood out, because we were in Germany with four black guys and they did face some opposition. One of the biggest concerns was stopping the locals stealing the steel pans, which would have stopped the band playing. Plus, they were outdoing the local groups, who were playing traditional folk music. However, the many visiting seamen, including those from the Caribbean, enjoyed hearing a band that reminded them of home."

It was this important fact, and that the steel band was playing contemporary music, that made them so popular. Woodbine and Williams returned to Liverpool, but had a problem. They had lost some of their musicians. Everett stayed as bandleader on tenor pan but after he left, James took over as bandleader, accompanied by Clive, "Bones" and "Slim". They were supplemented by other local musicians.

With the Royal Caribbean Steel Band playing almost every night, James and his friends were the talk of the town. Williams soon saw the opportunity to hire out the band, which took them to several important and prestigious locations in the UK, including stately homes where they rubbed shoulders with the aristocracy. "Nobody had seen anything like us before," said James, "so we were very popular. The money started to roll in and we could afford nice clothes and a more comfortable lifestyle. We were a novelty, but if I have to hear 'Yellow Bird' one more time I think I will go mad! But Allan gave us these opportunities and deserves so much credit."

Now that the group was resident in The Jacaranda, I asked James if he had any interaction with The Beatles, who were being managed by Williams. "We all knew John and Paul in particular, because they were hanging out in The Jac all the time. I won't claim that we were best friends, but we would talk together. They were obviously interested in the sound that we were making, and observing what we did. Paul was a great guy, though John was more stand-offish. To me, Paul was a keen observer and a smart guy who was always trying to learn something new. He could pick things up really quickly. I do remember seeing them in Liverpool when they were raw, and I feel that I saw the real Beatles, before Epstein cut their hair, put them in suits, and cleaned them up. I remember when I had moved to London and was playing in the Speakeasy, Paul and Linda came over to talk to me and we had a really nice chat because he still remembered me. People then came up to me and wanted to know how I knew Paul, and I told them a bit, but I never wanted to boast about it.

"What I did see in those early days," James added, "was the influence of the black musicians from America, like the Motown artists, The Isley Brothers, Smokey Robinson, Chuck Berry and Little Richard. They loved that black music and they could hear lots of it in Liverpool at the clubs. They were clearly influenced by them and it was not just because of the charts. It was being played in the clubs in Liverpool.

"When I arrived, there were signs on the guest houses that said 'No Blacks, No Irish, No Dogs'. I learned about racism in Liverpool because it was all new to me, and quite a shock, because we had nothing like it in Trinidad. We played at The Jacaranda, but we were the only black guys there. In fact, if I walked into town, I would get monkey-sounds directed at me because I stood out. Black people kept to their areas and did not go into town. We had our own clubs where we could get together safely. I rose above it because the gangs had toughened me up to cope with anything."

It's interesting to note that John and Paul had no problem hanging out in the black clubs of Liverpool because they did not see a colour divide. They simply heard good music and sought it out.

"By the mid-1960s," continued James, "rock 'n' roll had taken over Liverpool, so we were less in demand. I followed The Beatles' career and never really talked about knowing them. I even bought a Beatle suit and was there on the streets of Liverpool when they came home for the Civic Reception in July 1964. I decided to change my instrument and moved onto congas and percussion and had success in several bands. I played with Paddy Chambers, who had been in Paddy, Klaus and Gibson, and then moved to London in 1967. I was playing at clubs in the heart of the West End of London where I could witness the 'swinging sixties' in Carnaby Street."

In October 2012, on a trip to the UK, James sought out Allan Williams and I helped to reunite them in The Grapes Pub in Mathew Street, just 100 yards from The Cavern Club. The two old friends hadn't seen each other in almost 50 years and reminisced about those historic days in The Jacaranda.

"We stayed at The Jac because Allan looked after us, treated us well and loved us," explained James, who was emotional on meeting the man who had such an impact on his life.

The Rialto, on the corner of Princes Road and Upper Parliament Street.

"Jimmy" James (far right) playing with Paddy Chambers (second from right).

"They were unique," added Williams. "I've heard steel bands all over the world and they were the best, playing in my club. Everyone was a master musician in their own right, and they even made their own pans with a hammer and chisel! The problem was that it was so dark down there that you couldn't see the band!"

"Only if we smiled," joked James, "but then I was the only one with gold teeth, so you could pick me out."

The discussion turned to the music they were playing which was, in my mind, traditional Caribbean calypso. Williams and James put me straight on that point. "They were playing all the latest songs around at the time," explained Williams. James quickly added, "We played all the songs from the charts, but with a calypso style and rhythm, so everybody recognised the tunes."

"Everett, who played the lead tenor-pan, had a good ear for music," explained Williams, "and he could pick up a melody and translate it to the pan in no time. He could play any tune. He was also the master pan-maker. I would drive him to the scrap yards to pick out the oil drums to make the pans. The guys in the yard were staring at him as he went around tapping the drums to see if the tone was good enough. He would then stand outside The Jac on Slater Street with his hammer and chisel making the pans. It was a work of art.

"It was well worth it," Williams continued, "because the tone that he could get from the pans was perfect. On a summer night, you could hear the music a mile away, drawing the crowds, but they couldn't get in, because The Jac was always packed. We had artists, nurses, professional people and off-duty policemen, which meant that there was never any trouble, because the criminal element kept away."

"And after we had finished," added James, "we all used to walk up to the Blue Angel, Allan's other club. That was an exclusive club for the groups, visiting actors and celebrities. The first time we went up there, the bouncer on the door, a mixed-race giant of a man known as "Snowy", told us to get the hell out of there! We had to get Allan to come and tell him to let us in! Black guys weren't usually found in these clubs. After the Blue Angel, we would walk up to Allan's house in Huskisson Street and continue the party."

"Even the bad days were good," recalled Williams. "We never had any

"Jimmy" James with Allan Williams in The Grapes Pub, Mathew Street, in 2013.

Inside Allan Williams' club, the Blue Angel.

The area of Liverpool 8 where many of the black clubs were situated.

bother or arguments, except when they were arguing between themselves." This reminded James of a personal battle he fought when he joined the group in 1960. "Everett and I used to argue because we had different styles. I had brought with me a more jazz style, which was different to his, but we soon learned to work together and became very good friends. When Everett left, Allan came to me and said, 'can you carry on?' so I said 'yes', and that was it. I had passed the audition.

"We looked forward to going to work, because it was great fun, and it helped to get the girls, too! All the gyrating and dancing closely on stage was really good. We were the only black guys in a white club."

What is already well-known is that the Royal Caribbean Steel Band played regularly at The Jacaranda and that John, Paul, George and Stuart were often in the audience. There was an influence on the music of Lennon and McCartney that has its roots in the black community of Liverpool. "The steel band was playing six nights a week," explained Williams, "and there was no other band like them. They were playing four or five hours a night, with only a fifteen-minute break, and the band evolved and improved every night. John and Paul were always there, carefully watching and observing this new musical phenomenon.

"I then started letting The Silver Beatles rehearse in the afternoons on a Monday," continued Williams, "and I gave them some work. They were a very expensive noise!" Although the steel band sometimes had Monday off, James occasionally went down to the cellar of The Jac to watch them rehearsing. "I would go down to see them if I was in the building, and I have to admit that I did not care for them at that time," he said candidly. However, he loved the great rock 'n' roll band they became.

James obviously wanted to pay tribute to his former manager Williams and took this opportunity to say what he really felt about his contribution to his career. "You wouldn't find people like Allan anymore," explained James, "or a club like The Jac. He gave us the chance, and what he contributed should be recognised more fully. He changed my life, and I love him."

Vinnie Ismael

Another black Liverpool musician who had an influence on the young Lennon and McCartney was Vinnie Ismael, a Somali-Irish rhythm guitarist from the Granby area of Liverpool 8. James McGrath wrote a thesis for his doctorate on the influence of the black musicians and his investigative work has been important in researching this topic. "He would have been known to The Beatles and many other Liverpool musicians," noted McGrath, referring to Vinnie. "In the early 1960s, he led his group, Vince and His Volcanoes." Ismael went on to perform with The Harlems. McGrath interviewed Vinnie's manager, George Roberts, who witnessed a significant meeting that took place in 1961. "Vinnie was showing John and Paul how to play a certain Chuck Berry chord," recalled Roberts, "which they called the 'string bar seventh', or just the seventh. They were having trouble mastering it. The person who showed it to them was the only black guitarist on the scene."

Vinnie Ismael (centre back) and his group The Harlems.

As McGrath observed, The Beatles had a great many Chuck Berry songs in their set, so this small piece of tuition was vital to their performances. Roberts observed Vinnie showing Lennon and McCartney guitar chords on numerous occasions. They were learning new techniques from one of the leading black musicians around. Although the first meeting took place at The Cavern, many of the further lessons took place at the Starline Club in Windsor Street, the club that was managed by Roberts.

Odie Taylor

Various witnesses saw this happening. The black Liverpudlian bandleader George Dixon remembers Lennon and McCartney watching him and the guitarist Odie Taylor at the White House pub. The Nigerian-Liverpudlian singer Ramon Sugar Dean recalls the way their music developed: "I heard them jamming in The Cavern club and the rhythm had changed. They'd got some chords off Odie."

Zancs Logie

The Guyanese guitarist Zancs Logie was another willing teacher. In 1995, Lord Woodbine told Derek Murray, author of a forthcoming book on black music: "Zancs was always showing Lennon something." With all of these influences, their repertoire was expanding, which would equip them for what would happen next.

For John and Paul, as well as George, Stuart and Pete, the clubs around the Upper Parliament Street area of Liverpool 8 were a source of inspiration, influence and importance as they absorbed the unique culture that was Liverpool in the 1950s and early 1960s. As we saw in the earlier chapter on the story of the Cunard Yanks, the latest black American music was being brought into these clubs and The Beatles were mentally absorbing it, waiting for it to manifest itself in their future music.

Paul McCartney recently spoke about how The Beatles' music was influenced by Liverpool's ethnic communities. In particular, he mentioned "calypsos via the Liverpool Caribbean community," which, he proudly added, "was the oldest in England." McCartney said that sailors and immigrants made Liverpool a "melting pot" of different ethnic sounds, and he added, "We took what we liked from all that."

They found their calypso beat – in the heart of Liverpool 8.

How important were the experiences of John and Paul in the black clubs of Liverpool 8? After talking to a number of friends, it is apparent that John and Paul, as well as George, Pete and Stuart, were hanging out in these clubs between 1960 and 1962, listening to the music, talking to the musicians and absorbing the culture and music of the black artists, both local and international. As Paul said, they were happy to take whatever they could from everyone they came into contact with, even if they only picked up a few chords or a couple of new rhythms. Those days spent in the Liverpool 8 clubs were obviously important as they continued their musical education. They learned a great deal from the black musicians who were hanging out there, and credit should be given to them. Although there isn't much evidence of the calypso rhythm in The Beatles' music, what musicians like Vinnie Ismael showed them was how to properly perform the music of Chuck Berry, which would be central to their set list for the next two years.

How big was the influence of Lord Woodbine? Allan Williams boldly said that without Lord Woodbine, there would be no Beatles. Is this hyperbole, exaggeration and mischief, or is there some truth in it? As we have seen, for a short period in 1960, Allan Williams and Lord Woodbine were managing The Beatles. For some, Williams was just a booking agent, but what booking agent gets the group a drummer, puts them forward for auditions, arranges gigs and then pays for and transports them over to Hamburg? Booking agents just booked the acts. Even Paul McCartney in *The Beatles* A*nthology* referred to Williams as their manager.

Even those who will accept Williams as manager know little about the impact of Lord Woodbine. When I spoke with Williams recently, he again asserted the influence of his business partner on the group. If it hadn't been for Williams and Woodbine, The Beatles, who did not have a great reputation, would never have made it to Hamburg. If they hadn't made it to Hamburg, they wouldn't have become the best rock 'n' roll group in Liverpool. If they hadn't become a great band, Mona Best wouldn't likely have managed and encouraged them to the point that Brian Epstein could take them on, refine their act and make them the phenomenon they became. This period in 1960, with Allan Williams and Lord Woodbine was the make-or-break time for The Beatles, and its importance cannot be over-emphasised.

What's also clear is that The Beatles, once they were famous, were

Upper Parliament Street, the heart of the black community of Toxteth.

quite prepared to run the gauntlet of adverse publicity when the subject of audience segregation came up during their American tours. They were due to perform a concert at the Gator Bowl in Jacksonville, Florida, on 11 September 1964. It was originally to have been racially-segregated, but The Beatles took a stand and refused to perform under such circumstances. "We never play to segregated audiences," said John Lennon emphatically, "and we aren't going to start now. I'd sooner lose out on appearance money." They had even had to change their hotel because there was a segregation issue. George said at a press conference, "We don't know about our accommodations at all. We don't arrange that. But, you know, we don't appear anywhere where there is (segregation)." While the Gator Bowl lease had stipulated segregated seating for concerts, this became a moot point by the time of The Beatles' show at the venue. The Civil Rights Act had become law in July 1964, thus allowing the group to play to an integrated audience.

When The Beatles returned to the U.S. in 1965, the contract for their appearance on 31 August 1965 at The Cow Palace in Daly City, California (San Francisco), specifically stated that they "not be required to perform in front of a segregated audience". For a pop band in a foreign country, when trying to sell records, this was a brave stance to take, and they should be applauded. They were greatly influenced by black musicians and singers, but were also friends with many from the black community in Liverpool, and were standing up for what they believed.

Perhaps the most significant statement from The Beatles was Paul's song, "Blackbird". As Paul remembered in an interview with KCRW's Chris Douridas in 2002: "I actually just remembered why I'd written 'Blackbird'. I was in Scotland playing on my guitar and I remembered this whole idea of 'you were only waiting for this moment to arise' was about the black people's struggle in the southern states, and I was using the symbolism of a blackbird. It's not really about a blackbird whose wings are broken, you know, it's a bit more symbolic."

Paul also said in a *Mojo* magazine interview in 2008 how it was a reaction to the racial tension and civil unrest in America in the 1960s: "We were totally immersed in the whole saga which was unfolding. So I got the idea of using a blackbird as a symbol for a black person. It was not necessarily a black 'bird', but it works that way, as much as then you called girls 'birds'. 'Take these broken wings' was very much in my mind, but it was not exactly an ornithological ditty; it was purposely symbolic."

Finally, although many sources will state that Bob Dylan turned The Beatles on to cannabis on 28 August 1964, that dubious honour went to the black community in Liverpool, where the locals contended that the best cannabis in the UK could be found. John Lennon put the record straight in a 1975 interview. "People were smoking marijuana in Liverpool when we were still kids," Lennon said, "though I was not too aware of it in that period. All these black guys were from Jamaica, or their parents were, and there was a lot of marijuana around. The beatnik thing had just happened. Some guy was showing us pot in Liverpool in 1960, with twigs on it. We smoked it and we did not know what it was."

This period in early 1960 when The Silver Beatles were associated with Allan Williams and Lord Woodbine is just a small part of the group's decade-long journey. However, the time they spent with these two men is no less important than The Quarrymen and Cavern days or their time with Tony Sheridan in Hamburg, with Mona Best at The Casbah or with Brian Epstein. Allan Williams and Lord Woodbine were vital cogs in the wheel, and they should be acknowledged for their contributions.

The Jacaranda Club, where the Royal Caribbean Steel Band played.

10 MAY 1960

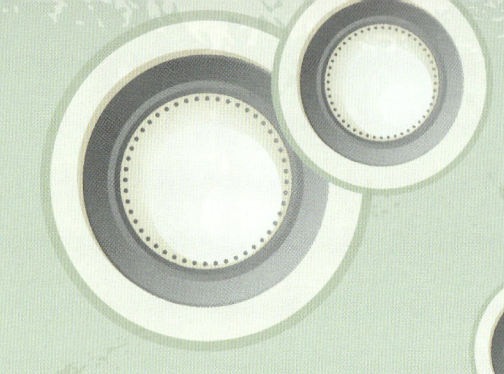

Cheniston K. Roland *photographs* *The Silver Beetles*

On 10 May 1960, the music promoter Larry Parnes was in Liverpool to audition local bands to back his stable of stars, like Billy Fury, Duffy Power and Johnny Gentle. Witness to that event, and official photographer for the day, Cheniston Roland took the first photographs of the group that would soon be changing its name from The Silver Beetles to The Beatles.

Cheniston K. Roland was born on 8 March 1932 in Liverpool and first lived in the spacious family home in Steble Street, The Dingle. He attended private schools, including the prestigious Liverpool College, which would a few years later also be attended by Brian Epstein. After receiving a Leica camera for his 21st birthday, Cheniston decided to become a professional photographer and opened a studio at 26, Slater Street in Liverpool, opposite The Jacaranda Club. Through Allan Williams, Cheniston became the official photographer for The Jacaranda.

As the club's staff photographer, Cheniston had to be at The Jacaranda every morning to receive any assignments, bringing him into contact with the great and the good of the Liverpool art scene. "The Jacaranda was like the old days of the Vienna Cafes", explained Cheniston, "where everybody from the town professionals to the everyday man in the street would meet together. All snobbery and class was abandoned, which meant it became the most successful club

Cheniston Roland, with the Leica camera he used to photograph The Silver Beetles.

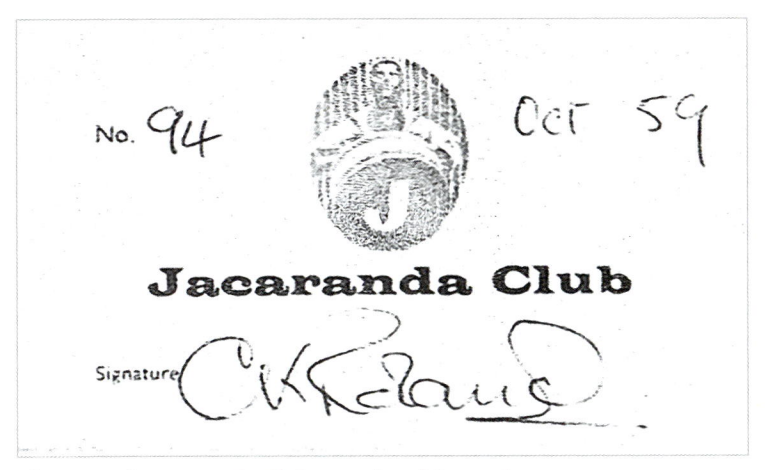

Cheniston's Jacaranda Club membership card.

Rory Storm and the Hurricanes at the Liverpool Stadium.

Gene Vincent performing at Liverpool Stadium

Cass and the Casanovas performing at The Jacaranda Club.

in Liverpool. You had artists, poets, musicians and writers all joining together in a creative collective consciousness."

On 3 May 1960, Gene Vincent headlined a marathon concert at the Liverpool Stadium, which also included such Liverpool bands as Cass and the Casanovas, Rory Storm and His (sic) Hurricanes and Jerry (sic) and the Pacemakers. "Our firm was appointed as the official photographers for the night," recalled Cheniston, "but we had to call in photographers from Peter Kaye. Kaye had been my mentor

The Fab one hundred and Four

The Blue Angel, formerly the Wyvern Club.

As soon as Williams had made the audition arrangements at his new club, The Wyvern in Seel Street, he enlisted Cheniston to be on call for the day to photograph all the bands. "There must have been over 40 musicians there that day," recalled Cheniston, "and they all had to tune up, rehearse and then perform. It was really busy, and loud, but most of the time I was concentrating on the photographs I was shooting, as opposed to the music. It was hard work.

"What I also remember," Cheniston continued, "is that it was a very serious affair, as there was a lot at stake that day for the bands, because this was a chance at a professional engagement, potentially with Billy Fury who was a massive star at the time."

when I was learning the trade and I would have done anything for him, day or night, so if I had the chance to repay the favour, I did. We ended up with about twenty photographers that night. We spent all day there and I saw Gene Vincent get through three bottles of whisky, but he was the nicest man – a real gentleman. It was hard work, but I remember the music was good. I especially liked Davy Jones – and Nero and The Gladiators had these incredible yellow and green suits."

The night was a success. Parnes was so impressed with the Liverpool groups that he asked Allan Williams to set up auditions at which groups would be chosen to back his stable of singers. Among the stars under Parnes' management was Britain's answer to Elvis Presley, Liverpool-born Billy Fury.

Cheniston managed to capture a unique piece of history that day and observed his new friends, John, Paul, George and Stuart, performing for Parnes. What he hadn't realised was that he had captured the only photograph of Tommy Moore drumming with The Silver Beetles. "I did not realise this until many years later, because I was just taking the photographs." Because Moore turned up late and was not present at the start of their audition, he was replaced by Johnny Hutchinson.

Cheniston looked back at the photographs he had taken, and what he remembered about their performance. "I have never thought about it until now," said Cheniston, "but The Silver Beetles and Billy Fury would never have worked together. They were too alike, as they both modelled themselves on Elvis, as you can see from the photograph of John singing without his guitar. For a backing band, working with Fury would have been a clash. They would have wanted to sing it their way, and Fury would have wanted to do it his way, and there would have been murder. Their styles were too close together and would have overpowered their lead singer."

One of The Beatles myths perpetuated since that day originated with Cheniston's photographs, showing Stuart Sutcliffe with his side to the camera. The story goes that Stuart was not playing, so he stood with his back to the audience. I asked Cheniston what he observed, and if he could put the record straight. "At that time, Stuart was not too proficient on the bass," observed Cheniston, "and he probably only knew a few notes. However, he was adequate for the day, but I did think that he angled himself carefully at the side to hide his limitations. He did not stand with his back to Parnes, or have his guitar unplugged."

Stuart and Cheniston became friends, and he was certainly closer to Stuart than John, Paul or George. "I used to see them all every day in The Jac, because they were always hanging out there. Stuart became a very good friend of mine. We were very close. He used to come over to my studio and we would talk for hours about art and photography. He was gentle, and what I would call an intellectual, too. He could sit and analyse a painting for hours. He would also study my photographs, and I remember him saying, 'You're a triangle man, Chen. Every picture has a triangle in it.' What he was saying that whenever I was

John Lennon (right) approaches Billy Fury for his autograph.

John and Paul singing, with Tommy looking on, as George concentrates on his guitar playing.

John singing with The Silver Beetles.

The Fab one hundred and Four

asking a subject to pose for the photograph, I would find a triangle in the shape of the arm to the body, or standing against a wall, and I had never realised it before, but Stuart spotted it."

Toward the end of the day of the auditions, John Lennon came over to Cheniston to talk to him and, in the moments that followed, Cheniston captured an historic photograph. He explains: "I had finished taking photographs and was talking to John and asking him, 'Why do you make so much noise?' They were loud. He stopped me and said, 'Hang on a minute. I want to go over to Mr. Fury and ask him if he'll sign this picture.' I remember him clearly calling him Mr. Fury, a real sign of respect. Lennon walked over to Billy and I followed him, as I wanted to speak to Billy and Larry Parnes. John leant forward and spoke to Billy. 'Mr. Fury, would you sign this drawing I've just done of you?' Billy answered him is his faux American accent, 'Yeah, sure. Have you got a pen?' John did not have one, so Fury turned to me. 'Hey Chen, have you got a pen I could borrow?' Lennon's face was a picture, and in a loud voice he said, 'Jesus Christ, he called him by his first name!' I just turned to Billy and said, 'Tell him how you know me'. Fury just turned to Lennon and said, 'A long time ago, I used to be one of his *Echo* newspaper delivery boys.'

"I had known Billy when he was just Ronnie Wycherley from The Dingle. He was a great guy, but always had a weak heart and sadly he died very young. He was a gentle man and a great singer. I was just taking the photo of Billy and not really concentrating on John. Otherwise I would have caught more of him in the photograph."

Cheniston went on to speak to Parnes, too, and I wondered what he thought of the legendary promoter. "I would say he was superior," explained Cheniston, "and not quite arrogant, but he was not friendly or easy to talk to. I would even say he was contemptuous, but he was very successful."

Cheniston had a six-year career as a professional photographer, which included photographing many of the famous musicians and actors who came to Liverpool. "I also went to the Blue Angel," continued Cheniston, "which Williams had renamed from the Wyvern after Marlene Dietrich's famous German film, and had the pleasure of photographing Marlene there. She was a bright woman and Allan was no match for her.

"The first photograph I took was of Cilla Black, but I also captured Dizzy Gillespie and Allen Ginsberg performing at The Jac, and watched Ginsberg as he read poetry at the Philharmonic Hall. The Beatles also played that night, a fact that isn't well-known."

Although he has made a good living as a photographer, Cheniston has also had a very successful life in a number of different fields. "I have worked for the BBC, sung in opera and written books on the violin as well as performing as a musician. I have lectured and been a radio broadcaster, but I suppose I would always like to be remembered as a violin historian."

For Beatles fans, however, he will be remembered as the photographer who captured the first pictures of the fledgling group who, within a few weeks, would be known as The Beatles.

Larry Parnes, Beryl and Allan Williams, with Billy Fury outside The Jacaranda Club.

10 MAY 1960

John Lennon, Paul McCartney, George Harrison, Stuart Sutcliffe and Tommy Moore

After Allan Williams became the group's manager, he immediately urged them to get a drummer. Having tried and exhausted their options, they asked Williams for help. Brian Casser of Cass and the Casanovas suggested Tommy Moore. Tommy was considered a good drummer and, although he was a few years older than the others, he was just what they needed. Cass even suggested a new group name: Long John and The Silver Beetles. They settled on The Silver Beetles.

There has been some doubt over his age, but the birth certificate shows that Thomas Henry Moore was born on 12 September 1931 to Stephen and Rhoda Moore. They lived at 16, Lockhart Street in Liverpool 8, the same street where Jack and Polly Lennon, John's grandparents, had lived at the turn of the century.

When Tommy started working at the Garston Bottle Works, he was living at 49, Fern Grove in Liverpool 8. At this day job he was a forklift truck driver, but he drummed when he could in the evenings. The age difference between Tommy and the other band members was a point of contention and led to several arguments among the boys, but particularly with John (who was nine years younger than Tommy). John was the undisputed leader of the group, yet Tommy had been a musician for several years, and was a working man providing for his

John, Paul and Tommy Moore at the Wyvern Club.

The Fab one hundred and Four

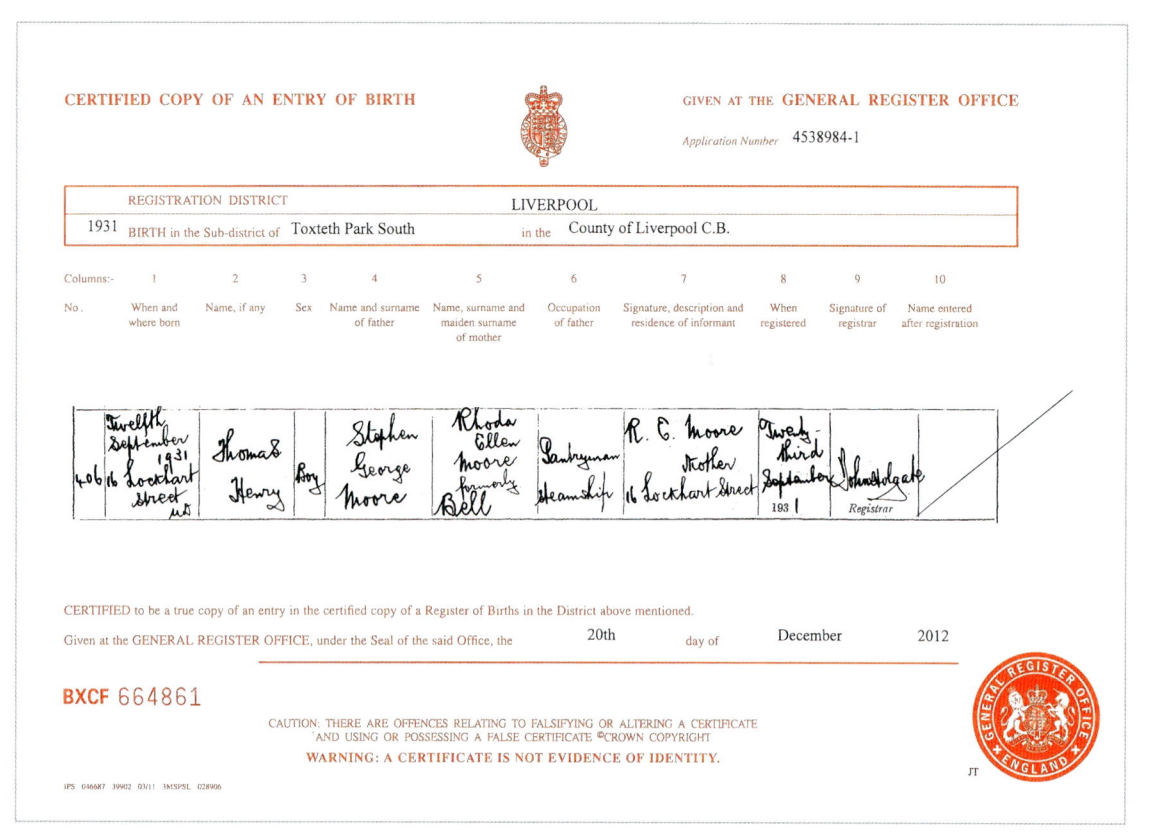

Tommy Moore's birth certificate, showing Tommy's date of birth as 12 September 1931.

Johnny Hutchinson stood in until Tommy arrived and finished the audition. Parnes noticed that he was older and did not seem to fit in too well, but this did not stop Parnes from booking The Silver Beetles as Johnny Gentle's backing band for a tour of Scotland. Paul was impressed with Tommy's drumming skills, in particular his ability to reproduce the tricky drumming on the Everly Brothers' number "Cathy's Clown".

Allan Williams used to see Tommy around Liverpool and remembers one conversation they had about John. "I did not like Lennon," Tommy told Allan. "I couldn't stand him. He had some awful ways. He was an absolute gannet where food was concerned. He'd wolf down everything in his path in such

family. Those responsibilities were still a few years away for his bandmates. It was more a difference in maturity than purely their age.

Allan Williams considered Tommy a great drummer and recalled that George was also positive about him. "Tommy Moore was the best drummer we ever had at any time," Williams recalls George saying in Ringo's presence! Tommy rehearsed with the group in The Jacaranda for hours before they began playing anything resembling good rock 'n' roll. From that point on, the band vastly improved. "You could detect a day-to-day improvement," Williams observed.

Because Williams felt that the group was now ready, Tommy and The Silver Beetles were invited to audition for Larry Parnes at the Wyvern Club on 10 May 1960. However, Tommy turned up late, which did not impress the band or Parnes, who considered this a black mark against them.

an obnoxious and beastly – that's the only word – ill-mannered way, it would make me physically sick and put me off my food just to watch him." Referring to the Johnny Gentle tour of Scotland, Tommy said, "He [Lennon] always insisted on getting the best accommodations available. We got two bedrooms between the five of us. Lennon would never sleep three in a room. He was always the one who went into the double for the extra comfort it might afford. He was a very aggressive boy."

When Tommy was dragged out of the hospital, dazed and confused from the van accident in Scotland, all he remembered was Lennon laughing at the state of his bruised and battered face. It's no surprise that on his return from the tour, Tommy's thoughts turned to quitting the group. "I'd had a belly full of that Scottish tour when we got back," recalled Moore. "And I'd had my belly full of Lennon. You know, I think he was sick. He seemed to love watching the fights that broke out in the dance halls between the rival gangs. He'd say, 'Hey look at that guy putting the boot in there'. He got a sadistic delight out of it all. At least his conduct indicated this. When our train got into Liverpool, the rest of the lads went to the tea van that used to be sited just across the road in Lime Street. I said, 'Goodnight lads,' and took a cab home. I was pissed off with Lennon. I had had enough of him."

Tommy made a few appearances with them during May and June 1960, but when he failed to turn up at a gig at the Grosvenor Ballroom in Wallasey on 11 June 1960, he left the group in an awkward position. Williams took them to Tommy's house where they were greeted by his girlfriend, who informed them that he had quit the band. She'd given him an ultimatum. It was either her or The Silver Beetles. Tommy had returned to work full-time at the Bottle Works, so they jumped into the car and drove to Garston, where they confronted their drummer.

Despite their pleading, Tommy refused to come with them. He made it clear that his time with the band was over. "I've got mouths to feed," explained Moore. "I'm not like the rest of you. I'm a working lad who has to make some money to feed the people who depend on me. I can't go on living like this anymore. Honest I can't, she'd kill me," he said, referring to his girlfriend. "Sorry lads, I need more than a measly fiver a week to keep me and mine. You ought to know that. I don't mind going on a diet, but starving is a different kettle of fish. Sorry boys."

One of Tommy's friends would later reveal that Moore's girlfriend suffered with depression, and was prone to violence, too. Their relationship did not survive, as Tommy's granddaughter, Michelle, told me. "Tommy married Vera Hughes, and they had two daughters, my mum Veronica and then Angela, but the marriage didn't last and they separated when my mum was about four or five." Tommy moved to the Belle Vale area of Liverpool and settled there. He would talk about his time with The Silver Beetles with fondness and was not bitter about what had happened. He was a big fan of The Beatles and followed their career, collecting all their albums.

He even attended the early Beatles conventions in Liverpool and was interviewed in 1971 for a BBC Television documentary. He was asked what life was like for him now, compared to his time with The Silver

Garston Bottle Company, where Tommy worked as a fork-lift driver.

Beetles. "Same as it was for me back then," said Moore, "a bit downhearted, and still making a couple of pounds a night. We weren't making any headway at the time, so we made this contract with a guy and did a tour of Scotland, where we started to make some money – to earn a few shillings. It was about £2 10 shillings a night."

Moore was then asked by interviewer Bernard Falk if he had any regrets when he sees what became of The Beatles. "Wouldn't anybody?", he answered honestly. "They are millionaires and so popular." When asked why he left the group, he replied that "because of a car accident, I ended up in hospital for three weeks, and when we came back to Liverpool, I did not play, and then someone walked off with my drums from Allan's club – I mean, stole them – it left me a bit puzzled as to what to do about it. So I considered it was no use to me, and went back to my job at the Garston Bottle Works as a fork-lift truck driver."

Tommy died from a brain haemorrhage on 28 September 1981. Only eleven people attended the funeral, including Cavern compère Bob Wooler. Those who knew him and saw him play regarded him as a great drummer. According to Allan Williams, Tommy was far more than that: "He was the best drummer The Beatles ever had."

One of the few people to have interviewed Tommy was Bob Cepican, when carrying out research for his book, *Yesterday Came Suddenly*. "I never met Tommy in person, just over the telephone," explained Bob. "I sent away for a Liverpool telephone directory to help me locate people in Liverpool. There were a number of T. Moores and several Thomas Moores listed in the book. I called randomly, hoping to find the right Tommy Moore. Luckily, Tommy was listed and we began our telephone chats.

"I liked Tommy a lot. He never made a big deal out of his association with The Beatles, and Lord knows that there are so many people out there who knew The Beatles for a minute and made careers out of that minute! To me, Tommy was one of these guys that you occasionally meet and right away you become good friends. He was that approachable, that down to earth and truly a very nice guy. I also sensed a sadness about him: that life had victimised him from time to time. He lost his drum kit when Allan Williams' Top Ten Club burned down and as far as I could tell, he never played again because he couldn't afford to buy a new drum kit.

"He told me that he played music for fun. He didn't think that it would lead to a career as a professional drummer. Tommy played in a variety of trad. jazz bands and some beat groups, just for fun, and to make a few bob. One of the things I found remarkable is that he was happy for The Beatles' success. Whenever I spoke with him, he never lamented on 'what could have been;' never kicked himself for not staying with the group. So, he had no regrets. I found that remarkable."

Tommy had met the group once before at the Temple Restaurant in Dale Street, a gathering place for musicians to meet and jam together in a room above the restaurant. "When they arrived at the Temple," recalled Tommy, "they were known as The Quarrymen. As far as I was concerned, they were playing novelty music."

After a week of rehearsals in The Jacaranda Club (The Jac), Allan Williams began to book the group with the understanding that he would receive ten percent of its earnings. Williams found work for The Silver Beetles, but in Tommy's opinion, Williams was not their manager. "In the time that I was with them," says Tommy, "he looked after us. I wouldn't say that he was a manager. He was only interested in the money or whatever he could get out of it. He never attended any of the rehearsals or gigs. As far as I know, he just made the bookings through other people. We used his van and were paid in pennies at the end of the night. I don't know much about it, because there was too much going on behind my back. Allan wasn't involved with it that much. He had his club to run, so I don't see how he could get involved."

The Silver Beetles' first professional booking was on 20 May 1960 at the Grosvenor Ballroom in Wallasey. For the next month, the group played steadily around Liverpool, mostly in Wallasey and Neston, on The Wirral. These were rough places and fights often broke out between rival Teddy-boy gangs and bouncers while the groups were performing. "John Lennon loved the fights," said Tommy, "and he used to think it was funny watching someone get kicked in the head. He'd say, 'Ooh, did you see that?' He gloated at anything like that."

The Silver Beetles alternated sets with the Royal Caribbean Steel Band in The Jac. "I lost a lot of sweat in The Jac," says Tommy. "We used to play from midnight to about four in the morning for cups of coffee and a jam buttie (sandwich). I don't remember getting paid. The only time we got paid was when we played outside of The Jac,

Stuart (left), with John and Paul sharing a microphone as Tommy Moore drums in the background.

Tommy Moore poses with his drumsticks in 1970.

and Allan was more interested in keeping us in The Jac because we were bringing in the people."

The Silver Beetles' repertoire consisted of songs by Jerry Lee Lewis, Little Richard, Fats Domino, Gene Vincent, and the Everly Brothers. "It was just a matter of rattling songs off, one after the other, just to make the night go by," recalled Tommy. "We played one Everly Brother tune in particular, 'Cathy's Clown.' I remember that the drum part was difficult for me at the time. We did a couple of good blues numbers, too. All that mattered to us was that it rocked." Tommy, who was a jazz enthusiast, often persuaded the others to play a couple of jazz tunes. "There was no way they could have played jazz and made a living of it," he says. "They just couldn't get it. Lennon and McCartney continued to write songs together, but their tunes were never heard by the public because they didn't have the confidence to include them in the group's repertoire, and in fact seemed embarrassed when anyone asked about them."

Tommy gained a unique insight into his fellow band members. "I didn't like John Lennon at all," he said. "I saw him in those days as a down-and-out – a bit of a tramp. He was so hard-headed; you couldn't insult him, no matter what you said. He was a bit of a beatnik and wore a dirty old jumper, denim jacket, sandals, long hair combed back over his collar, and glasses. Paul was a real homely lad, but a nice fella. I didn't have too much to do with George. He was the electrician of the group and used to do all the spot work on the equipment. And Stuart was a bad bass player, but he tried his best. The others never gave him any encouragement. They were always kidding him.

"I used to do me own bit on the drums," continued Tommy. "A solo to keep the crowd happy and on the floor while the others were off and had a bit of a break behind stage. So I'd be playing for some time and I'd turn around every so often to see where they were and when they were coming out, and all I'd see is John Lennon pulling faces at me from behind the curtain." Tommy took his drumming seriously, but wasn't impressed by the lack of professionalism of his colleagues. "I was getting a bit fed up with things," he said. "No one was telling me how much we were supposed to get paid for a gig or what job was down the line. Everything was so secretive. So I said to John one day outside The Jac, as we were getting our equipment into the van, 'You know what John? I'm getting a bit cheesed off with all this business here.' John said, like a typical Scouser, 'Why? You're getting paid, aren't you?' I said, 'Well, yes, but what are we getting paid? Buttons!' He said, 'What else do you want, then?' I said, 'There's nothing happening, nothing is materializing. In the near future, I'm bailing out and going back to me old job in the factory.' He said to me, very seriously, 'I'd sooner die first, mate, than go to work.'

This, of course, was the reputation that John, Paul and George had gained for doing anything except work. They would sign-on to receive state benefits, known as the 'Dole', and try and play as often as possible to make some cash to stop them having to find real jobs. Allan Williams always referred to it as 'rock 'n' dole'. Tommy was used to being a working man, and earning a living as a forklift truck driver at Garston Bottle Works, so the idea of avoiding work at all costs was anathema to him.

The big break for The Silver Beetles was at the Wyvern Club, when auditioning for Larry Parnes. The group turned up without Tommy,

Tommy Moore drums on an old tin box.

who couldn't get there for the start, so Johnny Hutchinson stepped for him until he arrived. That didn't impress Parnes. However, they performed well enough for Parnes to book them to support Johnny Gentle on a small tour around Scotland. For Tommy, it was a disaster. "When we went up to Scotland, we didn't have any money at all. It was Allan's idea that the money would be sent to us in advance from Larry Parnes in London. All I was interested in was getting on with the tour; I wasn't interested in who was doing the business. It was our understanding that Allan was looking after the financial part of it and that the money would be sent to us from London to hold us over." The deal was that each of the musicians would receive £15 per week, and even before the tour started, John rang Larry Parnes demanding, "where's the bloody money?" It didn't arrive, and so the penniless Silver Beetles arrived in Scotland.

Johnny Gentle was shocked at their appearance. "I wondered what on earth Parnes had sent me," remembered Gentle. "They were the roughest-looking bunch I had seen in my life, hopelessly fitted out with no stage gear. Paul and Stu had black shirts. I lent John a shirt of mine and went out and bought one for George, but we were so broke that we couldn't afford to buy one for the drummer, so he wore white." Lennon told Gentle, "This is our big break. We've been waiting for this!"

During the first week of the tour, John, Paul, and George constantly teased Stuart while they performed. The teasing, according to Tommy, was always instigated by Lennon. "Stuart wasn't the type of lad to argue over anything," said Tommy. "They used to mock him because of his ways. They'd get on him about his playing, shout at him on-stage. He had something none of us had: looks. It was often said by the many girls we knew in Liverpool that he would have made another James Dean. Believe me, he was the image of him – a real good looking lad. I don't know what it was with them, but if anybody looked better than they did, they'd give him a rough time. Lennon would try and give me a rough time, so I'd give him one back and threaten him. The way they were carrying on in general, I thought, 'What the bloody hell is going on here? Once I get back to Liverpool, this is it!'"

There have been stories that Stuart played his bass without being plugged in to his amplifier, and one such incident occurred in Scotland. However, it was not because Stuart couldn't play. Tommy recalled what happened. "One night during a performance, John unplugged Stuart's bass guitar from its amplifier while his back was turned. As Stuart struggled to play the proper notes, the others watched in silent hysteria, particularly Paul, who enjoyed seeing 'James Dean' make a fool of himself. At the end of the show Sutcliffe asked them how he did. Lennon said he didn't know, and that next time Stu should be sure his guitar lead was plugged into the amp. Confused by John's comment, Stu looked at his amp and saw that the jack was lying on the stage. Paul and George exploded with laughter; Stuart blushed in embarrassment."

This practical joke nearly became the end of the road for the group, as several girls complained to the tour promoter, Duncan McKinnon, about how bad the group sounded. McKinnon, who had heard similar comments the nights before, wanted to send them home. "We all sat down together in a bar in Inverness and went over each number until the boys got the right sound," said Johnny Gentle. "They were terribly depressed. I felt sorry for them and persuaded McKinnon to let them finish the second week. One night, after we'd finished a show, a girl came up and asked for their autographs. John was so thrilled, he couldn't stop talking about it and asked me if I thought they should chuck up everything and go full-time."

With the tour not going well, and money in short supply, their initial thrill of being on tour was waning. "On the way up there, it was fairly exciting," said Tommy. "The idea of just travelling was exciting. After the first few dates, things got a bit sticky and I started getting funny feelings about the tour, particularly about Allan. I told the others in a hotel, 'I don't like the looks of this at all.' We literally had to scrounge for food. In the hotel we were staying at, I felt like a tramp. We kept getting telephone calls saying that the money was on its way, but it never came." They smuggled food from the restaurants they ate in – saltines, bits of cheese wrapped in paper, slices of bread and dinner rolls – back to their hotel rooms and divided their haul. Once John was so hungry that he ordered a huge meal and walked out of the restaurant without paying. "We walked in front of him and he sort of used us as a shield," says Tommy.

Tommy's tour took a turn for the worse when the van they were travelling in was involved in a crash near Banff. "Johnny Gentle could never go on stage unless he had a few drinks," remarked Tommy. "He was just starting out on his first tour, and whenever we were with him, he was always under the influence. One night Johnny had a few drinks and after the show he suddenly got it into his head that he would drive the minibus. Well, he got behind the wheel and took a wrong turn and – bang! All I remember was waking up in a hospital. They were in a sticky position. I was in the hospital, things weren't going well on the tour, and they couldn't find another drummer. Even if they did, there wasn't enough time to rehearse. So against doctor's orders, I left the hospital."

Tommy arrived at the theatre drowsy from the effects of the drugs and with stitches in his upper lip, two teeth missing, and a bandage around his head. John exploded with laughter upon seeing him, and mocked and needled him throughout their performance, making faces, trying to stretch the stitches in Tommy's lips by making him laugh. Occasionally John would turn around while performing, look at Tommy, and burst out laughing. "Lennon must have thought, 'This is it, this time I'm gonna have a go at him,'" said Tommy.

The tour ended in Dundee in late June 1960, "We said goodbye to each other at the railway station," says Johnny Gentle, "and as my train pulled out, they were still saying, 'Ask Larry Parnes if he wants us again!'" According to Tommy Moore, the tour was a disaster; all five of them returned to Liverpool penniless, and the behaviour displayed by Lennon, McCartney, and Harrison finally forced him to quit the group. However, it was not really a disaster: this was vital experience that would serve them well in Hamburg in just a few months.

Tommy Moore, photographed with his family in 1970.

10 MAY 1960

John Lennon, Paul McCartney, George Harrison, Stuart Sutcliffe and *Johnny Hutchinson*

Regarded as probably the best drummer in Liverpool, Johnny Hutchinson, better known as Johnny Hutch, made his first appearance with John, Paul, George and Stuart at the Larry Parnes audition at the Wyvern Social Club.

Born on 18 July 1940 in Malta, Johnny Hutch grew up in Liverpool and made his name with Cass and the Casanovas, appearing on the bill with Gene Vincent at the Liverpool Stadium gig on 3 May 1960. Such was the success of the Liverpool groups that night that Parnes wanted to find the best groups to back his stable of singers.

Cass and the Casanovas was formed in December 1959 by Brian Casser, who also used the names Casey Valance and Casey Jones. He had completed his National Service, and during his stint in the army, formed a skiffle group with Bill Wyman, later to become a founding member of The Rolling Stones. After he left the army, Cass turned down Wyman's offer to join a group with him and teamed up with Adrian Barber, a Yorkshire musician who had arrived in Liverpool. For a short time, they had a drummer called Brian Hudson, but Johnny Hutch replaced him. According to Adrian, "He could do all the patterns that Brian couldn't. He was a rock 'n' roll man." Johnny made his debut with them at the age of eighteen at the Corinthian Club in Slater Street. He also did the occasional gig with a modern jazz band. One of Johnny's masterstrokes was to bring Johnny Gustafson, better known as Johnny Gus, into the group, as they needed a bass guitarist. However, he did not have a guitar so Adrian converted a Hoyer Acoustic for him and put bass strings on it.

Johnny Hutch was called into action when The Silver Beetles turned up at the Larry Parnes audition without their drummer, Tommy Moore. Brian Casser had recommended Moore to the group, and maybe with a pang of guilt or embarrassment, Casser asked Hutch to sit in with The Silver Beetles until Moore turned up. Casser, in addition to providing the band's drummer, had suggested they call themselves Long John and The Silver Men. While they rejected his recommendation, they did indeed keep the "Silver" in their name when they became The Silver Beetles.

At the end of the audition, Parnes booked Cass and the

Johnny Hutchinson

Casanovas, Derry and the Seniors and The Silver Beetles to back his singers. The Casanovas would accompany Duffy Power while The Silver Beetles would back Johnny Gentle on a tour of Scotland.

Johnny Gus revealed that The Casanovas had to change their line-up. "Cass was both the founder and leader, and the rest of us were getting increasingly fed up with him. So we hatched this plot to disband and reform without him." Cass left for London at the end of 1960, missing out on the entire Mersey music scene. For a short time, he became manager of the Blue Gardenia Club in St. Anne's Court, Soho.

The group became The Big Three, with Johnny Hutch, Johnny Gus and Adrian Barber. They were considered the best group, musically, in Liverpool, and became one of The Beatles' biggest rivals, as the two bands were often in direct competition with each other. This would have a bearing on the next time Johnny Hutch and The Beatles crossed paths. Johnny's opinion of The Beatles was that they "were not worth a carrot" and that did not change. This created an interesting situation as shortly after Brian Epstein signed The Beatles, Hutch approached him about taking on The Big Three (which Brian agreed to do). The arrangement would be short-lived and unsuccessful.

When Pete Best was dismissed in August 1962, Brian wanted Johnny to replace him, and offered the job to him. His response was straight to the point. "Brian asked me to join The Beatles and I said, I wouldn't join The Beatles for a gold clock," Johnny said. "There's only one group as far as I'm concerned and that's The Big Three. The Beatles can't make a better sound than that, and Pete Best is a very good friend of mine. I couldn't do the dirty on him." Johnny sat in with John, Paul and George for the three engagements before Ringo joined. It is generally accepted in Liverpool that Johnny Hutch and John Lennon in the same group would have spelled disaster and probably ended up in a fight.

Adrian Barber had never been happy with the idea of Epstein managing the group because Brian tried to impose the same methods on The Big Three that had worked so well with The Beatles. However, it did not have the same result. The Big Three had creamy yellow and pink suits, which Epstein said they had to discard. He also informed them that they couldn't smoke on stage and dictated what music they had to play, insisting they introduce soft numbers into their act.

The band fought Epstein at every stage, and Adrian took the lead, but was surprised that the others did not back him up more. The crunch came when Epstein said that, for their tour to Hamburg, they had to be a four-piece band, as the contract demanded they had to be a quartet. They recruited Brian Griffiths, former guitarist with Howie Casey and the Seniors. Adrian decided it was time to leave. "After all, we were supposed to be The Big Three, not the Big Four," he said.

Brian set up a recording session at Decca, but it did not go well. He told them to record "Some Other Guy". "This was actually a demo tape for Decca," said Gus. "My voice was completely gone. We had come back from Hamburg that very morning and were thrown into Decca's No. 2 studio in the basement. It was horrible. We were croaking like old frogs. Eppy wouldn't let us do it again and we went berserk. The bass sound was non-existent and the drum sound was awful."

The Big Three were disgusted when they found out that Decca would be releasing their test recording. They had built such a strong

Johnny Hutchinson drumming with The Silver Beetles.

The Fab one hundred and Four

Johnny Hutchinson (centre) with his band The Big Three.

reputation on their live performances, which they wanted to recreate on record, but they had been let down by Epstein. "Some Other Guy" peaked at number 37 in the UK charts on 11 April 1963. If that was not bad enough, Epstein and Decca decided that they should record more lightweight, pop songs. They gave them a Mitch Murray tune, "By The Way", which became their next record. Although it did better than their first, it only made it to number 22 on 11 July 1963. It was a case of record it or lose the record deal.

In 1963, their Liverpool-born A&R man Noel Walker recorded them live at The Cavern. Decca engineers had spent three days experimenting with microphone positions and the recording took ten hours because of technical problems. The EP, *The Big Three At The Cavern*, featured an introduction by Cavern compere Bob Wooler and the tracks "What'd I Say?", "Don't Start Running Around", "Zip-A-Dee-Doo-Dah" and "Reelin' And A Rockin'".

That same year, Epstein decided to present a series of shows with a number of his artists, like The Beatles, Gerry and the Pacemakers, Billy J. Kramer and the Coasters and The Big Three. This was not enough to satisfy the members of The Big Three, so on 20 July 1963, Epstein and The Big Three parted company.

By the time *The Big Three At The Cavern* was released on 22 December 1963, Johnny Hutch had quit the group. He would not change his mind, despite an offer to join Kingsize Taylor, and he decided to put down his drumsticks and turn his back on the music world.

Johnny Gus approached Faron and Paddy Chambers of Faron's Flamingos and asked them to join him, although they did not last long. The new lineup of The Big Three recorded an EP at the Oasis Club in Manchester, which contained "Money Honey", "Cruel Cruel World", "New Orleans" and "Whole Lotta Shakin'". This was followed in June 1964 by the single "If You Ever Change Your Mind". Paddy Chambers left, and was replaced by Paul Pilnick, and they released "Bring it On Home To Me".

Hutch is now a property developer and still lives in Merseyside, though whenever I speak to him, we never discuss The Beatles. It is disappointing that The Big Three were never able to transfer their incredible live sound onto vinyl. Those who missed The Big Three in their heyday missed seeing one of the best rock 'n' roll bands Liverpool produced.

Johnny Hutchinson pictured in 2013.

14 MAY 1960

The Silver Beats –

John Lennon, Paul McCartney, George Harrison, Stuart Sutcliffe and Cliff Roberts

Appearing as The Silver Beats – the only time they used this name – the group played at Lathom Hall, in the north of Liverpool, on 14 May 1960. Their drummer Tommy Moore was with them, but because he did not have his kit, they asked Cliff Roberts to fill in. In many reference books, there is confusion over which Cliff Roberts played that night, and most of them refer to Cliff Roberts and The Rockers. However, the Rockers' Cliff Roberts was a singer and guitarist, not a drummer. The Cliff Roberts who played with The Silver Beats was the drummer with The Dominoes.

Roberts had started a group, The Sinners, with friends Sam Hardie and Arthur Baker after they left Waterloo Grammar School in 1957. Roberts assembled a basic drum kit. Hardie was a great pianist and Baker could do a decent impression of Little Richard and Elvis. They made their debut at Caradoc Mission Hall in Seaforth, north Liverpool.

The group added George Watson and Charlie Flynn on guitar and vocals and, in 1958, also added Ted Taylor. They changed their name to The Dominoes. Ted "Kingsize" Taylor, so called for his 6' 5" height, joined as lead vocalist and guitarist. Over the next two years, Baker, Watson and Flynn all left. Bobby Thompson, with whom Taylor had played in another skiffle group, the James Boys, joined as bassist and vocalist. The group was completed with John Kennedy (rhythm guitar) and Geoff Bethell, who often stood in for Hardie on piano. The band played local clubs and Taylor, known for his vivid checkered jack-

The Dominoes, with Cliff Roberts on drums.

ets, developed a reputation as one of the best rock 'n' roll singers in the Liverpool area.

By summer 1960, the group was being billed as Kingsize Taylor and the Dominoes and were playing at some of the best clubs in Liverpool. "By now we were playing interval spots at Litherland Town Hall," recalled Roberts, "the most prestigious venue in North Liverpool. That meant free admission for the band and our girlfriends, plus free refreshments. We were local celebrities now. We'd made it!"

They first performed at The Cavern Club in January 1961 and featured seventeen-year-old singer Cilla White, who was mistakenly renamed Cilla Black later that year in an article Bill Harry wrote for in his music paper *Mersey Beat*. Soon after that appearance, Kennedy and Roberts left the band to join another group, Ian and the Zodiacs, and were replaced by John Frankland (rhythm guitar) and Dave Lovelady (drums). At the beginning of 1962, the band placed sixth in a *Mersey Beat* readers' poll, topped by The Beatles.

Roberts recalled The Silver Beats' appearance that first night: "They were a scruffy bunch whose drummer hadn't brought his kit and asked if he could borrow mine. I had a brand new Olympic kit that I hadn't even used on stage myself, so I naturally refused." However, he agreed to play with The Silver Beats and they performed six numbers together, as Roberts recalled, "four rock 'n' roll standards that all the groups played, and two originals that they had to teach me."

Kingsize Taylor remembers that night, too: "We had just finished our set and were getting off to have a couple of pints at the International Pub. Then Brian Kelly asked Cliff if he would sit in with the band, which he duly did."

As a result of The Silver Beats' brief performance, Kelly booked them for the following week, on Saturday 21 May. He publicised the event, which was the first time the group had officially appeared in an advertisement which stated the bill as "Silver Beats, Dominoes, Deltones".

In spite of the top billing, they did not turn up for the gig. Instead, they left for a tour of Scotland as Johnny Gentle's backing band. In the process, they'd failed to inform Kelly, who consequently did not book them again for several months until Bob Wooler talked him into it.

Roberts says that the group then disappeared. He did not see them again until eight months later when they appeared on the bill at the Alexandra Hall, Crosby on Thursday 19 January 1961. He recalled the evening: "They wore black leather, had brand new instruments and played brilliantly."

What a difference a few months, and a gruelling apprenticeship in Hamburg, could make to a band.

Advertisement for The Silver Beats' appearance at Lathom Hall on 14 May 1960, the only time they used this name.

MAY 1960

John Lennon, Paul McCartney, George Harrison, Stuart Sutcliffe
and *Johnny Gentle*

One of the most confusing personality crises the group would ever face occurred on their tour of Scotland. For starters, everyone but drummer Tommy Moore and headliner Johnny Gentle decided to use stage names. Then, after being selected by Larry Parnes as the backing band on a Scottish tour by his artist, Johnny Gentle, The Silver Beetles became the designated "Group" in what would be billed "Johnny Gentle and His Group". Although the publicity for the tour called them "His Group", Parnes referred to them as The Silver Beetles. By the end of the tour, Gentle was introducing them as The Beatles, though on a set of autographs the group signed for a fan on the tour, Stuart Sutcliffe called them "Beatals", the name he had suggested at the beginning of the year.

Johnny Gentle was born John Askew on 8 December 1936 in Nightingale Square, off Scotland Road in North Liverpool. It is perhaps ironic that a son of Scotland Road should make his name on the road in Scotland.

Askew became an apprentice ship's carpenter and in 1957, after discovering a love for music, he read an article about how to make a guitar. "After I completed the guitar," recalled Askew, "I took lessons to play. My tutor was amazed at the sound of my guitar. He always played it when I came for my lesson".

He started performing with his friend Bobby Crawford at various pubs and clubs doing two-part harmony songs by The Everly Brothers. Like so many other artists, they attended auditions for agents whenever they could and, at one particular club in Walton, Liverpool, they would get their bookings.

In 1958, after completing his apprenticeship, he became a ship's carpenter on a cruise liner. On leave, he decided to enter a talent competition under the name of George Baker, the first of many pseudonyms he would use. The competition was at Butlin's Holiday Camp, but he did not win. That accolade went to a school friend of John Lennon's at Dovedale School: Jimmy Tarbuck. George Baker did not make another appearance, as Askew soon changed his stage name to Ricky Damone in honour of Ricky Nelson.

Johnny Gentle on stage in Alloa, Scotland.

246

When he won a competition at the Locarno, he was given some contacts in London, including Larry Parnes, one of the top promoters of the day. Parnes gave Johnny an audition with Philips Records and he signed a six-record deal with them.

Parnes also decided to sign Johnny as an artist, but needed to find the right stage name for him. His first suggestion was Tim McGhee, but Johnny did not like that. As he was called Johnny and was perceived as a quiet guy, he was given the name Johnny Gentle.

Gentle began composing his own songs, and one of these originals, "Wendy", became his debut single in March 1959. It was not successful, but was followed with "Milk From The Coconut" in August 1959 and "Darlin' Won't You Wait" in January 1960. It was because of this limited chart success that Larry Parnes decided to send him on a tour of Scotland. But first, he would need a backing band.

By now, Parnes had a stable of stars, all with their own unique stage names: Billy Fury (Ronnie Wycherley), Duffy Power (Ray Howard), Vince Eager (Roy Taylor), Dickie Pride (Richard Knellar) and many others. Billy Fury was his most successful artist to date, so Parnes headed to Liverpool. If the city could produce two singers like Fury and Gentle, then perhaps it would also be the place to find bands to back them.

The auditions were set up through Allan Williams at his Wyvern Social Club on 10 May 1960. Among the local bands attending were The Silver Beetles, consisting of John, Paul, George, Stuart and drummer Tommy Moore. There are many stories about this day, some truths and others myths. First, Tommy Moore was late for the audition, which did not endear him to Parnes. It has also been reported that John Lennon refused to back Billy Fury because Parnes wanted the group to drop Stuart. Other accounts say that The Silver Beetles failed the audition.

What actually happened was that The Silver Beetles were not considered good enough to back Billy Fury, but they were selected to support Johnny Gentle on his tour of Scotland. This was by no means a failure. The fee for the tour, which was billed as the "Beat Ballad Tour", was £120, including their travelling expenses. It would begin on 20 May 1960.

Inside the Locarno Ballroom, 1950.

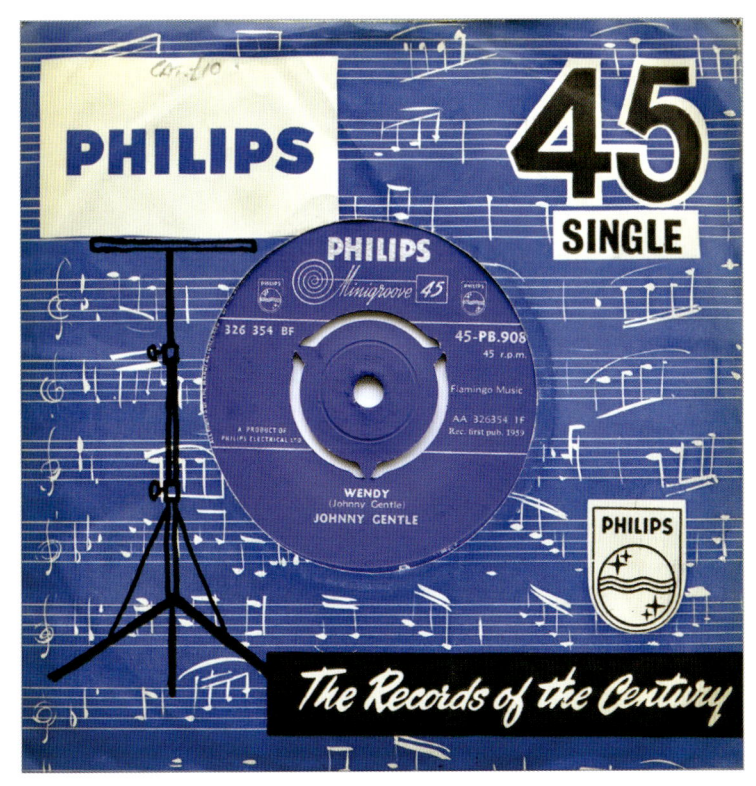

"Wendy" by Johnny Gentle.

Since they were not billed as The Silver Beetles anyway, the group devised their own stage names for this tour. While Tommy Moore opted out of this idea, John Lennon became Johnny Lennon, Paul McCartney decided he would be Paul Ramon, George would be Carl Harrison and Stuart would be Stuart de Stael.

As Paul later commented: "John did not wish to be known as 'Long John' any longer and I did not wish to be known as Paul Ramon. It was just an exotic moment in my life. It made it all sound professional and real. It sort of proved you did a real act if you had a stage name". Although Paul suggests John used the name Long John, the evidence of autographs obtained on that tour show John using the name, Johnny Lennon, not Long John.

Many authors have labelled this tour a complete disaster, but it was far from it. This was their first time away from home on tour and a forerunner for what was to come a few weeks later in Hamburg.

John recalled how important it was: "It kind of opened our eyes. We played literally hundreds of gigs before we made it. That first tour was the first time we had seen what it was like to be on the road. It was bloody hard work. There's no doubt that Scotland gave us a taste for whatever it was we were looking. It was a turning point of sorts". Ken McNab, author of *The Beatles In Scotland*, examined the tour in detail.

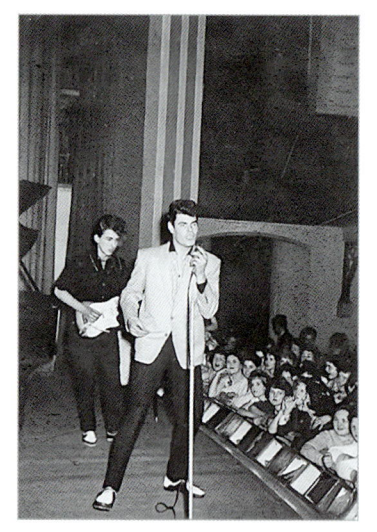

Johnny Gentle, with George Harrison looking on.

The tour programme was as follows:

20 May 1960	The Town Hall, Marsh Hill, Alloa, Clackmananshire
21 May 1960	The Northern Meeting Ballroom, Church Street, Inverness
22 May 1960	Day off
23 May 1960	Dalrymple Hall, Seaforth Street, Fraserburgh, Aberdeenshire
24 May 1960	Day off
25 May 1960	St. Thomas' Hall, Chapel Street, Keith, Banffshire
26 May 1960	The Town Hall, High Street, Forres, Morayshire
27 May 1960	The Regal Ballroom, Leopold Street, Nairn, Nairnshire
28 May 1960	The Rescue Hall, Prince Street, Peterhead, Aberdeenshire

The tour was eventful, to say the least.

Autographs from 23 May 1960, showing the group's pseudonyms, and the first time the name, The Beatles, appears.

20 May 1960 Alloa

The Silver Beatles left Liverpool's Lime Street railway station and headed for Glasgow, before changing trains for the trip to Alloa. They made it to the Town Hall at 8:30pm, one hour before the concert was due to start. There was no time to rehearse before the tour started so, with 20 minutes to go before curtain-up, Johnny Gentle and His Group had their first meeting and first practise. They quickly discussed what songs they were going to do after a brief introduction.

Johnny Gentle was less than impressed on their first meeting. "I did wonder what Larry Parnes had sent me," recalled Gentle. "They were dressed in jeans and sweaters and were the roughest bunch of lads I had seen in my life. John and Stu were at Art College and they looked it. Their hair fell over their collars and Stu had a beard. George was serving an apprenticeship and looked like it, as did Paul who was studying for his A-Levels. John told me excitedly; 'This is our big break'".

The opening night repertoire for Johnny Gentle and His Group consisted of Ricky Nelson's "Poor Little Fool", Jim Reeves' "He'll Have To Go", Elvis Presley's "I Need Your Love Tonight" and Clarence Frogman Henry's "I Don't Know Why I Love You But I Do".

Johnny would then hand the show over to The Silver Beatles, whose set was more rock 'n' roll. In addition to playing a couple of their own songs, "Hello Little Girl" and "One After 909", they performed The Everly Brothers' "Bye Bye Love", Little Richard's "Tutti Frutti", "Lucille" and "Long Tall Sally", Eddie Cochran's "Twenty Flight Rock" and "Hallelujah I Love Her So", Buddy Holly's "That'll Be The Day", Gene Vincent's "Wild Cat" and "Be Bop A Lula", Elvis' "Stuck On You", Ray Charles' "What'd I Say", Chuck Berry's "Little Queenie" and The Olympics' "Hully Gully".

The first night wasn't very good and the promoter, Duncan McKinnon, made sure that they knew it. They also didn't dress the same, so Johnny gave George a black shirt that matched those worn by John and Paul. Johnny was less than impressed by McKinnon, whom he described as "more like a farmer than a man who put on shows in dance halls".

However, there was a small contingent of screaming girls who loved the idea of seeing a pop star like Johnny Gentle. Jean Morrison was one of those fans. She and a friend even accepted a lift in the group's van. "John came up to me and put his arm round my waist, and said 'Hi, my name's John'. He said he was coming back in a couple of weeks and that we should meet, but it never happened." As for the ride home in the van, John had said they were going her way and offered the two girls a lift. "I sat on his knee on the way home. It was just a cuddle and a lift home in the van."

Johnny Gentle with the crowd in Alloa, Scotland.

Alloa Town Hall.

The Fab one hundred and Four

21 May 1960: Inverness

From Alloa, it was 150-mile drive north to the highlands of Scotland. Their driver, Gerry Scott, was their roadie and responsible for getting their Austin van all the way to Inverness. The next day's gig was at the Northern Meeting Ballroom in Church Street, Inverness. The group was much improved over the previous night's effort. They rehearsed during the day together and gave a more polished and professional performance which was well received by the audience.

After the concert had finished, there were girls waiting for autographs outside, which was new experience for the group. "This is great," John commented. "This is the life. Do you think we should give everything up and go full-time?" They were starting to enjoy the tour and it would only get better.

The following day, they rested before their next performance in Fraserburgh. It was while they were relaxing that Johnny Gentle was playing around with a song he was writing called "I've Just Fallen For Someone". He couldn't get the middle-eight to work. John was with him, so he asked him for his opinion. Lennon quite happily helped him with the song. "This might fit", Lennon told him after writing something that could work. With little effort, Lennon provided the words for Gentle to use. "I instinctively knew", said Gentle, "and he just picked up my home-made guitar, closed his eyes and sang these lines: 'We know that we'll get by, just wait and see, just like the song tells us, the best things in life are free'." Gentle recorded the song a few years later under another pseudonym, Darren Young. Adam Faith recorded it, too.

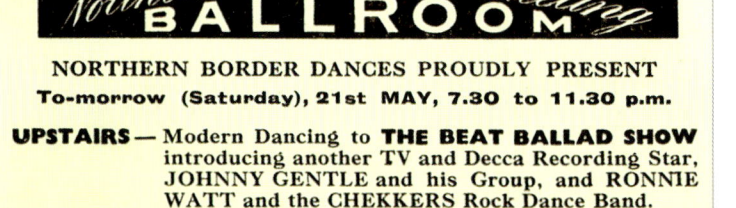

Ticket for Johnny Gentle's appearance at the Northern Meeting Rooms in Inverness.

23 May 1960: Fraserburgh

By the time they were on their way to Fraserburgh, money was already running out. There was a problem with the driving, however, as Gerry Scott was hung over from the night before. It fell to Johnny to take over at the wheel. With Scott in the back, Lennon sat up front alongside Gentle, though he quickly fell asleep.

As they approached a crossroads outside of Banff, Johnny suddenly swerved to the left to avoid an oncoming car, which was occupied by a couple of pensioners. As he hit the brakes, Tommy Moore was thrown on top of Lennon, who had bashed into the dashboard. Moore's face was covered in blood, so they took him to the hospital. There, he was informed that he had lost a tooth and had a concussion. He told Lennon that he was in no state to play. Without a care for his drummer's health, Lennon made his feelings clear. "You listen to me," Lennon yelled. "You're bloody playing! We need a drummer and you're it. Let's go!"

Poor Tommy Moore. With a banging headache, he was soon banging his drums behind the group that signed autographs after the show using the new name they had been toying with: The Beatles. This is the first known use of the spelling of the name that would soon be forever etched in history.

The evening performance at Dalrymple Hall in Fraserburgh was the first time that Johnny Gentle noticed a change in the audience's reaction. The screams for The Beatles were louder than the ones for him.

Margaret Adams was in the audience that night and told Stan Williams what she remembered: "It was bedlam! I couldn't quite understand it because Johnny was always the main attraction for me. After the show, The Beatles all ran out of the back door and piled into my dad's Vauxhall estate car because the girls were chasing them. We then drove back to my parent's house. We had a bit of a sing-along and I remember Paul McCartney singing the Jim Reeves' song "He'll Have To Go" to my mum. John spent the night talking to my dad. George was very quiet and I can't remember if Stuart was there. When I look back on the show now, I feel that I was in at the start of Beatlemania."

The next day, the boys realised that they were running out of mon-

Dalrymple Hall in Fraserburgh.

ey. Even though Gentle had written to Parnes, there was not even enough to pay for their room at the town's Station Hotel. John, Paul, George and Stu wandered on the beach. In the dunes were Margaret Moffat and a friend, both of whom had been among the screaming fans the night before.

"We recognised them right away as the band from the night before," Margaret said. "We did not see many strangers in Fraserburgh at that time. It was very tight-knit. They were quite a scruffy bunch. We just stood and watched them. Then we ran like fury down the other side of the sand dune so we could bump into them accidentally on purpose and appear very nonchalant. We got talking and we told them we had been at the show the night before. John Lennon then asked us if there was a café nearby so we said, yes, there was a café down the road and we would take them to it. That meant a walk of about a quarter of a mile, which suited us because it meant we would be walking with the band.

"We walked back along the beach to Joe's Café and discovered that they had virtually no money. There was some story about someone having absconded with the money and they were going to be thrown out of the Station Hotel because they hadn't paid their bill. John had one shilling left which is 5p in today's money and he spent it on a chilled orange for him and one for me. And that is my claim to fame. John Lennon spent his last sixpence on me."

They talked about the previous night's show. John told them that their black stage shirts had been torn by the over-enthusiastic female fans. As they had to wear them for the next night, they had a problem. The girls quickly found a solution.

Margaret said, "We went back to my house and my friend and I stitched up the shirts, ironed them and made them some bread rolls. John Lennon was in my bedroom but it was all perfectly innocent. He did ask me out, but it just was not possible, and I never saw him again."

25 May 1960 Keith

Next, the group headed for Forres, one of Scotland's oldest agricultural towns. It was the obvious place to choose, as it lay directly between Keith and Nairn, where the band was due to play on 25 and 27 May. The concert in Forres itself was sandwiched in between.

Due to their lack of cash, Lennon decided it was time to raise the stakes. Grabbing the telephone, he rang Larry Parnes at his Oxford Street office in London. Johnny Gentle remembers Lennon shouting at Parnes, "Look Larry, where's the bloody money? We're broke."

Parnes remembered it well: "We used to pay the groups £15 by post on a Thursday so they would get it on Friday or the very latest on Saturday. I always remember the second week that The Silver Beatles were working for me and I was sitting in my office on a Monday morning at about 11 o'clock and a phone call came through for me, reverse charge. 'Who's on the line?' I asked my secretary. 'John Lennon', I was told. 'Oh well', I replied, 'you had better put him on to see what he wants'," he recalled.

"John comes on the phone and says, 'Larry, where's the bloody money?' 'What money?' I asked. 'We're broke, we're skint', John replies. I said, 'But you haven't even worked the week out yet, John. In fact, you haven't even started the week.' John says, 'Larry, you said if we get a short week we could have a sub.' So I said, 'You can have a sub, how much do you want?' 'Well about five pounds each.' 'Oh all right,'

St. Thomas Hall, Keith.

I replied. 'We'll send you up five pounds each.' It was funny really because both weeks he worked for us, he would either come on the phone on the Monday or the Tuesday or the Wednesday. He was the spokesman and he would always say the same thing – 'Where's the bloody money?'"

The Silver Beatles and Johnny spent the night having a few – and, in George and Paul's case, illegal – beers in the lounge of their hotel. After a long night, the lads lay in bed until late morning, but had to be up for rehearsals in the afternoon. They wanted to try out a few new songs, among them Buddy Holly's "Words of Love" and Little Richard's "Kansas City", and also to work on their own composition, "One After 909".

By now, George Harrison's guitar playing had greatly improved and the close harmonies of Lennon and McCartney were near perfect. Suddenly, they were making the kind of rock 'n' roll they had only dreamt about. Johnny Gentle remembers a band that suddenly found their best form. "They had already backed me more than adequately", said Gentle. "But when it came to their own set, they simply stunned the audience. Their own songs were cheered as loudly as the others, but the most successful song of the night was 'Kansas City' and it remained a part of their repertoire for many years to come.

"Duncan McKinnon had arrived just in time for The Beatles' performance and he was shocked by what he heard," Gentle continued. "They did not sound anything like the crummy band he'd wanted to send home just five days earlier in Alloa. I thought we had just seen the future of rock 'n' roll. I just thought they were going to make it. I had seen enough backing bands to know that these guys were different. Maybe Stuart and Tommy did not quite fit but the other three were a rock 'n' roll triumvirate to be reckoned with. Next morning when Larry Parnes called to check on the tour, I advised him to sign The Silver Beatles. I said sign them up now while you can. They're gonna be big. In fact, I thought they were going down better than me. But, to his regret, he was not listening. He said he did not have the time." Parnes became yet another who was to miss out on signing The Beatles.

26 May 1960 Forres

Once again, the previous night's performance had been an improvement on the one before, and Forres was no different. As usual, Johnny's show-stopping moment came when he pulled up a chair and sang his ballad "Have I Told You Lately" beneath a single spotlight. Behind him, in the shadows, The Silver Beatles strummed their guitars.

When he finished his last song, Johnny bowed and then, for the first time, announced his support group like they were the headline act. "Ladies and gentlemen... a big hand for The Beatles". The group had their first ovation with Johnny. As Lennon recalled: "I'll tell you one thing. It's better than working."

27 May 1960 Nairn

The next night, they were at the Regal Ballroom in Nairn. As Gentle left the stage, Lennon took his place at the microphone, feet firmly

The Town Hall, Forres.

The Regal Hall, Nairn.

planted on the stage and guitar at the ready. McCartney stood next to Lennon. Harrison stared at his red Grazione guitar. Sutcliffe held his bass guitar in anticipation and the moody Moore just showed his lack of interest behind the drums.

Local musician Johnny Douglas did not rate their musical prowess. As he recalled: "They arrived in this old Austin 16 van. They were so poor they slept in this van. They were all nice guys and they would talk away to you. They would drink bottles of beer. All the kids were doing it. They were typical youngsters but, from what I saw, they seemed to be enjoying themselves. They had wee, tiny amplifiers. I was amazed they got any sound from them at all. They were absolute rubbish."

28 May 1960 Peterhead

If there was one thing that brought them back down to earth, it was sleeping in the van that carried them through the Highlands of Scotland. Their final engagement was at the Rescue Hall on Prince Street in Peterhead. Parnes had even sent more cash through to Duncan McKinnon, which enabled them to check into a small bed and breakfast.

There was a nice surprise waiting for them at the hall where McKinnon, now delighted that the tour had turned in a healthy profit, had delivered a crate of beer to their dressing room. Gentle was finishing on a high, turning in the best performance of the tour. He and his much-improved backing group celebrated in style by working their way through the crate of alcohol.

With thumping heads and reddened eyes, Gentle and His Group met up at the singer's hotel to say goodbye and congratulate each other on a tiring, but successful tour. A couple of nights earlier, Johnny even considered hiring them as a permanent backing band, but he did not dwell on it for long.

In many narratives, the Johnny Gentle Tour of Scotland has been written off as a failure, reinforcing the misconception that The Silver Beatles were not that good, and that Hamburg was their real proving ground. However, the fact is, the Scotland tour saw them improve in leaps and bounds. Hamburg would only make them better.

Stuart Sutcliffe sent a postcard to his friend Rod Murray from Scotland, which gave his impression of the tour. "Going like a bomb, love every minute. Scotland beautiful here particularly. See you Monday – I hope. Look after yourself. Stuart."

While it is true that going to Hamburg would be the springboard that propelled them to superstardom, let's give credit to Johnny Gentle and Larry Parnes for offering them the opportunity to hone their skills in the small halls in Scotland.

However, for Tommy Moore, the short time spent on the road with the group was enough, and he would soon quit the group to drive a forklift truck at the Garston Bottle Works. So much for rock 'n' roll.

Postcard sent to Rod Murray by Stuart Sutcliffe while he was in Fraserburgh.

JUNE 1960

John Lennon, Paul McCartney, George Harrison, Stuart Sutcliffe *and Janice the Stripper*

Allan Williams booked The Silver Beetles at the strip club he co-owned with Lord Woodbine at 174a, Upper Parliament Street. It was an old cotton merchant's house with big white pillars and black railings. Williams had auditioned a well-proportioned Manchester stripper named Janice who demanded live music for her act, unlike the other strippers who performed to a record player. Williams agreed because he knew she would be good for business. He convinced the lads to play there, even though they were against the idea. They backed Janice on a stage that was seven feet square and, in return, received 50 pence a man per night for a week.

As they were drummerless, Paul played the kit that week. Janice fancied young George – though she was warned off. The punters often complained about The Silver Beetles because they couldn't concentrate on Janice.

After some initial resistance, the four Silver Beetles had haggled out an equitable financial deal. Supposedly, Stuart was a tough negotiator and got them a fairly decent fee. "Why so much?", Williams had asked them during the negotiations. Paul had replied, "For the indignity. The bloody indignity of it all!"

Lord Woodbine recalled the club, and The Silver Beetles' appearance, very well. "Allan Williams and I used to run some clubs together, and The Beatles used to play there. There were actually two clubs. In the first one, they used to play at dinner time (noon) until 3:00pm. The second was a striptease club in a basement, called the Cabaret Art-

Lady identified as Janice, photographed at The Jacaranda, by Cheniston K. Roland.

174 Upper Parliament Street on the corner where, in the basement, at 174a, was the Cabaret Artists' Social Club.

And so, for one week only, The Silver Beetles backed a stripper in a strip club. They were determined that they would never again sink so low as to work in such a place. After all, they were professional musicians. How ironic, then, that only two months later, The Beatles would be settled in the heart of the red-light area of Hamburg, surrounded by strip clubs.

ists' Social Club. Their job was to play music for the strippers. The strippers used to get them to play very slow numbers, which The Beatles did not really like. There was only one who wanted an up-tempo song. She used a hula hoop in her act. The Beatles weren't interested in the strippers or the music. They just did it for the money."

Paul obviously remembered the occasion very well, in a private letter to Bill Harry, for inclusion in *Mersey Beat*. "John, George, Stu and I used to play at a Strip Club in Upper Parliament Street," recalled Paul, "backing Janice the Stripper. At the time we wore little lilac jackets, or purple jackets, or something. Well, we played behind Janice and naturally we looked at her, the audience looked at her, everybody looked at her, just sort of normal. At the end of the act, she would turn round and, well, we were all young lads, we'd never seen anything like it before, and all blushed, four blushing red-faced lads.

"Janice brought sheets of music for us to play all her arrangements. She gave us a bit of Beethoven and the 'Spanish Fire Dance'. So, in the end, we said 'We can't read music, sorry, but instead of the 'Spanish Fire Dance' we can play 'The Harry Lime Cha-Cha', which we've arranged ourselves, and instead of Beethoven you can have 'Moonglow' or 'September Song'. Take your pick. Instead of the 'Sabre Dance' we'll give you 'Ramrod'. So that's what she got. She seemed quite satisfied anyway."

Janice poses in The Jacaranda.

The *Fab* one hundred and *Four*

14 JUNE 1960

John Lennon, Paul McCartney, George Harrison, Stuart Sutcliffe *and* Ronnie 'The Ted'

After Tommy Moore quit the group to return to his job at the Garston Bottle Works, The Silver Beatles still had to fulfil a performance that had already been booked for 14 June 1960 at The Grosvenor Ballroom, Wallasey. Without a drummer, John tried to make a joke about their absent band member and asked if there were any drummers in the room. Not expecting a response, he was shocked when Ronnie 'The Ted' (Teddy Boy) stepped up and, using Moore's drum kit, bashed away at the skins for the evening. It turned out that Lennon and The Silver Beatles were too scared to challenge this intimidating man.

Allan Williams remembered the night clearly. "When The Beatles went on stage, there was the usual mob of kids determined on mischief. I knew the reputation of the Grosvenor, and they couldn't just not turn up, as there would be murder! The lads set up, and I could see one of the gangs had a leader, who we now know was Ronnie. He had a mass of red hair and was about six feet two inches tall, and around seventeen years old. He had hands like anchors, shoulders like a brick outhouse and piggy eyes which gleamed out uncertainly, madly, at a highly suspect world. Ronnie liked hurting people, and was responsible for hospitalising a number of victims. Most of all, he had his gang around to back him up. You did not take him on.

"When Lennon joked that they could play without a drummer, but it would be better if they had one and then stupidly asked for volunteers, there was only one person to step forward, and that was Ronnie. When he stepped up, the lads looked at Lennon and Lennon looked at Ronnie. He realised what he had done, but couldn't get out of it now. They knew Ronnie and had seen him in action at the Grosvenor before. There was nothing else they could do but let him bash away. Ronnie even asked John if he could join them permanently!

"I was back at The Jac when there was a phone call from John. He brought me up to speed with what had happened, and sounded really afraid, which was not often the case with John. I drove over there as fast as I could and, by the time I arrived, the lads had finished and were in the band room with Ronnie and some of his gang. I introduced myself and helped the lads pack up, with Ronnie chatting away to me. I was thinking on my feet, because I'm only five

The Grosvenor Ballroom, Wallasey, where Ronnie 'The Ted' joined The Silver Beatles on stage.

feet small! I did have my bouncer with me, but wanted to get away without a fight. As we finished packing up, Ronnie approached me. 'Well, you're the manager, what about it?' obviously wanting me to appoint him as the group's new drummer. I tactfully explained that Tommy was still our drummer, and he was just busy this night. And then I left him with a promise. 'The lads are playing here again next week. If we haven't got another drummer by then, you can sit in with the boys. How about that?' Ronnie was happy with that compromise, and we escaped.

"We went back to Tommy and convinced him to play one more time with us, but after that, he was finished."

For one night only, Ronnie 'The Ted' was the group's drummer.

Despite several public appeals on Merseyside, Ronnie 'The Ted' has never come forward and revealed his identity.

18 JUNE 1960

John Lennon, Paul McCartney, George Harrison, Stuart Sutcliffe *and* Norman Chapman

Probably one of the strangest lineups in the story includes Norman Chapman: John, Paul, George, Stuart and Norman. The Silver Beetles had struggled to find a regular drummer, having fallen out with Tommy Moore, who quit the group to return to a regular job.

Norman's daughter Ann-Marie who gave me an exclusive insight into Norman's life and his brief time with the group.

"Dad was born on 31st December 1936 and lived in a three-bedroom maisonette in Pitt Street, Liverpool," said Ann-Marie. "He was the youngest of eight children. He had four brothers and three sisters, and my Auntie Maria used to dote on him. His mother, Sarah, was a cook and well-known for her pies, which she would cook, sell, and then give all the proceeds to her local church, St. Michael's. Maria would walk Norman to St. James' School every day and she remembers that, from a young age, he was interested in being a picture framer. No one knows why, but that is what he wanted to be, and from school, he went straight into work as a picture framer.

"Dad learned to play the drums in the Boy's Brigade and was given his first set of cymbals by a guy called Red Carter. He went down to Hessy's to get his first set of drums on finance."

Seeking inspiration, The Silver Beetles were with Allan Williams in their usual hangout, The Jacaranda Club, wondering where they could they find another drummer to join them? "One night, we

Norman Chapman drumming with Ernie Mack's Saturated Seven.

heard the sound of drums coming from the street," recalled Williams, "so we went outside to find out where it was coming from. There was a drummer rehearsing across the road from The Jac – in what became the Bamboo Club – and the company repaired old cash registers."

In the only known interview that Chapman gave, he told author and broadcaster Spencer Leigh in 1980 how he joined the group.

"I worked in a shop in Slater Street originally, Jackson's Art Shop, and I was practising in a place further down from there with my drum kit: I was practicing in a workshop I used to work in Slater Street. I think the drum kit cost about £20, and I was dead keen on playing, but never had any thoughts of playing with a group. One afternoon in Jackson's, my boss Mr. Brewer said somebody wants to see you downstairs at the front of the shop. When I went down to see who it was, it was Paul McCartney, and he had heard me practising and he asked me if I would like to sit in with the band that night, which I did." Norman was a picture framer at R. Jackson & Sons, situated at 20, Slater Street. At six feet two inches, Norman cut an im-

Norman's passport photograph.

Ann-Marie, Norman's daughter, with her children Avie and Hayley.

R. Jackson & Sons, opposite The Jacaranda, where Norman Chapman worked above the shop.

The *Fab* one hundred and *Four*

posing figure in the doorway. Trying not to appear desperate, they quickly "invited Norman to join the group. "It was just sit in and play and just one of those nights where you just go down and do your thing. There was no rehearsals or band calls, it just happened you know, the twelve-bar blues stuff and general music like that." After that, Chapman was into the group for real. "Dad spent a lot of time rehearsing with them," explained Ann-Marie, "and soon showed that he was a talented drummer. We know that he did rehearse with the lads at John's Aunt Mimi's home, "Mendips", among others places, and they quickly became friends." Norman proved to be a natural fit for the group, appearing with them for three consecutive Saturday night performances at the Grosvenor Ballroom in Wallasey, on 18 and 25 June, and 2 July 1960.

In his book, The Man Who Gave The Beatles Away, Allan Williams remembers Norman fondly. "He was a big guy, about six feet two, and spoke in a very quiet, gentle voice. His drumming was a hobby and he hadn't even sat in with a band before. I told him about the band, and that they were playing around Merseyside, earning about ten pounds a night, and asked him if he was interested. 'I sure am,' he told me, 'I could do with the money because drum kits are so expensive. That'll help me pay off the money for the kit.' The others liked him too."

Williams met up with Norman many years later and talked about those days. "Those guys really loved the game," he told Williams. "You could tell even then that they had something special going for them. Everything they did and said was directed at making their sound better and better, day by day. I remember Paul as the dominant one, not John, although everyone nominated John as the leader. One night when we were playing at the Grosvenor Ballroom in Wallasey a fight broke out. Fights were always breaking out. There were chairs flying through the air, bottles whizzing about and bodies hurling in every direction. The police charged in and they were carting bodies out and stacking them on the lawns outside. What a scene. We kept playing the music all the way through. John was hiding behind the curtain and laughing his head off and Paul was somehow crouched under the piano. The music never stopped. What a night.

"John and Stuart were on a poetry kick at the time and they asked

Norman Chapman (left) with friends, including Liverpool singer, Derry Wilkie (right).

me to go down to London with them to play while some guy read his poetry out. I was married at the time so I did not go with them. John's flat in Gambier Terrace was a scream of a place. It was so dirty and untidy. They never cleaned the ashes out of the fireplace and things got so bad the ashes stretched from the fireplace to the middle of the floor."

Just as Norman was getting to know his new friends, disaster struck the group. "Being slightly older than the others, Dad was called up for National Service," recalled Ann-Marie, "and was conscripted into the army, joining the Liverpool Scottish Guards for two years. He was soon heading for Kenya and Kuwait to complete his two years of active service." Suddenly, Norman's brief but important stint in the group was over. Ann-Marie is naturally proud of her father's contribution. It was also a twist of fate because National Service was soon to finish, meaning that John, Paul and George wouldn't have to do two years National Service, a mandate which could have spelled the end of the group. "Dad is thought by many to have been one of their greatest drummers. We gave his drum kit to The Jacaranda Club in Slater Street, where they have been on permanent display."

Norman was philosophical about his time with the group. "It was just one of those things, me being called up for the army," he said. "I never rose above private, and when I came back to Liverpool, The

Beatles were getting really big so there was no opportunity for me to go back with them. I sometimes think that maybe I should be rich by now, but I had no control over the situation at the time so it doesn't really worry me. It's not as though I parted with The Beatles voluntarily."

George Harrison recalled Norman's time with them: "I remember him well, Norman Chapman. Big feller, did not talk much. In fact, I can't remember a word he ever said to me. He was a good drummer, though, and that's for sure." Ringo later commented on Norman, too: "The boys told me they had this drummer they heard rehearsing on his own. They thought a hell of a lot of him."

Ann-Marie told me more about Norman. "Dad and mum married in 1959," she explained. "My mum was called Anastasia Peloe and she was the youngest of nine children. My granddad, mum's dad, was Walter Peloe who was a sea captain and Nanna Peloe was called Josephine. They lived in Kensington, Liverpool. I was born in 1961, but, sadly, the marriage did not last and after about three years, they got divorced. I went with my mum to live with Nanna Peloe in Kensington. She enrolled me in St. Sebastian's Catholic Primary School in Fairfield and she used to take me to mass every day!

"Mum then met a man called Lenny Gilbert and we moved to Wavertree. They had two daughters, Susan and Janet, my half-sisters.

Norman with his son-in-law, Michael, and grandchildren Hayley and Avie.

Norman with his granddaughter Hayley in Sefton Park, Liverpool.

However, mum made it clear that I was not allowed to see my dad, but I was allowed to visit my Nanna Chapman. If my dad called when I was there, I was not allowed to see him and vice versa. I didn't know that this subterfuge was taking place until I was an adult."

Ann-Marie wouldn't see her dad again until she was in her twenties. She left home at the age of only nineteen after falling out with her mother and stepfather. Ann-Marie then met her future husband, Michael Opone, who was from Nigeria. Michael left Africa for England on a scholarship and ended up in Liverpool studying Marine Engineering. After the falling out with her mother, Ann-Marie left home, never again having any contact with her.

Ann-Marie continued: "Michael and I married and we had a daughter, Hayley, and a son, Ovie. I then had a phone call from Auntie Maria who asked if I wanted to meet up with my dad again. Of course, I said yes, and it was wonderful. We would meet up in Sefton Park with the kids and he bought them bicycles. We had a lovely time getting to know each other again. Michael moved to Brighton in 1990 with his work while I finished my degree at Liverpool John Moores University. I graduated with a First Class Degree in 1993 and followed Michael down to Brighton, where we still live. Michael moved to Brighton in 1990 with his work while I finished my degree at John Moores University. I graduated with a First Degree in Psychology in 1993 and followed Michael down to Brighton, where we still live. Dad came and stayed with us and we shared Christmas together. It was a lovely time."

Norman then set up a picture-framing business in Southport. "Dad did work with some of the famous local footballers," explained Ann-Marie, "but he never tried to make a lot of money. He was not interested in making money, just enjoying what he did. He played drums for many years, including in a group called Ernie Mack's Saturated Seven (a play on words with the more famous Temperance Seven, a group that had a number one hit in 1961 with "You're Driving Me Crazy", produced by future Beatles producer, George Martin). His longest lasting friendship was with 'Old' Joe Royle, father of the former Everton Football Club manager, Joe Royle. They enjoyed playing gigs together for many years until Joe passed away. Dad used to go round to Joe's house every week and cook him his favourite fish. Young Joe still keeps in touch with Auntie Maria, who steadfastly respects her brother's wishes to maintain a dignified silence about his time with The Beatles.

"Dad contracted lung cancer and ended up in hospital," Ann-Marie said. "We were travelling up from Brighton to see him when I received a phone call to say we were too late and that he had passed away. I don't know why they did not tell us he was so ill or we could have got up there sooner. He was only 58. He never got to meet his third grandchild, my son, Efe."

Norman Chapman was a shy man and never wanted to talk much about his time with the group that, as The Beatles, would conquer all before them. "Dad was never jealous or bitter about his short time with the group and was also conscious of never wanting to cash-in on their fame for his own rewards. He was just happy with his life and got on with it."

As Chapman said to Spencer Leigh, "Being in music has cost me quite a lot actually, domestic-wise and otherwise, unfortunately, but

Norman at work in his picture-framing business, Southport.

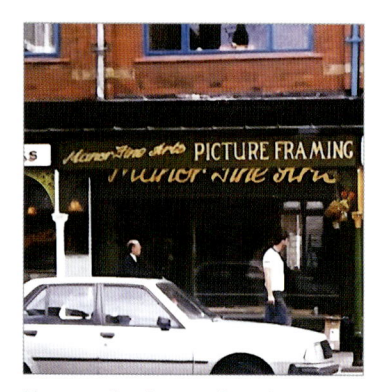

Norman's picture-framing business, Manor Fine Arts, in Southport.

The record, "Down By The Old Mill Stream", that Norman played on.

Norman's workshop, where he made his frames.

I've also met some very nice people through being involved with music and also people who like to shoot The Beatles down. I don't know why, in their early stages, because they said they were semi-skilled and couldn't tune instruments or whatever, but who could at an early stage in their profession or starting off in music? Do I miss the fame, the fortune, whatever? Well, I don't. I'd like a few shekels from time to time but I wouldn't say I've missed it all that much, but people want me to have this down on everybody."

A gentle giant, Norman was popular in the group during his short tenure with them. "He would probably have still been with them," observed Allan Williams, "as he got on well with them. Norman died young and I went to his funeral. I hardly knew him, but he was a nice man."

When he died in July 1995, his sister Maria paid a warm tribute to him. "He was very talented and I'm not just saying that because he was my brother. Many people said he was much better than Ringo ever was. But he was also a lovely man." When asked whether Norman was bitter because he had missed out on fame, Maria was unequivocal in her response. "He was not that sort of person. His philosophy was 'what will be, will be'. He loved music and he loved the drums."

Norman's story is one of those 'what if?' scenarios. He was a great drummer and may very well have permanently filled the slot had fate not intervened.

As Norman joined up with the army, the group was once again left with a vacancy for a drummer. With the Hamburg trip just days away, the position would have to be filled very quickly.

Ernie Mack's Saturated Seven, the group Norman played drums with.

Norman with his grandson, Ovie.

Norman (left) playing drums with Ernie Mack's Saturated Seven.

Norman Chapman.

"Make It A Party", by the Ernie Mack's Saturated Seven. Norman is second from the right.

The Ernie Mack's Saturated Seven's record sleeve, with Norman on drums, second from right.

Norman, second from right, with friends.

24 JUNE 1960

Royston Ellis and The Beetles

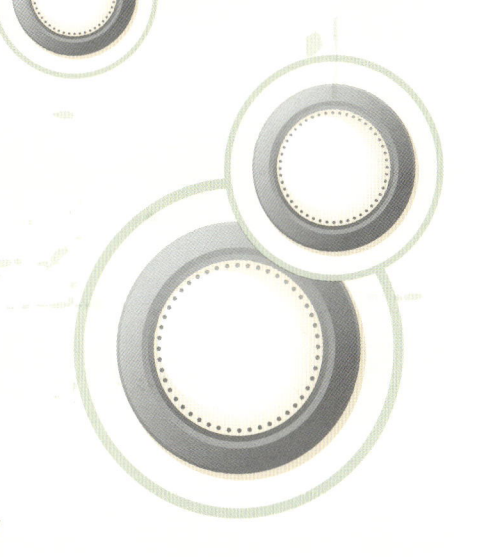

Royston Ellis first met John, Paul, George and Stuart when he visited Liverpool in the summer of 1960, when the group was still virtually unknown. They became one of the numerous bands that backed the young British Beat Poet. Royston was born on 10 February 1941 in Pinner, England and left school at sixteen with one goal in mind: to be a writer.

I tracked Royston down to his idyllic home in Sri Lanka. He told me more about that famous first encounter with The Beatles and how his 1961 book, *The Big Beat Scene,* has now been reissued.

Royston Ellis was considered one of the UK's leading exponents of beat poetry, very much in the style of the American beat poets like Allen Ginsberg. From the age of sixteen, he was hanging out in the jazz clubs and coffee bars in Soho, London, and committing his observations to poetry. In 1959, he teamed up with Cliff Richard's group, The Drifters, and performed what he called "rocketry" – rock 'n' roll poetry – on stage and on television. He was the first biographer to write about Cliff Richard (*Driftin' with Cliff Richard*) and the group that backed Cliff for many years, The Shadows (*The Shadows by Themselves*).

The Big Beat Scene, written in 1961 before The Beatles became famous, gives us a glimpse into Royston's thoughts and experiences with them, unlike many books written with the rose-tinted benefit of hindsight. Royston came to Liverpool in June 1960 as part of a tour of cities and clubs, performing his poetry. While seeking out the best place to find the beat generation of Liverpool, he was directed to The Jacaranda. There, he found the bohemian lifestyle in abundance, as the club was frequented by students from the Art College. These included two members of Allan William's resident group, John and Stuart, as well as their band mates Paul and George.

"Among the crowd I spotted a boy with a mass of hair framing a thin face," Royston told me. "Although he was dressed

Royston Ellis pictured in 1959.

The Fab one hundred and Four

Gambier Terrace, where Royston was invited to stay with Stu, Rod and John.

more like a yob than a beatnik, I nodded at him and he came over. 'Hi, whack,' he said in a thick accent. Haven't seen you around here before.' He couldn't hear my reply above the music. His name was George."

During their conversation, Royston told George that he was in Liverpool to perform at an arts festival. George decided to take him for a walk up the hill, past the Anglican Cathedral and to 3, Gambier Terrace.

Royston continued: "The hall was stacked on both sides with canvasses, easels, lumps of rock and clay chipped into weird shapes. The wallpaper was spluttered with splotches of oil paint. Thanks to the destructive enthusiasm of the wild group of art students who lived there, the luxury of this particular flat was a myth. I was supposed to be the King of the Beatniks. Well here was a real beatnik pad, so naturally I should feel at home.

"A lot of floor space was taken up with mattresses strewn on a bare wooden floorboards. Each had an assortment of tattered bedclothes on them. As I grew accustomed to the gloom and the stench of unwashed bodies, I realised that, on each mattress, there was a boy and each one was dressed in a similar manner to George, with jerkin, jeans and T-shirt.

BIG BEAT SCENE
By Royston Ellis Four Square Books 2/6

ROYSTON ELLIS, a bearded teenager who made a name for himself on the television programme 'Living For Kicks', visited Liverpool last year. Appearing at Liverpool University's 'Festival of the Arts' where he recited his poetry, he was threatened by students who wanted to set fire to his beard. Later, he recited 'poetry-to-rock' at the Jacaranda coffee club, Slater Street, backed by the Beatles.

His published works include the books of poems 'Jiving To Gyp', 'Rave', and 'The Rainbow Walking Stick', and 'Driftin' with Cliff Richard' written in corroboration with Jet Harris. His latest, 'The Big Beat Scene' is a fairly comprehensive history of rock and roll.

The blurbs on the jacket of the pocket-book scream 'an outspoken expose of the teenage world of rock and roll', 'uncensored' with their usual sensationalism, giving one the feeling that rock and roll is a form of entertainment of the luridness of strip-tease. Nothing within the covers of the book seem to justify the outcry as the report is a straightforward account of an entertaining musical medium.

The scene begins in the early fifties with the James Dean cult, the Teddy-boys and the 'creep', setting the background for the explosive impact Bill Haley made on the young generation with his music in 'The Blackboard Jungle' and 'Rock Around The Clock'. We are shown how his popularity built up to fantastic proportion, and then began to wane when he arrived in England for his tour. Elvis Presley's career is traced from its early beginnings, through his army service, his return to the recording field and films, and his present position in the scene. Ray Charles (the favourite of many Merseyside rock groups) also rates a detailed biography. Although Elvis is the undisputed leader of the field, with an almost electrical sex appeal, Charles is the genius of rock and roll. Incurably blind from the age of six, he has faced life with such determination and courage that he has mastered almost everything he has tackled. A singer of intense feeling, he is also a pianist, saxophonist, band leader, arranger and writer. Strangely enough, he is rarely in the hit parade and his records never seem to sell as they should.

Fats Domino, Gene Vincent, Ricky Nelson, Connie Francis and the majority of American vocalists are mentioned, along with Buddy Holly, Ritchie Valens, the Big Bopper, and Eddie Cochran still remembered for the joy they brought to millions. This section of the book contains many interesting items: Eddie Cochran, when returning from a two-week trip to Canada, had three hundred dollars' worth of clothing destroyed by screaming teenagers; Jerry Lee Lewis wrecked his career by marrying a thirteen-year-old girl; Ricky Nelson has been a popular television star since he was eight years old; the record 'Rock Is Here To Stay' was the swan song for Danny and the Juniors; Fabian was signed for his looks alone, and has never been popular with the British public, due to the fact that he can't sing.

Rock came to Britain simultaneously with skiffle. Tommy Steele's career is traced in detail up to the present day, and we find that his brother, Colin Hicks, found the handicap of being 'Tommy Steele's Brother' too much. He is now a popular singing star in Italy. Terry Dene, Laurie London, Jim Dale, were all there when it started, now, not as popular, they are still performing, better than ever. Skiffle has almost faded away, but Lonnie Donegan is still as popular as he was during the skiffle craze. 'Rock Island Line', 'Don't You Rock Me, Daddy-O' and 'The Battle of New Orleans' were just a few of the many hits he produced. Nowadays, appealing to a wider audience, he varies his style of singing, introduces comedy sketches in his television show, and is a pantomime favourite. Other idols of the skiffle days have faded into near obscurity. Charles McDevitt and others now enjoy a small following as folk singers. The skiffle era was fantastic; amateur groups were springing up by the thousands, playing with home-made instruments, very often with a bass made from a tea chest. It cannot be denied, however, that skiffle was responsible for providing many youngsters with the desire to play an instrument themselves.

The rest of the book covers the British scene intimately — via rock and roll on television; the creation of such idols as Cliff Richard, Adam Faith and Billy Fury; the jazz scene; personalities such as Lionel Bart and Jack Good. For anyone interested in rock and roll, this book is certainly the most comprehensive and interesting publication obtainable anywhere.

Leo Rutherford

Leo Rutherford has provided us with a brief history and the aims of his group, the line up of which is: Leo Rutherford, clarinet; Tom Burns, trumpet; Pete Williamson, trombone; Brian, banjo and guitar; Tony Snow, piano; Jon Thompson, drums; Malcolm Harrison, bass; and Shena, vocals.

"We formed the band during 1960, and our aim is to play a basically traditional style of jazz without deliberately copying any professional band. We have a varied repertoire and include a fair proportion of out-of-the-rut numbers which give the band more scope than some of the hackneyed four-chord standards! We also feature several of our own compositions, the most notable of which is Tom Burns' "Dreary Wirral Blues!"

The latest member to join the ensemble is our singer, Shena, who is a well-known Merseyside artist in her own right. She has made a considerable impression everywhere she has sung with us.

The band is based in the Hoylake and West Kirby area where we are quite well known, and we are currently featured at the Beach Club, Fort Perch Rock, New Brighton."

Bill Harry's review of Royston's book, *Big Beat Scene*. Image © Bill Harry.

Photograph of the Gambier Terrace flat that was featured in the *Sunday People* newspaper.

The Liverpool University Students' Union in 2012, where Royston Ellis performed.

They were introduced by George as being the rest of the group he played with: John, Paul and Stuart. He told me they were guitarists by night and art students by day. It was a glorious communal atmosphere, and I fell for the set up straight away. There was a record playing in the room that evening when I arrived, one I hadn't heard, by a Negro blues shouter. John proudly explained that he liked to listen to imported records that weren't part of the Top Ten."

Royston began telling John about his association with Cliff Richard and The Shadows and the other beat stars of the day, and why he was in Liverpool. John was clearly interested. Lennon would later refer to Ellis as "the converging point of rock 'n' roll and literature". Ellis added, "I was quite a star for them at that time because I had come up from London and that was a world they did not really know about."

On Friday 24 June, Royston took part in an "Afternoon of Poetry" for the Liverpool University Poetry Society, beginning at 2:30pm. The programme from the event lists him after the interval, stating "A reading of 'Beat' poetry to jazz accompaniment by Royston Ellis (Britain's foremost exponent of 'Beat' poetry)". A further advertisement in the programme promoted his appearance the following day in the basement coffee bar at Liverpool University, giving a "Reading of Beat Poetry".

John, Stuart, Rod Murray and Bill Harry were in the audience and Rod invited him to stay at their Gambier Terrace flat for a few days. "We went down to the Student's Union in Liverpool University to watch Royston Ellis read some of his poetry," Rod recalled. "After the event, like you do when you're on holiday, you say 'you must come and stay with us', but he did. We all went back to Gambier Terrace, where he famously introduced us to the drug experience with the Vicks inhaler."

John was certainly more taken with Royston than the others. Paul told biographer Barry Miles in *Many Years From Now* that 'A poet named Royston Ellis arrived in Liverpool with his book, *Jiving to Gyp*. He was a beat poet. Well, well, Phew! You just did not meet them in Liverpool. And it was all 'Break me in easy, break me in easy'. It was all about shagging sailors, I think. We had a laugh with that line. John became quite friendly with Royston."

Royston famously introduced them to their very first experience of a drug. He cracked open a Vick's inhaler and showed them the strip of Benzedrine inside. It was nicknamed a "spitball" and you chewed it. The amphetamine kept you awake in a state of excitement all night.

Royston later recalled, "Yes, the Vick's inhaler story has become part of drug legend. I was shown how to do that by a singer who later became Neil Christian and his guitarist, who used to accompany me in those days, Jimmy Page."

John recalled the encounter in a letter to Barry Miles about Allen Ginsberg in May 1973:

> 'By the way, the first dope, from a Benzedrine inhaler, was given to The Beatles (John, George, Paul and Stuart) by an (in retrospect) obviously 'English cover version of Allen – one Royston Ellis, known as beat-poet (he read poetry whilst we played 12-bar blues at the local in-place!).
>
> So give the saint his due.
> Love,
> John Lennon

Following Royston's University appearance in June 1960, the *Liverpool Daily Post* gave a great review of his performance.

John Lennon's letter about Allen Ginsberg.

Liverpool University report about Royston's appearance at the Student's Union.

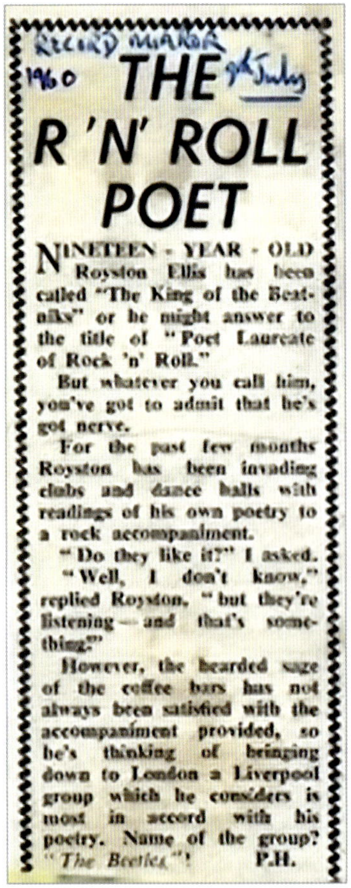

THE R 'N' ROLL POET

NINETEEN - YEAR - OLD Royston Ellis has been called "The King of the Beatniks" or he might answer to the title of "Poet Laureate of Rock 'n' Roll."

But whatever you call him, you've got to admit that he's got nerve.

For the past few months Royston has been invading clubs and dance halls with readings of his own poetry to a rock accompaniment.

"Do they like it?" I asked.

"Well, I don't know," replied Royston, "but they're listening — and that's something."

However, the bearded sage of the coffee bars has not always been satisfied with the accompaniment provided, so he's thinking of bringing down to London a Liverpool group which he considers is most in accord with his poetry. Name of the group? "The Beetles"!
— P.H.

The Record and Show Mirror article where Royston mentions The Beetles.

Royston Ellis, 2012.

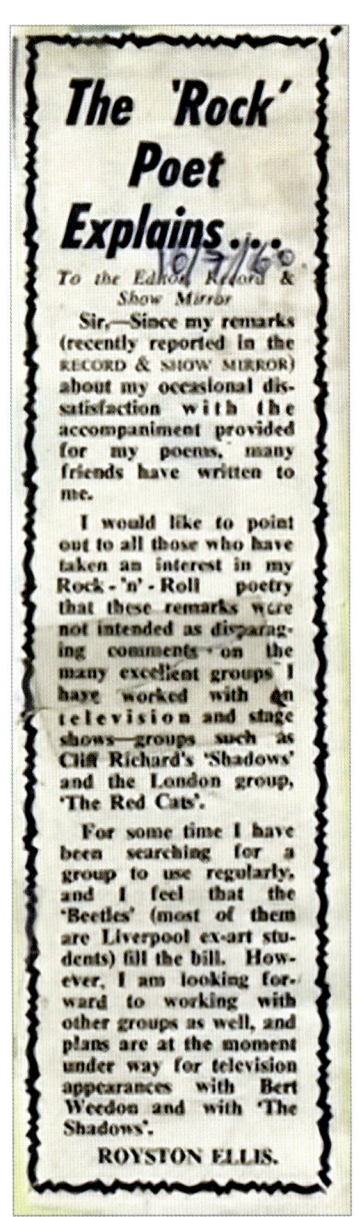

The 'Rock' Poet Explains...

To the Editor, Record & Show Mirror

Sir,—Since my remarks (recently reported in the RECORD & SHOW MIRROR) about my occasional dissatisfaction with the accompaniment provided for my poems, many friends have written to me.

I would like to point out to all those who have taken an interest in my Rock-'n'-Roll poetry that these remarks were not intended as disparaging comments on the many excellent groups I have worked with on television and stage shows—groups such as Cliff Richard's 'Shadows' and the London group, 'The Red Cats'.

For some time I have been searching for a group to use regularly, and I feel that the 'Beetles' (most of them are Liverpool ex-art students) fill the bill. However, I am looking forward to working with other groups as well, and plans are at the moment under way for television appearances with Bert Weedon and with 'The Shadows'.

ROYSTON ELLIS.

The Record and Show Mirror where Royston emphasised how great The Beetles would be to work with.

"Thanks to the Liverpool University students' festival of art, 'Beat' poetry reached the academic groves yesterday afternoon... Royston Ellis did not give his listeners a lot of boom and bant. He let the matter speak for itself – which effectively it did – as he moved about here and there, sometimes taking a seat in the front row, or on the edge of a table.

It was frank, down-to-earth stuff, with plenty of vigour and vision, centred on the progress of two characters in dance halls, coffee-bars, jazz clubs. The denizens are vividly conjured. There is plenty of alliteration and unrhymed couplets, while staccato phrases lend a punch and a jab.

We might here well have a the rudiments of a significant new free-verse medium."

When John read the review, he was so impressed that he suggested Royston join them at The Jacaranda, where they were playing each week. This "Poetry-to-Rock" session at The Jac involved John, Paul, George and Stuart. The Beetles took to the stage and played for about half an hour before John announced their special guest. Royston came onto the stage. "The change in style was slow to register," recalled Royston in his book, *The Big Beat Scene*, "but gradually the fact that there was a newcomer on stage seeped through to the kids in the cellar. It did not matter that I was not singing, just shouting out the words of a poem, while John and the others strummed their guitars."

George carrying Royston's books from the plane.

To capture the atmosphere of what Royston called 'rocketry', he has allowed me to reproduce the poem he performed that night:

> Easy, easy,
> Break me in easy.
> Sure I'm big time,
> Cock-sure and brash,
> But easy, easy,
> Break me in easy.
> Sure they've been others,
> I know the way,
> But easy, easy,
> Break me in easy.
> Let me hide,
> Warm, deep and wet,
> Under the blanket
> And between your thighs
> And easy, easy,
> Aaah – break me in easy!
>
> *Courtesy Royston Ellis*

Royston Ellis with The Shadows.

Royston at Cambridge, with a young Jimmy Page in the background.

"As I came off stage, leaving the boys to wind up their set, my mind was in a complete whirl," recalled Royston. "The kids in the cellar seemed to like it. Hands reached for me from all directions and voices babbled in my ear. 'That was gear… hey… what's yer name?'"

This was witnessed by what Royston considered to be 'John Lennon's other band', Rod Murray and Bill Harry, who together with Stu and John called themselves The Dissenters. The Dissenters was the name given to this foursome who, one night at Ye Cracke, after attending Royston's performance at Liverpool University, decided that they would put Liverpool on the map – John for his music, Stu and Rod for their painting, and Bill for his writing.

The Record and Show Mirror of 9 July and 16 July 1960 reported that Royston Ellis had been searching for a group to use regularly and was thinking of bringing a Liverpool group called The Beetles to London to back him on his poetry readings, but nothing came of it.

"There is famously a letter from *Record Mirror*", Royston recalled, "in which I said I was planning to bring to London a group of Liverpool art students to back me after appearing with them in Liverpool, named The Beetles. I told them to spell it Beatles as I was a beat poet and they liked the beats of the USA and played beat music."

John and Royston spent a long time talking, and one of the issues they discussed was John's future. "John told me that he was keen to take up playing music full time," said Royston, "but was worried about leaving Art College. I told him that, if he believed in himself as a musician, he should give up schooling. I explained that I had myself left school as soon as I was old enough. I put myself forward as an example of what dedication to an art form, like writing or music, could achieve. 'As a musician,' I told him, 'you have a great future. As an artist you might go into advertising or become a schoolteacher. Where's the fun in that?' I urged him to follow his conviction and be a true beatnik, leave college and do what he believed in. He never did go back."

Royston discussed taking the group to London for stage and TV appearances. "John and George liked the idea, although I think Stuart and Paul were less keen." Royston promised to get them advance publicity, get the work and then send for them. "I asked John what name he was calling the group. He said The Beetles. I asked him how it was spelt and he said B-E-E-T-L-E-S."

This is evidenced in the article that appeared about Royston in *The Record and Show Mirror* on 9 July 1960:

However, the bearded sage of the coffee bars has not always been satisfied with the accompaniment provided, so he's thinking of bringing down to London a Liverpool group, which he considers is most in accord with his poetry. Name of the group? The Beetles!

The same paper followed this up a week later with another article, in which the name Beetles appears again.

> "Since my remarks about my occasional dissatisfaction with the accompaniment provided for my poems, many friends

Royston Ellis poses with The Beatles.

have written to me. I would like to point out to all those who have taken an interest in my rock 'n' roll poetry that these remarks were not intended as disparaging comments on the excellent groups I have worked with on television and stage shows – groups such as Cliff Richard's Shadows and the London group, The Red Cats. For some time I have been searching for a group to use regularly and I feel that the Beetles (most of them are Liverpool ex-art students) fill the bill."

When Royston sent the cutting to John, Allan Williams contacted Royston in London and told him that the group had arranged a booking in Hamburg. John had suggested that Royston go with them as a 'poetical compere', an offer that Royston turned down.

Royston had some involvement with the change in the spelling of their name from "Beetles" to "Beatles": "I suggested that since they liked the beat scene and they were coming to London to back me, a beat poet, why not spell it with an 'A'?" When John later explained in the first issue of *Mersey Beat* how "the man on a flaming pie" gave him the idea, Royston also claims that he was behind that, too. On the night he and John talked about changing the second 'E' to an 'A', they were in the Gambier Terrace flat. "I had bought a chicken pie and mushrooms for dinner. I might have had the money but I did not know much about cooking, and the result was that I overcooked the mushrooms and burnt the chicken pie. I have always assumed that gave rise to John's reference to 'a man on a flaming pie' suggesting they call themselves Beatles with an A."

Stuart was originally the one who suggested "Beetles" as a tribute to Buddy Holly's group, The Crickets. They used Beatals, Silver Beetles, Silver Beatles and Silver Beats in early 1960, yet still hadn't made a definitive choice. Royston may well have helped John decide that it should be The Beatles, because, when they left for Hamburg just a few weeks after meeting the beat poet, they were, and would forever be known as, The Beatles.

"Polythene Pam"

On 8 August 1963, The Beatles played at the Auditorium, Guernsey, in the Channel Islands, where Royston Ellis was working as a ferryboat engineer. Lennon recalled how the song "Polythene Pam" came about: "That was me, remembering a little event I had with a woman in Jersey. Royston Ellis, a beatnik that looked like a beatnik who was from Liverpool, took me to this apartment of his in Jersey. So, this poet took me to his place and asked me if I wanted to meet this girl, Polythene Pam, who dressed up in polythene bags. She did not wear jackboots and kilts – I just sort of elaborated – and no, she did not really look like a man. There was nothing much to it. It was kind of perverted sex in a polythene bag. But it provided something to write a song about."

In 1961, at the age of 20, Royston decided to leave the UK to travel the world, beginning with a trip to Moscow, where he appeared with Russian poet Yevtushenko before heading to the Canary Islands. While there, he appeared with Cliff Richard in the film *Wonderful Life* and wrote three novels. Between 1966 and 1980, he lived in Dominica, where, using the penname Richard Tresillian, he published the Bondmaster series of historical novels and became the President of the Dominica Cricket Association. Since 1980, he has been a resident of Sri Lanka, where he has continued to write guidebooks, novels, biographies and travel features.

It is probable, however, that he will be best known for his connection with The Beatles in the summer of 1960.

AUGUST 1960 – AUGUST 1962

The Beatles to The Fab Four

With the group now known as The Beatles, they lost drummer Norman Chapman, quickly found a replacement in Pete Best and, just a few days later, they were on their way to Germany. On arrival in Hamburg, The Beatles had a rude awakening. They found themselves lodging behind a cinema in the heart of the red light district. The clubs they played were vastly different to those they'd played at home and performing up to eight hours a night meant that there was a steep learning curve for the young musicians. The improvement was almost immediate.

Now they could join fellow Liverpool groups Derry and the Seniors and Rory Storm and the Hurricanes on stage. For the first time, on 15 October 1960, they served as a backing band for the Hurricanes' Lu Walters as he recorded in a Hamburg studio. Pete and Stu did not join them, so Lu asked the drummer from his group, Ringo Starr, to accompany them. This would be the first time John, Paul, George and Ringo appeared together on record.

When club owner Bruno Koschmider decided to split the bands, Stuart played with Howie, Stan, Derry and a German drummer in a new group. However, just as they were settling in, George was deported for being underage, closely followed on the journey home by Paul and Pete. Within days, John was also on his way back to Liverpool. Stuart stayed behind with his new girlfriend, Astrid.

Back home, The Beatles were joined for four appearances by Chas Newby on bass. Early in 1961, Stuart decided to quit the group and

George, John, Pete and Paul in their leathers, outside The Cavern in Mathew Street, 1961.

The Fab one hundred and Four

The Top Ten Club, Hamburg.

was almost replaced by Klaus Voormann, but Paul took over the role.

Over the next year, The Beatles recorded with Tony Sheridan in Hamburg, generating great interest back in Liverpool, and bringing them to the attention of future manager Brian Epstein.

On 26 November 1961, the advertisement for their appearance at Hambleton Hall, described The Beatles as: John Lennon ("The Singing Rage"), Paul McCartney ("The Rockin' Riot"), George Harrison ("The Sheik of Araby") and Pete Best ("The Bashful Beat"). They were making a name for themselves in Liverpool.

At various venues around Liverpool, they were joined on stage by Ray McFall, Johnny Gus, Davy Jones, Rory Storm, Gene Vincent and Roy Young. They even joined forces with Karl Terry and Gerry and the Pacemakers as the Beatmakers for one night only.

Stuart would eventually play with a German band called The Bats in Hamburg, though only for a short time. Within a few weeks, on 10 April 1962, he would die unexpectedly.

On securing a recording contract with George Martin at Parlophone, John, Paul, George and Pete were expected at Abbey Road at the beginning of September 1962. However, the most controversial change of personnel happened in August when, without warning, Pete Best was dismissed and replaced by Ringo Starr. Ringo was the most experienced musician among them, having played with The Eddie Clayton Skiffle Group, The Darktown Skiffle Group, plus the various names that Alan Caldwell (aka Rory Storm) used for his group.

A couple of weeks after Ringo joined The Beatles, they were recording their debut single "Love Me Do". However, George Martin decided that he needed a session drummer, so Andy White was brought in to play on the record.

Pete drumming with The Beatles on stage at The Cavern, 1961.

Between then and the end of 1962, they backed young singer Simone, pop star Craig Douglas and Liverpool singing sensations, The Chants. They rounded off the year at the Star Club in Hamburg, joined on stage by their friends Horst and Freddie Fascher.

The Fab Four were now ready to take on the world.

12 AUGUST 1960

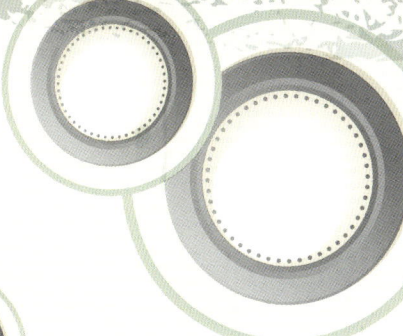

The unknown drummer nearly joins The Beatles

The advertisement in the *Liverpool Echo* on 8 August 1960 was quite simple: "Drummer. Young. Free KP 60." After investigation, KP is a personal number at the newspaper, to protect the advertiser's identity.

Not much was given away, but it was enough to catch the eye of the drummerless Beatles, who were heading to Hamburg in a matter of days. Paul McCartney took it upon himself to respond to the advertisement, though what happened after that is as much a mystery as is the identity of the drummer.

In 2011, the letter written by Paul turned up at auction, having been found inside a cheap book purchased at a car boot sale (flea market).

The letter said:

"Dear Sir, In reply to your advertisement in Echo, Wed. night, we would like to offer you an audition for the position of drummer in the group. You will, however, need to be free soon for a trip to Hamburg (expenses paid £18 per week (approx.) for 2 months.) If interested, ring Jacaranda Club, Slater St. [ROYAL 6544] and ask for either a member of the 'BEATLES', Alan Williams [sic], or else leave a message, stating when you will be available. Yours sincerely Paul McCartney of THE BEATLES."

ARTISTES AND DANCING
ALTO free 13th.-Formby 4205-
DRUMMER -young free,-KP 60 Echo

Advertisement placed by the unknown drummer seeking work.

The letter was written on 12 August 1960, the same day that Pete Best was due for his audition with The Beatles. Best came down to the Wyvern Social Club and was offered the position with the group. He was soon packing his bags for Germany.

Nobody knows what happened to the unknown drummer or whether he could have been the recruit they were seeking. In the end, Pete Best was installed as the group's drummer, and his "atom beat" was soon drawing the crowds into the Hamburg clubs.

The mystery letter went to auction and reached nearly £35,000, as it demonstrated quite clearly that the group now considered themselves to be The Beatles, having dropped "Silver" from their name.

The Fab one hundred and Four

12 AUGUST 1960

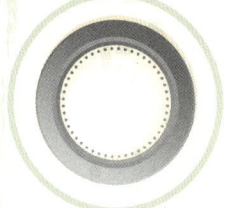

John Lennon, Paul McCartney, George Harrison, Stuart Sutcliffe *and Pete Best*

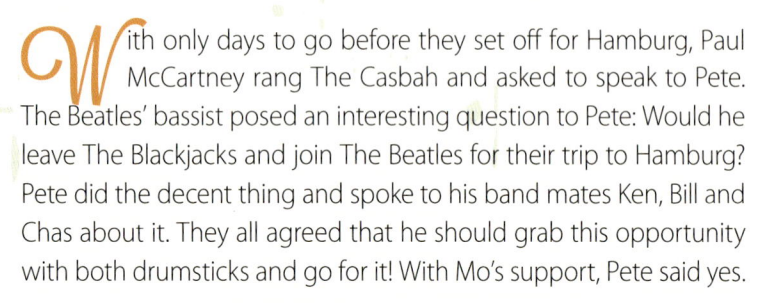

With only days to go before they set off for Hamburg, Paul McCartney rang The Casbah and asked to speak to Pete. The Beatles' bassist posed an interesting question to Pete: Would he leave The Blackjacks and join The Beatles for their trip to Hamburg? Pete did the decent thing and spoke to his band mates Ken, Bill and Chas about it. They all agreed that he should grab this opportunity with both drumsticks and go for it! With Mo's support, Pete said yes.

Not only did The Beatles gain a good drummer, they also found a new manager to help them reach the big time: Mona Best. Mother and son would both contribute a great deal to the group over the next two years.

Mona Best

Mona, or "Mo" as she was known, was born in India on 3 January 1924 and was training to be a doctor when she met Johnny Best, a fitness instructor working with the army during World War II. They married in India and on 24 November 1941, Randolph Peter Best was born in Madras. Pete's brother Rory was born in 1944 and, at the end of the war, the Best family joined the last troop ship out of India, arriving back in Liverpool at Christmas 1945.

The Best family was well known in Liverpool, as they had been involved in boxing promotion at the Liverpool Stadium. Johnny often compered the fights at the stadium his father's family had helped to build. After living in a few rented properties, the family settled at 17, Queenscourt Road in West Derby. However, when Mona's parents decided to retire and move from India to Liverpool, it was clear that their home would not be able to accommodate everyone. Having lived in large houses in India, Mo wanted a similar home in Liverpool, but found it difficult to locate the perfect one. Whenever she did, Johnny Best wanted no part of it.

After Rory spotted the old Conservative Party Headquarters in Haymans Green up for sale, he ran home to tell Mo. She fell in love with the property and though she agreed to buy it, she had no money of her own and Johnny refused to move. Undaunted, Mo took her jewelry to the pawnbroker and sold it. She then went to the betting shop, where she looked at the horses running in the English Derby. At great risk, she decided to back a 33-1 outsider called Never Say Die, ridden by a little-known jockey named Lester Piggott. Mo's vision of a winning horse was spot-on as it finished first, giving her enough money to buy the house with a balance

Pete with his kit in Hamburg, 1960.

of cash and a small mortgage. Mo, together with Pete and Rory, though not their stubborn father, moved into 8, Haymans Green. A few weeks later, Johnny realised he couldn't win, and turned up with his suitcases.

While watching the television with friends one evening, Mo became interested in a feature on the 2i's Coffee Bar in London, where some of the leading British music stars like Tommy Steele, Marty Wilde and Cliff Richard had been discovered. Rory Best remembers what happened next: "Mo stood up and declared, 'I'm going to turn the basement into a little coffee club'. My father turned round and said, 'Over my dead body'. He just kept repeating the phrase 'You're crazy' while shaking his head. I won't tell you what was said, but the next day, we were clearing the cellars!"

The Casbah Coffee Club was now a reality and George re-formed The Quarrymen to open the club on 29 August 1959. Mo had enlisted John to paint the "Aztec" ceiling, which he managed to do properly by the third attempt. Paul painted the "Rainbow" ceiling, Pete and John painted the "Spider" room and all of them painted the stars on the ceiling of the coffee bar. As Paul was later to say, "I think it's a good idea to let people know about The Casbah. They know

The Aztec ceiling painted by John Lennon.

The rainbow ceiling, painted by Paul, above the first stage area where The Quarrymen opened The Casbah Club. Also pictured are the original club record player, speakers and microphone stand.

about The Cavern, they know about some of those things, but The Casbah was the place where all that started. We helped paint it and stuff. We looked upon it as our personal club."

Mo had created one of the first rock 'n' roll clubs in Liverpool and, over the next three years, showcased the talents of most of the top names to emerge from the city in the 1960s. To many of those bands, Mo was the 'Mother of Merseybeat'.

Her impact on Pete's musical career started when he was young. Pete was always fascinated by rhythm. As his brother Rory recalls: "Pete was always tapping on something and it would drive me mad! He was tapping his fingers on the table, or drumming with pencils on tins." Mo decided that she would encourage her eldest son by investing in a set of bongos for him. "That was even worse," exclaimed Rory. "It just meant that he was hitting something different, but this time more loudly!"

Pete says he had several influences as a drummer: "Some of my earlier influences were Gene Krupa, who is jazz-orientated, Joey Morello, and Buddy Rich, which goes without saying. I suppose you introduce things in your work, different influences. You don't exactly copy, but it's like everything else, it contributes to it and you develop your own style."

Pete told me how special Mo was to him and the club members. "I could sit here and talk for a year about her," said Pete. "She was our mother first, and then a mother to all the club members. We became like a family to all the members, and she would hand out advice when asked, even to some of the parents. She was a diplomat and a politician. She was the matriarch, who had a clear vision of what she wanted The Casbah to be. At the time, we did not realise the ideas that she had."

The Blackjacks: Pete Best, Ken Brown, Bill Barlow and Chas Newby

As Pete got more and more interested in percussion, an opportunity arose at The Casbah. The Quarrymen's loss of Ken Brown was Pete's gain, leading to the formation of Pete's first group, The Blackjacks. Ken asked Pete, Bill and Chas to join him in the group. There was only one problem for Pete: he had no drums! Without a second

Pete posing for the camera in Hamburg.

thought, Mo invested in a full set of drums for him and, of course, a regular club to play. Soon, The Blackjacks were pulling the crowds in at The Casbah. Although they'd walked out of the club, threatening to never play there again, John, Paul and George, now accompanied by Stuart Sutcliffe, became regulars and noticed the progression of Pete's drumming.

Although it's been suggested that The Beatles dropped the 'Silver' from their group name on the way to Hamburg, Pete was never asked to join The Silver Beatles. "When Paul called me," he said, "he asked me if I wanted to join The Beatles and come with them to Hamburg. He never mentioned Silver Beatles. I was then asked to come down to the Wyvern Club, where I would do an audition with them, to make sure we could play together. We played a few songs through, and then it was time to go home and pack my bags and get ready to travel to Hamburg."

An onlooker that day was Pete's brother, Rory. "I went with Pete to the Wyvern Club," Rory recalled. "I don't know why they did an audition because they weren't trying other drummers out. They played about a dozen songs through and I have to say, they weren't that good. But, I did not tell our Pete, because I did not want to put him off."

Allan Williams confirmed what Rory said. "They remembered Pete

John (left) watches as the van is loaded.

from The Casbah," said the former Beatles manager, "and he was now playing on his new set of drums, which sealed it. They did not ask anyone else. Therefore, I acted like a manager should and said he needed an audition, so Pete came down and played a few songs but he had the job anyway. Pete learned along with them out in Hamburg."

Pete headed off to Germany with The Beatles in a small van, at the expense of Allan Williams. "So we set off for Hamburg in our little van with all the equipment on the roof," recalled Allan. "Dockers did not want to load it on to the ship, so I had to plead with them. There were ten people in the van. There was me, my wife Beryl, Barry Chang, who was Beryl's brother, Lord Woodbine, John, Paul, George, Stuart, Pete and the translator Herr Steiner, who we picked up on the way. They did not have money for the trip, so I lent them money for food and clothes, like black T-shirts, trousers and pumps. I still have an 'I.O.U.' from Paul for £15, which he hasn't paid. I had to feed them and pay for the ferry and for the minibus."

Allan continued: "We had trouble getting on to the ship as the famous photo shows with all their gear on the roof. We landed at the Hook of Holland and took a wrong turning somewhere and we were lost. We had arrived about 7am and, of course, we were driving on the wrong side of the road. I remember it was like a sea of bikes. Lennon was telling them all to f**k off and to stop leaning on the van. We arrived at the Arnhem War Memorial and that famous photograph was taken by my brother-in-law Barry Chang, which was a bit prophetic: 'Their Name Liveth For Evermore'. John was not in it, as he did not want to be involved. I don't know if he was just being miserable, but seeing all of those little white crosses as far as the eye could see commemorating the hundreds of soldiers who lost their lives attempting to liberate Holland got to us all. It was sickening.

"We all then went into Arnhem. They went into a music shop and all came out laughing. I asked them why, they laughed again, and John produced a mouth organ that he had stolen from the shop. I thought, we aren't even going to get to Hamburg at this rate. What if he'd have been caught? We had a real job getting through the customs. We had to say we were students on a holiday with all this equipment and we were going to play in a coffee bar. We did not have the visas. They had to itemise each piece of equipment we had. The lads were messing around and, in the end, the customs just said to go. We finally arrived in Hamburg about 1am and pulled up outside the Kaiserkeller and saw Derry and the Seniors. They all thought this was great. But Herr Koschmider came over and said, 'you don't play here, you play at The Indra.' We went over there and it had a striptease artist on. They said, 'We've not come to Hamburg to back a stripper.' Remember, they had already done that in Liverpool.

Allan concluded: "It was Koschmider's second rock 'n' roll club – he thought he could keep them both going. They played there for a couple of weeks and then there was trouble. A woman who lived above the club did not mind the strip music, but when the loud rock 'n' roll music started, she complained, so they had to stop. They went over to the Kaiserkeller. Their accommodation, of course, was appalling. They were in the filthy dump in the Bambi Kino. The only water was in the toilet block of the cinema, so they had to wait until it was closed to get any water. The place was disgusting, the filth was thick on the walls, but they were young enough to cope."

After playing in Hamburg for a few weeks, the sound The Beatles were producing amazed everyone, including themselves. The necessity of having to play for up to eight hours a night meant that they not only had to learn new songs, but also how to make the songs they did know last longer. At that time, most bands just played the songs as you would hear it on the record. However, as most only last around two and a half minutes, you would need a lot of them to get through the evening. The Beatles had to experiment, ad-lib, improvise and learn quickly not only how to be the best performers, but how to attract the public into the club to listen to them play.

It's here that Pete developed his famous 'atom-beat'. I asked Mike Rice, drummer with the Liverpool band The Senators in the 1960s, to

The Beatles pose for the cameras at The Indra Club, Hamburg.

The Beatles take a boat trip in Hamburg.

The Beatles performing at the Top Ten Club, Hamburg.

explain. "Pete was dynamic," he said, "with the sound he was punching out. People tried to analyse it. It was the bass drum that stood out – the atom beat – but there was so much more to it than that. He could use his snare and put a variety in the beat, not just the straight 4/4 atom beat." Pete's pounding bass drum could be heard outside in the street and drew in the crowds, giving a harder edge to The Beatles' music. Pete put the beat in The Beatles – and the crowds loved it.

However, when they tried to move to the competing Top Ten Club, an angry Koschmider reported to the local authorities that George Harrison was seventeen, under age and out after the curfew. He was arrested and deported – sent back to Liverpool. Pete and Paul went back to their dimly-lit Bambi Kino lodgings to gather their belongings and stuck a lighted condom on the wall so they could see better. This left a small scorch mark that Koschmider used to his advantage, having them arrested and jailed for the night. Never mind that the wall was concrete and wouldn't burn! Stuart Sutcliffe voluntarily gave himself up and reported to the Police Station. After making statements, it was decided that Pete and Paul would also be deported, but Stuart could stay.

Pete returned home, dejected. There was a real possibility that The Beatles would have ended.

1st Dec. 60.

Dear Mum,
        Surprise, surprise. We finished in Kaiserkeller last week. The Police intervened because we had no work permits. Paul and Peter the drummer were deported yesterday and sent in handcuffs to the Airport. Now only John and I remain. John goes home tonight, and I stay at Astrid's house till Xmas. (Her mother will feed and keep me in cigarettes till then.) It's better for you that I stay away till then because I would not be able to find work so late, and you would not be able to keep me. The last few days have been rather hectic, and we've not known

2.
what has been happening next. We were supposed to work in the Top Ten but the Police again intervened. So you see how the position is. I haven't written sooner, because I wanted to see matters settled. I'm rather unhappy about the money situation — if we had worked in the Top Ten I could have sent you 100 marks a week, for at least two weeks. I don't think Ive had any letters from you for some time so I assume you are rather

Letter from Stuart explaining about his time in Hamburg, and how they were locked up in the cells.

The Fab one hundred and Four

4 OCTOBER 1960

Derry and the Seniors –
Howie Casey, Derry Wilkie, Stan Foster, Brian Griffiths, Billy Hughes, Paul Whitehead, Jeff Wallington
and The Beatles

The band that began as Derry and the Seniors soon became Howie Casey and the Seniors. This was the first Liverpool rock 'n' roll band to head to Hamburg, allowing them to witness first-hand The Beatles' evolution from a group with a poor reputation to the best rock 'n' roll group in the world. Derry and the Seniors played on stage with The Beatles in Hamburg. I spoke to Howie about his musical career, and going to Hamburg and working with The Beatles.

Howard W. Casey was born on 12 July 1937 in Liverpool and grew up in Altmoor Road in Huyton. "In those days, you did not get to learn much music in schools, apart from the recorder," said Howie. "I got interested in progressive jazz through my cousin, John Howard, who was listening to people like Stan Kenton." Kenton was a sometimes controversial American band leader who developed what became known as the "Wall of Sound", upon which Phil Spector would later build his reputation. His style of jazz was innovative and creative. Howie also listened to the great jazz saxophonist Charlie Parker Jr. who was an influential musician, and he cites Parker, known as the "Bird", as his greatest inspiration.

Like most of his contemporaries, he was fascinated with modern music, and, in August 1954, with his friends Georgie and Tony,

Derry and the Seniors, with Howie Casey playing saxophone.

formed a group with the intention of playing Christmas parties. "We had to choose our instruments," said Howie, "and I fancied playing the drums, but Tony claimed that job, so I chose the saxophone. How different my life could have been. In the end Tony did not become a drummer anyway!"

In 1955, Howie was called up for National Service and signed on for three years in the King's Regiment military band. It was a tough regime. "We had a fierce bandmaster", Howie remembered with a laugh, "and we would practise from 9am to 12:30pm solid. Then, in the afternoon, we would have the usual army routines, and then we would have extra rehearsals. We had to learn quickly or else! We were taught to take our instruments apart, clean them and put them back together again. For the first few times I had pieces left over, but eventually learned how to do it right. It was a great skill to learn and without that army discipline, I would never have knuckled down and learned to read music and practise so hard. There was always something to distract me at home.

"We were stationed in Bury St. Edmunds, Norfolk for the first twelve months, which, as well as learning how to drink, was great training for being back home in Liverpool, and for the future. Unfortunately, while I was still getting used to the speed of drinking, my bandmaster spotted me being dragged out of the pub, and bellowed at me: "Casey! I don't want to see you in town drunk again!"

Howie's trip to Hamburg in 1960 was not his first visit to Germany. "For my second and third years in the army, I was posted to Osnabruck, in West Germany, where I remained until I was demobbed in 1958. I got on well with the locals and even had a German girlfriend who taught me a lot, too. I learned to speak the basics in German, like ordering beer and food. One thing it also taught us in the army was independent living, so that when I was on the road with the band, I knew what I was doing, unlike the other lads."

Although playing in the regimental band was the main focus, the individual musicians would form their own groups, playing jazz and rock music together. In 1958, when it was time to leave the army and return to Liverpool, he got a job at English Electric in Kirkby, but music was his passion. He was really just waiting for his lucky break. This arrived from an unlikely source: his father.

"My dad had an electrical business, and he used to service and repair the PA equipment at some of the local halls, like Wilson Hall in Garston. While he was there, he was talking to Charlie McBain who ran the dances there. My dad mentioned that I played the sax and he told my dad to send me down. So I joined "The Rhythm Rockers" who played at Wilson Hall. They played Traditional Jazz, which I loved, so we had a great time. But then he asked me to join the dance band, and that was for the old fogeys and pretty boring, so I did not enjoy that.

"I left the band and formed one with my friends. Coming from Huyton, a district in Liverpool, we called ourselves the Hy-Tones. We had Stan Foster on piano, Billy Hughes on guitar and Derek Gill – who was dating my sister at the time – on drums. We played a few local places, like Hambleton Hall. We were then introduced to Brian "Griff" Griffiths, a great guitarist who went on to be a member of The Big Three, and Jeff Waddington. We did not even have a bass player at first. We changed our name to The Seniors.

We started to play at bigger clubs, and one night at Holyoake Hall, near Penny Lane, Bob Wooler, who was acting as promoter and emcee, mentioned to us that there was a young lad standing at the side of the stage, and would we let him come on and sing with us. We were quite happy to, and invited him on to the stage. That was Derry Wilkie, a young black singer from Kent Gardens in Liverpool city centre. He was an incredible singer and we invited him to join the group. We became Derry and the Seniors. He was into the music that we were into – gutsy rock 'n' roll, like Little Richard, Fats Domino and Ray Charles. In fact, when he later married and had sons, he named them Richard Penniman Wilkie (Richard Penniman is Little Richard's proper name) and Ray Charles Wilkie."

Derry and the Seniors soon became one of the top groups in Liverpool. When Gene Vincent came to Liverpool to play at the Liverpool Stadium, Allan Williams, who was promoting the event locally for Larry Parnes, needed to fill the programme after the tragic death of Eddie Cochran. Williams turned to Derry and the Seniors, along with other local groups, to play that night. It was a significant night for those bands, but also for four musicians watching in the audience: John, Paul, George and Stuart. It was after this gig that they approached Allan Williams to become their manager.

The *Fab* one hundred and *Four*

THE SILVER BEATLES
Howie Casey tells *Mersey Beat* of The Beatles' First Trip to Hamburg

The first time I ever saw the group was at an audition Larry Parnes was holding in Liverpool. Other groups who attended were Gerry and the Pacemakers and Bob Evans' Five Shillings. The group were called The Silver Beatles then. I sat down to watch them go through their paces and was surprised to find that Stuart Sutcliffe, the bass player, performed with his back to the audience. This, I learned, was because he was so self-conscious and critical of his musical ability. Quite frankly, I wasn't too impressed, and can't remember the group singing. I believe they played a lot of instrumentals and Shadows numbers.

Through Alan (sic) Williams, The Seniors obtained work in the Kaiser Keller (sic) in Hamburg Later, The Beatles came to the city and played at The Indra and as soon as we heard them we realised that the improvement in them was nothing short of fantastic–they were great! At the beginning they still played a lot of The Shadows' numbers, but gradually turned to R & B with such numbers as "Roll Over Beethoven" by Chuck Berry.

When they came over they had very, very pointed shoes in grey crocodile. They had mauve jackets, black shirts and pants and also had brown jackets with half-belting at the back. The length of their hair caused a great stir around the area – it was thick at the back, almost coming over their collars. They used to sit in with Tony Sheridan at the Top Ten Club – he helped them and they learned a lot from him.

They used to sleep in the dressing room of a cinema and practised a great deal. In fact, when we were asleep in the club we were frequently awakened by the sound of guitars. The girls used to rave over Pete Best – he was the star boy. He was a great fellow and the one I liked the most. He was very quiet and didn't rave as much as the others. Pete really did fit in with the group then – but their style is more sophisticated now as they have improved musically. He used to swap ideas with our drummer Jeff Wallington.

Paul had terrific talent and used to play left-handed guitar. He didn't actually play it, he had the amp turned down low. The manager of the Kaiser Keller (sic) decided to discontinue having a juke box in the interval – and wanted to put a group on instead. So he split our group into two. He arranged for Stu to play with us. So the second unit of The Seniors was myself on sax, Stan Foster on piano, Stu on bass and a terrific German modern jazz drummer.

He used to sketch around the club, drawing patrons and members of the groups such as Derry Wilkie. In fact, he left the group during the trip and remained in Germany to study at the Hamburg Art College.

Derry Wilkie, lead singer with Derry and the Seniors.

Parnes was impressed with the night and when he was looking for groups to back his singers, like Liverpool's Billy Fury, he approached Williams to arrange some auditions at the Wyvern Social Club. Derry and the Seniors were asked to audition, along with other Liverpool groups like Cass and the Casanovas, Gerry and the Pacemakers, Cliff Roberts and The Rockers, Bob Evans and The Five Shillings and The Silver Beatles. They all hoped to be Billy Fury's backing group, but Derry and the Seniors were selected to support another of Parnes' singers, Dickie Pride.

Howie continued: "On the strength of this upcoming tour, we knew we had to turn professional, so we gave up our jobs for a life on the road. Of course, as we all know, the tour was cancelled and we were stuck with no jobs. We went straight to Allan Williams and told him to sort it out! So, when he told us he was going to take us to London to the 2i's Coffee Bar in Soho, we went along with him, blindly trusting him. So we went to London in two cars and Allan spoke to Tom Littlewood, who said we could play at lunchtime in return for a piece of cake! As luck would have it, in the audience was Bruno Koschmider, a club owner from Hamburg who was looking for a group to replace Tony Sheridan at the Kaiserkeller. Koschmider signed us up and we became the first Merseybeat group to go to Hamburg."

The trip proved to be anything but easy, as Howie remembered clearly: "We did the usual boat and train journey, crossing the country to catch the ferry to the Hook of Holland. We asked Allan about work permits, which I knew we would need having spent two years in Germany, but Allan told us not to worry as we would pick them up when we got there, and if anyone asked, we were to say we were tourists! Well, as we crossed the border from Holland into Germany, the border control asked us where we were going. We told them we were on holiday, but they took one look at the musical instruments and amplifiers, and we tried to say we liked playing on holiday, but they knew we were lying and threw us off the train. By coincidence, the place where we were ejected from the train was Osnabruck, where I had been stationed in the army.

"We were panicking, so I tried to ring the Kaiserkeller, but got no answer, so I rang Allan, who rang Koschmider who spoke to the Police and explained the predicament. Thankfully we made it safely to Hamburg."

Considering that Brian Griffiths was only sixteen, and the other lads were seventeen and eighteen, it was quite an experience for them. Howie was 22 and, unlike his band mates, had been abroad before. They had very little money, no work permits and had no idea what to expect from Hamburg. They were in for a shock.

"We went to the Kaiserkeller, and they had these bright fluorescent posters, and that is where I had to help Derry when translating the poster. It said 'Der Seniors' in big letters, and then underneath it said 'mit der Neger Sanger Derry Wilkie'. I had to convince Derry that it was their way of saying 'black' or 'negro', which he accepted.

"Bruno Koschmider came and met us and took us to the strip clubs, gave us whisky, had strippers come and sit on our knees and showed us all of the clubs and venues. The next day, we started playing! Hamburg was madness!"

I wanted to know what it was like for a group of lads from Liverpool to be confronted by the red light district of Hamburg for the first time. "There were neon lights everywhere," Howie told me. "Brilliant and stunning and nothing like Liverpool at all."

How did your parents let you go to Hamburg in the first place? Howie explained: "It was not so much of a problem to me, as I had been to Germany before with the army and I was 22 years old. The others were younger and I don't think any of them had been much beyond Liverpool. Of course, Brian was only 16 and shouldn't have been there as he was too young, as George was to find out later. You had to be over 18 because of the curfew, so if you were under 18, you had to be at home by 10pm, so they could have got into trouble at any stage."

Casey described The Kaiserkeller, their new club. "It was bigger than the clubs we were used to playing in Liverpool and looked totally different, too. With Hamburg being a major port, there was a nautical theme to the Kaiserkeller. There was fishing nets around the stage and the seats were laid out like rowing boats. The waiters were dressed like sailors, too.

"A lot of the clientele were tourists and out-of-towners just visiting for the day. They would be German people making a day trip to Hamburg and wanting to see what this place was like, including the strippers and bars and clubs. The rest were the hardcore locals, and we got to know them. The locals were often smartly dressed, with the men in suits and the ladies in posh hats with feathers. Others drifted in looking for the more curious clubs where there was live sex on stage."

Keeping in touch with Liverpool was a difficult process because, unless it was an emergency, "You would not use the telephone," remarked Howie, "and so all communication was by letter." Howie, on receipt of a letter from Allan Williams, famously wrote back to him about his proposal to send The Beatles over to Hamburg. As Howie recalled: "I know I will be remembered for it, but at that time, we did not really know much about them, and the only time we had seen them was at the audition in the Wyvern Club for Larry Parnes, when they weren't very good. Tommy Moore turned up late and it was a bit of a disaster."

Howie wrote to Williams, pleading with him not to send that "bum group" over to Hamburg as they could "ruin it for everyone". He felt that they were onto such a good thing, that only the best groups should be sent over. The Beatles, at that time, were not in that category.

Now with Pete Best in their ranks, The Beatles arrived in Hamburg

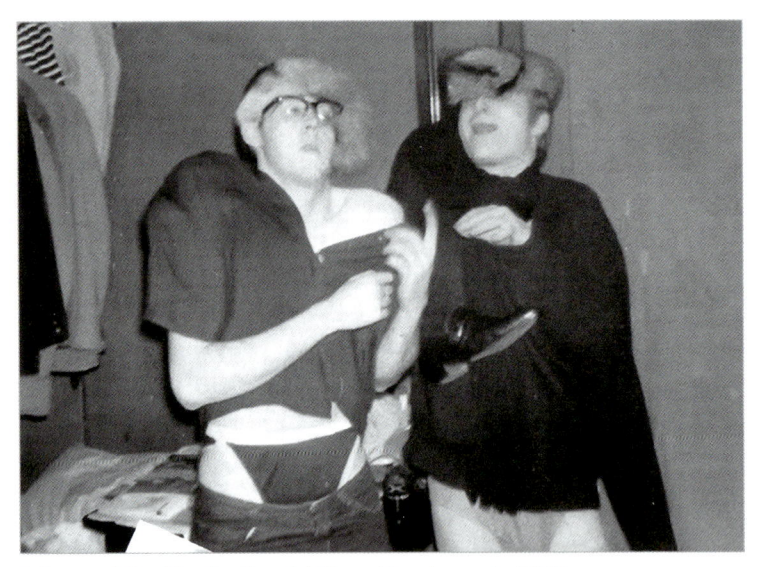

John and Paul in the Bambi Kino, Hamburg, in 1960.

and, on 18 August 1960, began to play at The Indra Club, which was a little club just off the Reeperbahn. After finishing their set, they would come over to the Kaiserkeller to watch Derry and the Seniors. "The Beatles would always come over to see us and they would get up on stage with us and we'd jam, so they became recognised in the club."

This was an important step for The Beatles, which showed the progress they had made on their way to becoming the top band in Hamburg.

Howie went on to have an extensive career, touring and recording with some of the biggest names in popular music, like Paul McCartney and Wings, Ringo Starr, Cliff Richard, The Who, Mott The Hoople and many more. He is now a regular in the Incredible Roy Young Band and appeared with the band at The Casbah Coffee Club in August 2012.

Howie Casey at The Casbah Club, August 2012.

15 OCTOBER 1960

Lu Walters, John Lennon, Paul McCartney, George Harrison and Ringo Starr

Wally Eymond, whose stage name was Lu Walters, was the bass player and second vocalist from Rory Storm and the Hurricanes. Walters was an accomplished ballad singer with the group and the opportunity to commit his voice to record was too tempting to resist.

During his band's eight-week residency at the Kaiserkeller in Hamburg, Allan Williams arranged a recording session for Saturday 15 October 1960 at the Akustik Studio, which was a small booth on the fifth floor of 57, Kirchenalle (The Klockmann-House). Williams asked John, Paul and George from The Beatles to play and sing harmonies for Walters on the recording.

Pete Best was in town supposedly buying drumsticks, so Ringo played drums, which was the first time John, Paul, George and Ringo played and recorded together. There are conflicting reports as to which songs were recorded and these may never be resolved as the documentation and the original discs have long since vanished. Beatles historian and author Hans Olof Gottfridson has studied the evidence for that day.

In a 1963 edition of *Mersey Beat*, it is claimed that three separate acetates with the individual songs "Fever", "September Song" and

The Hurricanes at the Kaiserkeller, Hamburg, December 1960. (Lu Walters second from left).

The Fab one hundred and Four

287

Lu Walter's demo of "Summertime".

Lu Walters, second from right, with Rory Storm and the Hurricanes.

"Summertime" were recorded. Gottfridson concluded that "Fever" was probably recorded at the session, but there is no evidence that it made it onto disc. However, there is a photograph in Allan Williams' book, *The Man Who Gave The Beatles Away*, which shows a 78 rpm record with the words "Beatles and Wally Demo" and "Summertime" across the label. In *Mersey Beat*, both Lu Walters and Johnny "Guitar" Byrne from the Hurricanes supported the claim that "September Song" was also recorded.

Bill Harry, writing in *Mersey Beat*, recalled that, to his knowledge, John, Paul and George only backed Lu on "Summertime", whereas Johnny "Guitar" Byrne and fellow Hurricane members Ty Brian and Ringo Starr backed Lu on "September Song" and "Fever".

"The B-side of the acetate contained no music," observed Gottfridson. "Instead, it comprised commercials for goods sold by the Klockmann Company who had a leather bag store in the bottom floor of the building."

Investigating these early recordings often means relying on the memories of men who were swept up in the craziest times of their young lives. They had neither the time nor the desire to maintain extensive diary notes for the benefit of inquisitive fans over fifty years later. Johnny "Guitar", who kept a brief day-to-day diary, simply recorded on 14 October 1960: 'Wally and Beatles going to make a test recording tomorrow.' At least this confirms the date of the recording. Sadly, Byrne's diary entries cease on that day until the end of December 1960.

In March 1962, Lu left Rory Storm to join Derry and the Seniors, but by September of that year, he had rejoined the group when the Seniors split up. His time with the Hurricanes lasted until February 1965 when he finally quit the group for good to concentrate on his career as a psychiatric nurse.

Wally (Lu) still lives in the Merseyside area and is a frequent visitor at local rock 'n' roll nights.

NOVEMBER 1960

Howie Casey, Derry Wilkie, Stan Foster, Stuart Sutcliffe *plus* a German drummer

With Derry and the Seniors doing well at the Kaiserkeller and The Beatles making similar progress at The Indra, Bruno Koschmider was quite happy. "For Koschmider, we were to be the magnet to draw them in from the street," recalled Howie Casey, "which is why the famous cry 'mach Shau' became the norm. We had to stop the people from leaving by keeping the music going."

However, Koschmider had a problem. "When we had finished our 45-minute slot, there would be a break of about 15 minutes when the jukebox was played. People started leaving in the break, which was bad for business, so he needed to have continuous live music, which meant having another band that could alternate with us.

"The solution for Koschmider was to bring The Beatles across from The Indra where they were playing, which was also owned by him, to the Kaiserkeller. He then split the Seniors and The Beatles to create new bands that could play continuously. I was given Stuart Sutcliffe, along with Derry Wilkie and Stan Foster, and we used a German drummer."

So Stu Sutcliffe played with Howie Casey and his new group, continuing his musical education while the other Beatles headed home to Liverpool, contemplating whether the group was finished or not.

Howie Casey & The Seniors' record, "Twist At The Top", which was released in February 1962.

The Fab one hundred and Four

NOVEMBER 1960

John Lennon, Paul McCartney, Stuart Sutcliffe and Pete Best

Recently, in an interview with author Spencer Leigh, Uwe Fascher mentioned that The Beatles had played at a club that he was associated with, Studio X, in Hamburg.

After George had been deported on 21 November 1960, Uwe invited the remaining Beatles to play at Studio X. As it was only a small club, they only played for a couple of nights. John, Paul and Pete would soon be joining George back in Liverpool, with Stuart left behind with Astrid. It could have been the end for the band.

The Grosse Freiheit in Hamburg.

George in the Bambi Kino, Hamburg. Soon after these photos were taken, George was heading home.

The *Fab* one hundred and *Four*

17 DECEMBER 1960

Mona Best becomes The Beatles' Manager

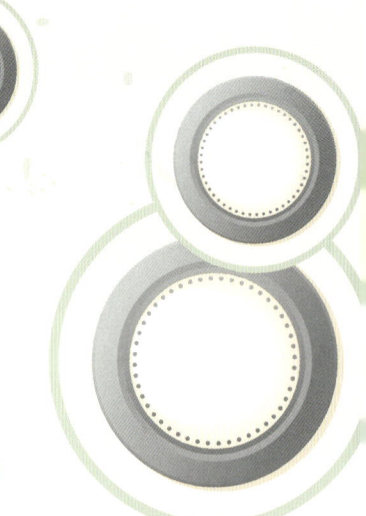

Although Mona had created The Casbah Coffee Club, was instrumental in getting The Quarrymen back together, and supported Pete in his desire to be a drummer, she was about to play an even greater role in Beatles' history.

"If Brian Epstein has been credited with polishing the rough diamond to create the biggest and best group of all time," said Pete, "then it is surely Mo who helped to produce the rough diamond in the first place. She saw the potential in The Beatles when we came back from Hamburg. Derry – from Derry and the Seniors, the first Merseybeat band to conquer Hamburg – had come back from Hamburg and told Mo how good The Beatles were. When we came back and played that Christmas at The Casbah, we were the best rock 'n' roll group around."

They had returned in disarray, and Paul admits doubting whether they had a future. His father made him go out and find a job. Stuart wrote home about Johnny and Paul going to Paris and the group splitting up. With Stuart now living in Hamburg with Astrid, The Beatles could have called it a day.

Enter Mo. She knew they possessed something special. She arranged for them to play at The Casbah twice and, through local promoters, they played Litherland Town Hall and The Grosvenor Ballroom, Wallasey, with Chas Newby on bass guitar.

When Mo saw us, she saw that we had something extra and was determined to do her best for us, not just because of me," Pete said. "She helped arrange bookings outside The Casbah – forming Casbah Promotions. It was Mo who rang Ray McFall at The Cavern to get

Mona Best.

us our first lunchtime appearance. The Casbah is Mo. Yes, we had our part to play, and it was a family thing, we all helped, but The Casbah is Mo's legacy. Maybe it is karma."

Mona Best has never been given the credit for managing them during 1961 and keeping them together. It has even been suggested that one of the reasons for Pete being dismissed from The Beatles was because Mo was a tough character who wanted to tell Epstein how to run the group. Epstein had to get rid of Pete to get rid of Mo. Pete enlightened me: "Epstein came to see Mo. They had a chat and Mo was happy to hand over the running to Epstein. By this time in her life, she had her mum living with her, who was seriously ill with cancer. She died in the spring of 1962. Then of course, Roag was on the way – he was born in July 1962 – and the work at The Casbah was taking it out of her, so she was more than happy to pass on the responsibility to Epstein. He asked her if she had any reservations and she said 'No. Just promise me that you will do a damn good job of looking after them, as they deserve it.'" They eventually signed their contract with Epstein at The Casbah.

One of Mona's dreams was to get The Beatles on to local television, and so, in the summer of 1961, she approached Granada Television with regards to showcasing the group. On 21 September 1961, Mona received a letter from the television station confirming that they would consider The Beatles for their programme, *People and Places*. Producer David Plowright was true to his word and, with an ironic twist of fate, Granada Television filmed The Beatles at The Cavern on 22 August 1962. Sadly, for Mona, this was a week after Pete Best had been dismissed from The Beatles.

The Casbah Coffee Club closed on 24 June 1962, with The Beatles signing off in style. Having just signed with George Martin and Parlophone, Pete was looking forward to a successful recording career. Unfortunately for him, the others had a different idea in mind. The execution of that idea has become one of the most controversial mysteries in the history of The Beatles – why was Pete Best dismissed?

After The Beatles, Pete was offered the chance by Brian to join The Merseybeats and make them into the next Beatles. Pete turned this offer down. In September 1962, he agreed to join Lee Curtis and the All-Stars. Within twelve months, largely due to Pete's popularity, Lee Curtis and the All-Stars were voted into second place behind The Beatles in the *Mersey Beat* Poll Winners contest. They toured the UK and Germany to packed audiences.

Casbah Promotion ticket for St. John's Hall, Tuebrook, only a five minute drive from The Casbah.

Pete with Lee Curtis and The All Stars.

Directors: Sidney L. Bernstein, Cecil G. Bernstein, Denis Forman, Maurice King, Victor A. Peers, John S. E. Todd, Joseph Warton, Richard J. Willder.

GRANADA TV NETWORK LIMITED

GRANADA HOUSE WATER STREET MANCHESTER 3

GRANADA MANCHESTER TELEX

DEANSGATE 7211

21st September 1961

Dear Mrs. Best,

Thank you for your letter telling me about "The Beatles". I will certainly bear them in mind and will contact you again if it is possible to invite them to take part in our programme PEOPLE AND PLACES at any time.

Yours sincerely,

David Plowright
Producer

Mrs. M. Best,
8 Hayman's Green,
West Derby,
Liverpool, 12.

DP/AI

Letter from Granada Television replying to Mona's request to feature The Beatles. © Mark Naboshek

In a strange twist of fate, Mike Smith, A&R man for Decca who had turned The Beatles down in 1962, decided to sign the band. However, they split from Lee Curtis and formed a new band, now called The Pete Best Four to reflect Pete's popularity. They released a number of singles and made TV appearances, too. After changing their name to The Pete Best Combo, they embarked on a European tour, followed by a trip to America. Once there, they recorded with Bob Gallo's Cameo Label and then set off on a tour of the United States and Canada.

By 1968, Pete decided that it was time to call it a day. He hung up his drumsticks. He worked as a baker for a while, before gaining employment as a civil servant and only came out of retirement when Mo suggested in 1988 that he and his brother Roag, who is also a drummer, play together. It was such a success that the Pete Best Band was formed. The group has been performing around the world ever since, musically recreating Pete's early days with The Beatles in Liverpool and Hamburg.

Not long after seeing Pete and Roag perform together for the first time, Mo suffered a heart attack and died at the age of only 64. Her sons have since re-opened The Casbah for fans to visit the true birthplace of The Beatles.

Pete Best at The Casbah Club.

The Casbah Coffee Club where, on 17 December 1960, John, Paul George, Pete and Chas Newby made their debut appearance as The Beatles.

In 2008, The Pete Best band released an album called *Haymans Green* to international acclaim. The album, an autobiographical look at Pete's life, The Casbah and his time with The Beatles, was placed on the Official Ballot for the 2010 Grammy Awards for Record of the Year ("Step Outside"); Album of the Year (Haymans Green), Song of the Year ("Gone"), Best Pop Performance By A Duo or Group with Vocals ("Step Outside"), Best Pop Instrumental Performance ("Beat Street") and Best Pop Vocal Album (Haymans Green). Unfortunately it did not win any awards.

The Fab one hundred and Four

17 DECEMBER 1960

John Lennon, Paul McCartney, George Harrison, Pete Best and Chas Newby

After Ken Brown left The Quarrymen, he and Pete Best asked Bill Barlow and Chas Newby to form a new band, The Blackjacks. As The Blackjacks, they often played at The Casbah, which gave Pete his first taste of drumming with a band, and the opportunity to play in front of John, Paul, George and Stuart. Consequently, when they needed a drummer for Hamburg, they knew where to look. After The Beatles recruited Pete and he left The Blackjacks, they ceased to perform as a group and Chas Newby headed off to University. However, just before Christmas 1960, he was about to create his own part of Beatles' history.

Charles "Chas" Newby was born in Blackpool on 18 June 1941, exactly one year before Paul McCartney and Ivan Vaughan were born. Due to air raids in Liverpool, his heavily-pregnant mum had been evacuated. "I grew up in Queens Road, Anfield," explained Chas, "a street long since demolished. I went to Anfield Road Primary School and then on to The Collegiate from 1952-59, where I befriended Pete Best, Bill Barlow and Ken Brown. We formed our own skiffle group – The Barmen. We even had a mention in the *Liverpool Echo*.

"As with most skiffle groups, we entered local competitions, including an appearance at the Empire, playing alongside The Vipers and Jim Dale. We also appeared at The Cavern in 1957."

When his musical career started, he first played acoustic guitar, later progressing to the bass guitar. "I never wanted to be a professional musician," he explained, "as I had always longed to be a scientist.

Chas Newby, who played bass guitar with The Beatles.

After leaving school, I joined Pilkington's (the glassmakers) and left for London. As a student, I would come home for the holidays. It was for this reason that I was home over the Christmas holidays in 1960."

In December 1960, The Beatles needed a bass player and Chas was the man for the job. "Stuart Sutcliffe did not return from Hamburg," recalled Chas, "and so The Beatles were in need of someone to play the bass guitar. As I was a friend of Pete's and we'd played together in The Blackjacks, he asked me to play with them over the Christmas holiday. Our first engagement was at The Casbah on December

17th, 1960. There was confusion as Mo Best billed us as 'The Fabulous Beatles – Direct from Hamburg'. The crowd was expecting a German band, and when they saw us, they realised they had seen us before in The Quarrymen and The Blackjacks. The screams were great and the applause was fantastic. The second appearance was at The Grosvenor Ballroom in Wallasey, where we appeared alongside Derry and the Seniors."

Pam Roberts (née Thompson) remembers The Casbah well. "I have lots of memories of The Casbah. My friend Sheila and I went to The Casbah most weekends and some weeknights. It was not very big and was usually packed. They had bouncers, mainly ex-boxers from the Liverpool Stadium, on the door. The first room on the right was a bar that sold soft drinks. The next on the left was where the band played and there was another room on the right for dancing.

"We first heard about The Casbah from Pete after we met him and a friend in Southport. After they moved to Haymans Green, Pete told Sheila that they were opening a club in the basement. John helped to paint the ceiling. Mrs. Best was always the driving force in The Casbah. Pete was very good. The girls fancied him. His value was having a club in the basement of his house. When Chas played with them, he was my boyfriend, and I would sit upon the stairs waiting for him while he practised with them in Pete's bedroom.

"We would often have all-night parties after the club had finished. Sometimes, The Beatles would be there, and Paul's brother Mike was a regular. On one occasion, George was there wearing his best suit. He had had rather a lot to drink, and as he was only about fifteen, it had had quite an effect on him: his face was green! We took him outside and gave him a concoction of tomato juice and various other ingredients to help him dispose of the alcohol, and it had the required effect! He was really worried about his suit as it was brand-new and his parents had bought it for him. Sometimes after an all-night party, we would go to Ainsdale Beach in Mrs. Best's Consul car and on at least one occasion, someone travelled in the boot! Mona Best was quite a character. Our first port of call was always to see her in the kitchen and have a chat, and then we went into the room next door to see 'gran': her Mum.

"There was a narrow staircase that led from the club to the main house. On one occasion, I was at the top of the stairs when John came up (there was not room to pass) and he kissed me (my claim to fame!). He was very charismatic but also very scary with a very caustic wit. Paul was always the nice one."

What did she remember about that incredible night when they returned from Hamburg?

"I remember when they went to Germany and then when they came back and performed at The Casbah. They were always very good, so we accepted that as the norm, though I don't remember them ever performing any of their own songs. When they came back from Hamburg, they had changed, more mature and confident. The club was packed on their first night. We thought that they were 'stars'

Chas Newby and Bill Barlow at The Blackjacks reunion at The Casbah, 24 August 2013.

then because they had performed in Germany! They were always better than the other groups, apart from Gerry and the Pacemakers in my mind.

"I can't remember what they played. We did not know that history was happening in front of us then, but I think that there was a sense of them having taken a step up from the other groups. It was normally impossible to dance in the spider room, but we always managed to get a ringside stand! It was very hot and humid, with no health and safety back then, but we wouldn't have missed it for anything. I can't remember anyone not enjoying a night at The Casbah."

The Beatles' most important gig – often seen as the pivotal moment in the start of Beatlemania – was at Litherland Town Hall on 27 December 1960. Again, billed as "The Fabulous Beatles, Direct from Germany," this was one of their first adventures into North Liverpool. The local fans also assumed therefore, that they were German. "We were lined up on the stage, behind the curtain," recalled Chas. "As the curtains opened, Paul launched into 'Long Tall Sally'. The buzz in the atmosphere was incredible. In the main, bands played as the people in the hall danced. Partway through, the dancing stopped and the crowd came towards the stage and watched. We were performing to a crowd, like you would do now. They were shouting and screaming.

"I remember sitting in the dressing room afterwards with Bob Wooler. Bob was excited, as was promoter Brian Kelly. Beatlemania had begun. No one had witnessed scenes like this before – frenzied and screaming teenagers. Kelly took his diary out and booked The Beatles then and there for thirty-six dances between January and March 1961."

On 31 December 1960, Chas played one last time with The Beatles at The Casbah and his career with them was over. "I have no regrets about my temporary flirtation with fame, and I wouldn't have changed my plans for my career just for a shot at playing music professionally. I never wanted to be a full-time musician."

I remained in contact with my friends in The Blackjacks – Pete Best, Ken Brown and Bill Barlow. We got together to perform at The Casbah in 1999. I've also come out of musical retirement and picked up my bass guitar again. At the end of 2002, I joined a band called The

The Blackjacks reunion at The Casbah Club in 1999.

Chas Newby in The Casbah.

Rackets. We play for fun and to raise money for charity."

After four appearances as The Beatles' first left-handed bass player, Chas Newby returned to a normal life. However, his band-mates went on to take Liverpool and the world by storm.

SPRING 1961

John Lennon, Paul McCartney, George Harrison, Stuart Sutcliffe, Pete Best and Steve Calrow

In the spring of 1961, Bob Wooler had begun to introduce The Beatles at The Cavern Club. They had made their lunchtime debut on 9 February 1961 and their first evening performance was on 21 March 1961. Between these two dates, and before Stuart returned to Hamburg on 15 March 1961, Steve Calrow, a local performer who Wooler had seen at Holyoake Hall, made a brief appearance at The Cavern with The Beatles.

Calrow was there one lunchtime when he heard his name called over the tannoy system. "If Steve Calrow's in, will he come to the band room," Calrow recalled. "So I went and John, Paul, George, Stuart Sutcliffe and Pete Best were there. Bob said to me 'do you want to get up and sing with them because they can hardly talk, never mind sing?' They'd done fourteen days of gigs on the trot and they'd worn their voices out completely."

Calrow already knew Paul, as his Auntie Ethel lived opposite the McCartney home in Forthlin Road. "I used to see him walking down the road and sometimes we would get the same bus. One day he told me they were going to do the television show, *Scene at Six Thirty*. "I knew Paul and George more than I knew John but we all lived around the same area, which is why I think they worked so well together because they knew each other well."

Naturally, when he got the opportunity to sing with them, he didn't have to think for too long about it! "We did two Elvis songs – 'Blue Suede Shoes' and 'So Glad You're Mine' – and one Little Richard number, 'Rip It Up'. The lineup was John, Paul, George, Stuart and Pete, and they were really fun on stage, and a great backing group. John and Paul were behind me as I sang, with George stepping forward to do the lead guitar. They were incredible."

Steve had his ten minutes of fame. Though he did ask if there was any chance of working with them on a more permanent basis, The Beatles were well established by then. However, he was one of only a handful of people who can claim to have had The Beatles as a backing band.

Steve Calrow, who was backed by The Beatles at The Cavern.
© Andrew Teebay/ Liverpool Echo

The Fab one hundred and Four

15 MARCH 1961

Rory Storm and the Wild Ones:
Rory Storm, Lu Walters, Johnny Guitar, Ty Brian, Ringo Starr, John Lennon, Paul McCartney and George Harrison

Beatles promoter Sam Leach ran regular shows at the Iron Door and the Cassanova Club, where he would book Rory Storm and the Hurricanes and The Beatles to perform. However, as some of the Hurricanes still had jobs, Rory Storm created a band called the "Wild Ones", which consisted of whoever was available at the time.

Leach remembers it well. "There was a great one at the Cassanova Club in Dale Street, where they appeared at an afternoon session one Sunday – the launch of the club. The Beatles were playing regularly at The Cavern and Ray McFall, The Cavern's owner, told The Beatles they couldn't play at the Cassanova. I had promoted the concert but I was in a dilemma. Suddenly, The Beatles turned up.

"Apparently, someone had let off stink bombs in The Cavern," recalled Leach with a smile, "and they had to shut it down for the afternoon. So they turned up and played for me. The Beatles were threatened with being banned from The Cavern. What would have happened then? The Beatles never officially appeared again at the Cassanova, but billed as Rory Storm and the Wild Ones, John, Paul and George would come along and play – whoever was free at the time got up on stage".

There was therefore a combination of Rory Storm, Lu Walters, Johnny Guitar, Ty Brian and Ringo Starr who appeared on stage with John, Paul and George as the "Wild Ones", though the exact combination of musicians is not recorded.

Rory Storm and the Hurricanes, with Ringo on drums, playing at the Iron Door, 1960.

Handbill promoting **Rory Storm and the Wild Ones** at Liverpool Jazz Society.

'Swinging Lunch Time Rock Sessions'
AT THE
LIVERPOOL JAZZ SOCIETY,
13, TEMPLE STREET (off Dale Street and Victoria Street),
EVERY LUNCH TIME, 12-00 to 2-30

RESIDENT BANDS:
Gerry and the Pacemakers,
Rory Storm and the Wild Ones,
The Big Three.

Next Wednesday Afternoon, March 15th
12-00 to 5-00 Special
STARRING—
The Beatles,
Gerry and the Pacemakers
Rory Storm and the Wild Ones.
Admission—Members 1/-, Visitors 1/6
" Rocking at the L. J. S. "

The Victor Printing Co 230. West Derby Road, Liverpool. 6

APRIL 1961

Klaus Voormann – almost The Beatles' bass player

Klaus Voormann was born on 29 April 1938 in Berlin, Germany, and is associated with The Beatles from their early days in Hamburg.

He was part of the group known locally as The Exis (short for Existentialists), who were very much a part of the art scene in Hamburg. He was very close friends with Astrid Kirchherr and Jürgen Vollmer. In November 1960, when the trio discovered The Beatles playing in Hamburg's Kaiserkeller Club, they all became good friends and, of course, Astrid and Stuart fell in love. Astrid and Klaus had been a couple, but even he could see that Astrid and The Beatles' bassist were madly in love.

Klaus, as well as training to be a commercial artist at the Meisterschule für Gestaltung, was very keen on music. "When I came to Hamburg," explained Klaus, "I worked hard. I started drawing people with long fingers and developing my style of drawing. I was listening to Chet Baker and Miles Davis and then rock 'n' roll came along. I wanted to play these simple, stupid songs. I was not intellectual. The songs were just three chords most of the time. It did not have much to do with music. It was just a rhythmical feeling and it really interested me, and so I decided that is what I wanted to do.

"I never played what was written down on the music sheet. I played what I felt, because nobody ever told me what to play, which I'm very proud of."

So how did Klaus nearly become a Beatle? Stuart's time with The Beatles was running out and there was a chance that Klaus could have become their new bass player. Astrid Kirchherr remembers what happened: "Klaus used to watch the guys on stage, bright-eyed and full of desire. And later, when we visited the Top Ten Club, while Stuart preferred to sit with me, Klaus played the bass, but he had no heart to play on stage."

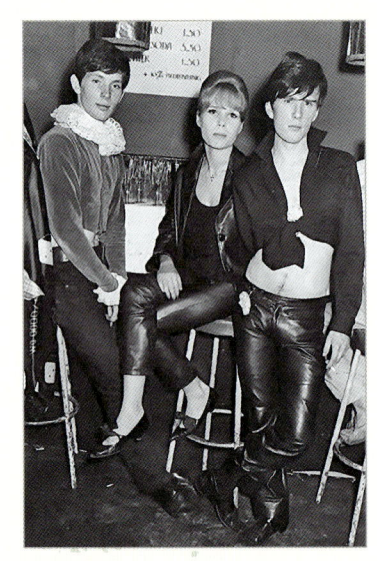

Klaus Voormann, Astrid Kirchherr and Stuart Sutcliffe in Hamburg, 1960.

Klaus remembers the first time he was asked to play with The Beatles. "One day, Paul said, 'Hey Klaus, come on and play the bass. Stuart wants to sit down.' So he gave me the bass and said, 'Come up on stage.' I said 'No, I can't do that. I'm not going on stage.' This was at the Top Ten Club. So, I took a chair and sat on the dance floor and the band was playing on the stage. I think they played a Fat's Domino number. It went okay because playing the bass guitar was not difficult for me. I played classical piano when I was young, so it was not new to me to play anything. I don't know why, but from the word go I had the sort of feel you need to play the bass guitar."

The Top Ten Club, Hamburg.

Stuart did not rehearse very often, preferring to pursue his love of painting. He decided to quit the band. "He sold his bass to me," said Klaus, "and I said, 'Well John, how about me playing the bass in your band', but he said, 'sorry, Paul has already bought the bass. He's going to be the bass player', and that was it."

Klaus was not to be denied a career in music. In fact, he has become one of the most successful bass players in music history. He formed Paddy, Klaus and Gibson and suddenly became one of the most sought after bass players. In the late 1960s, he was a member of Manfred Mann and had several successful years with them. But it

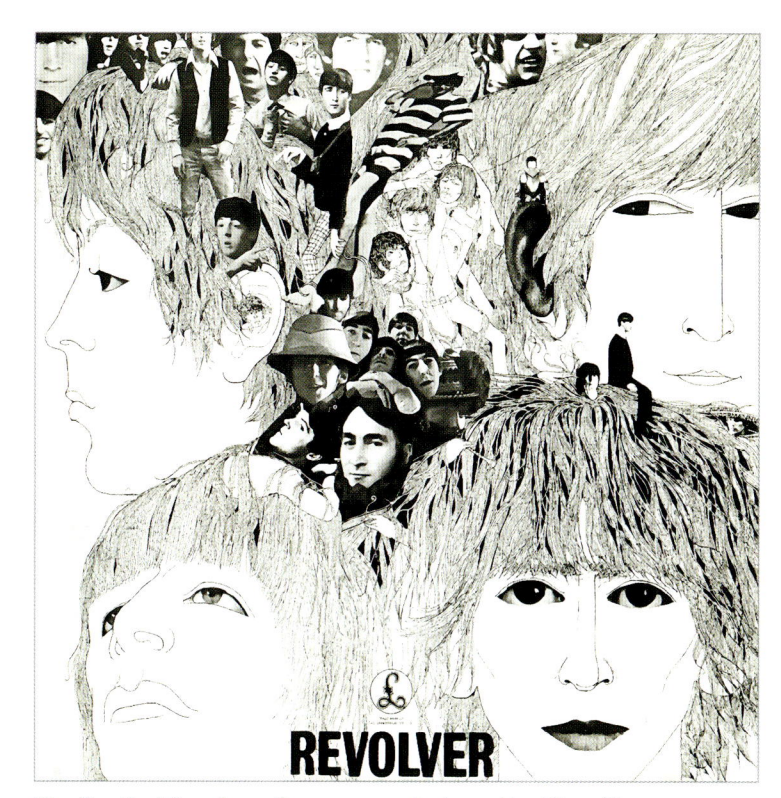

The Beatles' *Revolver* album cover, designed by Klaus Voormann.

was his association with The Beatles that would bring him everlasting fame. In 1966, his talent as a commercial artist would be showcased for all time when he designed the cover for The Beatles album, *Revolver*. For his work, he would win a Grammy for Best Album Cover, Graphic Arts. He continued to work with several other bands and musicians as an artist and graphic designer, but also became a noted session player, performing and recording with a veritable Who's Who of the top musicians of the 1970s, including Harry Nilsson, Carly Simon, James Taylor, Billy Preston, Randy Newman and his old mates John, George and Ringo. He was a member of Lennon's Plastic Ono Band and, in 1972, won his second Grammy for his performance as bassist in George Harrison's band on the LP, *The Concert for Bangladesh*. In 1995, he was commissioned by Apple Records to design the covers for *The Beatles Anthology* albums, which he also painted with help from his artist friend Alfons Kiefer. And, on top of all that, he almost became a Beatle!

The Beatles at the Top Ten Club, April 1961.

Klaus currently lives with his family near Munich, Germany.

The *Fab* one hundred and *Four*

SPRING 1961

The Beatles back Tanya Day and Buddy Britten in Hamburg

While at the Top Ten Club in Hamburg, The Beatles provided backing for two British singers, managed by Reg Calvert. Tanya Day, from the Birmingham area, and Liverpudlian Geoff Glover-Wright, who enjoyed minor success under his stage name Buddy Britten.

Tanya Day

Tanya was from Walsall, near Birmingham, and during the early 1960s was a singer with The Mark Dean Combo and The Tremors. She was famous around the clubs of the Midlands in the UK, but also spent time in Hamburg. It was during her time in Hamburg in the spring of 1961 that Reg Calvert arranged for Tanya to be backed on stage at the Top Ten Club by The Beatles. Tanya later appeared at the Star Club, Hamburg, in 1962.

On 5 October 1962, the day when "Love Me Do" was released in the UK, The Beatles played at the Co-operative Hall in Nuneaton. On that momentous day, one of the support acts was Tanya Day and The Vampires.

In 1964, she released a single as Tanya Day and the Somebody's

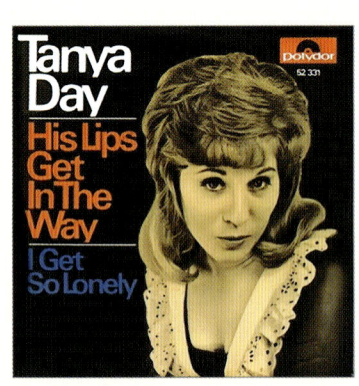

Cover for Tanya's single, "His Lips Get In The Way".

"I Get So Lonely" by Tanya Day and the Somebody's.

called "His Lips Get In The Way"/"I Get So Lonely", which featured the session guitarist Ritchie Blackmore, who went on to achieve international fame as one of rock music's greatest guitarists with Deep Purple and Rainbow. However, Tanya was not to achieve much success beyond her native Midlands.

Buddy Britten

Reg Calvert had made a career out of finding tribute acts who could perform like some of the top stars of the time. Buddy Britten, as the stage name suggests, did a very passable tribute to Buddy Holly. Born Geoff Glover-Wright in Liverpool, he formed Buddy Britten and the Regents in October 1960 and was touted as Britain's answer to Buddy Holly, partly because he also looked like the rock 'n' roll star. The Regents were a London-based group, for whom Keith Moon played for a short time before joining The Who.

While in Hamburg, Buddy Britten was backed on stage by The Beatles at the Top Ten Club, and Buddy was so impressed with his hometown backing band, he even suggested to his manager that he should sign The Beatles. Calvert, however, was not impressed by them, and said that he did not want to manage a scruffy Liverpudlian group.

Buddy Britten and the Regents released ten records between 1962 and 1966, achieving minor success on the Piccadilly, Decca and Oriole record labels.

In June 1967, The Beatles opened Apple Publishing, before Apple Records was established. Liverpudlian Terry Doran, a good friend of Brian Epstein, was responsible for signing several potential stars of the future, one of which was Buddy Britten. Three of Britten's previously unreleased songs were featured on a retrospective album *94 Baker Street Revisited*: "It's You", "It's Better to Have Loved" and "You Still Haven't Told Me".

Seeking further success, Glover-Wright decided to dispense with his "Buddy Britten" image, and changed his name to Simon Raven, as singer with the Simon Raven Cult. He released "I Wonder if She Remembers Me" in 1966, but with the record not achieving success, the band folded the same year. One of the band's members, Nick Simper, was to join forces with Ritchie Blackmore's new group, Deep Purple, in 1968.

"Zip-A-Dee-Dooh-Dah" released in 1963 by Buddy Britten.

Buddy Britten (centre) and The Regents.

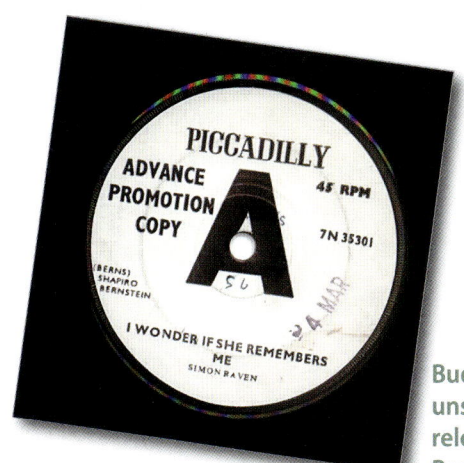

Buddy Britten dropped his unsuccessful stage name and released "I Wonder If She Remembers Me" in 1966 as Simon Raven.

24 JUNE 1961

John Lennon, Paul McCartney, George Harrison, Pete Best *and Tony Sheridan*

When The Beatles went to Hamburg, they hoped to make an impression on the clubs and learn their trade. They wanted to gain experience and grow as a band, but they did not realise that they were about to be educated by the single most important influence on their career so far. After exchanging pleasant emails, I had arranged to interview Tony Sheridan at the end of 2012. However, before we could talk, he was taken seriously ill and, sadly, in February 2013, Sheridan died.

To find out more about Tony's life and career, I spoke to his childhood friend and biographer, Alan Mann, with whom he'd been working on a new book, *The Teacher – The Tony Sheridan Story*.

Anthony Esmond Sheridan McGinnity may not be the most familiar name but, as Tony Sheridan, he had an almost immeasurable impact on the story of The Beatles.

Tony was born on 21 May 1940 in Norwich, East Anglia, but he went on to make Hamburg his town. Alan told me about his childhood friend. "I first came across Tony McGinnity (as he was then) at age 5," around 1945 and at the tail-end of the second World War. We were both playground urchins at the Bignold Infants School in Norwich, a city situated in the heart of Norfolk on the east coast of England. Norwich, the county seat, had been particularly vulnerable to the airborne onslaught waged by Germany in the early 1940s and was hit frequently during a series of over 40 air raids on the city over a three-year period.

"My earliest memory of Tony is playing in the school playground and around and about on the numerous nearby bombed-out sites. Tony and I – I'm 6 months older, but we were both in the same school year – lived within a few hundred yards of one another close to the school. Tony lived in a fairly large bay-windowed property in York Street, the eldest of a growing family – he was actually a stepson – whereas my family lived on Suffolk Street in a smaller terraced house occupied by just my mother, father – although he was mostly away at war – and an elder brother Graham.

"Thereafter, Tony and I would lose sight of one another when I moved to the other side of the city in 1947 and this obviously also meant moving schools. If life were not, in fact, a series of coincidences strung to-

Tony Sheridan in Hamburg.

Poster from the Glasgow Empire, 1960, featuring the Tony Sheridan Trio on the Gene Vincent and Eddie Cochran tour.

The Tony Sheridan Trio.

gether, our paths would never have crossed again. We both went on to pass our Eleven Plus exam and ended up at the largest grammar school, the City of Norwich School (CNS), as part of an intake of around 150 pupils who reported for lessons in September 1951. Did we meet up again then? I'm not sure as we were placed in different classes. It was not 'til the next year that the classes were streamed and we found ourselves thrown together in class 2A. Thereafter, for a few years, we were classmates and also appeared in the big annual Gilbert and Sullivan shows that the school put on each December. Mark you, it was always a humble role in the chorus for yours truly, whereas Tony, a prodigious musical talent from a very early age, got drafted in to play a principal role in *The Mikado* of December 1951. Then, when his voice began to break, he also ended up in the back row as a humble chorister!

"I remember him as an extremely lively individual who did not really mix that much with the mainstream pupils – indeed I was probably as close to him as anyone back then. This was probably because he was not very sporty and played hockey, as opposed to the football that we all played. He was also forever ensconced in musical projects, being a member, and a youthful soloist, in the hi-brow Madrigal Society. He was also a first violinist in the School Orchestra, while I was a reserve violinist, and he even went on to become the leader of that same orchestra.

"But, as he got older, he got noticeably wilder. I vividly remember walking across Norwich one day with him and his language was quite appallingly blue. I was no saint, but he really did start becoming quite anarchic whilst still at school, and the police were called in one day. He actually left school early. I don't think he was expelled. He just lost interest in the academic side of things but would go on to Art School.

Tony's skiffle group, The Saints.

The 2i's Coffee Bar, London.

"Around the same time, he'd joined a Youth Club and formed a skiffle group called The Saints, that would ultimately see him making his way to the 2i's Coffee Bar in London seeking fame and fortune. This led to him being a cast member of the *Oh Boy!* TV show and becoming a professional musician. It was then that he took on the stage name of Tony Sheridan, Sheridan being one of his Christian names. The Tony Sheridan Trio would, in 1960, become the opening act on the Cochran-Vincent tour, which made its way around the country and which had a tragic outcome, with the death of Eddie Cochran. This probably acted as much as anything as a trigger for Tony to migrate to Hamburg, Germany."

Tony and his band, The Jets, received an offer to play a gig in Bruno Koschmider's Kaiserkeller Club in Hamburg. The Jets moved to The Top Ten Club and, while they were there, Rick Hardy of The Jets remembers The Beatles coming over from the Kaiserkeller and playing on stage with them. However, despite making the long trip there, his band mates soon packed up and left Germany. Tony remained behind, ready to cement his place in Beatles folklore.

When The Beatles arrived in Hamburg in August 1960, they played Koschmider's second club, The Indra, as Allan Williams had arranged. At last, the young and impressionable Beatles came face-to-face with the professional musician and TV star, Tony Sheridan. As well as playing together, they lived together and developed a close bond on and off stage. The apprentice Beatles soon gave Tony a nickname: "The Teacher". They studied the way he stood on stage, with his guitar high on his chest – a stance that John would adopt as his trademark. They loved the way he could take a 3-minute song and make it last for 20 minutes. This was the best education they could have hoped to receive.

Without a regular band to support him, Tony used many different musicians as his backing group. These various lineups simply became known as the "Beat Brothers". By 1961, The Beatles were established in Hamburg themselves. Now reduced to four members after Stu quit, they started playing with Tony, often as his backing band, though Tony would sometimes return the favour and join The Beatles on stage.

When Bert Kaempfert, the German Polydor producer/A&R man, saw the two acts together on stage, he suggested that they record together. Although Kaempfert viewed Tony as the only one with real star quality, he signed The Beatles to play on Tony's recordings as the Beat Brothers.

There have been many different stories and dates surrounding these recordings, so I consulted Eric Krasker, author of *The Beatles Fact and Fiction 1960-1962*. He has spent many years investigating the sessions, working to set the record straight. We know that The Beatles present for these recordings were John, Paul, George and Pete.

It's generally accepted that there were seven songs recorded with Bert Kaempfert. However, the evidence indicates that only four songs were recorded during Sheridan's two day-long sessions for Polydor on 22 and 23 June 1961: "My Bonnie", "The Saints (When The Saints Go Marching In)", "Why" and "Cry For A Shadow", all recorded at Friedrich-Ebert-Halle.

Sheridan and the four Beatles also recorded "Nobody's Child", "Take Out Some Insurance On Me, Baby (If You Love Me, Baby)" and "Ain't

Bert Kaempfert, record producer of "My Bonnie".

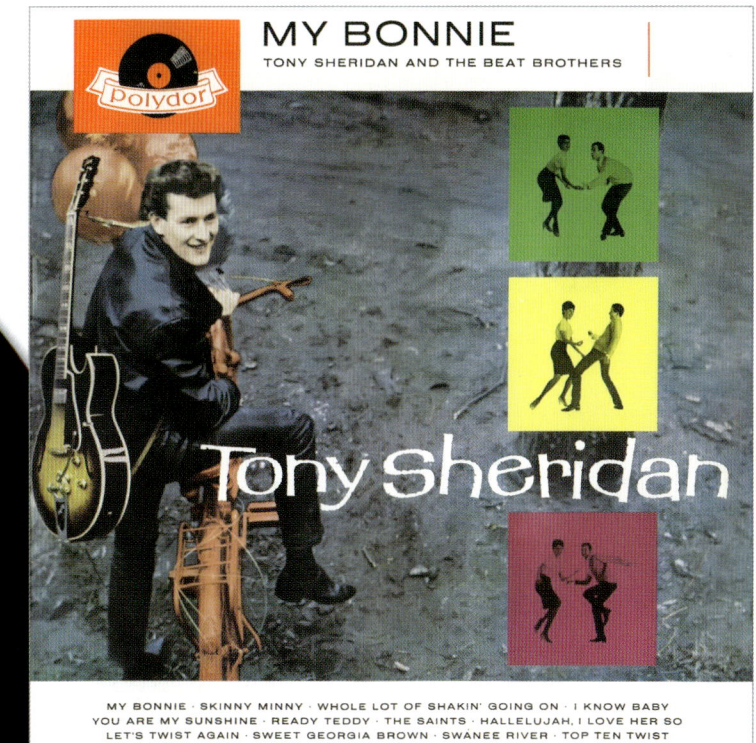

"My Bonnie" by Tony Sheridan and the Beat Brothers, released in October 1961.

Left: "My Bonnie" signed by Pete Best.

She Sweet", probably at the same sessions, but there isn't any documentation to confirm this. These three latter tracks were stored away and only issued at the beginning of 1964 as The Beatles' popularity grew. "My Bonnie" was released in October 1961 as a single by "Tony Sheridan and the Beat Brothers", but later releases list them as "Tony Sheridan and The Beatles", clearly a ploy to cash in on their new-found fame.

Tony had the opportunity to return to Liverpool and join The Beatles, but he stayed in the place he knew best – Hamburg. How could he have known what was about to happen?

Ringo Starr also briefly played in Tony's backing band during early 1962, having been recruited by Peter Eckhorn. However, he soon returned to Rory Storm and the Hurricanes, reportedly unhappy with Tony performing songs he hadn't rehearsed with his band. Ringo also considered him too unreliable and, by leaving, narrowly missed playing on Tony's debut album.

Tony Sheridan went on to have a successful singing and playing career in Hamburg at the Star Club for a number of years, but eventually lost his recording contract with Polydor.

He reflected on his time with The Beatles in conversation with Alan Mann, who offered these insights. "I spent many hours interviewing Tony both at his home in Seestermuhe in 2007 and later on during 2010 in Little Melton where I live. He was always tremendously pleased that as musicians they'd been flung together and it was a real arena for them to learn their trade together. But it has to be said that Tony is a stickler for musical proficiency, so he was unimpressed with Stuart Sutcliffe whose talents lay in the world of art and not that of a bass player. Pete Best and Tony also had their moments and it's chronicled that he and Pete would have an epic fist fight after Pete refused to toe the musical line.

"As to Ringo, Tony is adamant that he helped Ringo to develop the drive and application that he needed before becoming so important to The Beatles. Paul was, and still is, a musical genius, but Tony and he were never particularly close although he had the utmost of musical respect for Paul. On a personal basis, he gelled far more with John and George, particularly John, whose hard attitude was similar to that of Tony's.

Tony and the Beat Brothers in Hamburg, early 1962.

"It's interesting to learn that Tony recognised right from the start that George was an old soul. Having seen Tony perform on the *Oh Boy!* show, George was frantic to get whatever guitar tips he could from Tony."

Tony did make many a pithy comment about all six.

"Firstly, Tony on Stuart. 'He was a lousy bass player, a pleasant chap, a deep thinker, but, like George Harrison, an important catalyst for The Beatles.'

"Pete Best: 'Pete's style of drumming lacked a heavy backbeat. Most of the drummers, to my way of thinking, were a bit insipid. I was a stickler for strict timing and a hard taskmaster. But Pete and I would settle our differences and reflect back on our times together in Hamburg with a sense of camaraderie.'

"As to George and Ringo: 'George acted as a catalyst between Paul and John with Ringo as regulator and stabiliser. Obviously a good drummer needs to be these, but Ringo was these also in a higher sense. For all his young years, George was an amazingly stable character.'

"John Lennon: 'His vehicle for personal growth and fruition was rock 'n' roll. He'd jumped on with skiffle music and now he was well and

Author Alan Mann and his friend Tony Sheridan at Alan's home in 2010.

truly married to his chosen art form. So, in Hamburg, he let it ALL hang out... as we all did!'

"On Paul: 'Sitting with Paul and two guitars would, in a matter of minutes, produce an idea for a song. His cultured and somewhat effeminately outward appearance told me that here was a striving musician whose sensitivities would enrich anything he touched.'

"The main thrust of everything Tony said was how grateful and lucky he was to have met these remarkable musicians. It had all come together at a moment in time, but as he would forever lament, 'nothing we ever did was taped! What an opportunity was lost!'"

While The Beatles went on to worldwide fame and fortune, Tony had become disillusioned with his Beatle-brought fame. By 1967, he was more concerned by the Vietnam War. He agreed to perform for the Allied troops. While in Vietnam however, the band that he had assembled was fired upon and one of the members was killed. Reuters incorrectly reported that Tony himself had died. For his work entertaining the Allies, Tony was made an honorary Captain in the United States Army.

In February 2013, after a short illness, Tony died. Paul McCartney said, "Tony was a good guy who we knew and worked with from early days in Hamburg. We regularly watched his late night performances and admired his style. He will be missed."

27 JULY 1961

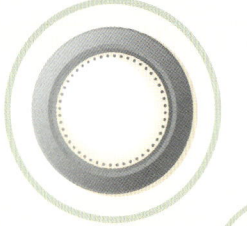

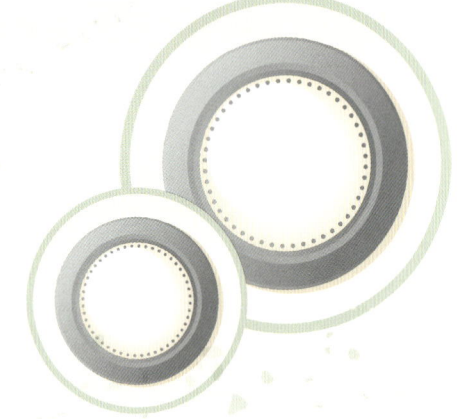

The Beatles and Cilla Black

One of Brian Epstein's most cherished artists, after The Beatles, was the Liverpool singer Cilla Black. With a string of hits and a career in television that's still going strong, she must rank as Epstein's other major success story. His prediction was quite emphatic: "She's going to be the biggest star in Great Britain for thirty or forty years."

Priscilla Maria Veronica White was born on 27 May 1943. She was brought up in a two-up two-down on Scotland Road in the north of Liverpool by her father, a docker, and mother, who ran a market stall. She attended St. Anthony's Junior and Secondary Schools before leaving at the age of 14 to begin a typing course at Anfield Commercial College. By the age of 20, she had progressed from student to full-time Dictaphone typist. But Cilla had greater ambitions.

Her love was performing and she was determined to become an entertainer. "It's no wonder that I knew I wanted to be a professional singer from a very early age," Cilla says, "because I was surrounded by music in our house. My father played the mouth organ, my mother and aunts used to sing, and it was not unusual for families to get together and make their own music in the fifties."

She sang impromptu with several Liverpool groups. She was encouraged to start singing by Liverpool promoter Sam Leach, who booked her first gig at his Cassanova Club, where she appeared as "Swinging Cilla". She became a guest singer with Rory Storm and the Hurricanes, Kingsize Taylor and the Dominoes and, later, with The Big Three. On 27 June 1961, she was encouraged to join The Beatles on stage at St. John's Hall in Tuebrook. She was also a waitress at the Zodiac coffee lounge, where she would meet her future husband Bobby Willis.

It was purely accidental that Cilla White became Cilla Black. In an article in the first edition of the local music newspaper

Cilla Black.

Mersey Beat, Bill Harry mistakenly referred to her as Cilla Black, rather than White. She decided she liked it and made it her stage name. She signed her first contract with long-time friend and neighbour, Terry McCann, but this contract was never honoured as she was underage. Consequently, her father signed her with Brian Epstein, who had offered her a contract after John Lennon introduced her and convinced him to give her an audition.

Cilla's first audition, at the Majestic Ballroom, Birkenhead, was a failure, partly because of nerves and partly because The Beatles, who backed her, played the songs in their vocal key rather than hers. In her autobiography *What's It All About?*, she writes: "I'd chosen to do 'Summertime', but at the very last moment I wished I hadn't. I adored this song, and had sung it when I came to Birkenhead with The Big Three, but I hadn't rehearsed it with The Beatles and it had just occurred to me that they would play it in the wrong key. It was too late for second thoughts, though. With one last wicked wink at me, John set the group off playing. I'd been right to worry. The music was not in my key and any adjustments that the boys were now trying to make were too late to save me. My voice sounded awful. Destroyed – and wanting to die – I struggled on to the end."

Thankfully for Cilla, she was to get another chance, as Bill Harry recalled. "Cilla had asked me to be her manager and I'd said 'no', because I was busy with *Mersey Beat*. One night in the downstairs bar of the Blue Angel, Brian Epstein was with Andrew Loog Oldham. I then saw Cilla by the stairs with her friend Pat Davis. I had an inspiration. I took her over to Brian, introduced her and asked if he'd do me a favour and listen to her. He said, 'yes'. I then asked Cilla if she could sing 'Boys' with the band on stage, The Masterminds. I went up to the group and asked if they could back Cilla and they said, 'yes'. She did the number and I brought her over and introduced her to Epstein. She then came to me and said he'd asked her to come to his office at ten the next morning. She phoned me later that day to say he was going to sign her."

She became his only female client on 6 September 1963. Brian introduced Cilla to George Martin who signed her to Parlophone Records and produced her debut single, the Lennon-McCartney composition "Love of the Loved". The record was released only three weeks after she had signed her contract. It peaked at a modest number 35,

THE DOMINOES

It is a well known fact that the Dominoes were the first rock group to appear on Merseyside (at least this is the view shared by the Dominoes). They also claim the distinction of being the first Merseyside group to have broadcast on the airwaves of Radio Luxembourg, although this is a little known fact. There have been many changes in the line-up of the group during the years it has been in existence, although it is felt that the present format is probably the best to date. Specialising in Rhythm & Blues and Rock type of music the group performs

SWINGING CILLA. Exclusive "Mersey Beat" photograph by Dick Matthews.

many types of numbers which usually are not very well known to the general listening public. This obviously has its points for and against, but as a rule this procedure is appreciated by the fans as a change from the stream of Hit Parade material churned out night after night by the majority of other Rock groups.

Ted "Kingsize" Taylor featured with the James Boys over five years ago, but after a short period with this group, switched to the Dominoes line-up in August '57. He is still a keen fan of many of the original Rock artists, and speaks very highly of the "Fingers-on-fire" guitar playing of Arthur Smith. Ted first commenced playing the guitar when he received a lesson from the famous North of England guitarist, Billy Sullivan. Since then he has developed a style of his own which many guitarists have unsuccessfully tried to imitate. He also has a distinctive style in his voice, but the rest of the group reckon that he sounds more like Alan Breeze of the Billy Cotton Show fame.

Keith "Sam" Hardie. The only member of the group who performed with the original Dominoes. He is a competent exponent of the Little Richard style of keyboard hammering, although it has been known for him to play classical type music when the moon is full. Left the Dominoes for a period of two years to serve as a member of the Lancashire Constabulary, but terminated his employment with same as he found the beat was too strong and he was only working for coppers.

Dave Lovelady, sometimes known as Dave, has been percussioning the drums since a very early age. Also performs well on piano, violin, trumpet, double bass and guitar. Well nigh four tenths of a decade of his musical career was spent performing with The Zodiacs musical ensemble and upon leaving to join The Dominoes had to drastically change his style to fit in with The Dominoes brand of music. His drumming was first influenced by Louis Bellson, of Skin Deep fame, and enjoys playing swing and modern jazz.

Bobby Thomson was first discovered hiding behind a pair of spectacles in Lulu's Place, Soho. Originally played rhythm guitar for the James Boys and took up bass guitar 18 months ago when his rhythm was smashed up in a car crash. Was influenced by non-one in particular and plays as if he's not particular. Emphatically states that a bass guitar should be played in the same style as a double bass and not as a guitar. He is a big Country and Western fan and this can be noticed by the influence of same on his singing, namely in such numbers as "Wild Side of Life" and "You Win Again."

1962 promises big things for the Dominoes and should see the introduction of Swinging Cilla into the permanent line-up of the group. The Dominoes would like to take this opportunity of expressing their appreciation to their loyal fans for voting them No. 6 in the "Mersey Beat Popularity Poll" and hope to improve their popularity in 1962.

As a post-script The Dominoes would like their van driver, 'Jim' to be mentioned.—Jim.

Swinging Cilla featured in *Mersey Beat*. Image © Bill Harry.

"It's For You", a Lennon/ McCartney song which was a top ten hit for Cilla, released in July 1964.

a relative failure compared to debut releases of Epstein's other artists. But all was not lost. Her second single, a cover of the Bacharach-David composition "Anyone Who Had a Heart", was released at the beginning of 1964 and reached number 1 in Britain, selling 800,000 copies. Her second number 1, "You're My World", was an English-language rendition of the Italian popular song "Il Mio Mondo" and sold over 1 million copies.

This was followed by another Lennon-McCartney composition, "It's for You". Paul McCartney played piano at the recording session and the song proved to be another major international success.

Cilla became the first artist to cover multiple Lennon-McCartney compositions. She also recorded "Yesterday", "For No One" and "Across The Universe", all of which were critically-acclaimed. McCartney said Cilla's 1972 version of "The Long And Winding Road" represented the way he always intended the song to be sung.

In August 1967, only days before his death, Brian Epstein instigated Cilla's switch to television. It proved to be a fantastic career move as, through her own eponymous variety show for the BBC, she regularly commanded audiences of between 18 and 22 million until the show ended in 1976. Her immense popularity continued throughout the seventies and into subsequent decades through an array of successful primetime entertainment shows. Most recently, these have included *Surprise! Surprise!* and *Blind Date* – the latter earning Cilla an award from the British Academy of Film and Television Arts.

In 1997, she was notably honoured with an OBE (Order of the British Empire) by Queen Elizabeth II for her achievements in the entertainment industry.

It seems that Brian Epstein's prediction proved quite accurate.

17 AUGUST 1961

The Beatles
and Johnny Gustafson

"Just to be with you", released by Johnny Gus in 1965.

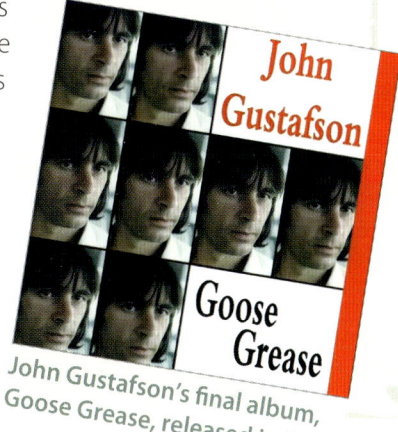

John Gustafson's final album, Goose Grease, released in 1997.

Amongst the great musicians who emerged from Liverpool in the 1960s, there was John Gustafson, better known as Johnny Gus, bass player for what was arguably Liverpool's top band musically – The Big Three. Johnny Gus, lead guitarist Adrian Barber and drummer Johnny Hutchinson – who was offered the chance to replace Pete Best in The Beatles – were the players destined for fame and fortune, until The Beatles got there first.

During June 1960, The Silver Beatles were playing regularly at the Grosvenor Ballroom in Wallasey. On one of those nights, Johnny also played all of The Silver Beatles' second set on guitar, replacing an ailing George Harrison. Johnny only turned up by accident to meet his girlfriend, not knowing who was playing that night. When he went backstage to see them, Lennon said, "You're on".

On 17 August 1961, at St. John's Hall in Tuebrook, Liverpool, Johnny Gus played bass with The Beatles while Paul was at the microphone singing "What'd I Say". He was also to make another appearance with The Beatles at The Cavern, as Paul recounted: "I remember arriving at The Cavern for one of the famous lunchtime sessions and realizing I had forgotten my Hofner bass. As I was left-handed – and still am! – nobody could lend me one, so I quickly drove half an hour to my house, picked up the bass but arrived back in time for the end of The Beatles' set, having been replaced by a bass player from one of the other groups. I seem to remember it was Johnny Gustafson of The Big Three. Was I gutted? Oh yeah."

However, Johnny Gus still remains relatively unknown to many people. Although The Big Three never achieved the success that their talent deserved, Johnny Gus carved out an incredible solo career as one of Britain's greatest bass players. When you look at the musicians he accompanied, it's no wonder he is held in such high regard. He was a member of several groups, such as Bullet, The Spencer Davis Group, Roxy Music, The Ian Gillan Band and also played with Gordon Giltrap. He even appeared on the original recording of the musical *Jesus Christ, Superstar*. He had a successful career as a session musician, too, working with a number of the leading UK artists in the 70s, like Ian Hunter and keyboard wizard Rick Wakeman.

When asked how he considered his talents were best described, Johnny was quite philosophical: "My Musician Union listing is 'Bass Guitar, Guitar, Vocal', but I guess I started as a bass player who sang a bit. When I started in The Casanovas, Cass, the main singer and rhythm guitarist, left the group, so I and the drummer John Hutchinson were then the lead singers. The remaining trio became The Big Three featuring Adrian Barber on guitar. This went on until we were signed by NEMS at the suggestion of John Lennon, as we were a favourite of his. Lennon even sat in with The Big Three at The Jacaranda Club and played Duane Eddy's 'Ramrod'."

Johnny's last musical release was a solo album *Goose Grease*, as John Gustafson, which he recorded in 1975, but did not release until 1997.

The Fab one hundred and Four

17 OCTOBER 1961

Paul McCartney and Pete Best

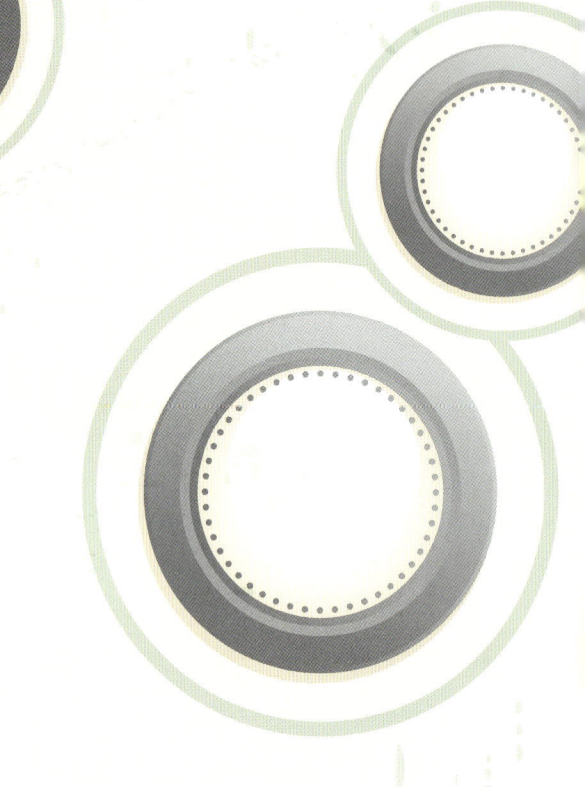

Inside of the David Lewis Theatre.

On this day, The Beatles Fan Club hired the hall at the David Lewis Theatre in the shadow of the Anglican Cathedral. The Beatles had no PA equipment and were forced to improvise. The crowd, which included Paul McCartney's father, watched as his son and Pete Best each belted out a few tunes.

Paul crooned some of the ballads from their usual set list, while Pete sang robust versions of "Matchbox", "Peppermint Twist", and a song made famous by Elvis Presley – "A Rose Grows Wild in the Country". When Pete forgot the words, he leapt around the stage and shook hands with the fans.

It did not go down as a legendary event, but was a bit of fun. It showed that the bond between The Beatles and their fans was so strong that they could get away with an impromptu music-free performance. Within a matter of weeks, they would have Brian Epstein as their manager, which leads one to wonder what he would have thought about his "boys" putting on a performance like this.

The David Lewis Theatre, where Paul and Pete entertained the fan club members.

Dressed in their official Beatles Fan Club sweaters—Anne Collingham, Bettina Rose and Freda Kelly in their Liverpool hotel to-day.

Anne Collingham, Bettina Rose and Freda Kelly from the official Beatles Fan Club.

The David Lewis Theatre (centre, right) in the shadow of the Anglican Cathedral

The Fab one hundred and Four

19 OCTOBER 1961

The Beatmakers – John Lennon, Paul McCartney, George Harrison, Pete Best, Gerry Marsden, Freddie Marsden, Les Chadwick, Les Maguire and Karl Terry

Gerry Marsden at the microphone at Hulme Hall.

Gerry and the Pacemakers at Hulme Hall, 1962.

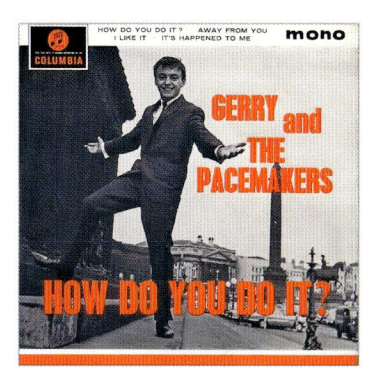

"How Do You Do It", the hit single from Gerry and the Pacemakers.

The Beatles and Gerry and the Pacemakers joined forces with Karl Terry at Litherland Town Hall on 19 October 1961 to perform as The Beatmakers. There was George on lead guitar and Paul playing rhythm, with the drumming duties split between Pete Best and Freddie Marsden. Les Chadwick played bass guitar and John Lennon played piano with Karl Terry joining in the vocals. Finally, Gerry Marsden played guitar and sang, while Les Maguire played the saxophone.

Gerry Marsden formed the Pacemakers in 1959 with his brother Fred, Les Chadwick and Arthur McMahon. They rivalled The Beatles early in their career, playing in Liverpool and Hamburg. In 1961, McMahon was replaced on piano by Les Maguire. The band's original name was Gerry Marsden and The Mars Bars, but they were forced to change this when the Mars Company, who produced the chocolate bar, complained.

The band was the second group to sign with Brian Epstein, who later signed them with Columbia Records (a sister label to The Beatles' Parlophone under EMI). Their first single was 1963's "How Do You Do It?", the Mitch Murray song that The Beatles recorded at George Martin's request, but chose not to release. The song was instead recorded by Gerry and the Pacemakers while The Beatles went on to release their own composition, "Love Me Do".

"How Do You Do It?" was produced by George Martin and became a number 1 hit in the UK, the first by an Epstein Liverpool group to achieve this on all charts, until being replaced at the top by "From Me to You", The Beatles' third single.

Gerry and the Pacemakers' next two singles, Murray's "I Like It" and Rodgers and Hammerstein's "You'll Never Walk Alone", from the musical *Carousel*, both also reached number 1 in the UK Singles Chart. "You'll Never Walk Alone" had been a favourite of Gerry Marsden's since seeing *Carousel* when he was a young teen. It was soon adopted as the anthem sung at every football game by the fans of Liverpool Football Club, a tradition which continues to this day.

Despite this early success, Gerry and the Pacemakers never had another number 1 single in the UK. Marsden wrote most of the group's songs, including "It's Gonna Be All Right", "I'm the One" and "Ferry

Gerry and the Pacemakers at Hulme Hall, 1962.

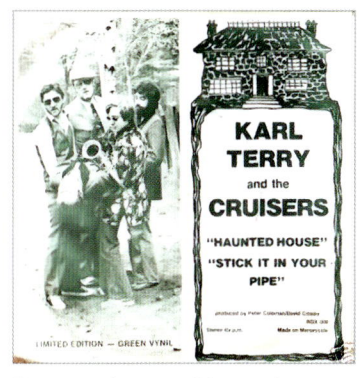

"Haunted House" by Karl Terry and the Cruisers.

Gerry Marsden pictured in Liverpool in 2008.

Cross the Mersey" as well as their first and biggest U.S. hit, "Don't Let the Sun Catch You Crying" (which peaked at number 4.)

They also starred in a film called *Ferry Cross the Mersey* in 1965, for which Marsden wrote much of the soundtrack. The title song was revived in 1989 as a charity single for an appeal in response to the Hillsborough football crowd disaster, an incident which took the lives of 96 Liverpool fans at a match in Sheffield. This record, which featured other Liverpool stars like Paul McCartney and Frankie Goes to Hollywood's Holly Johnson, gave Marsden another British number 1 hit.

This was not Gerry's only appearance with The Beatles, as Beatles Fan Club secretary, Freda Kelly remembered. "Although Gerry was good at larking about, the other Pacemakers wanted to have a more structured show. Once George or Paul did not turn up and Gerry went on with The Beatles. They got an orange box from the Fruit Exchange so he could sing into the same mic."

Karl Terry

The other member of The Beatmakers was Karl Terry, who started singing when he first heard "Rock Around The Clock" and hasn't stopped singing since. He joined a skiffle group, The Gamblers, which evolved into Terry and the Teenaces and eventually Karl Terry and the Cruisers. As well as sharing a stage with The Beatles, he appeared on the bill with some of the biggest names in pop history, like Tom Jones, The Shadows, Gene Vincent, The Crickets and many more. He has also appeared in TV movies and on stage shows. A truly original performer, he was nicknamed "The Sheik of Shake" by Cavern compere Bob Wooler. Karl is known for his flamboyant costumes and imperious stage presence. He is still performing around Liverpool today.

24 NOVEMBER 1961

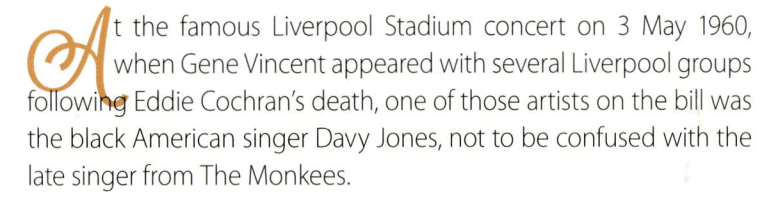

The Beatles
and Davy Jones

At the famous Liverpool Stadium concert on 3 May 1960, when Gene Vincent appeared with several Liverpool groups following Eddie Cochran's death, one of those artists on the bill was the black American singer Davy Jones, not to be confused with the late singer from The Monkees.

Jones returned to Liverpool at the end of 1961 and during The Beatles' appearance at Sam Leach's second "Operation Big Beat", he got up on the stage as an unannounced guest and sang two numbers with the group.

This was shortly followed by two official appearances. First, Jones was booked by Ray McFall to appear at The Cavern on Friday 8 December 1961. Since he was a solo singer, Jones needed a backing band, so McFall arranged for The Beatles to support him. The session was photographed for *Mersey Beat*.

That same evening, Leach was promoting another event at the Tower Ballroom in New Brighton and once again had Jones on the bill. As at The Cavern, The Beatles were booked to support him. Leach had advertised Jones as the *Saturday Spectacular* television star and highlighted Jones' status as a successful recording artist.

Davy Jones.

Jones was also one of the many American performers who made the trip to Hamburg to play at the famous Star Club. Bob Wooler remembered Jones' appearance at The Cavern, and an unfortunate experience with cocaine. "We did not have a strong drug scene by any means," recalled Wooler. "Originally, it was just purple hearts, amphetamines, speed or whatever you want to call it. When The Beatles went down south, they sometimes brought back cannabis and gradually the drug scene developed in Liverpool. There was a rare instance of cocaine when Davy Jones appeared at The Cavern. He was a Little Richard/Derry Wilkie type, very outgoing and bouncy. His big record was an oldie, 'Amapola', and its lyric about the 'pretty little poppy' must have appealed to him.

"Alan Ross, who was a local compere, brought Davy down to The Cavern, and that's when I had cocaine for the first and only time in

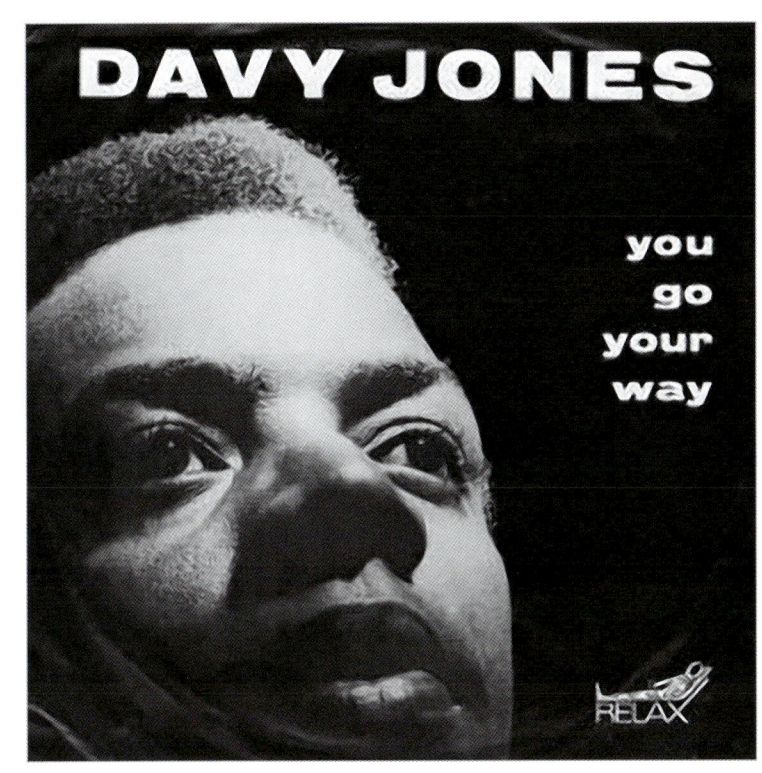

"You Go Your Way", a 1967 hit for Davy Jones, written by Bob Dylan.

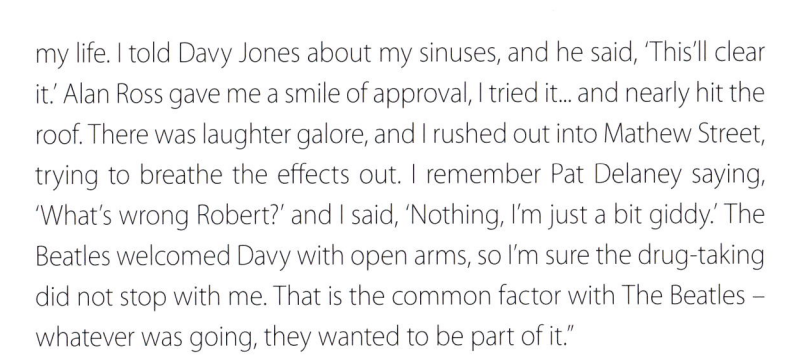

"Amapola", by Davy Jones, released in 1960.

my life. I told Davy Jones about my sinuses, and he said, 'This'll clear it.' Alan Ross gave me a smile of approval, I tried it… and nearly hit the roof. There was laughter galore, and I rushed out into Mathew Street, trying to breathe the effects out. I remember Pat Delaney saying, 'What's wrong Robert?' and I said, 'Nothing, I'm just a bit giddy.' The Beatles welcomed Davy with open arms, so I'm sure the drug-taking did not stop with me. That is the common factor with The Beatles – whatever was going, they wanted to be part of it."

Karl Terry remembered Jones' performance with The Beatles. "I saw Davy Jones at The Cavern and he was a real showman. I thought he worked with the cramped conditions better than I did."

Jones had several hit records, from "Amapola" in 1960 through to "Voodoo Ju Ju Obsession" in 1969, and he recorded as a solo artist, as Davy Jones and the Blue Sounds, Paul Nero's Blue Sounds and Davy Jones, and Davy Jones and the Voodoo Funk Machine.

Jones was a great showman, and in Hamburg he was renowned for changing into a gorilla costume as he performed, "I Go Ape". It was in Hamburg that Jones first came across The Beatles, which is why they were delighted to have the opportunity to back him when he came to Liverpool.

1 FEBRUARY 1962

Paul McCartney, George Harrison Pete Best *and* Rory Storm

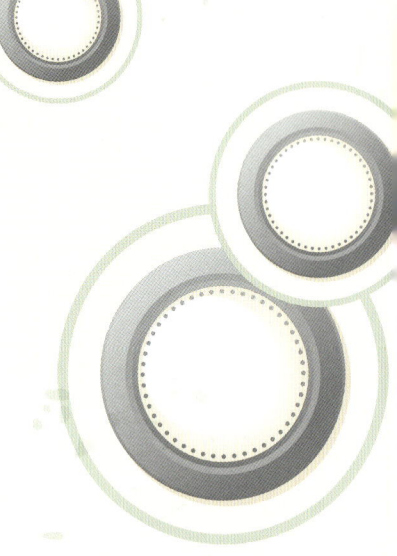

Back in Liverpool, during The Beatles' first engagement with Brian as their manager, a problem arose when it was discovered that John Lennon had laryngitis. Not wishing to cancel the appearance at the Macdona Hall on the Wirral, Epstein turned to Rory Storm to step into Lennon's shoes. For one night only, the Hurricanes' lead singer became a Beatle alongside Paul, George and Pete.

At one time, Ringo considered joining the Seniors but, on 30th December 1961, Peter Eckhorn enticed him back to Hamburg to play behind Tony Sheridan at the Top Ten Club, with the offer of a large fee, a flat and the use of a car. However, he found Sheridan's eccentric style of performing too hard to cope with and returned to the Hurricanes. While he was absent from the group, Derek Fell from the Blackpool group The Executioners replaced him.

During the Skegness summer season with the Hurricanes, Ringo received a letter from Kingsize Taylor offering him £20 a week to join The Dominoes in Germany as a replacement for Dave Lovelady, who was leaving the group to complete his studies. Ringo agreed.

Rory Storm, who sang with The Beatles.

Opposite: The Cavern in 1965.

The Fab one hundred and Four

5 APRIL 1962

John Lennon, Paul McCartney, George Harrison, Pete Best, Ringo Starr, Ray McFall, Billy Hatton, Dave Lovelady and Brian O'Hara

Ray McFall was the manager of the historic Cavern Club. He was born on 14 November 1926 in Garston, Liverpool. McFall became the owner of The Cavern on 3 October 1959 after founder Alan Sytner decided to sell the two-year-old club to him. Under McFall, it continued to be one of the best jazz clubs in Liverpool. However, by the end of 1960, rock 'n' roll was taking over from jazz as the most popular music in Liverpool. The Casbah had been rocking since 1959, and other former jazz clubs around Liverpool had already been converted into rock 'n' roll venues.

On 25 May 1960, The Cavern held its first beat night, featuring The Big Three and Rory Storm and the Hurricanes. Although the club was still promoting its jazz nights, McFall had decided to expand the rock 'n' roll sessions to lunchtimes. The lunchtime beat sessions started on 18 October 1960 and were a resounding success. In early 1961, Mona Best spoke to McFall about booking The Beatles, so he decided to find out more about them from the leading local authority on rock 'n' roll groups, Bob Wooler. On his recommendation, The Beatles made their lunchtime debut at The Cavern on 9 February 1961.

Paul, John and Ray McFall clowning around in The Cavern.

"The first time The Beatles came back from Hamburg," recalled Bob Wooler, "they wore leather jackets and jeans, not leather pants. They got those in Hamburg on their second visit and then they performed in full leather. Ray McFall did not like The Beatles playing in jeans. Jeans spelled trouble in his book and he said to me, 'You know the policy at The Cavern. I don't allow people in with jeans, so they can't play in them.' I groaned as I did not want to tell them. The Beatles were terrible when they ganged up on you – all of them, Pete Best as well. Their tongues could be savage if you criticised them for arriving late or messing around on stage. I knew that John would say, 'Who the f*** is he to tell us what to wear?' I went back to Ray and asked him to tell them himself. He put on his pained expression, which meant 'Aren't you capable of doing it yourself?' He went into the dressing room to see them and I waited for him to come out. There were no four-letter words then as he was the guy with the pay packet."

McFall remembered it, too. "Bob Wooler would say to me 'That's the way they are. Listen to their music.' They were different and they were very well rehearsed because they had come back from three months of torture in Hamburg. The other groups were like Cliff Richard and the Shadows, but The Beatles' music was so vibrant. As Bob said, 'They had ear and eye appeal.' However, I did not like them wearing jeans which were taboo in The Cavern. Our doormen would stop anyone wearing jeans. I felt that if people were wearing good, clean clothes they would be more likely to behave themselves as they wouldn't want them getting dirty and damaged."

McFall relented and allowed them to play in their leathers and jeans because the reaction to them was so great that their appearance virtually guaranteed a large attendance. Ray McFall got on very well with The Beatles, spurring them on to new projects in every possible way.

The Beatles responded to him in kind. McFall loved to sing. On 5 April 1962, The Beatles Fan Club were holding a special night at The Cavern, which Bob Wooler remembered. "Brian Epstein hired The Cavern on a Thursday night in April 1962 and it was for The Beatles to thank their fans and they had The Four Jays as their guests. Because it was a special night, they asked me to sing with them and I said no. On the other hand, Ray McFall did sing two songs with them – the Elvis song, 'Can't Help Falling In Love', and the title song of the film *Tender Is The Night*, which had been recorded by Vic Damone. The Beatles played a few chords behind him and the audience dutifully applauded. He had a good voice and he did well."

Author Spencer Leigh asked Ray McFall about his performance. "It was good fun but I should have stuck to the one song they knew. The second song was an unwise choice, but how could they refuse me? I owned the club."

The same night, The Beatles did a song they wrote, "Pinwheel Twist" and they swapped instruments. Pete Best emerged from behind his drums and took to the dance floor, dancing with his girlfriend

Outside The Cavern in 1973, just before it closed.

Kathy – the future Mrs. Best. Paul replaced Pete on drums as usual. But that wasn't the end of the musical fun, because they decided to invite members of The Four Jays onto the stage. Billy Hatton from The Four Jays, later The Fourmost, remembered it well. "This was one of the most fulfilling nights we had at The Cavern. We were chuffed about it: it was The Beatles Fan Club night and the only bands were The Beatles and The Four Jays. Frieda Kelly had asked who they wanted and they settled for us. I remember doing 'Mama Don't Allow' with The Beatles. Paul was on piano, John stayed on guitar, I played guitar, we had two drummers with Ringo and Dave Lovelady, and Brian O'Hara brought out an old violin. George Harrison found an old trumpet and he was blowing that. It sounds good but it was ten minutes worth of crap." It is worth noting that when it came to making up the new group, Ringo Starr was preferred to The Beatles' current drummer, Pete Best. The Fourmost went on to have hit singles with Lennon's "Hello Little Girl" in August 1963 and a Lennon-McCartney song "I'm In Love" in November 1963.

George, Paul, John and Pete outside The Cavern.

The Beatles in The Cavern dressing room, wearing their leathers.

John at The Cavern in early 1961, just after Ray McFall booked them.

APRIL 1962

The Beatles and Gene Vincent

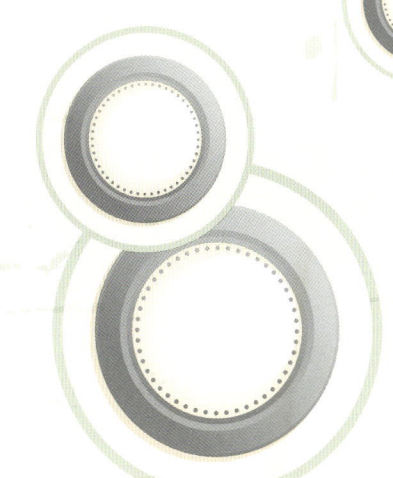

Vincent Eugene Craddock was born on 11 February 1935. The future rock 'n' roll pioneer showed his first real interest in music while his family lived in Munden Point, Virginia, near the North Carolina border where they ran a country store. He acquired his first guitar at the age of twelve when he was visiting a friend in West Virginia who had a guitar-playing sister. This friend gave him the guitar and told him to keep it. He joined the U.S. Navy in 1952 at age seventeen, but three years later, a tragic accident ended his career. He changed his name to Gene Vincent, formed a band called the Blue Caps and the rest, as they say, is history.

Vincent was one of The Beatles' favourite rock 'n' roll stars. His 1956 hit "Be-Bop-A-Lula" was quickly added to The Quarrymen's repertoire and John proudly performed it for the first time on 6 July 1957 at the Woolton Village Fête as Paul McCartney watched. Vincent's 1956 rock interpretation of "Ain't She Sweet" was also an inspiration and John began performing it with The Quarrymen.

According to Beatles drummer Pete Best, when the group first went to Hamburg, "John did his best to imitate Gene Vincent, grabbing up the microphone as if he was going to lay into the audience with it."

The Beatles met their idol in Hamburg in April 1962 when both acts appeared at the Star Club. They became friends and The Beatles often backed him. John even asked Gene for his autograph. When later asked by Sounds Incorporated what Hamburg was like, Gene told them, "Oh, it's OK there. I had a nice band backing me up. They're called The Beatles."

First issue of *Mersey Beat*, 6 July 1961, with Gene Vincent on the cover. Image © Bill Harry.

Gene had a pronounced limp, the result of a 1955 motorcycle accident while he was in the Navy. While he was riding his new Triumph, a woman in a Chrysler ran a red light and hit him. He was rushed to a naval hospital with a severely smashed left leg. Doctors seriously considered amputation, which would have been devastating, but Gene begged his mother not to allow the operation. He received a medical discharge and spent the rest of the year in and out of the hospital. His leg was permanently affected and he was forced to wear a steel brace for the remainder of his life.

By early 1956, with his leg still in plaster, Gene started to hang around the WCMS radio station in Hatteras, North Carolina, occasionally singing with the staff band, The Virginians. He regularly appeared on its *Country Showtime* programme and would perform "Be-Bop-A-Lula".

The Fab one hundred and Four

With "Be-Bop-A-Lula" selling like hot cakes, Gene's manager Ken Nelson wanted him and his Blue Caps back in the studio to record enough material for an album and another hit single. Between 24 to 27 June 1956, Vincent cut sixteen tracks including "Bluejean Bop", which Paul McCartney covered on his *Run Devil Run* album. This song became not only the title of his first album, but also the A-side of his third single. Like "Be-Bop-A-Lula", "Bluejean Bop" went gold.

After a short tour in 1957 in Ohio with Sanford Clark, Carl Perkins and

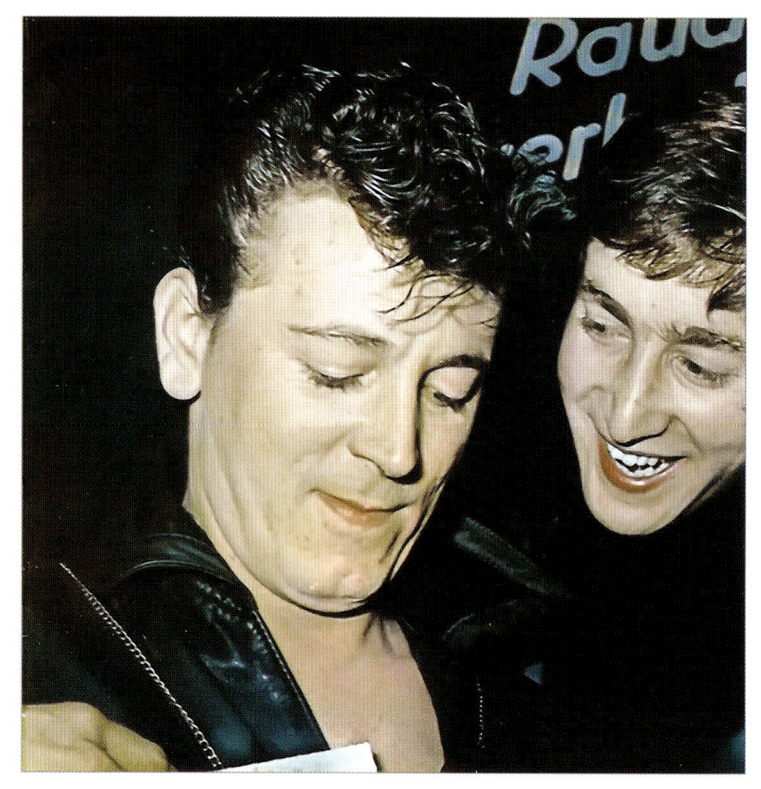

Gene Vincent with John.

"Be-Bop-A-Lula"

There are three versions of the origins of "Be-Bop-A-Lula". The song was supposedly based on a comic strip heroine called Little Lulu and Gene said he co-wrote it with fellow hospital patient Donald Graves. Then Sheriff Tex Davis, a local DJ, saw some potential in Gene and the weird song he sang and decided cut himself into the writing credits by buying Graves' song rights for a mere $25.

Another story ignores Graves completely and claims that Gene and Sheriff Tex wrote the song together one afternoon while listening to a 78 rpm recording of "You Can Bring Pearl with the Turned-Up Nose, But Don't Bring Lulu".

A third version has Graves writing the song entirely on his own and selling it to Gene for $50. The real story remains a mystery, although Sheriff Tex did sign Gene to a management deal, and later did co-write songs with him.

Gene Vincent's famous hit single, "Be-Bop-A-Lula".

Roy Orbison, Gene and his Blue Caps found themselves on a week-long series of shows in Philadelphia with Eddie Cochran.

In December of 1959, he arrived in London having been invited to headline a number of appearances on the popular *Boy Meets Girl* show. Gene's decision to tour the UK and appear on British TV was crucial. He arrived on 6 December 1959 to a hero's welcome, even though he hadn't had a major UK hit for over three years. Jack Good, the British impresario who had booked Gene for his television shows, was less than impressed upon meeting him for the first time. Good had this vision of a wild rock 'n' roller who had destroyed motel rooms across America, but Gene came across as an extremely polite Southern country gentleman, addressing him as "Sir".

Good decided to change Gene's image, dressing him from head to toe in black leather and draping a silver chained medallion around his neck. Many of his British fans identified with the black leather "biker" image and his popularity duly soared, especially after his much-talked-about first appearance on *Boy Meets Girl*. He created a TV image that, for the many fans who saw it, has failed to diminish to this day.

To add to the on stage excitement, Gene was joined by his old pal Eddie Cochran for the famed but fateful "Anglo-American Beat Show" tour put together by Larry Parnes. On 17 April 1960, after hurriedly leaving a Bristol gig, Gene, Eddie Cochran and Eddie's girlfriend, Sharon Sheeley took a late night taxi en route to London. They were all in the back seat. In the town of Chippenham, Wiltshire, around 1:00 am, the cab rounded a curve and hit a cement post at 70mph. The accident ended Eddie Cochran's life and severely re-injured Gene's leg, leaving him with a limp for the rest of his life.

Gene's own words on the accident: "When the three of us traveled together, Shari always sat in the middle. But because of the crowd of fans, I got in the cab first, then Eddie, then Shari last. With Eddie in the middle, the only way he could have flown out that door was if he tried to cover Shari. The only way I came out alive was because I had taken a sleeping pill. After the crash, I woke up and carried Eddie over to the ambulance even though I had a broken arm. I was in such a state of shock that I thought nothing was wrong with me. Eddie died two days later on Easter Sunday. Somehow, I did not."

By the end of 1965, Gene's health and career had both hit rock bottom, so he returned to California and retired for 18 months. However, he couldn't afford to stay retired for too long. In 1967, he hit the road again, touring in Europe, but unfortunately he returned to his self-destructive lifestyle.

Gene managed to get through two shows at the Wookey Hollow Club in Liverpool on 3 and 4 October '71, before his health completely gave out and he flew back to California.

Vincent Eugene Craddock died on 12 October 1971 in Newhall, California, from a bleeding ulcer. He was only 36 years old.

Gene Vincent meets John, Paul, George and Pete at the Star Club, Hamburg, in the spring of 1962.

APRIL 1962

John Lennon, Paul McCartney, George Harrison, Pete Best and *Roy Young*

In April and May 1962 while at the Star Club in Hamburg, boogie-woogie piano player Roy Young joined The Beatles on stage. Roy also joined The Beatles on backing vocals when they recorded "Sweet Georgia Brown" and "Swanee River" with Tony Sheridan on 24 May 1962.

I've had the pleasure of speaking with Roy on a number of occasions during the writing of this book and finally met up with him when he played at The Casbah Club in August 2012. Roy is a true cockney, born within the sound of 'Bow Bells'.

I began by asking him where the passion for his music originated. "I started to play piano when I was eight years old," Roy recalled, "and I really wanted to play boogie-woogie but my hands were only little. My mum, who was a good piano player, told me that I had to wait until my hands grew bigger, then I would be able to play a full octave. I measured my hands on my pillow to see if they had grown. I hated lessons, because I could see my friends through the window playing outside and I wanted to be out there with them."

Roy's desire to play with his friends was greater than his patience at piano lessons – so I asked him how he developed into such a great keyboard player. "I only learned to play when I formed my first band when I was twelve," Roy continued. "We would bunk into the music room in our school and play boogie-woogie on the piano there. Needless to say, I was caught, sent to the headmaster and caned! 'You should be playing this piano properly, Young, not this rubbish!' he yelled at me. I was not interested in anything apart from music, so I missed lessons, and when I was told I couldn't take part at the Christmas variety show, I decided I would give up and go to town. Of course, I was punished and taken back into normal lessons, with no music. I left school as soon as I could the following year at the age of fourteen."

With not many prospects of work for an unqualified fourteen-year-old, Roy had to bide his time. When he was eighteen, he joined the Merchant Navy. "I had to wait about three or four weeks, submit my forms and then have a medical," said Roy. "You were then set your grade for entry onto the ship, and I was soon made Head Steward in charge of the shows. I performed many shows for the crew and passengers with the Baggage Steward, who was Russ Conway, who later recorded several hit songs. When we were in Australia, I went to watch the movie *Rock Around The Clock* and I loved it so much, I stayed in the cinema just to listen to the music again, but I was thrown out. I never enjoyed any

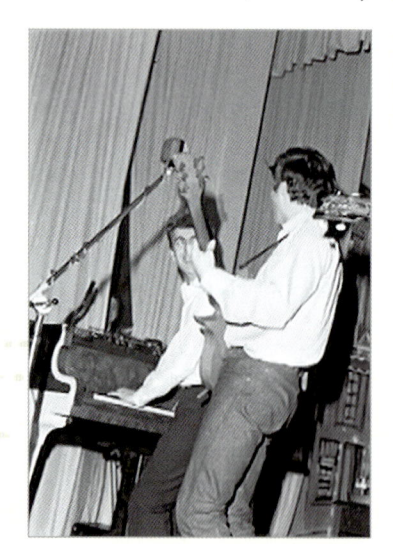

Roy with John Lennon at the Star Club, April 1962.

of the music theory at school, but this just increased my desire to play rock 'n' roll. I was influenced by such Boogie players as Meade Lux Lewis, Pete Johnson and Albert Ammons at a very young age. It was all I really wanted to do."

Roy returned to the UK and spent three months walking around London visiting different agencies, trying to break into the recording business. He eventually signed with Jack Fallon's Cana Variety Agency and, on that same day, found himself dubbed 'Roy Rock 'em Young' and performing his first professional engagement with Johnny Duncan and the Bluegrass Boys, a well-known skiffle group.

In the late 50's, Roy auditioned for the one-hour rock 'n' roll television show, *Oh Boy*, with famous British producer, Jack Good, who was also a Little Richard fan. He performed a Little Richard number and was immediately hired, only to go on and become "England's Little Richard". He later followed it up with a series of rock 'n' roll shows for the BBC entitled *Drumbeat*, backed by The John Barry Seven. During this time, Roy was regularly releasing singles on the Fontana/Phillips label. He then began extensive tours throughout England, Ireland and Scotland with Cliff Richard and The Shadows. This was followed by engagements as 'Roy Young' in clubs, theatres, variety shows and cabaret dinner venues all over England, including the 2i's Coffee Bar in London.

Roy (right) performing on the TV show, *Drumbeat*.

One of the many stars he worked with was Adam Faith. "I knew Adam really well," recalled Roy, "and I remember one day we were practising a song in my bedroom at home in front of the mirror, and Adam was struggling with the vocal. I told him how I had received a fabulous singing lesson from this old woman, who put her hand on my belly and told me to sing from there. I asked him where he was singing from, and it was clear that it was from his throat, which is why he was struggling. I showed him what I had been taught. He was always grateful to me because, soon after, he released 'What Do You Want' which became a huge hit. He had a number of top hits after that, with his distinctive voice. That's what we all did, we helped each other."

By 1961, Young's music had reached the European market scene where he regularly played the legendary stages of Germany. Along with Tony Sheridan and Ringo Starr, he formed The Beat Brothers, the house band at the Top Ten Club. "To me, Liverpool became the centre of rock 'n' roll in the UK," said Roy emphatically. "London was still too jazz-orientated back then, so it needed somewhere else, and Liverpool was the focal point for that. When the Liverpool groups came to Hamburg, everything changed for the better."

This naturally brings us to Roy meeting The Beatles in Hamburg and that offer to join the group:

"In the spring of 1962, I was offered the very first contract to appear at Hamburg's famous Star Club," Roy recollected. "Tony Sheridan and I formed the Star Combo and became the Star Club's first house band. As well as performing, it was my job to scout for and enlist the talent, which I did. I brought The Beatles, Ray Charles, Little Richard, Chuck Berry, Fats Domino, Gene Vincent, Bill Haley and Jerry Lee Lewis among others to the club. I was having the time of my life.

"Manfred Weissleder had asked Horst Fascher and me to come to Liverpool in early 1962 to book some of the bands for the Star Club. I came over and booked The Beatles, Gerry and the Pacemakers and Kingsize Taylor and the Dominoes. I knew I had to have the best Liverpool groups at the Star Club.

"It was here that a friendship began between myself and The Beatles and, before long, they had me up on stage playing piano and singing back-up vocals with the band. We got on so well, they were a

"I loved them! They were such great musicians, but lovely people, too. We got on so well and I enjoyed playing with them on stage. I suppose Paul and I got on the best, because he was fascinated with Little Richard, and wanted to play like him, too. I therefore gave Paul lessons in how to play boogie-woogie piano and he learned quickly. What a talented guy. I could also see how well John, Paul and George worked together, and Pete will always be a good friend of mine. Great drummer and what a beat he laid down. The girls fell in love with Paul, but if you spent half an hour with John in a room, you would fall in love with him. He was a great buddy. We made some

Roy Young playing piano with Tony Sheridan's Beat Brothers in Hamburg, 1962.

great bunch of lads. Manfred, who was running the Star Club, offered me whatever I wanted. I asked for a car, and he gave me this incredible Ford Taunus. It was luxurious, and I felt great driving around Hamburg in it. Then of course, The Beatles keep asking for a ride, and would I take them to the seaside in it. I gave in, and we headed off to the beach in the car. Once we got there, it was manic. They were kicking seawater at each other, and me. I was in my best suit, real leather, and not wanting to get it dirty, but Paul and John had other ideas. John drove my car into the sea and then they dragged me out of the car, still wearing my suit! The suit, of course, was ruined. When they all got back in the car, full of seawater, it all drained onto the seats and wrecked them, too. I took it to the car dealership and after they extracted seaweed and shells, the whole of the interior of the car had to be renewed. Thanks boys!

Poster from the Star Club, where Roy worked.

The Beatles and Roy Young on stage at the Star Club.

Roy playing with The Beatles at the Star Club, Hamburg, April 1962.

great music together. We even tried writing together, John, Paul and me. We would scribble on pieces of paper, and they were mainly just thrown in the bin. What could they be worth now?

"After coming off stage one night, Brian Epstein came to me and asked me if we could speak privately. He was very polite and said to me: 'I have been talking to the four lads and they have asked if you would come to England with them and go to London, where we are procuring a record deal. Would you think about it?' I was under a three-year contract at the Star Club, which I had only recently signed, and I had a new car and I'm working with the top rock 'n' roll stars on the planet, so I turned him down. 'I'm going to refuse your offer,' I said to Epstein. 'I know you won't be happy, but at the moment I must do my own thing.' So, I turned down The Beatles! I was not ready for it. I just felt that I had my thing going here in Hamburg and had to see that through, wherever it would lead.

Roy concluded: "As we know, The Beatles went on to become the best thing on the planet, and good luck to them, because they deserved it."

I did not even need to ask the next question, because it's been asked of him a thousand times. Roy starts to chuckle with his infectious laugh. "You're going to ask me if I regret it, aren't you? Well, I now give the same answer: Every night I bang my head on the wall ten times to get to sleep for being so stupid!" Roy and I laugh almost uncontrollably after he gave me one of the best interview answers ever! "You can't have regrets, and I don't. I have had an incredible life, and I can say I played with The Beatles, and considered them good friends."

Roy eventually returned to England, where he joined Cliff Bennett and the Rebel Rousers, who were managed by Brian Epstein. They joined The Beatles on their 1966 tour of Germany and later worked with the band to produce a version of "Got To Get You Into My Life", with Paul McCartney joining Roy on keyboards. He formed the Roy Young Band and has released albums on several record labels, such as EMI, Columbia, Ember, Phillips (Germany), RCA Victor and British MCA (Decca GB). He even made a live recording on tour with Chuck Berry of 'My Ding-a-Ling' which went to number 1 in the UK charts.

In 1974, while recording an album with Jeff Beck, Roy received a call

Roy performing at The Casbah in 2012.

from David Bowie asking him to help record his new album, *Young Americans*, which contained the song "Fame". Unfortunately, he couldn't join Bowie for that one, but he later helped Bowie record his album, *Low*. Roy has also worked with Long John Baldry, Ian Hunter and many other big stars. He was reunited with Tony Sheridan and Howie Casey in 1985 to record a CD and video, and made a personal appearance with Yoko at a John Lennon art show. He recorded a tribute to George Harrison, "Never Give Up", which were the first words George would always say to Roy when they met.

Now back in the UK, he is still touring with the Incredible Roy Young Band, which includes Howie Casey, who played with The Beatles in Hamburg and with Paul in Wings. They made a guest appearance at Best Fest, held at The Casbah in August 2012. He has lost none of his incredible musical ability or that voice which is on a par with Little Richard.

Not bad for a boy from London who turned The Beatles down and bangs his head on the wall every night!

20 JUNE 1962

Paul McCartney and The Strangers –

Joe Fagin, Harry Hutchings and George Harper

On 20 June 1962, The Beatles shared the bill at The Cavern with The Strangers. A minor problem ensued when the group's drummer, Brian Johnson, developed cramp in his leg and couldn't go on.

In dire need of a replacement for the evening, one unlikely candidate came forward: Paul McCartney. The Beatles' bassist offered his talents and they were gratefully accepted. He got up on stage with The Strangers and drummed his heart out. Jeff Hall was there and remembers what happened.

"I guess I saw The Beatles play over a hundred times," Jeff recalled. "I saw them mostly at The Cavern, where they were at their best, and a few other venues such as Aintree Institute, Holyoake Hall, Litherland Town Hall and Knotty Ash Village Hall.

"Although I went to The Cavern for the evening sessions, the lunchtime sessions were superb. A shilling (five pence) to get in, a bowl of soup and a roll and then watch The Beatles for an hour. I worked at the Pier Head so I could make it to The Cavern in five minutes and managed to go most lunch times. Once, I was there and an old friend from school, now a drummer, was in a band playing the lunchtime session. He suddenly got a cramp and could not play his drums, so who should leap on the stage from the sidelines but Paul McCartney. Paul took over the drums for the rest of the session and went down so well. He was such a good drummer.

Chris Huston, guitarist with The Undertakers, also remembered the event: "Paul did sit in on drums with The Strangers at The Cavern, once. I was there for that one."

Once again, Paul showed what a competent all-round musician he was, impressing the crowd on drums before resuming bass guitar duties in his own band.

The Strangers were a great Liverpool band, originally known as Jet and The Tornados at the end of the 1950s. They were so popular that they were voted number 5 in the popularity poll of the *Mersey Beat* newspaper.

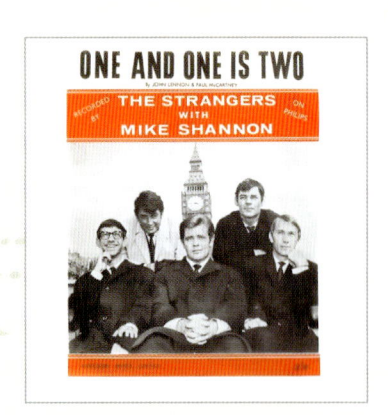

The Strangers' record, "One And One Is Two", written by John Lennon and Paul McCartney.

Pete drumming with The Pete Best Band in Liverpool.

16 AUGUST 1962

Pete Best is dismissed from The Beatles

One of the most controversial moments in Beatles history involves the dismissal of Pete Best just a few days before the group headed for London to record at Abbey Road on 4 September 1962.

In my book, *Liddypool: Birthplace of The Beatles*, I examined the many different theories that have been put forward over the years, and could easily dismiss those such as Pete not wishing to get a Beatles' haircut, or that he wasn't a good drummer. Since the book was published, I have continued to investigate this intriguing mystery, and uncover new information. I have spoken to Andy White, the session drummer brought in by George Martin on 11 September; Leslie Woodhead who arranged to film The Beatles at The Cavern for Granada TV; Joe Flannery who was a personal friend of Brian, and, most importantly, I have discovered an interview given by Ringo Starr to journalist Chris Hutchins in November of 1962, not long after Ringo joined The Beatles, giving a different sequence of events to the many we have read, which lead to Ringo replacing Pete as The Beatles' drummer.

"We were playing on the Wednesday evening, 15 August, at the Cavern," Pete told Beatles' biographer Hunter Davies. "We were due to go the next evening to Chester and I was supposed to be taking John. As we were leaving the Cavern, I asked John what time he wanted me to pick him up for Chester. He said oh no, he would go on his own. I said 'what's up?' But he was off. His face looked scared."

When I spoke to Pete, he recalled what happened next. "Brian saw me the night before and said that he wanted to see me in the morning, which was not unusual, as we often discussed the upcoming bookings. However, when I arrived there, Brian was agitated and I knew something was wrong. Finally, he came out with it: 'I don't know how to tell you this, Pete, but the boys want you out and Ringo is joining them on Saturday. They don't think you're a good enough drummer'. Epstein by this time was almost in tears."

Pete asked Brian for a definitive reason. "He said that George Martin wasn't too pleased with my playing. He said the boys thought I didn't fit in. But there didn't seem to be anything definite." Brian was clearly unhappy, as he told Beatles' biographer Hunter Davies. "The sacking of Pete Best left me in an appalling position," Epstein recalled. "This was the first real problem I'd had. Overnight I became the most disliked man on the beat scene. For two nights I didn't dare go near The Cavern because of the crowds shouting 'Pete for ever, Ringo never.' Ray McFall laid on a bodyguard for me.

"I knew how popular Pete was. He was incredibly good looking with a big following. I had got on well with him. In fact, he'd been the first one I'd got to know. I thought the way was through Pete because he was the easiest to get to know, the simplest. So I was very upset when the three of them came to me one night and said they didn't want him. They wanted Ringo. It had been on the cards for a long time, but I'd hoped it wouldn't happen."

At the time, Mona Best was quite clear of the reason. "Pete's beat had made them. They were jealous and they wanted him out. Pete hadn't realised what a following he had till he left. He was always so very shy and quiet, never shot his mouth off, like some people I could mention. He'd been their manager before Brian arrived, did the bookings and collected the money. I'd looked upon them as friends. I'd helped them get so much, got them bookings, lending them money. I fed them when they were hungry. I was far more interested in them than their own parents."

The point that Pete makes whenever he talks about this matter is why, if they had a problem with him, was he The Beatles' drummer for two years? Surely if he wasn't up to the job they would have replaced him earlier. And if they really wanted Ringo as their drummer, he was available and looking to leave Rory Storm and the Hurricanes at the end of 1961.

In fact, Ringo did quit the Hurricanes, joining Tony Sheridan in Hamburg for a short time before returning to Liverpool to re-join Rory. That being the case, why didn't The Beatles grab him then?

Pete was told that it was because he wasn't a good enough drummer, but very few people accept that as the true reason. In his *Wingspan* documentary, Paul did say: "Pete Best was a great drummer, but he just wasn't like the rest of us."

So why was Pete really dismissed? What we have to remember is that we can only look at the facts and opinions that were relevant in August 1962, and avoid any argument that relies on the benefit of hindsight. We know how well Ringo fitted in, became the perfect Beatle, and one of the world's greatest rock drummers, but nobody knew that at the time Pete was dismissed.

> ● Latest episode in the success story of Liverpool's instrumental group The Beatles: Commenting upon the outfit's recent recording test, Decca disc producer Mike Smith tells me that he thinks The Beatles are great. He has a continuous tape of their audition performances which runs for over 30 minutes and he is convinced that his label will be able to put The Beatles to good use. I'll be keeping you posted…

Tony Barrow reported that The Beatles were likely to be offered a deal by Decca.

Let's look at the chronology of events that surrounded Pete's dismissal in the summer of 1962:

1 January 1962 – The Beatles audition for Decca. They are turned down, but John, Paul and George do not tell Pete right away.

18 May 1962 – George Martin issues a contract for The Beatles and sends it to Brian Epstein, who signs and returns it to EMI.

4 June 1962 – Contract is effective from this date for 12 months.

6 June 1962 – The Beatles' first meeting and recording session at EMI with George Martin. It is after this session that Martin tells Brian that he will use a session drummer for the record.

July 1962 – Following this appearance, George Martin confirms the recording contract to Brian Epstein. He announces that the first recording session will take place on 4 September and that The Beatles should work on "Love Me Do" and "How Do You Do It".

July 1962 – Leslie Woodhead from Granada TV visits The Cavern and meets The Beatles to arrange to film The Beatles on 22 August.

11 August 1962 – John, Paul and George invite Ringo to the Blue Angel to meet Brian Epstein.

14 August 1962 – Ringo is asked to telephone Brian Epstein who offers him the role as Pete's replacement as drummer in The Beatles.

16 August 1962 – Pete Best is dismissed.

18 August 1962 – Ringo Starr joins The Beatles and performs with them for the first time as a band member at Hulme Hall, Port Sunlight.

22 August 1962 – Granada television film The Beatles at The Cavern.

23 August 1962 – John Lennon marries Cynthia Powell.

4 September 1962 – Second recording session at Abbey Road, this time with John, Paul, George and Ringo.

11 September 1962 – Third recording session at Abbey Road, with session drummer Andy White brought in to drum for the debut record, leaving Ringo to play the maracas and tambourine.

5 October 1962 – "Love Me Do" is released as The Beatles' first record, with Ringo on the drums, with the B-side "P.S. I Love You" featuring Andy White on drums. White's version of "Love Me Do" appeared on The Beatles' debut album, *Please Please Me*.

The Fab one hundred and Four

Abbey Road: 6 June 1962

What seems to be the catalyst for Pete's departure was the comment made by George Martin to Brian Epstein following the recording session at Abbey Road on 6 June 1962. Unfortunately, George Martin has given different versions of what he said, but the core facts remain the same. Martin recalled: "When I saw them – The Beatles – I thought the three front men worked well, but the guy at the back, Pete, was the best looking, but he didn't say much or have the charisma of the others. More importantly, his drumming was okay, but it wasn't top-notch in my opinion, so I mentioned it to Brian Epstein. I said, 'I don't care what you do with them as a group, but from purely a sound point of view, I would like to get someone else in to play drums on the record. Is that okay? They took it as the final word – the catalyst to bring about change and poor Pete got the boot. I've always felt a bit guilty about that, but I guess he survived."

Interestingly, Paul McCartney commented in *The Beatles Anthology* that "George Martin told us". This is a different scenario. It was always reported that George Martin spoke to Brian only, but Paul has clearly stated through multiple sources that George Martin spoke to him and probably John and George as well. A clear division was there for even Martin to observe. George Martin was not present at most of the June session and was only brought in later by his producer. He had delegated the responsibility of The Beatles' artist test to engineers Norman Smith and Ken Townsend and to producer Ron Richards, who oversaw the session. It was Richards who put Pete through his paces and admitted that no other regular 'live' drummers could have done what he asked – not even Ringo. "I just got a bit, oh God, where do we go from here", a despairing Richards had said. George Martin was only agreeing with, and passing on, the comments of his producer and engineers, who have admitted in hindsight that they were a bit harsh on Pete. Norman Smith said, "I personally didn't see a reason for a session drummer to be brought in."

Paul later recalled that when George Martin told them about changing the drummer, he thought, "'No. We can't!' It was one of those terrible things you go through as kids. Can we betray him? No. But our career was on the line. Maybe they were going to cancel our contract."

If Pete's drumming on 6 June resulted in his subsequent dismissal from the group, then it is clear that George Martin was going to use a session drummer to make the record. At the time, it was quite normal to have session musicians brought in for the purposes of making a record.

However, no session drummer was present on 4 September, so Brian must have informed Martin that they had changed their drummer and needed to re-assess the group. The easiest way to do this would have been to show George Martin the edition of *Mersey Beat* where Brian had convinced Bill Harry that Pete had voluntarily left and the parting was amicable. This would have appeased Martin's mind and made the replacement drummer story more plausible.

The Blue Angel: 11 August 1962

The earliest recorded interview with Ringo about joining The Beatles was conducted by *New Musical Express* journalist Chris Hutchins, who followed The Beatles' career through their American and UK tours, and was one of a handful of journalists to be trusted by The Beatles. In November 1962, just three months after joining The Beatles, Hutchins met The Beatles for the first time in Hamburg, and asked Ringo how he joined the group. It is very revealing, as for the first time it reveals how Ringo's place in the group was agreed in a secret meeting just days before Pete Best was dismissed. There have been many different stories about how Ringo was recruited, involving John, Paul, George and Brian, and various phone calls and even John and Paul driving to Pwllheli where Ringo was playing with Rory Storm. The following series of events makes the most sense, and was recalled by Ringo within a few weeks of joining the group.

"The Beatles were playing at a place called 'The Hot Spot', said Ringo. This was actually 'The Odd Spot' in Bold Street, Liverpool. The date was Saturday, 11 August 1962. "One Saturday morning," Ringo continued, "Elsie said that George Harrison had called and would I go down to see them at the Hot Spot (sic)? It was my night off and I couldn't think of a better way to spend it." Ringo had returned to Liverpool from Butlin's, Pwllheli, where he had been playing with Rory Storm and the Hurricanes. "During the break," continued Ringo, "John, Paul and George invited me to join them at the Blue Angel later on. Pete Best wasn't coming, they said.

"At the Blue Angel, I was introduced to Brian Epstein. We shook hands and he seemed a bit surprised by my appearance: I had a beard and a grey streak in my hair then. I thought no more about the meeting until the following Tuesday when, early in the afternoon, I received a message asking me to phone Mr. Epstein at midnight. I did and he said, 'Would you like to join The Beatles?' I said I would and he asked me if I could make it the next day as Pete Best had left, so I said no, but I would join them on the following Saturday afternoon. I turned up that afternoon in black corduroy jacket and trousers and a black polo-neck sweater, John said I looked like Billy the Kid.

"My first date as a proper Beatle was at Port Sunlight. Half the hall was in my favour and the other half called out 'Pete Best for ever, Ringo never!' One fellow kept shouting it and George yelled back at him, 'Shut Up!' Later on the fellow butted him for it." This incident was at The Cavern four days later, where it is recorded that George obtained a black eye and the cries of support for Pete are known to have been shouted all evening.

"About a month later, we went to London for our first recording session at EMI. I was very nervous and the others kept saying, 'Don't crack up now, Ringo.' The next time we went to the studio, I was horrified to see a set of drums that weren't mine and a man who definitely wasn't me to do 'Love Me Do' again and I played tambourine. I found it harder to get close to George Harrison. As the youngest Beatle, he tended to back off rather than try to compete for the limelight with the extrovert John and Paul.

Abbey Road: 4 September 1962

The new lineup of The Beatles turned up at Abbey Road for their second recording session at Abbey Road on 4 September. They recorded versions of "Love Me Do" and the Mitch Murray song, "How Do You Do It", which George Martin had asked them to work on for their first single.

In *The Beatles Anthology*, they revisited these events with yet another version, which does little to clarify things. "In September, we went down to London with Ringo and played for EMI again," said Paul. "By this time we did have a contract." Ringo was asked for his recollection of the eventful trip to London. "The response to us at EMI was okay, because we'd done the auditions and George Martin was willing to take a chance. On my first visit in September, we just ran through

Pete Best.

some tracks for George Martin. We even did 'Please Please Me'. I remember that, because while we were recording it, I was playing the bass drum with a maraca in one hand and a tambourine in the other. I think it's because of that that George Martin used Andy White, the 'professional', when we went down a week later to record 'Love Me Do'. The guy was previously booked anyway because of Pete Best. George didn't want to take any more chances and I was caught in the middle."

Ringo alludes to the session drummer being brought in to replace Pete, but there is no evidence to back that up.

Paul then contradicts Ringo's version in *Anthology*: "Horror of horrors! George Martin didn't like Ringo. Ringo at that point was not *that* steady on time. Now he is rock steady, it's always been his greatest attribute. But to George he was not as pinpoint as a session guy would be. So, Ringo got blown off the first record. George did the 'Can I see you for a moment, boys?' 'Yeah?' 'Um… without Ringo.' He said, 'I would like to bring another drummer in for this record.' George got his way and Ringo didn't drum on the first single." Both Paul and Ringo are convinced that Ringo didn't play on the first single of "Love Me Do".

Abbey Road: 11 September 1962

George Martin recalled this second recording date clearly, and that he had booked a session drummer to replace Ringo. "On 11 September 1962, we finally got together to make their first record. The boys meantime had brought along a guy and they said 'we're going to get Ringo to play with us' and I said 'we just spent good money and booked the best drummer in London. I'm not having your bloke in. I'll find out about him later. Poor Ringo was mortified and I felt sorry for him, so I gave him the maracas."

If we look at it from Ringo's perspective, we have to consider what he was or wasn't told when he was offered the drummer's position in The Beatles. When Ringo joined the group, he signed for £25 per week on a probationary basis. Peter Brown, who had worked closely with Brian Epstein as his personal assistant since their days at NEMS in Liverpool, said in his book *The Love You Make*: "The terms were that Ringo would be paid £25 per week for a probationary period, and if things worked out he would be made a member." At that stage, the other three Beatles were earning £50 per week, plus a share of the proceeds from their records and performances. Ringo did eventually become a full and integral member of The Beatles.

Was Pete treated as just the drummer as opposed to a fully-integrated fourth member of The Beatles? Was any drummer since Colin Hanton treated as more than just a drummer? When I spoke to Tony Barrow several years ago, he was quite clear that The Beatles revolved primarily around the songwriting talents of John and Paul as well as the musical partnership and friendship between John, Paul and George. John, Paul and George had been together since December 1957 and were closer than brothers. Between then and the moment that Ringo joined, The Beatles had engaged a succession of drummers, with Pete having the longest tenure.

After Colin Hanton, they had used Mike McCartney, Paul McCartney, Tommy Moore, Norman Chapman, Johnny Hutchinson and then Pete, as well as a few temporary drummers. It was the one role in the group that was fluid and, when looking back at the groups of the day, the drummer's role was not as important as it is today. Did the other Beatles consider Pete to be just a drummer and not *their* drummer? The evidence is clear, especially in the fact that John, Paul and George didn't even inform Pete that they had been turned down by Decca! However, it they really wanted to get Pete out of the group because of his drumming ability, surely the fact that Decca had turned them down was the perfect opportunity, and not after they had secured the contract with EMI?

John was quite brutal in his assessment of Pete: "The reason he got into the group in the first place was because we had to have a drummer to get to Hamburg. We were always going to dump him when we could find a decent drummer, but by the time we were back from Germany, we'd trained him to keep a stick going up and down (four-in-the-bar, he couldn't do much else) and he looked nice and the girls liked him, so it was all right."

As history proves, they had lost Tommy Moore and replaced him with Norman Chapman who, soon after, was called up for National Service. With only days to go before heading off to Hamburg, they had to find a drummer. On the day that Pete was auditioning, Paul was responding to an advertisement in the *Liverpool Echo* where a drummer had offered his services. Pete was recruited on 12 August 1960 and, on 16 August, they were on their way to Hamburg. It was a desperate situation and with drummers in short supply, they had to employ whomever they could get. That's why they chose Pete. He was someone they already knew and had seen drum at The Casbah. It was a close call. It could be argued, therefore, that The Beatles considered drummers to be a disposable asset.

Pete, like Tommy and Norman, was brought in as a drummer, not a friend. In contrast, Paul was introduced to John by a mutual friend, Ivan Vaughan. Paul introduced John to his friend George, so they were together through friendship. Tommy, Norman and Pete were drummers who joined them with no previous ties. Although they knew Ringo, what John, Paul and George also knew was that he was unhappy playing with the Hurricanes and was looking for a way out. Just as Pete was ready to leave The Blackjacks, Ringo was ready to leave the Hurricanes. As they needed a drummer at short notice to go to Hamburg, they now needed a drummer at short notice, as they were about to make a record. At that stage though, they were expecting to be using a session drummer, but it is likely that they didn't explain that to Ringo at the time.

Some have claimed that they were approached by either Brian or The Beatles to consider replacing Pete as the group's drummer. They include Joe Brown's drummer Bobby Graham and Johnny Hutchinson. Even former Quarrymen banjo player Rod Davis was asked, on a brief meeting with John in March 1962, if he played drums, because they needed a drummer for Hamburg. It is hard to verify them all, but it does seem to be accepted that The Beatles were on the lookout for a new drummer, several months before Pete was dismissed. Bobby Graham was an established drummer with a top star of the day, and Johnny Hutchinson was the best drummer in Liverpool.

Ringo eventually slotted in perfectly with John, Paul and George and, with the benefit of hindsight, nobody could disagree with their decision to enlist Ringo as the final member of The Fab Four. However, if he was the one they wanted, why did he feel that he wasn't fully accepted straight away? Ringo stated that "I had to join them as people as well as a drummer". Did John, Paul and George ever think that Pete joined them as people as well as a drummer, when many others had failed? Was this what Paul meant when he said that "Pete Best was a great drummer, but he just wasn't like the rest of us?" They didn't know if Ringo was going to be the perfect replacement, so did they just enlist him because they needed a drummer?

What reasons have been suggested for Pete's dismissal?

When dealing with the dismissal, we can only examine the evidence at the time of the decision in August 1962, and not with the benefit of hindsight.

Did He Fit In?

Paul said that "he wasn't like the rest of us." From Paul's point of view, Pete didn't fit it. For many people, this is one of the most likely reasons because even Ringo admitted he had to 'join them as a person as well as a drummer'. This, according to Ringo, took some time. However, Ringo's personality perfectly complemented those of the other Beatles and the four of them looked comfortable in each other's company. This conclusion, however, is based on what is now known and from observations of the group during their career in the 1960s.

There was a suggestion that Pete was moody. Bob Wooler described Pete as "mean, moody and magnificent" and many have taken this the wrong way. Wooler was a genius of alliteration and because Pete reminded him of a film star with those "bedroom eyes" and film-star good looks, he found an apt use for the phrase. Wooler took his inspiration from the poster from the 1943 film *The Outlaw*, where Jane Russell, draped in a sexually provocative pose was described as "Mean, Moody, Magnificent". Wooler was alluding to this description when describing Pete Best in this way.

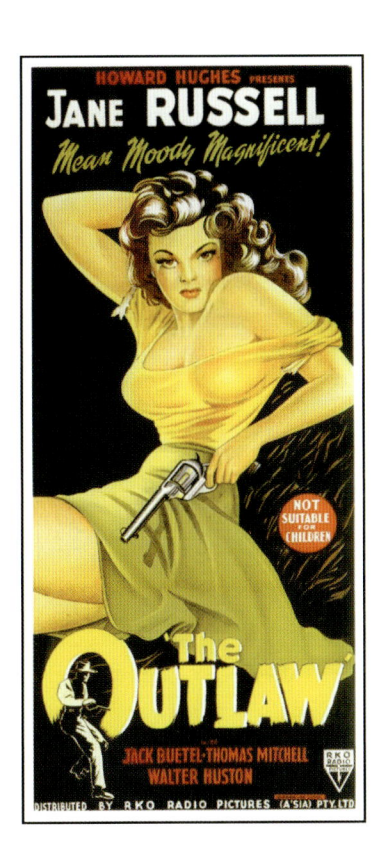

Was it jealousy?

Did Pete's popularity make the other Beatles jealous? Consider that when Bob Wooler introduced The Beatles at The Cavern with "It's time for John, Paul, George and... Pete", the screams reached an unbelievable crescendo. as happened at various other venues across Liverpool where the screams became ear-piercing at the mention of Pete's name.

It has often been suggested that Paul McCartney was the most jealous. During the *Teenagers' Turn* showcase in Manchester in March 1962, Lennon, McCartney and Harrison walked on stage to applause, but when Best walked on, the girls screamed. Pete was surrounded at the stage door afterwards by attentive girls, while the other members were ignored after signing a few autographs. Paul's father, Jim McCartney, was present at the time and admonished Pete by saying: "Why did you have to attract all the attention? Why didn't you call the other lads back? I think that was very selfish of you." Did this hasten Paul's desire to see Pete removed from the group? That their female admirers loved Pete is a matter of public record, and the more people I speak to in Liverpool, the more I hear the same comment: Pete was getting all of the attention at the expense of the other Beatles. However, when you are dealing with young men, egos are involved. Many believe that this would have been a significant factor.

Get rid of Pete, get rid of Mona?

Some authors have suggested that Brian had to get rid of Pete because his mother, Mona Best, was still trying to manage The Beatles even though Brian was now in charge. On the face of it, this does sound feasible, if she was being a nuisance. Mona was a forceful character and worked tirelessly encouraging and supporting The Beatles between 1960 and 1962. However, it was George Harrison, and not Brian Epstein, who had felt the full wrath of Mona's ire when, before an important gig, he was discovered drunk and slumped in a chair. Mona was so disgusted she told George that he was sacked from The Beatles! The others revived him and the performance went ahead, but this incident was remembered by George and Paul, and couldn't have helped Pete's position.

However, it wasn't managing The Beatles that Mona wanted to do, or was in a position to do any longer.

By the summer of 1962, Mona had been nursing her dying mother for months and had closed The Casbah in June 1962 because she couldn't cope with the pressure and had given birth to her third son, Roag, in July 1962. When would she have the time to handle The Beatles? It was this potential scandal of the birth of Roag from the relationship between Mona and Neil Aspinall that Brian described to his friend Joe Flannery as "very indiscreet: the last straw." Was this enough for John, Paul and George to convince Brian to dismiss Pete?

When Brian dismissed Pete, and Pete wouldn't accept a position in another of his groups, he turned to Joe Flannery to find a band for Pete. Joe was a popular promoter on Merseyside, and a close friend of The Beatles. However, as well as promoting The Beatles with Brian, he managed his younger brother Peter, better known as Lee Curtis. As Lee Curtis and the All Stars, now with Pete on drums, they were voted a close second to The Beatles in the *Mersey Beat* poll at the end of 1962. They were soon signed to Decca records, so Pete had a recording career that he had missed out on with The Beatles. However, Joe explained that Mona became an issue to him too. "It wasn't long after Pete had joined that we made the record, but Mona started to ring me constantly, so I could understand what Brian had gone through. It was clear to me that Mona wanted the All Stars to be about her son, just as she had done in The Beatles, and it wasn't long before the All Stars decided to split from Lee Curtis and were soon known as The Pete Best Four."

In Conclusion

This wasn't the first time that The Beatles had got rid of a band member. They had replaced many people over the years, like Nigel Walley, The Quarrymen tea-chest bass player who became their first manager; Eric Griffiths was replaced by George; Ken Brown was eased out of The Quarrymen at The Casbah over fifteen shillings (75 pence) because he didn't play; Allan Williams was dropped in Hamburg. So, why should Pete Best get the proceeds from The Beatles' records if he wasn't going to be playing on them? It made more sense to get Ringo and pay him just £25 per week.

John, Paul and George made the decision to get rid of Pete because George Martin had told Brian that Pete wasn't going to drum on the records. It could be surmised that they weren't sure how long fame would last and were scared that Pete's inability to satisfy Richards and Martin in the studio would endanger their future success. For them it was an easy decision: Pete had to go. As Allan Williams commented, "All groups are users. They are ruthless."

Alistair Taylor once said that Pete was simply not a Beatle. John Lennon made a similar observation: "Pete Best was a great drummer, but Ringo was a Beatle."

With the Abbey Road recording date looming on 4 September, and, more urgently, a television show to be filmed on 22 August, Brian had to act swiftly, as they couldn't appear in the charts with one drummer, and then on television with another. Once the date for filming was fixed, Brian had no option but to summon Pete into the office and give him the bad news.

Pete Best was a Beatle for two years and played an important role in the formation of the band. He was a vital cog in the band that took Hamburg and Liverpool by storm and secured a recording contract. For Pete, it was a shame that he wouldn't be with them on their road to fame and fortune.

Pete drumming with The Pete Best Band in Liverpool.

Ringo Starr,
Harry Graves, Marie Maguire, a "Teacher" and Red Carter

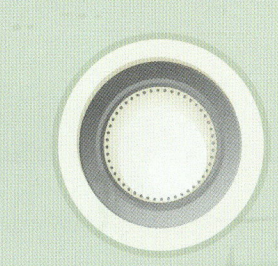

Ringo poses in August 1962.

Richard Starkey was born on 7 July 1940 at 9, Madryn Street in the Dingle area of Liverpool. His mother and father divorced when he was three, with Richard Sr. moving out of the house and back in with his parents at 59, Madryn Street. His paternal grandparents, John and Annie Starkey, often babysat young Richy, but the relationship between his parents was strained and living on the same street was awkward.

A bigger problem for Richy's mother Elsie was paying the high rent as a single parent. In order to make ends meet, she moved in 1945 to 10, Admiral Grove, just a few hundred yards across High Park Street. Richy was only five. Elsie married again when her son was thirteen, this time to Harry Graves. When Richy was nearly seven, his appendix burst and he was rushed to the Royal Liverpool Children's Hospital on Myrtle Street, Liverpool. He eventually recovered from his life-threatening illness, earning the nickname of 'Lazarus' given by his paternal grandfather for his miraculous recovery.

It was during this time that his love for drumming was stimulated by childhood friend Marie Maguire.

Born in The Dingle, Marie Crawford (née Maguire) remembers the young Richy Starkey well. Her family moved into 10, Madryn Street in June 1943, immediately opposite Elsie and Richy's house. "Everyone knew everybody else. You knew who your neighbours were and we helped each other out," explained Marie. "That was what it was like, and why I was happy to help out. Richy's dad had moved out when Richy was only three, and so Elsie had to work to pay the rent.

The Fab one hundred and Four

345

"Mum became good friends with Elsie Starkey, and I was regularly called in, and trusted, to babysit young Richy. This would often entail going to Richy's grandparents' house at the bottom of Madryn Street where I would collect him – often fast asleep. I would carry him home and put him to bed."

9, Madryn Street, birthplace of Richard Starkey on 7 July 1940.

Royal Liverpool Children's Hospital, Myrtle Street, where Richy was rushed suffering with a burst appendix.

Richy moved on to Dingle Vale Secondary Modern School at the age of eleven. However, he suffered another setback two years later when he contracted tuberculosis. This time, he missed more than a year of schooling when he was moved to the Royal Liverpool Children's Hospital in Heswall, across the River Mersey, on the Wirral Peninsula overlooking the Dee Estuary and North Wales. Here, the air was cleaner, giving children with weakened lungs a fighting chance to recover and build up their stamina.

"Liverpool was a breeding ground for tuberculosis, especially where I lived," remembered Ringo in *The Beatles Anthology*. "I had lots of time off with bad lungs, and it turned into tuberculosis. I was put in a greenhouse for a whole year. That second time I went into the hospital, there was Sister Clark and Nurse Edgington. Being thirteen or fourteen, it was puberty for me, and when the nurses would kiss us goodnight it was all quite frisky: 'Will you kiss me goodnight, nurse?' and I'd get a really good kiss off a lot of them. They were all young (they weren't old, anyway) about eighteen to twenty. We'd never ask the sister to kiss us goodnight!

"We had two wards separated by a partition, with girls in one ward and boys in the other. There was a lot of hot passion going on. We'd sneak in at night to the girls' ward and fumble around. We all had tuberculosis, of course, spreading those damn germs to each other."

One of way to keep the children entertained in the hospital was the use of music as therapy. The teachers would line the children up in their beds, outside in the fresh air, and give them various percussion instruments to play. "Playing drums for me started in the hospital in 1954, where, to keep us entertained, they gave us some schooling," recalled Ringo in an interview with Steve Goudie. "A teacher would come in with a huge easel, with symbols for instruments shown on a big piece of board. She gave us percussion instruments – triangles, tambourines and drums. She would point at the yellow and a triangle would sound and she would point at the red and the drum would sound. I'd only play if they gave me a drum.

"I was in the hospital band. I started using cotton bobbins to hit on the cabinet next to the bed. I was in a bed for ten months. It's a long time, so you keep yourself entertained; it was that and knitting. That's where I really started playing. I never wanted anything else

The Royal Liverpool Children's Hospital Sanitorium in Heswall, Wirral, where Richy was treated for tuberculosis.

kid they would let me do it. Everybody in Liverpool had their party-piece: you had to sing a song! My mother's was 'Little Drummer Boy'. She would sing it to me, and I would sing 'Nobody's Child' to her and she would always cry. Then I'd say 'I'm nobody's child, mum.' She'd say, 'Oh don't!' When I was about fifteen, I used to sing in the choir, for money. I'd been to Sunday school a little when I was younger".

from then on. Drums were the only thing I wanted and when I came out, I used to look in music shops and see drums. That's all I'd look at. My grandparents gave me a mandolin and a banjo, but I did not want them. My grandfather gave me a harmonica when I was seven: nothing. We had a piano: nothing. Only the drums.

"I was listening to music all this time. At fourteen, I bought three records: The Four Ace's 'Love Is A Many Splendoured Thing', Eddie Calvert's 'Oh Mein Papa' and David Whitfield's 'Mama'. The Four Aces lasted, and still holds up. I don't play the others too often now.

"I was never really into drummers. I loved seeing Gene Krupa in the movies, but I did not go out and buy his records. The one drum record I bought was 'Topsy Part Two' by Cozy Cole. I always loved country and western. A lot of it was around from the guys in the navy. I'd go to parties and they'd be putting on Hank Williams, Hank Snow and all those country acts. I still love country music. Skiffle was also coming through, and I was a big fan of Johnnie Ray. Frankie Laine was probably my biggest hero around 1956 – and I also liked Bill Haley.

"My first kit came on the scene about this time. I bought a drum for thirty shillings. It was a huge, one-sided bass drum. There used to be lots of parties then. An uncle would play banjo or harmonica, my grandparents played mandolin and banjo. There was always someone playing something. So I would bang my big drum with two pieces of firewood and drive them mad, but because I was a

With Richy in the hospital, Marie decided to buy him something to cheer him up. "He was at the convalescent home in Heswall," recalled Marie. "That is when I took him 'Bedtime for Drums', which he loved."

And so, inspired by Marie, and encouraged by the "Teacher", it was here that Richy developed his love for drumming. However, he did not have a set of drums, which is where his new stepfather, Harry Graves, comes into the story.

Harry, a painter and decorator who was from Romford in Essex, worked for Liverpool Corporation and married Elsie Starkey, née Gleave, on 17 April 1954 at Liverpool Register Office when Richy was thirteen.

"Harry, my stepfather, came into the picture when I was eleven," explained Ringo. "He worked as a painter and decorator up at Burtonwood which was an American army base. He made me laugh, he bought me DC comics and he was great with music. He used to lay music on me, but would never force any of it. He was into big bands and jazz and Sarah Vaughan, while I'd be listening to stupid people. He'd

"Bedtime for Drums", which Marie Maguire gave to Richy while he was in hospital.

The Fab one hundred and Four

347

say, 'Have you heard this?' That was always his line: 'Have you heard this?' He was a really sweet guy. All animals and children loved him. I learned gentleness from Harry.

"When someone in Harry's family died, he'd gone down to Romford and there was a drum kit for sale for £12," recalled Ringo. "The whole family collected together and he brought this drum set to Liverpool. I was given it for Christmas. Up till then I'd been playing drums at home. This kit was amazing. It was not just a drum, but drums: a snare, a bass drum, a hi-hat, one little tom-tom, a top cymbal and a bass drum pedal. I did not have to kick it any more.

"Once I'd got my drum kit, I set it all up in my bedroom, the back room, and off I went, banging away. And then I heard from the bottom of the stairs, 'Keep the noise down, the neighbours are complaining!' I never practised at home. The only way I could practise was to join a group. I got the drum kit on Boxing Day and I was in a group by February."

Although he always talked about the drums, Ringo had learned the piano accordion with the Orange Lodge, the Protestant organisation,

Ringo's mum Elsie and stepfather Harry inside 10, Admiral Grove.

Ringo playing the accordion in the back yard of his Admiral Grove home, with proud mum Elsie.

and would sometimes march with the band. He also learned to play the piano and organ and was occasionally seen with a guitar, too.

Although music was to become his career, he had studied at Riversdale Technical College in Aigburth before working on the St. Tudno ferry between Liverpool and North Wales, though that job did not last too long.

His first musical foray was not into rock 'n' roll though. In 1957, Richy became intrigued by a neighbour who was in a band. "Why did I not have a go? I thought it was a jazz group – I was mad on jazz. When it turned out to be a silver band, playing in the park and sticking to the marches and all that, I chucked it in. I lasted just one night."

His future would be with Rory Storm and the Hurricanes and The Beatles. For now, he had to find a group to join, because he did not enjoy drumming alone. He turned to his next door neighbour, Eddie Myles, to help fulfil that ambition.

Ernie Carter, better known as Red Carter, hailed from the Wirral, and was born in 1921. He started playing the drums when he was a child, and, with his flame-red hair, soon picked up the nickname for which he will be remembered. He joined a youth band in the 1930s and, after serving in the Royal Tank Regiment during the war, he formed his own band, called The Playboys.

Often playing with his own or other bands, he was to back a number of the biggest British artists, like Lonnie Donegan, Vera Lynn, Matt Monro and Cleo Laine at Liverpool's Cabaret Club in Duke Street.

When collecting stories for his book, The Beatles and Me, Dean Johnson came across one of Red's former student that told him how Red had given Ringo a few drumming lessons, and was responsible for Ringo's unique hi-hat style, which involves hitting it while open, instead of the usual way when it is closed. He also found an eyewitness who recalled how Ringo was a regular visitor to the Cabaret Club, when The Red Carter Trio was the resident band. Red also gave a number of Liverpool drummers lessons in his studio.

Ringo, in an interview with the BBC in 1966, did mention attending drum lessons. "I had about three lessons. Once I got interested in drums I said, 'Right, I'll go read music and learn how to play' but I went to this little man in a house and he played drums and he got a manuscript and wrote it all down. I never went back – I just couldn't be bothered. It was too routine for me, y'know, all those paradiddles and that – I couldn't stand it."

Without mentioning the tutor by name, this is the only tutor to have mentioned giving lessons to Ringo, so the story is very plausible, and there is a strong possibility that it was Red who gave Ringo the lessons. Red's studio, in Tempest Hey, Liverpool, was busy every Saturday morning with hopeful young drummers who had to bring their own sticks and manuscript paper, ready to learn from the master. He could play any style: rock 'n' roll, blues, swing, latin, waltz and his favourite, jazz.

Red continued to give lessons, and inspired local drummer Chris Sharrock, who has drummed with Oasis and Robbie Williams, and was a highly respected musician on Merseyside.

Red Carter's favourite quote was, "if anyone asks you what sort of drummer you are, don't tell them you're the best in the world, just say you're a 'competent' drummer; because competent drummers always work!"

Red Carter died in March 2013.

The *St. Tudno* Ferry, where Ringo worked for a short time, sailing up the River Mersey.

Admiral Grove, where Ringo lived from the age of five at number 10.

Red Carter (left) with his band.

Riversdale Technical College Engineering workshop, where Ringo trained.

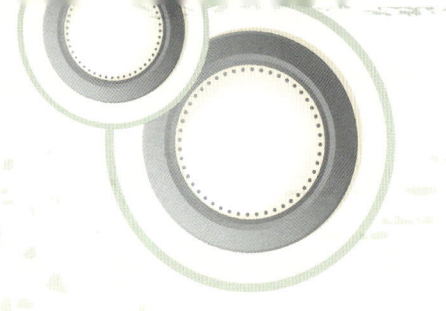

The Eddie Clayton Skiffle Group – Eddie Myles, Roy Trafford, Peter Healey, John Dougherty and Mickey McGrellis and Richy Starkey

Before he was Ringo, he was Richy. In February 1957, just a few weeks after getting his drum kit at Christmas, he joined his first group. "There was not a chance in hell that I could play by then," explained Ringo, "but neither could anyone else except the guitarist, who knew a couple of chords. The rest of us were making it up. We had no sense of time, though Eddie was a great player, one of those guys who, if you gave him any instrument, could play it. He was very musical."

The Eddie Clayton Skiffle Group was created from Richy's workmates at Henry Hunt & Son, just down the road from where he lived. The group consisted of his next-door neighbour Eddie Myles (often misspelled Miles), who played guitar; Roy Trafford on tea-chest bass and vocals; John Dougherty and Micky McGrellis on washboard; and Richy on drums.

"I was working in the factory, and we played for our fellow workmen at lunchtime in a cellar," Ringo said. "With a few of the other guys

The Eddie Clayton Skiffle Group in May 1957. Richy Starkey (far left), Roy Trafford singing (centre) and Eddie Myles (far right).

from the factory we built up the band. And then we started playing all the freebies we could get, playing clubs or weddings. We did a few weddings, like someone we knew was getting married, and we'd fetch the gear along and play for a few hours. Once a guy at work said, 'You've got to come and play at this wedding,' and then, the cheeky git, 'Can't I join the group if I get you the booking?' We said, 'OK,' and he joined and said, 'We're going to be all right here; it's a big fur-coat wedding. It's all shorts; there'll be none of that beer." However, when they got there, they were in for a surprise: it was all brown ale. Richy turned semi-professional, working during the day and playing at night, at various clubs and dances around Liverpool. "We'd play, and the girls would always be looking at the musicians," Ringo continued, obviously enjoying the memory.

Roy Trafford, who lived on Paulton Street in The Dingle, was Richy's best friend. I spoke to him about his time growing up with Richy and the Eddie Clayton Skiffle Group. "Richy and I were dancers, not fighters," said Roy. "We used to visit the Rialto for the dances, and

The Eddie Clayton Skiffle Group performing at Wilson Hall in Garston.

Windsor Street, centre, is the former premises of Henry Hunt & Son, where Richy worked and formed The Eddie Clayton Skiffle Group.

Kenyon's sweet shop (right) on High Park Street where young Richy worked, and whose telephone number he gave out for bookings.

The Fab one hundred and Four

being good dancers, we got the girls. One night, there was a gang who started beating up a couple of lads, and then they looked at us and said, 'you're next'! We just turned and ran home!" The Eddie Clayton Skiffle Group was the best skiffle group in Liverpool at the time. "I don't know why," explained Roy, "but we just kept winning the cups. I think a lot of it was down to Eddie Myles. He could play anything: the guitar, banjo, piano and even the violin! He filed down the frets on our guitars to lower the action and even made the pick-ups. He then made his own steel guitar too. Eddie didn't have the greatest singing voice, but, without blowing my own trumpet, I used to sing harmony and together we sounded good." When the Eddie Clayton Skiffle Group played at Wilson Hall, Richy only had a snare drum and a floor tom, and it was Roy who showed him how to play it. "Most of the skiffle songs we were playing were American railroad or folk songs, so I showed Richy how to use the brushes on the snare drum to make that unique rhythm that a train makes." Ringo immortalised his best friend in his song, "The Other Side of Liverpool". And so Richy's musical career was up and running, playing for the next year with the Eddie Clayton Skiffle Group.

Roy Trafford, pictured in Liverpool in 2013.

The Cadillacs
with Richy Starkey

Before joining The Darktown Skiffle Group and Rory Storm, Richy Starkey joined a group called The Cadillacs. As he told music journalist Chris Hutchins in November 1962: "Around the end of 1957, my best friend Roy Trafford and I started going to The Cavern Club. I used to admire the groups who played there and wished I could join one." Starkey told Hutchins how he formed the Eddie Clayton Skiffle Group with his friends at work and how they used to play in the cellar at lunchtime. "I did not take the full kit," he said, "just a snare drum and a cymbal and a pair of sticks in a shopping bag with me sandwiches each morning.

"Then I joined the Cadillacs in November of 1958. The leader had a car and used to pick me up, so for the first time I was able to take out the full kit. I still dressed like a Ted and I was going to dances and always getting into fights. So, when I got to join Rory Storm's group, I jumped at it. After all, I was fed up getting beaten up and it was a better way of meeting girls."

Unfortunately, no evidence has been found to confirm which Cadillacs group Ringo was referring to. There was a group, Eddie and the Cadillacs, who are commemorated on The Cavern Wall of Fame in Mathew Street. They played at The Cavern on 24 March 1957. There was also a group from Huyton, Liverpool, called Bobby and the Cadillacs, but no records exist to confirm which one Ringo was a part of.

Ringo signs an autograph for a Hurricanes' fan.

The Fab one hundred and Four

MERSEY BEAT

GREAT NEWS OF "THE BEATLES"

Photograph by Alan Swerdlow

THE BEATLES

In our last issue we promised our readers some exciting news about The Beatles. This is it: Impresario Brian Epstein informs Mersey Beat that he has secured a recording contract with the powerful E.M.I. organisation for The Beatles to record for the Parlophone label.

This is terrific news! And the many people who voted The Beatles the No. 1 Rock 'n' Roll group on Merseyside will now have the opportunity to vote again for their favourite beat music entertainers—this time by voting their first disc a hit and by buying copies as soon as it is released in July. At this stage, we regret we cannot reveal the titles of the disc, but further information will be given in our next issue.

Now here's where our readers can help us! We at Mersey Beat have often wondered which two songs, suitable for a single disc, our readers would most like The Beatles to record. There are so many numbers that this dynamic group does so well that we do not pretend the task will be an easy one. But please let us know what you think. Write in immediately giving reasons for your choice. We shall publish the results and award a prize to the writer of the best letter received, in the opinion of the Editor. Send your letters to this address: Mersey Beat, 81a Renshaw Street, Liverpool 1. The closing date will be next Wednesday, June 6th—so please hurry. We shall look forward to reading your letters.

Guitar Corner
by Bob Hobbs & Hu Birch

THE BLACK BISON
(Available at Rushworth & Dreaper)

This much-awaited new model has four pick-ups with two rotary switches allowing eight permutations in pre-set tone colours. The pick-up arrangement and wiring is designed to give a new system of Split-Sound. The bass frequencies can be eliminated on pick-up three which can then be auto-coupled to the bass on pick-up three. It has specially designed tremolo arm plus bridge unit and fitted in the heel of the neck is a precision "Gear Box" which is coupled to the steel truss rod in the neck and gives micromatic adjustment of the neck pitch.

The machine heads are completely enclosed, even the string barrels have a cover. Again, all metal parts are gold plated. Price: £157 10s. 0d.

SEE THE BEATLES
IN THE
BRUCE CHANNEL SHOW
at the TOWER. THURSDAY, JUNE 21st
TICKETS **4/6** (in advance) from usual agencies

---

the CAVERN

PRESENTS ITS EVENING SESSIONS

SATURDAY, 9th JUNE 7—12 p.m.

THE BEATLES
FIRST APPEARANCE FOLLOWING THEIR SUCCESS IN GERMANY

THE RED RIVER JAZZMEN
KEN DALLAS AND THE SILHOUETTES
THE FOUR JAYS

FRIDAY, 1st JUNE—
THE RED RIVER JAZZMEN
THE SEARCHERS

SATURDAY, 2nd JUNE—
THE SAINTS JAZZ BAND

SUNDAY, 3rd JUNE—
VINTAGE JAZZ BAND

TUESDAY, 5th JUNE—
THE MERSEY BEATS
THE SORRALS

WEDNESDAY, 6th JUNE—
THE BIG THREE
MARK PETERS AND THE CYCLONES
CLAY ELLIS AND THE RAIDERS

FRIDAY, 8th JUNE—
THE COLLEGIANS
THE DENNISONS
(READ ABOUT THEM ON PAGE 8)

SUNDAY, 10th JUNE (Whit Sunday)—
ERIC ALLANDALE'S JAZZMEN

TUESDAY, 12th JUNE—
THE BEATLES
MARK PETERS AND THE CYCLONES

WEDNESDAY, 13th JUNE—
THE BEATLES
THE DENNISONS

Headline from Mersey Beat in June 1962 announcing The Beatles' recording deal.

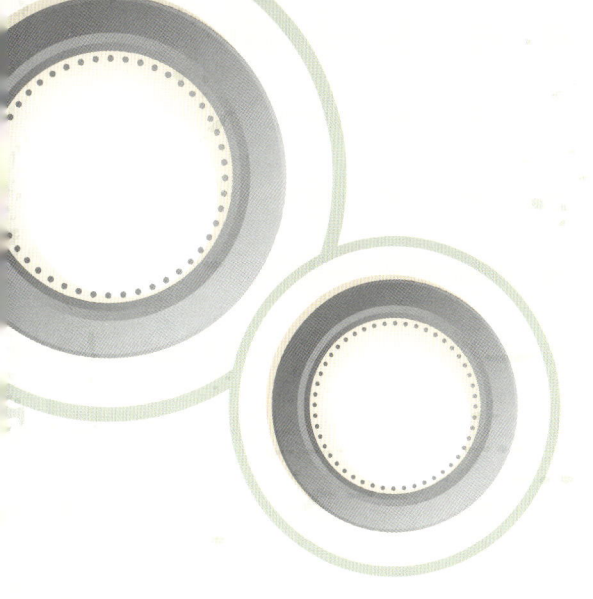

The Darktown Skiffle Group
with Richy Starkey

In early 1959, Richy briefly joined The Darktown Skiffle Group, widely regarded as one of the top groups in Liverpool at the time. The ensemble boasted several members in its short history, including Dave McKew, bass player Keith Draper, Alan Robinson, Kenny Irwin and David Smith on guitars, with Gladys Jill Martin on vocals. They had other drummers, such as Brian Redman and Kenny Hardin, but for a short time only, they had Richy Starkey in the drumseat.

Richy's time with The Darktown Skiffle Group did not last long as in March 1959, he would undergo his one and only ever audition for Alan Caldwell, who would soon start using the stage name of Rory Storm.

Ringo Starr drumming with Rory Storm and the Hurricanes at the Jive Hive, Crosby.

The Fab one hundred and Four

Rory Storm and the Hurricanes and Richy Starkey

The Eddie Clayton Skiffle Group first played at The Cavern on 31 July 1957 but, by 1958, the band had split up. Richy joined The Cadillacs and the Darktown Skiffle Group before being asked in March 1959 to join a group Alan Caldwell had formed called The Raving Texans.

The lineup consisted of Caldwell as lead singer, Johnny Byrne on lead guitar, Charles O'Brien on guitar and Wally Eymond on bass. The band went through several different name changes.

Rory Storm and the Hurricanes.

Iris Caldwell, Rory Storm's sister.

Rory Storm and the Hurricanes at Butlin's, summer 1962.

From The Raving Texans, they became Al Storm and the Hurricanes, then Jett Storm and the Hurricanes and finally, at the end of 1959, Rory Storm and the Hurricanes.

Their love for the "Westerns" inspired each of them to assume an alias in keeping with a cowboy theme. Al Caldwell settled on Rory Storm; Johnny Byrne became Johnny Guitar after the 1954 film of the same name; Charles O'Brien, who was now on lead guitar, became Ty Brian after the star of the *Bronco* TV series; Wally Eymond, the group's bass player, was given the name Lu Walters and, as history has shown, Richy Starkey became Ringo Starr.

Rory Storm and the Hurricanes became one of Liverpool's top groups and were asked to play the Liverpool Stadium gig of 3 May 1960, which featured Gene Vincent. By October, they were on their way to Hamburg, replacing Derry and the Seniors at The Kaiserkeller. They would achieve top billing and alternated with The Beatles during each twelve-hour shift.

But Ringo was feeling frustrated at not progressing past holiday camp bookings. In December 1961, with the promise of a good fee, an apartment and the use of a car, he left the band to return to Hamburg as drummer for Tony Sheridan. On the surface, that sounded like a good deal, but with Sheridan's erratic performances on stage, Ringo decided that he was better off with the Hurricanes. He returned to Liverpool and reclaimed the drummer's seat behind Rory Storm. It was during the Hurricanes' 1962 summer season at Butlin's that Ringo was offered the chance to join The Beatles following the dismissal of Pete Best. On 18 August 1962, at Hulme Hall in Port Sunlight, Ringo Starr made his debut as the new drummer for The Beatles.

The Fab one hundred and Four

To find out more about Rory Storm and the Hurricanes, I talked to Rory's sister, Iris Caldwell who spoke about her memories of growing up in the family home, known as "Stormsville", and being the girlfriend of two of The Beatles!

David: Your mum, Violet, obviously had a big impact on Rory, as well as many of the local musicians.

Iris: She was a wonderful person. Rory wouldn't do anything without asking my mum's advice first. I remember one day, he had picked up two new suits – one orange and one green. He asked mum which one he should wear, and she said the orange one was the best. And so, off he went in his orange suit. What they hadn't taken into account was that it was St. Patrick's Day, March 17th!

David: St. Patrick's Day has been celebrated by Irish Catholics for over 1,000 years, in honour of their patron saint. Their colour is green. The Protestant organisation opposed to the Catholics is the Orange Lodge, whose colour, naturally, is orange. It looks like Vi may have chosen the wrong colour for Rory to wear that night! What happened?

Iris: It was a disaster! They were playing at a St. Patrick's Day party, and there was Rory, dressed in orange! It all kicked off, with chairs and bottles being thrown. It got so bad that they rest of the group ran off stage, leaving just Rory and Ringo trying to save themselves. Ringo just hid behind his drum kit trying to avoid getting hurt. Rory tried to calm it down by singing 'Don't throw bouquets at me'. It did not work, so they got out of there as quickly as they could.

David: When you talk about him, you call him Rory. Do you think of him as Rory, or Alan?

Iris: To me, when I think of our childhood, I think of him as Alan. He was six years older than me, and I have some lovely memories. My teenage years were with Rory Storm, and so I think of him then as Rory.

David: How did you get on as brother and sister?

Iris: Like most families, I loved him, even if we were fighting when we were little. We used to play tricks on each other. He would catch big spiders, or daddy longlegs, and sneak in and put them in my bed, and wait for me to scream! I would go into his room and smash things up. I got battered by my mum for that. He did not! When I was little, I never wanted to go to bed, so he would take me to the bottom of the stairs and say 'I'll race you till morning' and so I would go to bed so I could get to sleep and be up before him.

Rory Storm in his athletic's kit.

David: Tell me what he was like.

Iris: He was very fit, and loved sports. He was a great swimmer, played tennis, was an excellent footballer and a fantastic athlete. He ran for Pembroke Harriers, and went running nearly every night. Sometimes he would run five miles, other times fifteen miles. When he got back from a run, he would take our dog, Toby, out for a warm down jog around the block. He loved Toby so much. There was a funny incident when he was in Amsterdam and he had taken a girl out for a meal. He asked her if she was any good at running, as he was. When the girl said 'yes', he said that it was good, because he'd forgotten his wallet, and they had to run as fast as they could, out of the restaurant, through the winter snow, with her in high heels too!

David: As many people know, he had a bad stammer that would affect him when he was talking, but disappeared when he sang. How do you think that affected him?

Iris: It was amazing. He visited many therapists, tried hypnotism and injections and so many different ideas, but none of them really worked. The other guys in the band would try and finish his sentences for him, often getting it wrong, which frustrated him. However, if he tried to talk in an American accent, the stammer would disappear, but he refused to go around talking like an American, because it was not him. However, the years of therapy helped a bit, because he lost a lot of his Liverpool accent. In between songs, as you can hear on the concert from March 1960, Rory is talking in one of his created accents, which allowed him to talk without his stammer. He sometimes struggled to say his name, Alan Caldwell, so he called himself 'Bobby Cornflakes'. I don't know why, but it was easier to say.

"I remember one unfortunate incident. We were in town and a man with a stammer asked him for directions. Rory tried to reply but, of course, started to stammer himself. In a flash, the other man punched Rory on the nose, as he thought Rory was laughing at his stammer. 'It's the only time somebody got a punch in first,' he said afterwards. I think having that stammer made him even more determined. Everything he did, he had to be the best at. He had to do everything better than anyone else, no matter how small or insignificant it was.

David: What was Rory Storm and the Hurricanes like as a band?

Iris: They were different to the other bands, including The Beatles. Everyone was doing covers of the same records, but Rory's group would be throwing in high kicking steps, dance routines, and really putting on a show.

David: Rory was known as Mr. Showmanship in Liverpool. What made him so different?

Iris: I went to the Broadgreen School of Dancing and Rory would come with me. He couldn't dance, but he would sing and do the songs for the shows. He learned all about the art of performing on stage, entertaining an audience and putting on a show. He learned about the importance of dressing up in costume and working the audience.

Rory Storm and the Hurricanes at Butlin's, summer 1962.

Ringo at Butlin's, 1962, when playing with Rory Storm and the Hurricanes.

David: Rory Storm was known as the greatest showman in Liverpool at the time, and this experience in the dance school certainly explains where he developed his talents on stage. He was known for some outrageous performances. Which do you remember?

Iris: The famous one was in New Brighton, where they were playing at the outdoor swimming pool. He climbed up to the top diving board, dived off, swam the length of the pool and got out, before singing, 'Splish, Splash'. He did that jump in the theatre, landing on the piano awkwardly and breaking his ribs. Nobody could perform like him. What I also remember is going with the band to the Jive Hive and, of course, we would have to travel on the bus, with all of the equipment, drums included. By the time we had finished, the last bus had gone, so it was my job to go to the side of the road, with the boys hiding behind the gates, and try and hitch a lift. When the car stopped, out would run two of the band, jump into the car and get a lift back. As there were so many of us, it would often take three cars for us all to get in. Rory and I would get in the last car.

The Fab one hundred and Four

David: Was there musical talent in the family?

Iris: My dad was a great singer and had a lovely voice. Every Sunday, he would go to St. Vincent's Hospice, take some sweets and magazines, and hand them out to the residents. He would then sing to them. Quite often, he would take Rory with him and encourage him to sing to them, too. On Christmas Day, he would dress up as Father Christmas and we would all go in and give out chocolate to everyone. One funny incident happened on Boxing Day when one of the residents told my dad, 'You should have been here yesterday. Father Christmas came to visit us!'

David: Did Rory show a talent at an early age?

Iris: We went to Butlin's as a family and entered the talent shows. I won the under-twelve's category and Rory won the older competition. To win meant you got entered into the national final, which was a free week's holiday in Butlin's. We never won the national final, but we got the holiday.

David: The band became successful in getting a summer season at Butlin's. Is it through the competitions that they got the booking?

Iris: That was through me. I had joined Billy Smart's Circus in Blackpool and was doing an 'Elephant Ballet'. As I was the youngest, I had the job of having the elephant step over me! I did not like it, so I ran away from the circus. I went to Butlin's to audition, and passed, so they asked me which camp I would like to go to, and I said 'Pwllheli'. I then asked if my brother could come with me, and they said yes, so I got them the booking at £125 per week for the band. I'd also got them a booking at the Pavilion Theatre in Rhyl, back in 1959, when I had a job there.

David: How did Rory's group get together in the first place?

Iris: It started when he had this idea of starting a Skiffle group. One day, he was listening out of the window, and could hear someone playing a guitar. He walked around until he found where it was coming from. The player was Johnny Byrne, who became Johnny Guitar. The group started from there.

Ringo (right) shares a beer with his bandmates.

David: The Morgue Club was opened by Rory on 13 March 1958. Tell me about the club?

Iris: Rory was looking around for a place to open a Skiffle cellar. He'd been to The Cavern, but that was a jazz club, so he wanted a club of his own. A friend of his, Paul Murphy, was dating a nurse from the nearby Nursing Home in Oakfield Park. They had an unused cellar so, with the Nursing Home's permission, they opened the club there. Rory knew some art students, so he asked them to decorate it. He wanted the walls painted black, and asked them what they could paint. When one of them said he was good at painting skeletons, he told them to do it, hence it was called The Morgue. He also used an ultraviolet light in there for extra effect. Lots of groups played there, and it did really well. You couldn't charge an entrance fee, so everyone coming in had to buy a bottle of coke. The problem came when they were going home. The members would throw their empty bottles over the walls of the nearby houses and make a noise. The neighbours complained, so the police came and closed it down after only a few weeks.

David: In the summer of 1962, Rory lost his drummer Ringo to The Beatles. How did that happen, as there are so many stories about who made contact with him?

Iris: John and Paul might have come down to Butlin's, but the first

Paul, John and Rory Storm.

contact was Brian Epstein telephoning Rory and saying that The Beatles wanted Ringo to join them. Of course, Rory was concerned about the summer season where they were and asked Brian if it would be alright if Ringo stayed for the last three weeks of the season. Brian said it would be alright.

David: This is possibly where the visit by John and Paul comes into the story as, quite suddenly, Ringo decided he was not going to stay for the three weeks and was leaving almost immediately.

Iris: It was Ringo's decision to say that he wanted to leave straight away, which left Rory in a difficult position, so he had to get a replacement drummer quickly. Rory understood, but he was disappointed that Ringo left straight away, after all he had done for him."

David: Tell me more about how Ringo came to be in the band, and how he was helped?

Iris: When Ringo wanted to join the group as a professional, his parents were against it, as he was serving an apprenticeship which they did not want to go to waste. Rory went down and pleaded with Ringo's parents to let him join. As he was still under 21 years of age, he needed parental permission. Then, when he needed a fuller set of drums, he was still too young to arrange finance, so my father acted as guarantor to enable him to purchase the drums. Ringo was also grateful to Rory because, on holiday, Ringo fell into the water and couldn't swim. Rory, a trained lifeguard, dived in and saved his life.

David: You and George dated when you were young. How did you and George meet?

Iris: My friend Ann and I used to go to the Ice Rink in Kensington and this boy asked Ann if he could walk her home. She said that she was with a friend and asked if he was with one of his friends. He said 'yes' and introduced himself as Arthur Kelly, and his friend was George Harrison. And so George walked me home. We must have been about twelve at the time. George came round to our house nearly every night. I remember one night, I realised there were raised voices at the front gate. I looked out, and there was George arguing with a boy from my school, still in his short trousers, over who was taking me out. It got so bad that the lady across the road came over with her big Alsatian dog to stop the fighting.

David: Who won the fight?

Iris: George did! The other boy ran home. George would often come for tea, and I remember one evening, after we'd finished eating, he asked to leave the table. My mum asked him to push his chair back under the table and he said, 'My gran always told me never to push a chair under a table, because it means that you'll not be coming back again.' He would also say the sweetest things, like he would hold me, and we would both close our eyes, and he said that he was squeezing me with his eyes.

Rory with his mum, Violet.

David: He obviously got on well with your mum, Violet.

Iris: He called her 'Violent Vi', but it was a term of affection. I remember that when The Beatles were just starting off, my mum would say 'You lot will never get anywhere, you need more personality!' Well, they

The *Fab* one hundred and *Four*

were filming a piece for television and when the camera was on George, he smiled straight at the lens. After it had been on, George rang my mum and said, 'Did you see me smile? That was for you!' My mum told him it was great, but he had to tell the others to start smiling too!

David: As well as dating George when you were younger, you dated Paul?

Iris: Yes, we must have been about seventeen at the time. I remember one funny story, as we were all busy and in town at different times, so the relationships weren't a fixture as such. So, at the same time, I was dating Paul and Frank Ifield, who was also a performer. Well, one evening, when Frank was playing at the local theatre, Paul bought two tickets for the show, so we went together. I sat nervously in the audience hoping that Frank did not see us. Well, as the performance came to an end, Frank looked straight at me and Paul, and sang 'Tell that man there with you, he'll have to go.' Well, I was so embarrassed and Paul just sank deeper into his chair, muttering 'Cheeky bugger'!

Paul and Iris dated between 1961 and 1963, but because she was a dancer and Paul was back and forward to Hamburg or on tour, they could only get together when they were back in Liverpool.

David: Many people have suggested that "Love Me Do" was written by Paul about you. Is that true?

Iris: No, definitely not! It was written before we were together, possibly about a former girlfriend, but it was not about me.

David: Did any of The Beatles keep in touch with you after they became famous?

Iris: Ringo did not, but George did occasionally. Paul always kept in touch and brought Jane Asher to meet my mum when they came up here. Paul even went to see Rory when he was in the hospital after having an operation, which was nice. I do remember one occasion when I was performing in cabaret, and Paul and Ringo came to watch. However, the bouncers threw them out as they weren't properly dressed!

Disaster was to strike the Hurricanes in 1967, when Ty Brian collapsed on stage during a performance and later died due to complications following an operation to remove his appendix. Storm disbanded the Hurricanes and became a disc jockey, working at the Silver Blades Ice Rink in Liverpool, in Benidorm (where he was also a water skiing instructor), in Jersey and Amsterdam. Iris, by now, had married singer Shane Fenton, later known as Alvin Stardust, and they had a baby boy, Adam. When Rory's father died, he returned from Amsterdam to Liverpool to be with his mother.

There have been many theories and stories about what happened next. On 28 September 1972, Rory and his mother were both found dead at "Stormsville". One myth is that Rory and Violet died in a suicide pact, so I asked Iris to tell me what really happened.

"There was no pact," confirmed Iris. "Rory had spent the day before at the dentist getting work done for a crown, so Mum had spent the evening with me, as Shane was working and Rory was having an early night, as he had toothache and a bad cold. Mum went home about 2am. The next day she called me at lunch time to see if I needed anything. I was feeding Adam, who was just a few months old at the time, and my friend Maureen spoke to her. Rory was 'still asleep'. Mum was going to the shops to get something for tea, but when I tried to call later there was no answer. That did not worry me as it was Wednesday and Mum always went to the library to change her book on a Wednesday and Rory should have been playing golf."

"That evening, I was teaching dancing at Winnie Macs School of Dance, which was the house opposite Mum's. I kept looking over, but the lights were off, so I assumed that as it was *Match of the Day* night on TV. They had gone either to Pete Vernon's or Auntie Doris' house as they often did, as both Pete and Doris had colour TVs. Mum's was black and white. But when I got home and let the babysitter go, I suddenly felt very strange and I phoned Pete who said they weren't there. Doris did not have a phone, so I phoned Winnie Mac and asked her to go over to Mum's and check. She came back to the phone and said that Rory's car was in the garage and all was dark. I rushed round. The house was tidy, and on the table were two fresh cream cakes (they did not have a fridge) that she'd got for tea and 40 cigarettes. Would she have bought them if they had made a pact? No!"

"In the hall on the floor was a note from Mum and it said they couldn't carry on, etc. but no note for Rory? She was still protecting him. She did not want me to blame him for her death, so she'd tried to make it look like a pact. But she had obviously found him dead and then made that decision. He had taken very few tablets, I think to help him sleep because of the toothache and cold, but he was also on anti-depressants. She, however, took over twenty and drank a lot of whisky (she was tee-total). Mum meant it, he did not. I'm sure of that. They were each in their own rooms. That was when my heart broke."

Rory was 34. It was a tragic end for a great performer and for his mother, who was known and liked by so many of the Merseybeat musicians.

The funeral for Rory and Violet was held at Oakvale Congregational Church, Broadgreen, on 19 October 1972. Mourners sang Rory's favourite song, "You'll Never Walk Alone", which had been a hit for Gerry and the Pacemakers and had been adopted by Liverpool Football Club as its anthem. The two coffins were carried from the hearse to Anfield Crematorium by former band members. Rory's remains were scattered on section 23 at Anfield Crematoriums Gardens of Remembrance. When Ringo was asked why he did not attend, he said, "I was not there when he was born either", a comment the family still struggles to understand or accept.

Billy Fury, whom Rory had met at the Wyvern Club auditions, later played the part of a singer called Stormy Tempest (a name inspired by Rory Storm) in the 1973 film *That'll Be the Day*. The film also featured Ringo Starr.

The Fab Four perform at The Cavern on 22 August 1962, just four days after Ringo joined The Beatles.

18 AUGUST 1962

The Fab Four –

John Lennon, Paul McCartney, George Harrison and Ringo Starr

On 18 August 1962, The Beatles' world changed when they unveiled their new drummer Ringo Starr in Hulme Hall, situated in the middle of the picturesque Victorian village of Port Sunlight. On 18 August 2012, the 50th anniversary of Ringo's debut with The Fab Four, I met Ian Hackett, who had a unique part to play in arranging that momentous event.

The Beatles' August concert had been arranged on behalf of the Port Sunlight Horticultural Society. Ian had suggested The Beatles for a Golf Club Dance in July 1962 and his father, Harry, booked the group for that legendary debut appearance of the first Fab Four lineup in August 1962.

"Our home overlooked the Dell, a particularly lovely landscaped part of the village," recalled Ian, "and was just a few yards from Hulme Hall, the Bridge Inn and the Men's Club. While selling the *Liverpool Echo* outside Lever's, I was approached by one of my customers, Monty Lister, editor of the *Port Sunlight News*, with an offer I couldn't refuse.

"Monty recruited me to assist him in his voluntary work producing record request radio shows for the local Clatterbridge and Cleaver hospitals, using records from his vast collection, to which he added every week. We put the shows together on tape in a studio in his parents' home where he still lived, and then played them over the hospitals' intercom systems. The best bit was that we also did interviews with visiting pop stars such as Emile Ford, Billy Fury and Joe Brown. This was an addition to all my other jobs and extracurricular activities. I dropped back a bit at school again – and just after the first time I had been persuaded to skip a day's school for a Beatles lunchtime session at The Cavern on March 16th.

A smartened up Ringo, ready to be a Beatle.

Gerry and the Pacemakers performing on stage at Hulme Hall.

Ian Hackett (centre) with Billy Fury (left) in Hulme Hall.

Emile Ford (right) at Hulme Hall.

"Back in the spring of 1962, Harry, in his role as Captain of the Golf Club, organised the Club's annual dance. He chose Hulme Hall as the venue, July 7th as the date and old favourites, The Modernaires, as the main band. Then he asked me if I could think of a band to fill in during the Modernaires' break. I suggested The Beatles.

"On 7 July 1962, the Port Sunlight Golf Club Dance at Hulme Hall finally came," recalled Hackett, noting the first of four appearances at Hulme Hall by The Beatles. "They went down really well with all my friends, although dad got some 'Call this music?' complaints about The Beatles in general and Pete Best's drumming in particular from his friends. They were probably a lot better than I appreciated at the time. I loved virtually all the bands I danced to around that time and would have put The Beatles up there with Gerry and the Pacemakers,

The Fab one hundred and Four

Hulme Hall, Port Sunlight, where Ringo made his debut.

Ticket for the Port Sunlight Horticultural Society Dance on 18 August 1962.

Poster for Ringo's debut with The Fab Four.

The Dennisons, The Big Three, Billy J. Kramer and the Coasters, The Fourmost and other great bands. But I was no judge. While on holiday at Butlin's in Pwllheli later that summer, I told an agent that The Beatles weren't as good as the band already playing there – the pink-suited Johnny "Petal" Peters and the Crestas, who were essentially a Cliff Richard and the Shadows tribute band. I remember this well because the guy I was with got really upset that I could say such a thing."

Ian's dad managed to fend off the criticism from the Golf Club members, and Ian was able to bask in the kudos of having recommended The Beatles for the dance. Just over a month later, the Port Sunlight Horticultural Society was holding its event and, once again, The Beatles were booked to headline the show, only this time by Harry. Little did Harry and Ian know that this was to be a milestone event in the life of The Beatles. Just two day earlier, with the dismissal of Pete Best, the lineup had changed and this appearance would be the debut of John, Paul and George with their new drummer, Ringo Starr.

Ian explained: "By having The Beatles back as headliners at

The crowd on the dance floor at Hulme Hall.

Hulme Hall on August 18th for their after-show dance, this showed that not all the village's adults were hostile to them. But there was a mass female chanting of 'We want Pete!' when they introduced their new drummer.

"The make-up of the audience was different for this show," remarked Ian, "as there were more young people than locals. The problem was that the local people were angry as the young interlopers had only one thing on their minds: to show support for the sacked Pete Best. The Beatles never stood a chance. I was glad for this one that my dad took the flak, and not me!"

In spite of the audience reaction, Ian was impressed with The Beatles that night: "I loved their treatments of 'Twist and Shout' and 'Besame Mucho' and John's harmonica in general, but especially on Bruce Chanel's 'Hey Baby'. At that stage, they weren't playing that many original songs."

Because of such a hostile reception, Ringo was not enjoying the night of his debut. "I ran into a miserable-looking Ringo in the gent's toilet during the break," recalled Ian, "and tried to cheer him up with a smile and an optimistic comment: 'Don't worry about tonight. Things can only get better.' And it was not long before they did".

However, this was the calm before the storm. The following day, Ringo was to make his debut with The Beatles at The Cavern. The group had no idea of the backlash they would face. News of Pete Best's dismissal had spread around Liverpool and the fans had planned a protest. Brian Epstein had used Bill Harry's *Mersey Beat* to put the story out that Pete had left the group by mutual agreement,

The toilets in Hulme Hall, where Ian Hackett spoke to Ringo.

which was an abuse of the relationship between Epstein and Bill Harry. The fans did not believe a word of it.

Jeff Hall was a regular at The Cavern, and remembers that night. "I don't think it was widely known what had happened over Pete, as his replacement by Ringo was done so quickly", Jeff recalled. "When The Beatles set up on stage and Ringo appeared on the drums, the place went frantic. The noise was chaotic as the protests rose, mainly from the girls, about Pete being sacked. Some even had placards supporting Pete and demanding his reinstatement. The Beatles were quite shocked by the reaction and Paul McCartney did his best to appease them, but the crowd was having none of it. The night continued to be one long protest and eventually the band ended their session. From what I remember, although the band was taken aback by the protests about Pete Best being replaced, they all did their best to carry on with the gig. Paul was just being his usual diplomatic self, but trying harder than usual, jollying the crowd.

Jeff continued: "Ringo just sat there and drummed away, keeping a low profile – the sensible thing to do in the circumstances – and I guess pretending that nothing was amiss. George was his normal self, concentrating on getting his guitar-playing spot on and John being his 'natural' sarcastic self. I don't think the band was happy at all, but seemed to take the attitude that this would all go away. Maybe because they were used to some of the riotous nights in Hamburg, this was something they thought they could see through. As it turned out, once Ringo had a few gigs under his belt, it all calmed down and it was as if Pete was never part of the band. Weird really.

"They did finish their gig as planned", Jeff said, "but they had to put up with banter all along, and people still made their feelings felt at the end of the gig. What happened next is unclear, but during the band's playing, George Harrison was getting increasingly edgy as a result of the crowd's reaction and the abuse the band was getting over Pete's departure. Soon after the band's last number, George ended up with a black eye. I never saw the incident and more than one version of how he got it has been bandied about. Next day, I was walking down Church Street and who was walking towards me, but George Harrison, with his long leather coat looking every inch the part, but sporting a black eye. I knew him to some degree from the chats with all The Beatles at The Cavern, so I stopped as he passed me to ask how he got the black eye, but he just walked away – not a happy man."

After a rocky start, Ringo was soon welcomed into the group and became an integral member of The Beatles or, as Tony Barrow would christen them, "The Fab Four".

Ringo Starr drumming with The Beatles.

Paul, John, Ringo and George (sporting a black eye) head for Abbey Road Studios in London.

11 SEPTEMBER 1962

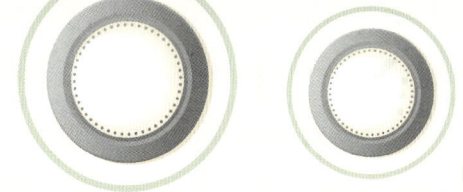

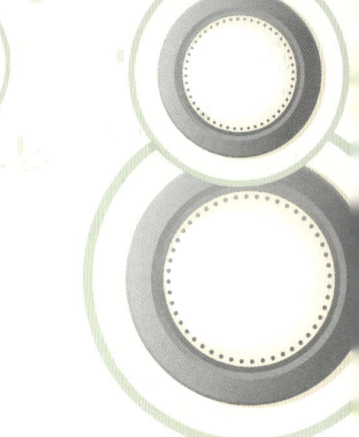

John Lennon, Paul McCartney, George Harrison, Ringo Starr and Andy White

For 24 hours, Andy White was a Beatle, and what a day it was. Brought in to replace Ringo on drums for The Beatles' first single, he spent the day with John, Paul and George in a session where he joined them recording "Love Me Do", "P.S. I Love You" and "Please Please Me". Relegated to the shadows for many years, nobody knew about White's involvement as, like many session musicians, his identity was not revealed to the public. I spoke to White and asked him about his career and that important day as The Beatles' drummer.

Andy White was born on 27 July 1930 in Glasgow, Scotland. He first played a side drum at the age of 12 in the local Boy Scout band, parading around the streets on the 'High days and Holy days'. "On V.E. Day, 8 May 1945," recalled White, "the band marched through the town for a parade, and I enjoyed it so much that I decided that I wanted to do this for the rest of my life."

He had to wait a few years before taking up the drums professionally. "From school, I joined an engineering firm, where I trained as an apprentice pattern maker," said Andy. "The pay was not great and, after five years as an apprentice, I was working 42 hours a week for £7 10 shillings per week.

"I got my first drum kit when I was about 21, and my professional de-

Andy White.

370

Andy White in 2008.

but was at a West Coast holiday resort. Some of the band were then offered a summer season on the Isle of Wight. It was while I was there that bandleader Vic Lewis contacted me and asked me to join his band. I then spent the next six years touring with Vic Lewis' orchestra, playing jazz and big band music.

"The musicians' union had got an agreement together so that if an American band came over to Britain, then a British band had to go on tour in America. And so, when one of the American bands came over here, the Vic Lewis orchestra went to the United States. We got to spend three weeks in America on tour. This was my first taste of rock 'n' roll, because we were on tour with some of the rock 'n' roll stars of America, like Bill Haley, Chuck Berry, The Platters and many other stars. We were only doing about three numbers each, so I got to experience and watch rock 'n' roll in America before it came to Britain. We were doing big-band songs, like those of Stan Kenton, but we were putting a back beat into it to give it our own twist, and fit in with what was really a rock 'n' roll tour."

After the success of the American tour, White was given an opportunity that would establish him as one of the busiest and most successful session drummers in Britain. "A friend of mine, Jackie Dougan, had the opportunity to appear in a television programme, *Boy Meets Girl*," explained White, "but he did not want the job, so he asked me if I wanted it. That was the start for me, and that lead to a career in rock 'n' roll and a number of television appearances and shows I was in demand from then on. I gained a reputation as a rock 'n' roll drummer."

In 1960, White played on Billy Fury's album, *The Sound of Fury*, which is regarded as Britain's first rock 'n' roll album. He also went on to play with Lulu on her classic song, "Shout"; Tom Jones' "It's Not Unusual" and with most of the top names in music in the sixties. However, it is his one day with The Beatles on 11 September 1962 for which he is best known. The subject soon turned to that momentous day and his memories of recording with The Beatles.

"George Martin was not in on most of the session, which was overseen by producer Ron Richards," explained White. Most accounts have mentioned that, as White had worked with Richards before, he was contacted by Richards for the job. However, White explains that this was not the case. "I received a call a few days before the session from the 'fixer' at EMI," said White, who then explained what a 'fixer' was. "Every record company had a guy, who often was a musician, who would contact the session musicians and book them for a particular gig. I received my call from EMI, and it was only when I walked in on the morning of 11th September that I realised it was Ron Richards producing the session."

White had worked with Richards several years before on that first TV show, and had picked up a little trick from one of the musical arrangers. "I think he was trying to catch me out," said White, "because instead of playing all eight beats to the bar, he wanted me to play seven beats, and miss the eighth beat, which was tricky, but I did it. When I walked into the studio to record 'Love Me Do' with The Beatles, Ron Richards wanted me to play that seven beats in the bar again, with the eighth beat played by Ringo on the tambourine. That is how you can tell which is my version."

This brings us on to the subject of Ringo, and what happened in the studio that day. "Ringo walked in with the others, and was obviously shocked to see me setting up my drums. It was clear that nobody had told him he was not going to be playing, and so we said a quick 'Hello', and that was it. He must have thought that I was going to replace him, but I was ten years older than him, and I'd have needed a wig after a year with them!"

What did he remember about the day itself? "As with any session, I had no knowing what I was going to be doing that day, so we sat down and discussed the songs. Most of the time I was talking with John and Paul, as they were the songwriters. Of course, they had no written music, but that was fine. They knew what they wanted to do, so we set to work. I was really impressed with them, and it was a nice change to be working on original songs, as a lot of my work was

"Love Me Do", released on 5 October 1962 in the UK.

with artists covering American songs. We worked through the routines and started rehearsing. Most of what I was trying to do was work with Paul and matching what he was doing with the bass guitar, to enhance the sound."

White first recorded "Love Me Do" and "P.S. I Love You", with his version of "Love Me Do" appearing on The Beatles' debut album, *Please Please Me,* and the U.S. single, while Ringo's version appeared on the UK single. White is also featured on "P.S. I Love You", the B-side of "Love Me Do". However, he also recorded the song "Please Please Me" with them that day, though many books suggest that it was not fully recorded, and was discarded as it was too slow. White refutes this suggestion.

"I don't know anything about a slower version, or not recording it properly. The version that was released had me on drums, because I can recognise the sound. Ringo's kit was very different to mine, and had a strange sound. I had a Ludwig Black Pearl kit with a distinctive sound, and also, how your kit is set up and tuned determines the sound, just like guitarists preferring a Fender to a Gibson because it has the sound they want. When I listen to "Please Please Me", I recognise my drumming and my kit, which had a much brighter sound. You can also hear the crash cymbal on my kit, which was a top of the range Zildjian cymbal, which made a crisper cleaner sound than the one Ringo was using at the time."

Although "Please Please Me" was recorded with White on that day, George Martin and The Beatles weren't happy with the results. Consequently, the song was re-recorded with Ringo on 26 November 1962, and that was released as the single version.

White was paid £5 10 shillings for the day he spent with The Beatles, and he continued with his career as a session drummer. He was asked to join the orchestra supporting Marlene Dietrich for two weeks at the Queens Theatre in London, and then a week in Edinburgh. It was

Andy White at the drums, with The Smithereens at a charity gig arranged by Tom Frangione (right) in New Jersey, 2008.

considered a success, so White and one of the guitarists were asked to go on tour with Dietrich. "We toured the world for the next eleven years," recalled White, "visiting America every other year with our orchestra. The conductor of the orchestra was a young Burt Bacharach who, of course, became one of the world's best songwriters. The travelling with Dietrich came to an end in Australia when the star fell down some steps and broke her leg. That was the end of her career, and so I returned to Britain.

"I applied for, and got, a job working for BBC Scotland, but after a long strike by musicians, I lost my job, and that was the end of that! I met my second wife, who is American, and so, in about 1983, we decided to settle in New Jersey where we've been ever since. I returned to my first love, pipe bands, and have been training drummers for many years now, which I love."

12 SEPTEMBER 1962

The Beatles and Simone Jackson

On Wednesday, 12 September 1962, a 15-year-old vocalist from London named Simone Jackson was appearing at The Cavern Club. The Beatles performed as her backing group. Bob Wooler later recalled that Simone was one of the most delightful people The Beatles had ever backed.

Simone Jackson (née Jacobs) was born in 1947, and at the age of only fifteen, having just left school, she was discovered by the rent man. Simone lived with her family in a flat in Bow, East London, and, when he called for the rent, he happened to overhear Simone singing in the house. In his spare time, the 22-year-old estate agent was a semi-professional drummer. "He heard me singing," recalled Simone, "and said that I should try and do something about taking it up. He said he could help me if I liked."

He was good to his word, and introduced her to Piccadilly Records, who then launched her career with her debut single, "Pop-Pop-Pop-Pie", which tied-in with the Popeye dance, a variation on The Twist. The song had also been recorded by an American teenage quartet, The Sherrys, who also released the record in the UK.

She had been performing professionally for all of five weeks when she was backed by The Fab Four. The evening's bill also included Freddie and the Dreamers. Jackson's recording career for Pye was brief and includes just three singles: "Pop-Pop-Pop-Pie" on her own, "Ain't Gonna Kiss Ya" with The Breakaways and "Tell Me What to Do" with The Babs Knight Singers.

Simone Jackson.

Demo record of "Ain't Gonna Kiss Ya", by Simone Jackson, released in 1963.

SWEET SIXTEEN SIMONE

From Mersey Beat, September 20 – October 4 1962

A new entertainer on the books of the Tito Burns Agency is beautiful Simone Jackson. The audience at the Cavern Club were pleasantly surprised by the sight of this sixteen-year-old vocalist who was backed by The Beatles.

Simone has only been singing professionally for five weeks, but Mersey Beat confidently tips he as a "Star of the Future". With her looks to delight the eye, she is ideally suited for television work– and the Granada T.V. Unit were at the Cavern again on the night she appeared.

The Fab one hundred and Four

21 OCTOBER 1962

The Beatles and The Chants – Joe Ankrah, Eddie Ankrah, Edmund Amoo, Nat Smeda and Alan Harding

One of The Beatles' favourite Liverpool bands was the all-vocal black harmony group, The Chants. The Beatles backed them on three occasions in 1962. The group originated in the Liverpool 8 area and I met founding member Joe Ankrah, who told me how it began.

"I grew up at 72, North Hill Street, and my father was the organist and choirmaster at the African Churches Mission, and so my brother Edmund and I were in the choir there. A lot of my upbringing with my dad and the church meant I did want to make something of myself."

Joe attended Upper Park Street Primary School and then went on to Wellington Road Secondary Modern. "When I left school, I wanted to be an artist, as I was quite good at art," Joe said. "There was a huge gap in opportunities between black people and white people. My dad was good at drawing, and when he was in the army, he was a draughtsman. He then did all kinds of rubbish jobs, and ended up as a ship's fitter over at Cammell Laird.

The Chants pose with their manager's car, a Zodiac.

Joe Ankrah with his painting of Pastor Daniels Ekarte.

The Fab one hundred and Four

The Rialto Ballroom, 1955.

"So I left school – and I'd been really popular at school with lots of friends – and suddenly, there were no friends and nothing to do. I decided that there was no way I was going to work in a chippy or something like that, so I put my portfolio together and headed for town and tried to get a job as an artist. It was possible back then, because posters and advertising hoardings were all painted by hand. However, of course, that kind of artwork was dying out and being replaced by photography and new ways of printing, and so I found myself out of work, and bumming around.

"One of the enjoyments for me and my friends was going to the Rialto, which was a cinema, and it also had a ballroom where we used to go and listen to music and dance. So we would head down there on a Monday night, all dressed up, stand around the ballroom, doing our moves. "There was a movie being shown at the Rialto called *Rock Around The Clock*, which we went to see, mainly because there were black singers like The Platters and Gene Chandler in it. We were impressed with them, even though the film was really about Bill Haley."

"I just realised that I wanted to start a group, and particularly a vocal-harmony group. My brother Eddie and I were bumming around and because my dad had been a choirmaster at the church, I knew about harmony."

The church that the Ankrahs attended was the Africa Churches Mission in Mill Street, Toxteth. The congregation was led by Pastor

Opposite: The Chants on stage at The Cavern in 1963.

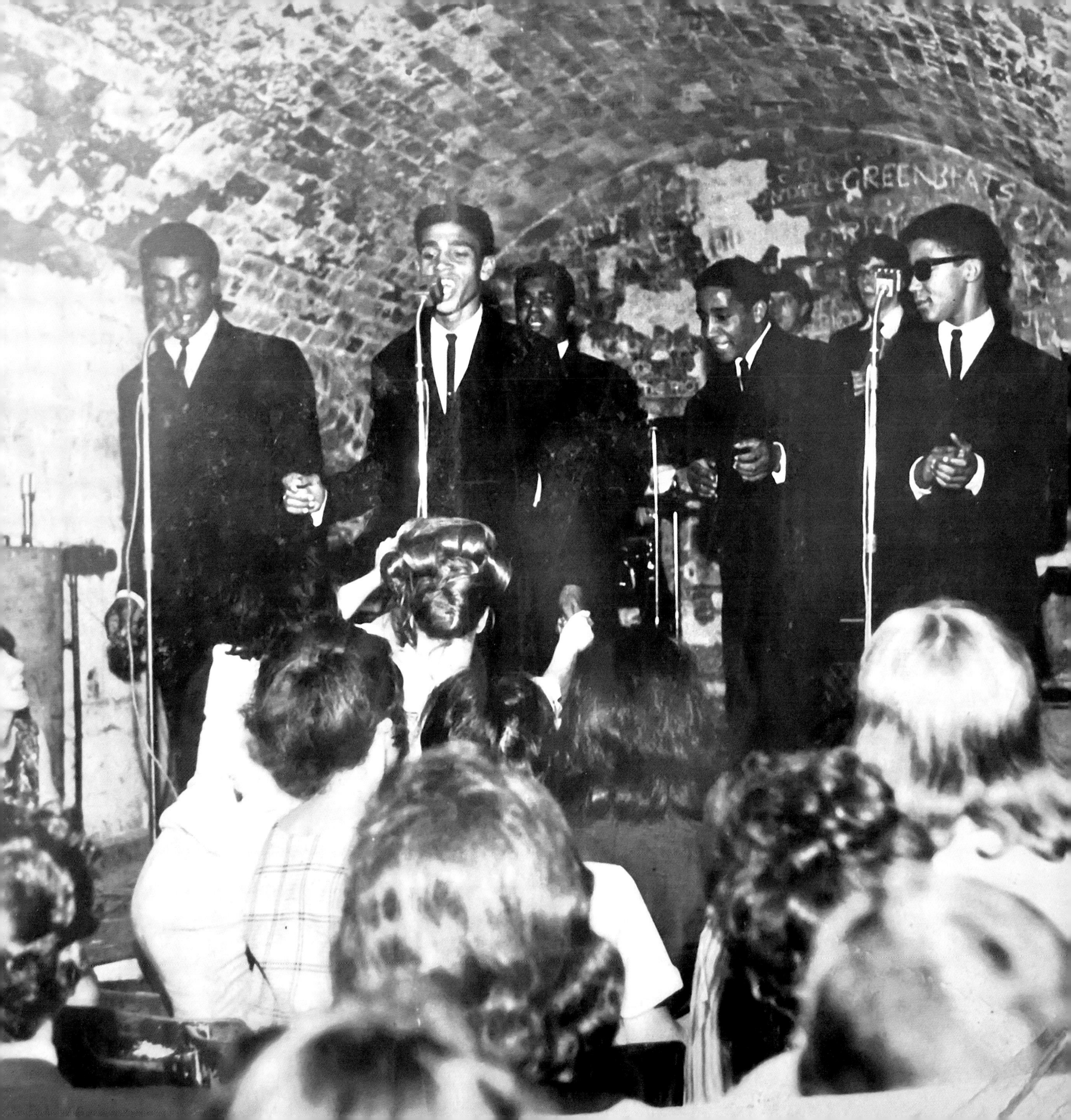
GREENBEATS

The former site of RAF Burtonwood.

Daniels Ekarte, who had set up the mission to help the poor, local community and immigrants with housing, food and clothing. Pastor Ekarte was known locally as the "African Saint" and he ran the mission for 30 years before the building was demolished in 1964.

"We were in the choir," said Joe, "and singing gospel songs and hymns, and there would be different voices, black and white voices, and I loved the harmonies, and I knew how to do it. So we got together with three other guys, Edmund Amoo, Nat Smeda and Alan Harding.

"We had moved from North Hill Street to Stanhope Street when my grandmother died. North Hill Street of course was a predominantly white area, and then we moved over Princes Road to this huge Victorian house at 92, Stanhope Street in a mainly black area. My life was turned upside down by my mother going to look after my grandmother's family. We used to go to bed at 7:30pm at our house in North Hill Street, but now we were still playing out at 9:30pm and playing our music loud. It was so different, yet we'd hardly moved very far at all. We then moved to 39, Upper Parliament Street, which had these huge cellars with great acoustics. We started singing together and doing these harmonies and were pleased with how it was turning out. I took charge, as I was the oldest."

At this point, apart from singing in their cellar, they had performed and practised a few times at Stanley House, the local youth centre, especially when his mother grew sick of them! There was a gang culture developing in Toxteth, as Joe explained: "There was the J's and the Shines. The J's were the white guys, the John Bulls (John Bull was a political character who symbolised England and British culture), and we were the Shines, because our skin was shiny. The younger ones in the group – Edmund Amoo, Alan and Nat – were involved in some of these skirmishes, gangs running up the street."

Joe continued: "I told them we were going to form a group and we started to practise in our cellar. I knew all the harmonies off by heart and that's how we evolved. People used to come around to the house and we would be singing on the corner. And even when we were rehearsing, there would be big crowds standing outside the house listening. Several American singers influenced us, and here we had an advantage. I have three aunties – Grace, Adah and Uzor – who were courting American GIs stationed at Burtonwood, just outside of Liverpool. They would bring their records down to my grandmother's house and we would listen to them.

P51 Mustangs on Upper Parliament Street, Toxteth, on D-Day, 6 June 1944, on their way to Burtonwood.

"We were bored with it eventually. What were we doing? Where were we going? All we seemed to do was rehearse. During one of those periods where we weren't singing or performing, I found out that Little Richard was coming over to Liverpool."

At this point, Joe makes an interesting observation about the music scene in Liverpool, which showed how the black and white communities were still segregated in the Sixties. "We did not know that there was a live music scene in Liverpool," observed Joe. "We did not know about The Cavern and clubs like that. I wouldn't have known how to get into the clubs and you wouldn't see a black person in town then. I had no reason to go into town, so I did not know what was going on there.

"I was a big fan of Little Richard and I had some communication with him. He told me he was staying at the Adelphi Hotel and to come and meet him. So I went down and he said to me, 'Hey man, I'm doing a thing at the Tower, a Mersey show', so I went to see him live."

The show was on 12 October 1962 at the Tower Ballroom, New Brighton, and it was one of Brian Epstein's marketing ideas to have The Beatles playing second to some of the biggest names around, a tactic that worked very well.

"I was backstage most of the time because I came with Little Richard," recalled Joe, "and The Beatles were on and Little Richard was doing his famous walking around the balcony, singing all of his songs. So we were back by his dressing room and everyone was around Little Richard, so I was just standing there, not trying to get near him. These two guys were there and asked me what I was doing there, so I told them I was there to see Little Richard. I asked them what they were doing there, and they told me they'd be on stage."

Without realising it, Joe was talking to John Lennon and Paul McCartney, who were also queuing up to meet their hero. Joe did not know most of the groups, or even their names. For that reason, he hadn't recognised John and Paul though, by now, "Love Me Do" had just been released and they had a huge following on Merseyside.

George and Paul at the Tower Ballroom.

Ticket for The Beatles' appearance at Operation Big Beat on 10 November 1961.

The Fab one hundred and Four

"I suppose I may have vaguely heard of The Cavern," Joe said, "but even if we went into town at night time and tried to get into any of the clubs, we were turned away, so we never really bothered. We just accepted it back then. That was how it was, and it was the way it was. We had our photograph taken with Little Richard and The Beatles, plus Derry Wilkie and Sugar Dean.

"I told John and Paul that I was in a band and they laughed a bit and asked what we played. I told them we don't, we just sing. They couldn't quite grasp it, but they said, 'Why don't you come down to one of the afternoon sessions at The Cavern, and we'll listen to your band.

"I remember the day clearly. I had gone back to the guys, we rehearsed for hours, and then on Wednesday 21st November, we went down to The Cavern and they wouldn't let us in while The Beatles were performing. Five black guys, standing outside The Cavern, which would have looked suspicious. So after they'd finished and everyone was coming out, they said we could come in then. The saving grace for us was that as we walked in, Paul remembered my name and said 'Joe, how are you?' I told him I'd brought the band, and he was great. It was a really nice atmosphere. It was dark, the stage was lit and people were clearing up around us. He asked us to sing, so we started to sing 'Duke Of Earl' and they were absolutely knocked dead, which was a buzz for us, because we'd been doing all of this rehearsing for twelve months and getting everything sharp without performing anywhere. It was refreshing to see people responding to what we were doing.

"Bob Wooler, The Cavern compere, was there and he heard us and said; 'I must go and get Brian. So he ran down Mathew Street to NEMS to see Eppy, and then came back to us. Bob told us that Brian can't come down now, but tell the boys not to speak to anyone or sign anything, and we were just bemused. The Beatles picked up their instruments and started playing. We were just happy to be playing with a band, as we were used to just singing together. I would start us off with the pitch and away we'd go."

Later that day, Brian Epstein arrived at The Cavern and was amazed to find that The Chants did not have musicians and objected to The Beatles providing the backing. However, after intervention from John

Advertisement for The Chants in *Mersey Beat*.

and Paul, he was overruled and The Beatles backed The Chants.

"We found ourselves appearing at The Cavern the same day and we turned up with these smart black shirts and suits. John or Paul said, 'I'd like to introduce you all to some friends of ours, The Chants', and then we walked on, wearing our dark glasses, our shades, being cool, all dressed in black, and we started singing. The place was in an uproar. We only had two microphones, with the lead singer on one, and the other four gathered around the second microphone, and doing our thing, and it was great. That's where it all started."

The Chants performed four songs that night: "Duke of Earl", "A Thousand Stars", "16 Candles" and "Come Go With Me".

"I can remember going up to the Blue Angel after The Cavern", Joe said, "and we did a few numbers with Paul playing the piano for us for Allan Williams."

"After appearing with The Beatles, I signed with Eppy on behalf of the band, which did not mean much really, as we were under 21. At least if people asked us to do anything, we could say no, because we were under contract. Epstein was certainly impressed with them, as he told a *Liverpool Echo* journalist, when asked if Bessie Braddock MP was right to promote the group. "Bessie is a good judge. The Chants and The Harlems have already worked for me five times."

"We played with The Beatles then a couple more times – once at The Majestic Ballroom in Birkenhead and then La Scala in Runcorn, which I remember because we went over the bridge to this little cinema. We played maybe another one or two times with them.

"Lots of our friends were starting up groups, but we were ahead of them, and had worked so hard on our stage presence. We were rough, but I had to tell the others that we can't be swearing on stage, and getting into arguments with the audience, but we had to watch what we said, how we said it. We once had a complaint from a member of the audience at the Playboy Club in London because one of us was sweating, and another one had different coloured socks than the others!"

There weren't many black groups around in the UK at the time, so where did they get their inspiration? Joe explained: "I watched a group called the Deep River Boys, who did all the moves on stage, dancing around the microphone and maybe a little more cabaret than us. We were a bit snobby about cabaret because we did not want to do that. However, artists like Frankie Lymon and the Teenagers, or the original Drifters, were a great inspiration to us. Furthermore, I would say all the black American vocal groups like The Marcels, The Del-Vikings, Marvin Gaye, Aretha Franklin and so many more. They were all fantastic."

One man who worked closely with them was Mal Jefferson. "In 1962, I formed my first group, Buddy Dean and The Teachers. I was on bass and vocals, the guitar player was Tony Cockayne and the drummer was Norman. We were asked to play at Stanley House one Sunday afternoon – it would have been late 1962 or early 1963. The three of us backed singer/guitarist Robbie Montgomery, who was excellent. The place was packed with young black guys, mostly around 14-16 years old.

"We did a few of these gigs and were able to leave our gear upstairs in a room where we could practise. The second time we were there these five young black kids were singing 'Duke of Earl' a cappella. We rehearsed with them and did about four numbers, including 'Write A Book'. They were terrific – very polished, professional and quite intent on getting every part of their harmony work completely accurate. They asked me if I would mind getting the band to play the numbers again and again. I told them that I was on their side, and that I could understand why they needed to be as polished as possible. I admired their determination and dedication to what was then the only harmony group in the city. No others ever came close.

"We then backed them a few times on the Sunday afternoon sessions, and they went down really well. Any record producer worth his salt would have snapped them up for recording. They looked great too – smart suits, shirts and ties, and polished, on-stage movements. They were true stars and should have been topping the charts."

With their career under the guidance of Brian Epstein, they should have had success, but it was not to be. "We did not do much with Epstein really, because he was busy with The Beatles, Gerry and Cilla," said Joe. "We did not see them again until after they had come back from America in 1964, because they had this civic reception at the Town Hall. We were invited, and we were the only other band there. I've got the picture from the day to prove it, but the photo has never really been seen before (see page 383), maybe because it had black guys in it. It is hard to believe that it was happening back then, but we just accepted that was the way it was.

"It was a great day, because we had this huge limousine come to our house in Toxteth to pick us up and drive us through the streets. It was crazy. There were thousands of people lining the streets and we were driving slowly past them, and you could see the girls fainting by the side of the road in the crowd. I wish we had gone out on the balcony now, just to experience it."

With a new manager named Ted Ross on board, they terminated their contract with Epstein and went on to make a number of television appearances. According to Joe, "This made us stars overnight. We were suddenly being recognised by our house and being followed down the road. We were trying not to be recognised, but it meant that we had to go and wash before we went out!"

Ross also managed to secure the group a deal with Pye Records and, on a special Beatles edition of the TV show *Juke Box Jury*, filmed in Liverpool, The Beatles were asked to review The Chants' new single.

The Beatles taped the episode at the Empire Theatre between 2:30pm and 3:15pm on 7 December 1963. *Juke Box Jury* was a popular show hosted by David Jacobs in which panelists voted on whether forthcoming singles would be hits or misses. In the audience were members of The Beatles' Northern Area Fan Club members. *Juke Box Jury* was broadcast later that evening between 6:05pm and 6:35pm, and was watched by an estimated 23 million people.

The Majestic Ballroom, Birkenhead, where The Beatles backed The Chants.

Stanley House, where The Chants made regular appearances.

The first song to be judged was "I Could Write A Book" by The Chants, and this is how The Beatles rated it:

John: "It's gear. Fabulous. Fab. It's it."

Paul: "I talked to The Chants recently about the disc. They said it's powerful. It is."

Ringo: "I'll buy it."

George: "It's great. Enough plugs and they've got a hit."

David Jacobs: "Are they being too generous?"

The Beatles unanimously voted the single a hit, but despite their support, it failed to achieve chart status. None of the group's other records fared any better: their debut single, "I Don't Care", released in September 1963; "She's Mine", released in June 1964; and their last single with Pye, "Sweet Was The Wine", from September 1964. Commenting on their period with Pye Records, Eddie Amoo commented, "They had no idea what to do with a black doo wop group. They just had no idea."

The group never found record success despite further releases with Fontana, Page One, Decca and RCA. They toured with box office stars like Helen Shapiro, Bobby Rydell plus The Searchers and went to Hamburg and played at the famous Star Club, where they were very popular. "All we had to do," recalled Joe, "was play two sets of twenty minutes, whereas the other groups were playing three or four hours each night. We had a great time there and Manfred Weissleder was very good to us."

Ticket for The Beatles' civic reception at Liverpool Town Hall, 10 July 1964.

The Chants toured around most of Europe regularly for a number of years and continued to release records, but none of them made a significant impact on the charts. When Eddie Ankrah fell in love with a girl while on tour in Sweden, he decided to stay there and get married. With his brother gone, Joe felt more isolated than ever in the group as the other three guys were friends. He decided to quit.

After they disbanded in 1975, Joey and Eddie Ankrah formed another group, OFANCHI, and enjoyed a degree of success on the television show *New Faces*. Eddie Amoo joined the Liverpool soul band The Real Thing, whose lineup included his brother Chris Amoo. They found UK chart success in June 1976 with "You To Me Are Everything", which reached number 1 in the UK and number 28 on Billboard's R&B Singles chart. Their follow-up UK hit, "Can't Get By With-

The Chants were guests at The Beatles' civic reception at Liverpool Town Hall. On the back row are Eddie, John, Edmund, Paul, Ringo, Nat and George, with Edmund and Joe in between the Lord Mayor and Lady Mayoress, plus local MP Bessie Braddock. The photo has been signed by Paul McCartney to Joe Ankrah and says, "To Joe, Cheers! Paul McCartney (great times man)".

The Fab one hundred and Four

The *Liverpool Echo* promotes The Beatles' appearance on Juke Box Jury, with host David Jacobs standing over John, Ringo, Paul and George.

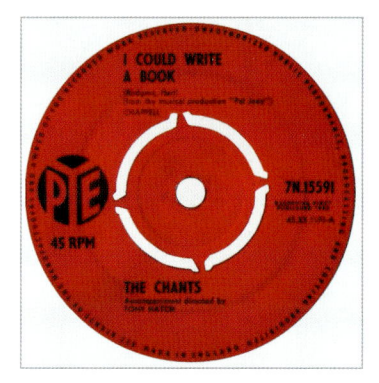

"I Could Write A Book" by The Chants, which was released in December 1963.

Ticket for The Beatles' appearance on Juke Box Jury.

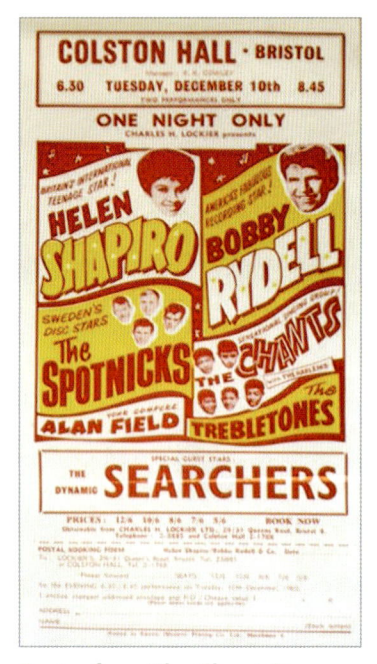

Poster from The Chants' tour with Helen Shapiro.

out You", reached number 2. They released a number of successful albums, including one named after the Toxteth area of Liverpool, their home turf. Their first suggestion was to call it *Liverpool 8*, the name Ringo Starr chose for his 2008 album because The Dingle is part of Toxteth, which is located in the postal district of Liverpool 8. However, the record company rejected the title and instead named it *Four from Eight*.

In addition to being a successful singer and performer, Joe Ankrah is a talented artist. Self-taught, he paints stunning portraits and has exhibited in local galleries. He is presently working on his autobiography, which will detail his remarkable life.

The Chants (left to right) Eddie, Joe, Alan, Nat and Edmund, with Helen Shapiro and Bobby Rydell.

28 OCTOBER 1962

The Beatles
and Craig Douglas

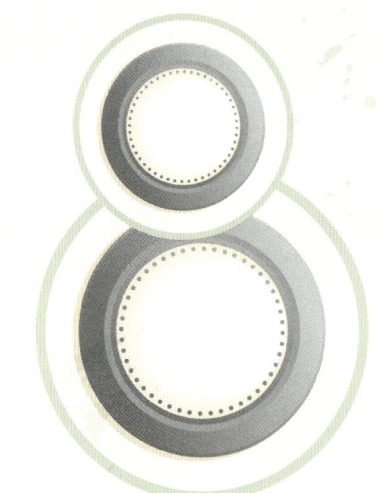

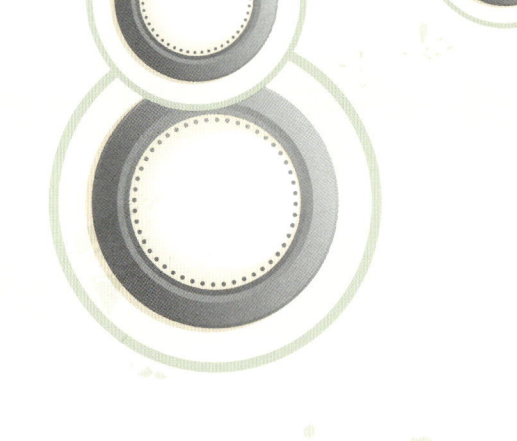

Craig Douglas is a British singer, who was a big star from 1959 to 1963, in the UK especially. Douglas was born Terence Perkins in Newport, Isle of Wight, on 12 August 1941.

As Terence Perkins, he was employed as a milkman before becoming a professional singer, and was known to many as the "Singing Milkman". His breakthrough came on the *Six-Five Special*, at that time the only real showcase for rock 'n' roll on British television. Douglas was booked on the show the same week that Cliff Richard and Joe Brown appeared, but he made an impression even in their company. A few days later, he was presented with two huge sacks of fan mail elicited by the performance. The *Six-Five Special* led Douglas to a recording contract and a string of successes. His manager, Bunny Lewis, gave him the name Craig Douglas, having seen it outside a house in Scotland. Douglas said that "Terry" was a common entertainment name at the time, and that was also one of the reasons for the name change.

Voted "Best New Singer" in 1959 in the British music magazine *NME*, Douglas went on to record nine Top 40 UK singles, eight of which were cover versions of former American hits. Amongst that tally, Douglas had a number one single in 1959 with "Only Sixteen", which easily outsold Sam Cooke's original version in the UK. It was recorded at EMI's Abbey Road studios, with whistling by Mike Sammes, and released through Top Rank records.

Craig Douglas' eponymous album, released in 1962.

In 1961, Douglas entered the *A Song For Europe* contest with his song "The Girl Next Door". It fared poorly, finishing last to The Allisons' effort, "Are You Sure?", which went on to represent the UK at the Eurovision Song Contest. Douglas' clean-cut, teen idol image was inspired by American performers like Pat Boone and Ricky Nelson. In 1962, he co-starred with Helen Shapiro in Richard Lester's feature film directorial debut *It's Trad, Dad!*, but his appearance did nothing to jump start an acting career.

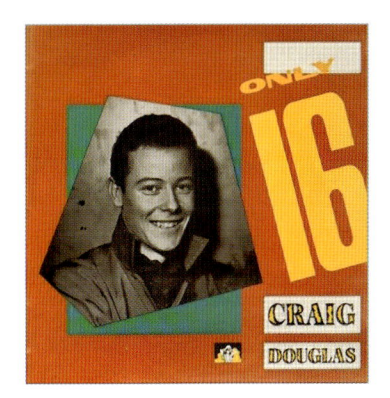

Craig Douglas' single, "Only 16", his only number one single from 1959.

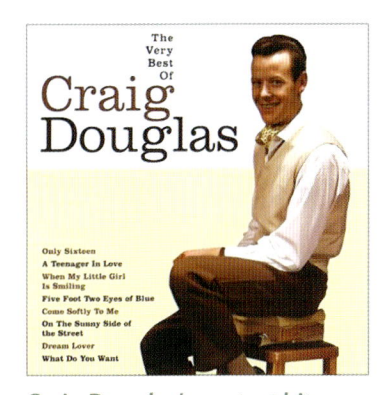

Craig Douglas' greatest hits album which came out in 2004.

Craig Douglas' meeting with The Beatles took place later that same year at the Liverpool Empire Theatre's Sunday concert, where the group backed him at the end of the first part of their first concert performance. This pairing with Craig Douglas was a prestigious one for The Beatles, not just because he was a star at the time but because the bill also featured several more top acts of the time.

On the bill, promoted by Brian Epstein's NEMS, were Little Richard, Jet Harris (previously with The Shadows), Sounds Incorporated (who opened for The Beatles at Shea Stadium in August 1965) and Kenny Lynch (who can be seen on the cover of the Wings album *Band on the Run*). Douglas was not originally scheduled to appear but, as he revealed in an interview with broadcaster Spencer Leigh, he had a call from Bunny Lewis, saying that Sam Cooke had to pull out of the Liverpool Empire gig. Douglas was asked if he would fill in for Cooke and, naturally, he agreed.

He and his keyboard player met with Brian Epstein at the Empire before rehearsals and Douglas asked Epstein about The Beatles' musical ability. "Do they read music?", he enquired. Brian told him they did not. A quick discussion between Douglas and his keyboard player followed and the pair tried to come up with a workable plan. They decided they could only write down what key the song was in and hope for the best. "John, Paul, George and Ringo were really good," explained Douglas, "and I think they already knew some of the songs. We rehearsed for a while, and then, later on, I was passing their dressing room and they were rehearsing the songs again, which I thought was lovely."

The Beatles did their slot, which was sensational, as their debut single "Love Me Do", had been released only three weeks before. The record was riding up the charts and here they were, performing in front of their home crowd. They would be a tough act for Douglas to follow. "I only did about 20 minutes", said Douglas, "which was fair enough. I had a photo taken with The Beatles, on which Paul wrote 'Craig's backing band', which was nice."

At the end of the night, Douglas had to head back to his hotel in Chester, which is about 25 miles from Liverpool. The taxi driver asked for change for the Birkenhead Tunnel (under the River Mersey) and Douglas realised he only had a £5 note. The driver had no change. "I went back into the theatre, and the first person I bumped into was John Lennon", he explained. "I asked him if he had change for a fiver, to which Lennon replied, 'Change one? I've never even seen one!'. John lent me half a crown (equivalent to 12.5 pence today) and I never paid him it back. It was a night to remember! Brian Epstein was a hell of a nice guy and you wouldn't have thought that a guy like that would have ended up as an agent. But he knew his business and he was very articulate."

Craig Douglas has several hits, including his million-seller "Only Sixteen", his only chart topper. His other records sold over 750,000 copies each. However, the emergence of groups ultimately spelt the end of Douglas' chart career, as solo singers were giving way to musical groups. His final chart entry came in February 1963 when "Town Crier" flopped at number 36. He then went into cabaret, most notably on cruise ships. He is still performing and releasing albums over 50 years after his first breakthrough.

NOVEMBER 1962

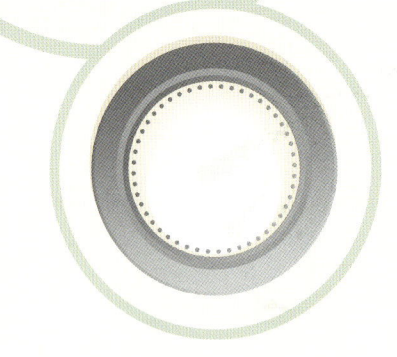

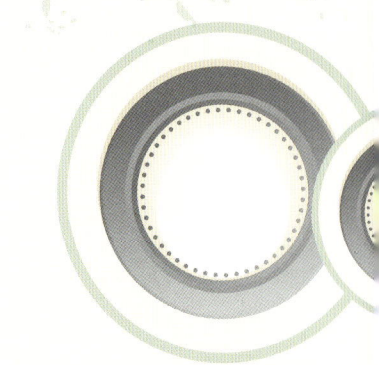

John Lennon plays solo in Hamburg

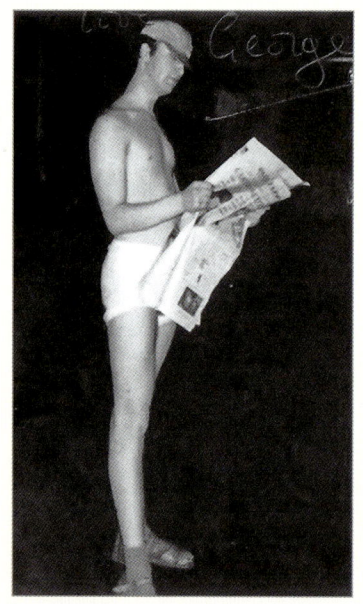

At the Star Club in Hamburg, November 1962, John Lennon told author Chris Hutchins that The Beatles were all struggling to make ends meet. Lennon revealed that he sent all his wages home to his new wife Cynthia, pregnant with their son Julian. Not everyone knew that John and Cynthia had wed in August: not even Ringo knew at that point.

Hutchins asked Lennon how he managed to send all of his wages home. "Easy," replied Lennon, "between sessions with the band, I go down to some of the strip joints and play guitar for the girls. That earns me my grub money." John did become cosy with one well-endowed German barmaid. "Bettina keeps me in drinks and pills, and Cyn keeps me in love," he said. "Bettina calls out for her favourite numbers when we're on stage. You can always pick out her voice."

Bettina was mentioned in the song "Red Light" on the *Haymans Green* album by the Pete Best Band, about Best's memories of his time with The Beatles.

John posing with a newspaper in Hamburg.

The Fab Four – ready to conquer the world.

The Fab one hundred and Four

31 DECEMBER 1962

The Beatles with
Horst and Freddie Fascher

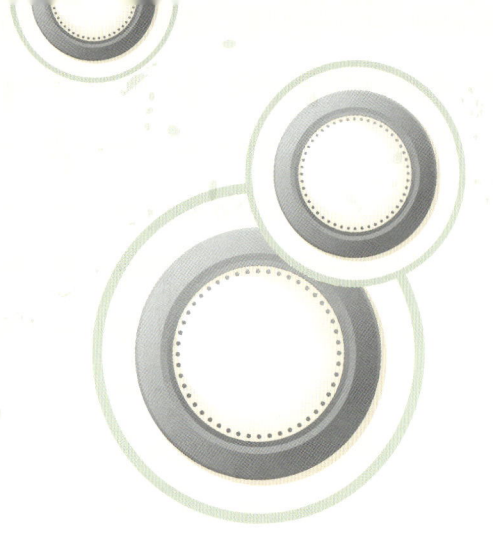

Horst Fascher was born on 5 February 1936 in Hamburg, the son of a housewife and a sailor. Like his three brothers, Horst was expected to follow his father into a career at sea. Encouraged by his father, he completed an apprenticeship as a ship's carpenter and boat-builder.

However, it was music, not the sea, that would eventually take over his life. In 1949, while walking down the Reeperbahn in Hamburg, he came across the rhythm and blues singer, George Maycock. Horst then discovered the British Forces Broadcasting Service where he listened to a concert on 27 October 1958 by Bill Haley and His Comets.

Prior to this, between 1953 and 1959, Fascher had been a professional boxer whose career was cut short when he had unintentionally killed a sailor in a street fight, leading to a prison sentence for manslaughter. This gained him a reputation among the locals and visiting band members as a man you wanted as an ally. Horst easily found work in the clubs along the Reeperbahn, mainly as a bouncer. On their first trip to Hamburg, he became friends with John, Paul, George, Stu and Pete.

"When he had to leave Hamburg for the first time," recalled Beatles drummer Pete Best, "Horst was very upset. Then, on our second visit, when we did three months at the Top Ten, he was there. He saw us every night, used to eat with us, drink with us, laugh and joke with us, and when we were leaving together for the first time to go back to Liverpool, he was in tears. Here was this outgoing man who had the reputation of being hard and could handle himself, openly shedding tears over the fact that his boys were leaving Hamburg and he did not know when he'd be seeing them again."

Over a two-year period, as they progressed from The Indra to the Kaiserkeller to the Top Ten and the Star Club, Horst was always on hand to look after his friends, trying to ensure he was working at the clubs they were playing.

At the beginning of 1960, he became the business manager of the Top Ten Club, but did not last long after falling out with the owner.

Horst Fascher with The Beatles.

He then worked as a waiter on the Grosse Freiheit before an opportunity arose to open the legendary Star Club. Here, he would work as both booking and business manager, bringing some of the biggest names in rock 'n' roll to the club.

"Many people called me a bouncer," said Horst, "and I was a bouncer at some of the clubs, but I was also a manager and a friend of the bands. When the British groups came to Hamburg, I tried to learn English because I loved the music they were playing. As a result, I became good friends with The Beatles. I was a 'Hamburger', like we say, and they were Liverpudlians, so I took care of them. I knew what was going on, especially in the St. Pauli area with all the prostitution and pimps, all the sailors and foreigners. I told them what was dangerous and how to take care of themselves."

Horst's friendship with The Beatles developed to the extent that he would occasionally join them on stage to sing. The most famous appearance occurred on 31 December 1962 at the Star Club, which resulted in the notorious live recording, which has been the subject of legal action on several occasions since then.

Horst was joined on stage by his younger brother Freddie, singing along with John, Paul, George and Ringo. He can be heard singing along to "Hallelujah, I Love Her So", while Freddie sang on "Be-Bop-A-Lula".

In his 2006 memoirs, *Let The Good Times Roll*, Horst talked about his friendship with The Beatles and the other Liverpool bands, as well as his life in Hamburg. On a trip to England, he came to London and Liverpool to look for new groups, and ended up managing Tony Sheridan. When the Star Club launched in April 1962, Horst, by virtue of his close friendship with The Beatles, was instrumental in bringing the group to the club. "On the opening night," he recalled, "we had The Beatles and other groups, and Brian Epstein also came. There were lots of drinks. The next morning, we all went to a club and Brian was a bit drunk and John Lennon poured beer all over him. There was a slight argument."

His association with the Star Club ended in 1965 when he was imprisoned for two years for breaking a customer's jaw. As a condition of his release, he was banned from the St. Pauli district, making a return to the club scene impossible. After his release, he worked with Tony Sheridan again and headed for Vietnam to entertain American

John and Paul singing in the Star Club.

The Beatles at the Star Club, Hamburg, December 1962.

GIs. While there, he met his wife Enry with whom he had a son, David, in 1970.

Horst later married Ali, the daughter of Merseybeat star Faron. They had a baby boy named Rory who died in a accident caused by a faulty cot. The relationship did not last and, with his next partner, he became the father of a baby girl. When his daughter was stricken with a rare heart condition, Horst contacted his good friend Paul McCartney who immediately arranged for a team to fly over from America and operate at the famous Great Ormond Street Children's Hospital in London. Paul also paid for Horst and his partner to stay in London.

Sadly, the baby couldn't be saved, and Horst had lost yet another child. He was plunged into despair at losing two children so young.

In 1976, he unsuccessfully tried to open a second Star Club, with both Ringo and George appearing on the first night, but it was a musical and financial failure and closed soon after. He passed on his musical touch to his son, who became DJ World Champion in 1991 and 1992.

Horst is still working and, in 2009, produced a DVD, *The Quarrymen: The Band That Started The Beatles,* working with the surviving members of the band.

Horst Fascher, centre, with The Quarrymen in Liverpool, August 2011.

And in the end...

We arrive at the end of 1962, with one hundred and four musicians, family members and friends having featured in the early history of The Beatles. Although John, Paul, George and Ringo were now recording artists with "Love Me Do" having hit the UK charts in October 1962, nobody could have predicted what was about to happen. By the end of 1963, Tony Barrow had christened them The Fab Four, and they'd topped the charts, toured extensively and, following their legendary appearance at the Royal Variety Performance, inspired a new phrase that would forever be a part of the English language: 'Beatlemania'.

At the beginning of 1964, their transatlantic appearance on *The Ed Sullivan Show* would catapult them to superstardom. Over the next few years, they became the most famous group in pop music history. Even so, they would occasionally recruit other friends and musicians to help them out. Just like in the early days, people like Jimmie Nicol, Eric Clapton and Billy Preston would step in to perform and record with them.

The Beatles had made it, with a little help from their friends.

the Fab one hundred and Four

The Fab one hundred and Four *(in order of appearance)*

#	Name	Description
1	Geoff "George" Lee	Gave John his first guitar and suggested that John start a skiffle group
2	John Lennon	The Beatles
3	Julia Lennon	John Lennon's mum who taught him to play
4	George Smith	John's uncle who gave him his first harmonica
5	Arthur Pendleton	Taught John to play harmonica
6	Pete Shotton	The Quarrymen
7	Eric Griffiths	The Quarrymen
8	Bill Smith	The Quarrymen
9	Rod Davis	The Quarrymen
10	Colin Hanton	The Quarrymen
11	Ivan Vaughan	The Quarrymen
12	Nigel Walley	The Quarrymen
13	Len Garry	The Quarrymen
14	Paul McCartney	The Beatles
15	Jim McCartney	Paul McCartney's dad who bought him a trumpet and guitar
16	Ian James	Taught Paul to play guitar
17	Michael McCartney	Paul's brother who played drums with the early Beatles
18	George Harrison	The Beatles
19	Harold Harrison	George's father, who arranged guitar lessons for his son
20	Len Houghton	Gave George Harrison guitar lessons
21	Geoff Nugent	Played guitar with George
22	Colin Manley	Gave George guitar lessons
23	Don Jefferson	Gave George guitar lessons
24	Peter Harrison	The Rebels
25	Arthur Kelly	The Rebels
26	Alan Williams	The Rebels
27	John Duff Lowe	The Quarrymen
28	John Brierley	The Vikings – played with Paul and George
29	Aneurin Thomas	The Vikings – played with Paul and George
30	Les Stewart	The Les Stewart Quartet
31	Ray Skinner	The Les Stewart Quartet
32	Ken Brown	The Les Stewart Quartet/The Quarrymen/The Blackjacks
33	Stuart Sutcliffe	The Beatles
34	Dave May	Gave Stuart Sutcliffe bass guitar lessons
35	Vinnie Ismael	Gave John and Paul guitar tips
36	Odie Taylor	Gave John and Paul guitar tips
37	Zancs Logie	Gave John and Paul guitar tips
38	Tommy Moore	Drummer with The Silver Beetles
39	Johnny Hutchinson	The Big Three – drummed with The Beatles, also known as Johnny Hutch
40	Cliff Roberts	The Dominoes – played drums with The Silver Beats
41	Johnny Gentle	Singer backed by John, Paul, George, Stuart and Tommy Moore on tour
42	Ronnie 'The Ted'	Played drums once with The Silver Beetles
43	Norman Chapman	Drummer with The Silver Beetles
44	Royston Ellis	Beat Poet backed by The Silver Beetles
45	Pete Best	The Beatles
46	Mona Best	Bought Pete his drumkit and managed The Beatles
47	Chas Newby	The Blackjacks/The Beatles
48	Bill Barlow	The Blackjacks
49	Howie Casey	Derry and the Seniors
50	Derry Wilkie	Derry and the Seniors
51	Stan Foster	Derry and the Seniors
52	Brian Griffiths	Derry and the Seniors
53	Billy Hughes	Derry and the Seniors
54	Paul Whitehead	Derry and the Seniors
55	Jeff Wallington	Derry and the Seniors
56	Lu Walters	Rory Storm and the Hurricanes
57	Ringo Starr (Richy Starkey)	The Beatles
58	Steve Calrow	Singer backed by The Beatles
59	Rory (Alan Caldwell) Storm	Rory Storm and the Hurricanes
60	Johnny 'Guitar' Byrne	Rory Storm and the Hurricanes
61	Charles 'Ty Brian' O'Brien	Rory Storm and the Hurricanes
62	Klaus Voormann	Rehearsed with The Beatles in Hamburg
63	Tanya Day	Singer backed by The Beatles in Hamburg
64	Buddy Britten	Singer backed by The Beatles in Hamburg
65	Tony Sheridan	The Beatles backed him as Tony Sheridan and the Beat Brothers
66	Cilla Black	Singer backed by The Beatles
67	Johnny Gustafson	The Big Three – played on stage with The Beatles. Also known as Johnny Gus
68	Gerry Marsden	Gerry and the Pacemakers/The Beatmakers
69	Freddie Marsden	Gerry and the Pacemakers/The Beatmakers
70	Les Chadwick	Gerry and the Pacemakers/The Beatmakers
71	Les Maguire	Gerry and the Pacemakers/The Beatmakers

72	Karl Terry	Singer who sang with The Beatmakers
73	Davy Jones	Singer backed by The Beatles
74	Ray McFall	Owner of The Cavern who sang with The Beatles
75	Billy Hatton	The Four Jays – joined The Beatles on stage at The Cavern
76	Dave Lovelady	The Four Jays – joined The Beatles on stage at The Cavern
77	Brian O'Hara	The Four Jays – joined The Beatles on stage at The Cavern
78	Gene Vincent	Singer backed by The Beatles
79	Roy Young	Pianist who played with The Beatles in Hamburg
80	Harry Graves	Ringo Starr's stepfather who bought him his first drumkit
81	Marie Maguire	Ringo's childhood friend who gave him "Bedtime for Drums"
82	"Teacher"	Teacher who encouraged Ringo to play drums
83	Red Carter	Drum tutor who gave Ringo lessons
84	Eddie Myles	Eddie Clayton Skiffle Group
85	Roy Trafford	Eddie Clayton Skiffle Group
86	Peter Healey	Eddie Clayton Skiffle Group
87	John Docherty	Eddie Clayton Skiffle Group
88	Mickey McGrellis	Eddie Clayton Skiffle Group
89	Alan Robinson	Darktown Skiffle Group
90	Dave McKew	Darktown Skiffle Group
91	Keith Draper	Darktown Skiffle Group
92	Gladys Jill Martin	Darktown Skiffle Group
93	David Smith	Darktown Skiffle Group
94	Colin Melander	Tony Sheridan and the Beat Brothers
95	Andy White	Session drummer who recorded with The Beatles
96	Simone Jackson	Singer backed by The Beatles
97	Joe Ankrah	The Chants – backed by The Beatles
98	Edmund Ankrah	The Chants – backed by The Beatles
99	Eddie Amoo	The Chants – backed by The Beatles
100	Nat Smeda	The Chants – backed by The Beatles
101	Alan Harding	The Chants – backed by The Beatles
102	Craig Douglas	Singer backed by The Beatles
103	Horst Fascher	Worked at the Star Club and sang with The Beatles
104	Freddie Fascher	Worked at the Star Club and sang with The Beatles

The Fab one hundred and Four

John Lennon *should have* said: "I met Pete Shotton, and he joined, and then Bill joined, and Eric joined, and Rod joined, and Ivan joined, and Nigel joined and Len joined… then I met Paul, and said, 'Do you wanna join me band', and then George joined, and Stuart joined and Tommy joined and Norman joined and Pete joined and Chas joined and then Ringo joined. We were just a band that made it very, very big, that's all."

"*We were just one hundred and four guys.*"

Index of The Fab one hundred and Four

Amoo, Eddie 14-15, 23, **374-385**

Ankrah, Edmund 14-15, 23, **374-385**

Ankrah, Joe 12, 14-15, 23, 33, **374-385**

Barlow, Bill 20, 178, 180, 278, **296-298**

Best, Mona 19, 25, 175, 177, 179, 225, 227, 276, **292-295**, 297, 326, 339, 343

Best, Pete 14-15, 20, 21, 75, 101, 153, 157, 164, 180, 186-187, 213, 241, 273-275, **276-281**, 285, 287, 291, 293-296, 298, 299, 306, 309-310, 315-316, 318-319, 324, 326, 328, 329, 332, 337, **338-344**, 358, 365-368, 388, 390

Black, Cilla 14-15, 21, 232, 245, **312-314**

Brierley, John 18, **174**

Britten, Buddy 14-15, 21, **304-305**

Brown, Ken 14-15, 18, 19, 20, 48, 49, **175-178**, **179-180**, 278, 296, 298, 344

Byrne, Johnny (Johnny Guitar) 15, 21, 23, 288, **300-301**, 357, 360

Calrow, Steve 14-15, 21, **299**

Carter, Red 22, 258, **345-349**

Casey, Howie 14-15, 20, 21, 28, 185, 186, 241, **282-286**, 289, 335

Chadwick, Les 14-15, 22, 41, **318-321**

Chapman, Norman 12, 14-15, 20, 180, **258-264**, 273, 342

Davis, Rod 12, 14-15, 16, 17, 28, 34, 37, 48, 49, 62, 63, 68, 73, **74-77**, 78, 82, 95, 96, 101, 108, 111, 117, 146, 162, 163, 169, 342

Day, Tanya 14-15, 21, **304-305**

Dougherty, John 23, **350-352**

Douglas, Craig 14-15, 23, 274, **386-387**

Draper, Keith 23, **355**

Duff, John 14-15, 18, 41, 42, 48, 49, 75, **167-169**, 172, 173

Ellis, Royston 14-15, 20, 180, 203, **265-272**

Eymond, Wally (Lu Walters) 14-15, 21, 23, 273, **287-288**, 300, 357

Fascher, Freddie 14-15, 23, 274, **390-392**

Fascher, Horst 14-15, 333, **390-392**

Foster, Stan 14-15, 20, 21, 186, **282-286**, 289

Garry, Len 14-15, 17, 40, 42, 48, 49, 65, 68, **97-99**, 109, 132, 169

Gentle, Johnny 14-15, 20, 179, 184, 200, 228, 234, 238, 239, 241, 245, **246-253**

Graves, Harry 22, **345-349**

Griffiths, Brian 14-15, 20, 241, **282-286**

Griffiths, Eric 14-15, 17, 34, 48, 50, **72-73**, 74, 76, 79, 96, 108, 162, 344

Gustafson, Johnny 14-15, 21, 240, **315**

Hanton, Colin 14-15, 17, 18, 48, 49, **78-82**, 98, 102, 107, 108, 114, 163, 167, 169, 172, 173, 203, 342

Harding, Alan 14-15, 23, **374-385**

Harrison, George **146-163**, **175-176**

Harrison, Harold 18, **146-163**

Harrison, Peter 18, **154-157**

Hatton, Billy 14-15, 22, **326-328**

Healey, Peter 23, **350-352**

Houghton, Len 18, **146-150**

Hughes, Billy 14-15, 20, **282-286**

Hutchinson, Johnny 14-15, 19, 180, 230, 234, 238, **240-243**, 315, 342

Ismael, Vinnie 19, 180, **208-227**

Jackson, Simone 14-15, 23, **373**

James, Ian 10, 11, 18, 48, 115, 118, 119, **127-138**

Jefferson, Don 18, **158-160**

Jill, Gladys 23, **355**

Jones, Davy 11, 14-15, 22, 230, 274, **322-323**

Kelly, Arthur 18, 49, 149, 154, **155-157**, 361

Lee, Geoff ("George Henry") 17, **50-51**

---

*The numbers in **bold green** are the main page ranges for that person*

396

Lennon, John **50-63**

Lennon, Julia 17, **53-63**, 74, 92

Logie, Zancs 19, 180, **208-227**

Lovelady, Dave 14-15, 22, 245, 324, **326-328**

Maguire, Les 14-15, 22, **318-321**

Maguire, Marie 22, **345-359**

Manley, Colin 18, 41, 49, 121, **158-160**

Marsden, Freddie 22, **318-321**

Marsden, Gerry 14-15, 22, 142, 143, **318-321**

May, Dave 19, 179, **181-202**

McCartney (McGear), Michael 125, **139-141**

McCartney, Jim 18, **120-126**, 139, 164, 168, 343

McCartney, Paul **107-145**

McFall, Ray 14-15, 22, 25, 274, 292, 300, 322, **326-328**, 338

McGrellis, Mickey 23, **350-352**

McKew, Dave 23, **355**

Melander, Colin 23, **189**

Moore, Tommy 14-15, 19, 20, 180, 184, 230, **233-239**, 240, 244, 246, 247, 248, 250, 253, 256, 258, 285, 342

Myles, Eddie 23, 348, **350-352**

Newby, Chas 14-15, 20, 21, 101, 178, 180, 187, 273, 278, 292, **296-298**

Nugent, Geoff 18, 49, 140, **151-153**

O'Brien, Charles (Ty Brian) 15, 21, 23, 288, **300-301**, 357, 362

O'Hara, Brian 14-15, 22, **326-328**

Pendleton, Arthur 17, **53-63**

Roberts, Cliff 14-15, 19, 180, **244-245**, 284

Robinson, Alan 23, **355**

Ronnie, 'The Ted' 14-15, 20, 180, **256-257**

Sheridan, Tony 11, 14-15, 21, 23, 157, 189, 227, 274, 284, **306-311**, 324, 332-335, 339, 357, 391, 397

Shotton, Pete 14-15, 17, 34, 48, 51, 52, **64-66**, 67, 68, 70, 74, 81, 85, 89, 94, 97, 98, 107, 119, 394

Skinner, Ray 14-15, 18, 49, **175-176**

Smeda, Nat 14-15, 23, **374-385**

Smith, Bill 12, 14-15, 17, 34, 40, 48, **67-71**, 96, 100

Smith, David 23, **355**

Smith, George 17, **53-63**

Starkey, Richy (Ringo Starr) **345-369**

Stewart, Les 14-15, 18, 49, **175-176**

Storm, Rory 11, 14-15, 21-23, 25, 143, 153, 157, 185, 229, 273-274, 287-288, **300-301**, 310, 312, **324**, 326, 339-340, 348, 353, 355, **356-363**

Sutcliffe, Stuart 12, 14-15, 19, 21-22, 37, 47, 53, 164, 179, **181-202**, 212, 231, 233, 240, 244, 246, 253-254, 256, 258, 276, 278, 280, **289**, 291, 296, 299, 302, 310, 397

Taylor, Odie 19, 180, **208-227**

A "Teacher" 11, 22, 306, 308, **345-349**, 397

Terry, Karl 14-15, 22, 274, **318-321**, 323

Thomas, Aneurin 18, **174**

Trafford, Roy 23, **350-353**

Vaughan, Ivan 14-15, 17, 40, 42, 48, 64, **83-88**, 89, 96, 97, 101, 108, 109, 296, 342

Vincent, Gene 14-15, 22, 119, 229-230, 237, 240, 249, 274, 283, 307, 321-322, **329-331**, 333, 357

Voormann, Klaus 14-15, 21, 182, 186-188, 190, 274, **302-303**

Walley, Nigel 14-15, 17, 40, 48, 64, 65, 73, 85, **89-93**, 96, 98, 344

Wallington, Jeff 14-15, 20, **282-286**

White, Andy 14-15, 23, 274, 338-339, 341, **370-372**

Whitehead, Paul 14-15, 20, **282-286**

Wilkie, Derry 14-15, 20-21, 210, 213, 260, **282-286**, 289, 322, 380

Williams, Alan 18, 49, **154-157**, 275

Young, Roy 14-15, 22, 23, 274, 286, **332-335**

*The numbers in **bold green** are the main page ranges for that person*

The Fab one hundred and Four

IMAGE CREDITS

Every effort has been made to correctly acknowledge the source or copyright holder of each illustration and Dalton Watson Fine Books Ltd. apologises for any unintentional errors or omissions, which will be corrected in future editions of this book.

Ankrah, Joe	11, 374, 377, 383, 385
Atherton, Mave	140
Baird, Julia	54
Bedford, David	10, 28, 31, 35, 44, 45, 47, 49, 52, 55, 57, 61, 65, 66, 69, 71, 73, 75, 77, 79, 82, 84, 91, 93, 96, 98, 99, 102, 108, 116, 118, 119, 122, 124, 130, 136, 147, 149, 152, 153, 155, 162, 164, 169, 173, 176, 177, 178, 192, 194, 193, 195, 196, 200, 202, 211, 214, 223, 228, 230, 235, 243, 259, 268, 277, 286, 295, 297, 300, 321, 335, 337, 344, 346, 349, 352, 366, 375, 382
Bedford, Ashleigh	105
Best, Peter	48, 178, 179, 284, 286, 292, 300, 301, 350
Blain, Gary	16, 60, 363, 377, 389
Bolland, Tony	142, 143
Bolt, Fred	87
Chang, Barry	210, 212, 279
Corbis Images	154, 161, 369
Davis, Rod	63, 65, 72, 76, 95, 109, 110, 111, 112, 113, 114, 115, 117, 392
Ellis, Royston	265, 266, 269, 270, 271, 272
Frangione, Tom	371, 372
Getty Images	237, 238, 239
Gunderson, Chuck	90
Hackett, Ian	365, 368, 379, 382
Harry, Bill	13, 144, 211, 267, 273, 313, 323, 329, 336, 354, 380, 395
Hill, Michael	95
Holmes, Tim	54
James, Ian	11, 134, 135, 137, 138
James, Fitzroy	209, 215, 216, 217, 218, 219, 220, 221, 222, 223, 224
Jones, David	24, 25
Kearney, Les	350, 351
Krone, Randy	384
Leach, Sam	178
Lee, Geoff	51
Liverpool Records Office	33, 34, 36, 37, 38, 39, 40, 41, 42, 43, 44, 46, 47, 52, 54, 55, 56, 57, 58, 59, 60, 62, 66, 68, 70, 81, 83, 85, 87, 91, 92, 95, 98, 100, 104, 120, 122, 124, 128, 129, 131, 133, 140, 141, 143, 148, 157, 163, 166, 168, 180, 191, 192, 193, 194, 201, 211, 213, 215, 222, 224, 226, 228, 247, 251, 255, 261, 266, 272, 327, 316, 317, 346, 347, 349, 351, 359, 360, 362, 365, 376, 382, 384
Mann, Alan	307, 308, 309, 311
McCartney, Angie	124
Mirrorpix	150, 348
Murray, Rod	19, 181, 182, 183, 184, 190, 196, 197, 198, 199, 200, 201, 253
Naboshek, Mark	17, 18, 37, 41, 46, 50, 53, 56, 64, 67, 70, 72, 74, 80, 82, 83, 94, 97, 120, 127, 132, 139, 147, 156, 158, 166, 167, 173, 187, 188, 257, 263, 281, 289, 294, 301, 311
Newby, Chas	21, 296, 298
Nugent, Geoff	151, 152, 153
Opone, Ann-Marie	20, 258, 259, 260, 261, 262, 263, 264
Phillips, Andrew	124
Phillips, Peter	170, 171, 172
Prytherch, Harry	160
radiosoundsfamiliar.com	12, 26, 27, 29
Rex Features	125
Rhind/LFI, Geoff	107
Roberts, Charlie	103
Roberts, David	318, 319, 320, 328, 329, 330, 365, 367, 379, 381
Roberts, Pam	298
Roland, Cheniston	229, 231, 232, 233, 235, 236, 237, 239, 240, 241, 244, 245, 254, 255, 260, 261, 290
Smith, Bill	68, 73
St. Peter's Church	106, 116
Stevens, Harvey	207, 249, 251, 252, 253, 256, 257, 258
Sutcliffe, Pauline	184, 185, 186, 190, 191, 197, 200, 201, 302, 312
Taylor, Ted	244, 249
Weissleder, Manfred	330, 331
White, Andy	370
Young, Roy	22, 332, 333, 334, 339, 340, 341

BIBLIOGRAPHY

Babiuk, Andy	*Beatles Gear*	Backbeat Books 2002
Baird, Julia	*Imagine This*	Hodder & Stoughton 2006
Beatles, The	*The Beatles Anthology*	Cassell & Co. 2000
Bedford, David	*Liddypool: Birthplace of The Beatles*	Dalton Watson Ltd. 2009
Best, Roag with Pete and Rory Best	*The Beatles – The True Beginnings*	Spine 2002
Clough, Matthew and Colin Fallows	*Stuart Sutcliffe – A Retrospective*	Liverpool University Press 2008
Davies, Hunter	*The Quarrymen*	Omnibus Press 2001
Davies, Hunter	*The Beatles – The Authorised Biography*	Granada Publishing Ltd. 1979
Ellis, Royston	*The Big Beat Scene*	Music Mentor Books 2010
Epstein, Brian	*A Cellarful of Noise*	Souvenir Press Ltd. 1964
Flannery, Joe with Mike Brocken	*Standing In The Wings – The Beatles, Brian Epstein and Me*	The History Press 2013
Frame, Pete	*The Beatles and Some Other Guys*	Omnibus Press 1997
Garry, Len	*John, Paul and Me Before The Beatles*	CG Publishing Ltd. 1997
Harrison, Olivia	*George Harrison: Living in The Material World*	Abrams, New York 2012
Harry, Bill	*Encyclopedia of Beatles People*	Blandford 1997
Harry, Bill	*The Ultimate Beatles Encyclopedia*	Virgin Books 1992
Harry, Bill	*The John Lennon Encyclopedia*	Virgin Books 2000
Harry, Bill	*The Ringo Starr Encyclopedia*	Virgin Books 2004
Harry, Bill	*The Paul McCartney Encyclopedia*	Virgin Books 2002
Harry, Bill	*The George Harrison Encyclopedia*	Virgin Books 2003
Harry, Bill	*Liverpool: Bigger Than The Beatles*	Trinity Mirror Publishing 2009
Harry, Bill	*Lennon's Liverpool*	Trinity Mirror Publishing 2011
Hill, Michael	*John Lennon: The Boy Who Became A Legend*	Penin Ink Publishing 2013
Hutchins, Chris and Peter Thompson	*Elvis Meets The Beatles*	Smith Gryphon Limited 1994
Krasker, Eric	*The Beatles: Fact and Fiction 1960-1962*	Seguier 2010
Leigh, Spencer	*Drummed Out*	Northdown Publishing 1998
Leigh, Spencer	*The Cavern*	SAF Publishing 2008
Leigh, Spencer	*The Beatles in Hamburg*	Omnibus Press 2011
Lewisohn, Mark	*The Beatles Live*	Henry Holt 1986
Lewisohn, Mark	*The Complete Beatles Chronicle*	Chancellor Press 2002
Lewisohn, Mark	*The Beatles – All These Years: Volume One: Tune In*	Little, Brown 2013
Mann, Alan	*The Teacher – The Tony Sheridan Story*	AMPS 2013
McCartney, Mike	*Thank U Very Much*	Granada Publishing Ltd. 1982
McNab, Ken	*The Beatles In Scotland*	Polygon 2008
O'Brien, Ray	*There Are Places I'll Remember*	The Bluecoat Press 2005
Pawlowski, Gareth	*How They Became The Beatles*	E.P. Dutton 1989
Pritchard, David and Alan Lysaght	*The Beatles: An Oral History*	Hyperion 1998
Roach, Kevin	*The McCartneys: In The Town Where They Were Born*	Trinity Mirror Publishing 2011
Roach, Kevin and John Gannon	*The Beatles: Living In the Eye of The Hurricane*	Liverpool Authors 2011
Shotton, Pete and Nicholas Schaffner	*John Lennon – In My Life*	Stein and Day 1983
Sutcliffe, Pauline	*Stuart Sutcliffe – The Beatles Era*	Timeframed Limited
Turner, Steve	*A Hard Day's Write*	Carlton Publishing 1994
Williams, Allan	*The Man Who Gave The Beatles Away*	Ballantine Books 1975

The *Fab* one hundred and *Four*

Layout & Production	Jodi Ellis Graphics
	Cara Seekell / Granite Graphics, LLC
Printer	Interpress Co. Ltd.
Printing	4 colour offset printing
Page Size	245mm x 245mm
Text Paper	130gsm Multiart Silk Coated
End Papers	140gsm Woodfree Paper
Dust Jacket	150gsm Gloss Art Paper, with gloss lamination
Casing	Foil stamping on front and spine, on black Geltex, over 3mm board
Body Text	11/14pt Myriad Pro Light
Captions	10/14pt Myriad Pro Semibold
Headlines/Subheads	Abraham Lincoln & Lavandaria